Balthasar Hubmaier and the Clarity of Scripture

Balthasar Hubmaier
and the Clarity of Scripture

A Critical Reformation Issue

GRAEME R. CHATFIELD

Foreword by
DIARMAID MACCULLOCH

◈PICKWICK *Publications* · Eugene, Oregon

BALTHASAR HUBMAIER AND THE CLARITY OF SCRIPTURE
A Critical Reformation Issue

Copyright © 2013 Graeme Ross Chatfield. All rights reserved. Except for brief quotations in critical publications or reviews, no part of this book may be reproduced in any manner without prior written permission from the publisher. Write: Permissions. Wipf and Stock Publishers, 199 W. 8th Ave., Suite 3, Eugene, OR 97401.

Scripture quotations marked (NIV) are taken from the Holy Bible, New International Version®, NIV®. Copyright © 1973, 1978, 1984, 2011 by Biblica, Inc.™ Used by permission of Zondervan. All rights reserved worldwide. www.zondervan.com. The "NIV" and "New International Version" are trademarks registered in the United States Patent and Trademark Office by Biblica, Inc.™

Pickwick Publications
An Imprint of Wipf and Stock Publishers
199 W. 8th Ave., Suite 3
Eugene, OR 97401

www.wipfandstock.com

ISBN 13: 978-1-61097-325-0

Cataloguing-in-Publication Data

Chatfield, Graeme Ross.

Balthasar Hubmaier and the clarity of scripture : a critical Reformation issue / Graeme Ross Chatfield, with a foreword by Diarmaid Macculloch.

xii + 410 p. ; 23 cm. Includes bibliographical references.

ISBN 13: 978-1-61097-325-0

1. Hubmaier, Balthasar, d. 1528. 2 Anabaptists—Doctrines. 3. Bible—Hermeneutics. I. Macculloch, Diarmaid. II. Title.

BX4946.H8 C417 2013

Manufactured in the U.S.A.

Dedicated to Heather. Without her support, self-sacrifice, and constant encouragement this work would not have been completed.

Graeme Chatfield
Australian College of Theology
Sydney Australia
August 3, 2012

Contents

Foreword by Diarmaid MacCulloch | ix
Preface | xi

1 Research Questions and Method | 1
2 Biographical Sketch of Balthasar Hubmaier | 9
3 Balthasar Hubmaier: Anabaptist Enigma | 25
4 The Plumb Line of Holy Scripture | 61
5 The Bright and Clear Word of God | 106
6 Against Those who Mutilate the Word of God | 134
7 Making a Patchwork of Scripture | 193
8 Judge Me According to the Word of God | 334
9 Hubmaier's Hermeneutic: "Truth is Unkillable" | 360

Bibliography | 383
Name Index | 395
Scripture Reference Index | 401

Foreword

I AM VERY HAPPY to commend this book to a wide readership, having seen it develop from a doctoral project under my supervision. Dr Chatfield is a reliable analyst of one of the most individual and remarkable among the radical theologians in the sixteenth-century Reformation. Balthasar Hubmaier has been unduly marginalized in the conventional narratives of the period. From Martin Luther onwards, it suited "mainstream" leaders at the time (and it has suited varied interest-groups since) to portray radicals as ill-educated fanatics, alien to the true spirit of the Reformation. As a scholarly preacher with a doctorate in theology (and indeed, a former pupil of Luther's great Catholic adversary Dr Johann Eck), Dr. Balthasar Hubmaier has been inconvenient for this narrative. Indeed, he is one of the great might-have-beens of the Reformation, with his church in Nikolsburg briefly gaining established status in that little territory, and showing how Anabaptists might have had a different future in sixteenth-century Europe. His martyrdom, and that of his devoted wife, brutally ended such a possibility. Now, in a very different Christian era, with the help of Graeme Chatfield's expert guidance, we can look at his theology of Scripture with fresh eyes, and see that one of the reasons that Hubmaier infuriated Reformers like Luther or Zwingli was that he took methods of interpreting Scripture which they themselves used, and came to very different theological conclusions from them. Yet he also struck out in his own direction, away from the conclusions that many of his radical contemporaries had drawn about biblical interpretation: their bitter disagreements remain fascinating. In an age when Western Christianity is riven by arguments about how the Bible should be interpreted, used, and applied to current society, it is highly instructive to listen to the voice of an independent-minded and deeply learned biblical theologian from another age.

Diarmaid MacCulloch
St Cross College, Oxford
January 2013.

Preface

THIS WORK IS ESSENTIALLY my doctoral dissertation submitted to Bristol University in 1992 in fulfillment of the requirements for the Doctor of Philosophy, conferred in 1993. To bring the literature review up to date I have rewritten chapter 3, Balthasar Hubmaier: Anabaptist Enigma.

This work explores the place of Balthasar Hubmaier in the broad context of Reformation studies, and more specifically Anabaptist studies, using the much-proclaimed idea of "the clarity of Scripture" as the interpretative lens to bring into focus his hermeneutic. Previous studies of Hubmaier's hermeneutic have drawn on a limited selection of his writings and not placed him in the broader Reformation context. This work draws on the whole corpus of Hubmaier's published works and compares him with key Reformation figures such as Martin Luther, Huldrych Zwingli and Desiderius Erasmus, as well as the Swiss Brethren and Hans Denck.

To orient the reader to the place of Hubmaier in the early Reformation period, a brief biographical sketch is provided in chapter 2. Chapter 3 is an assessment of Hubmaier's place in Anabaptist research, including an overview of research into Hubmaier's hermeneutic in the broader context of Reformation hermeneutics. Chapters 4 to 8 explore the development of Hubmaier's hermeneutic in his writings, which are grouped chronologically. While Hubmaier shares aspects of his understanding of the "clarity of Scripture" with Luther, Zwingli, Erasmus, the Swiss Brethren, and Hans Denck, he maintains his own position.

Hubmaier develops his hermeneutic over the period under investigation. His early understanding of the clarity of Scripture is at first much closer to Zwingli and Luther than to Erasmus. However, as Hubmaier adopts the practice of believers' baptism and is persecuted for that belief, he moves closer to the more literal interpretation of Scripture that typifies the Swiss Brethren. However, like the Magisterial Reformers, he too moves

Preface

away from his understanding of the clarity of Scripture as interpreted in the congregation, and back towards a more elitist position. Whereas the Magisterial Reformers place their emphasis on the necessity of understanding the biblical languages as the key to understanding Scripture correctly, Hubmaier adopts the method of distinguishing between different categories into which texts are placed, thus maintaining the unity of the Scriptures.

It is argued therefore that Hubmaier is closer to the Magisterial Reformers in his hermeneutic of the clarity of Scripture than to Erasmus, the Swiss Brethren, or the South German-Austrian Anabaptists.

1

Research Questions and Method

THIS WORK HAS THREE goals. Firstly, to provide a description of the hermeneutic of Balthasar Hubmaier based on the whole corpus of his work. Previous descriptions of Hubmaier's hermeneutic have been based on a limited selection of his writings relating to a specific doctrine, such as baptism, the Lord's Supper, or free will. This limitation of sources has not only introduced a distortion in the description of Hubmaier's hermeneutic, but also does not allow any firm conclusion to be reached regarding the question of change and development in his hermeneutic.

Secondly, Hubmaier's works will be assessed chronologically to answer the question of change and development. The critical edition of Hubmaier's works edited by Gunnar Westin and Torsten Bergsten will act as the basis for this undertaking. The English translation of that work by H. Wayne Walker Pipkin and John Howard Yoder, which includes some additional works of Hubmaier's, will be used to supplement the German text.[1]

---

1. Gunnar Westin and Torsten Bergsten, eds., *Balthasar Hubmaier: Schriften* (Quellen und Forshungen zur Reformationsgeschichte Band XXIX. Quellen zur Geschichte der Taufer IX. Gütersloh: Gütersloher Verlagshaus Gerd Mohn, 1962); H. Wayne Walker Pipkin and John Howard Yoder, eds. and trans., *Balthasar Hubmaier Theologian of Anabaptism* (Classics of the Radical Reformation 5; Scottdale, PA: Herald Press, 1989). Throughout this work the above works will be referred to by the abbreviations *HS* and *PY* respectively. References in footnotes will be given to both works. Where the English translation of Pipkin and Yoder is followed, it will be given first. Where English translations do not follow Pipkin and Yoder, those responsible for the translation will be identified.

Balthasar Hubmaier and the Clarity of Scripture

This description of Hubmaier's hermeneutic will also facilitate achieving the third goal of this work: to provide a reassessment of the place of Hubmaier within the Reformation. Various conclusions have been drawn as to Hubmaier's relationship to the Reformers and his Catholic contemporaries.[2] The trend of research appears to place Hubmaier closer to his Catholic roots than to the Anabaptists, Luther, or Zwingli. These assessments rely on a comparison of Hubmaier's theology with other contemporary theologians. Often they suffer from being based on a limited selection of Hubmaier's works. However, by using the rubric of hermeneutics, the whole of Hubmaier's works can be used, thus enabling a more accurate description of his relationship to his contemporaries.

The comparison of Hubmaier with other theologians of that time will be achieved by introducing them at the point where Hubmaier either engages them in debate on a specific issue, or where he takes up an issue they are involved in debating. For example, in his initial works Hubmaier, in part acting as representative for the newly emerged Anabaptists of Zurich, is engaged in debate with Zwingli on the issue of infant baptism. Thus, a discussion of the hermeneutic of Hubmaier, Zwingli, and the Swiss Brethren ensues from the examination of these early works of Hubmaier. Similarly, when Hubmaier takes up the issue of free will, the hermeneutic of Erasmus, Luther, and Hans Denck will be discussed. Finally, when Hubmaier discusses the relationship of the magistrate and the Christian, the hermeneutic of the Swiss Brethren as defined by *The Schleitheim Brotherly Union*,[3] commonly known as the *Schleitheim Articles*, comes to the fore.

To attempt a full description of the hermeneutic of all these other Reformers is beyond the scope of this work. Only a description of their hermeneutic on the particular theme being debated will be discussed. This will allow a comparison between them and Hubmaier on that issue.

It is the thesis of this work that Hubmaier's hermeneutic concerning the clarity of Scripture is closer to Magisterial Reformers, Zwingli and Luther, than to either the Swiss Brethren, (as represented by the *Schleitheim Articles*), or the South German-Austrian Anabaptists, (as represented by Denck and Hans Hut), or to Erasmus, or to the nominalist position of Hubmaier's early training as a Doctor of Theology. This work will attempt to demonstrate that Hubmaier's hermeneutic develops through a series of debates. In the initial debate with his Catholic opponents, Hubmaier

---

2. These assessments are the subject of chapter 3, Balthasar Hubmaier: Anabaptist Enigma.

3. Sattler, "The Schleitheim Brotherly Union."

Research Questions and Method

is in close harmony with Luther and Zwingli, not only in principles and method, but also in presuppositions. The debate with Zwingli over infant baptism sees him move away from Zwingli and closer to the hermeneutic of the Swiss Brethren. The Swiss Brethren adopted a more literalistic interpretation of Scripture that presupposed the priority of the New Testament over the Old Testament. This alignment with the hermeneutic of the Swiss Brethren is especially evident during Hubmaier's first six months in Nikolsburg.

In the second six months of his time in Nikolsburg a dramatic shift occurred in Hubmaier's hermeneutic. During that period he was involved in two debates. In the first debate on free will and necessity, he moved back towards his Catholic roots in his expression of presuppositions on the will of God, which reflects both the Old Franciscan tradition, and an older view concerning the tripartite nature of human beings that he adopted from Origen, possibly via Erasmus. However, he used a hermeneutic in his interpretation of Scripture that did not reflect his earlier nominalist training. Nor was it a duplication of the hermeneutic of Erasmus. Rather it was a complex amalgam of presuppositions and principles that reflected Hubmaier's continuing identification with Luther, Erasmus, and his earlier Catholic training. There is also some similarity with the hermeneutical method of Denck. However, Hubmaier does not share the presuppositions that underlie Denck's position.

The second debate concerned the relationship between the church and the magistracy. Hubmaier's work, *On the Sword,* gives evidence of his movement away from the hermeneutic of the Swiss Brethren towards the hermeneutic of Zwingli and Luther. This finds expression in two areas in particular. Firstly, Hubmaier gives the idea of forbearance, and the associated hermeneutic of faith and love, priority over the hermeneutic of truth, no matter the consequence for the peace of the church. Secondly, he emphasizes the role of the priest or preacher of the Word of God as the interpreter of the Word of God, at the expense of his earlier congregational hermeneutic. Both of these issues are fundamental to the hermeneutic of Luther and Zwingli as they seek to make Scripture not only understandable but also applicable to the life of the believer. However, in this last point in particular, Hubmaier demonstrates that his overall hermeneutic is closer to Zwingli and Luther, as he followed a similar course to them in the matter of redefining the clarity of Scripture.

All three begin by asserting that the Word of God is clear and understandable by lay people without any special education. However, when challenged from within their circle of supporters, they qualify their earlier position, and insist that the interpretation of Scripture must be limited to those who are authorized to preach the Word of God. For Zwingli and Luther, authorization to preach the Word of God depended on the candidate being educated in the biblical languages, Hebrew, Greek, and Latin, as well as receiving official recognition by the civil authorities. Hubmaier does not specifically declare himself on the necessity of languages, though he does make use of Hebrew and Greek in his argument for the first time in his second work on free will. He does, however, limit the interpretation of Scripture to the priests and preachers of the Word of God.

Before analyzing Hubmaier's works, it is necessary to outline questions that need to be addressed in order to determine his hermeneutic. Of primary importance are the questions that relate to Scripture. What constitutes Scripture? Are the books of the Old Testament, the New Testament, and the Apocrypha all to be considered as part of the canon of Scripture? How is the printed text of the Bible to be treated? That is, is every letter as it is written down to be understood as without error? What role does the concept of inspiration play in understanding a particular book of the Bible as being part of the Scripture? What is the relation of the church to the Scripture; who establishes the canon?

The Reformers often used the term "the Word of God" to describe the source of revelation that alone was to be appealed to as authoritative. However, the very term was ambiguous as it was used by the wide cross-section of the Reformers and their Roman Catholic opponents. Did the Word of God equate with the printed words in the Bible? Or was the printed text as used and interpreted by the Holy Spirit the Word of God? And if the Holy Spirit played a crucial role in taking both the printed text and the preached word and transforming them into the Word of God, what was the relationship of the Holy Spirit to the printed text and the proclaimed word? Or was the Word of God independent of both the text of the Bible and the proclaimed word from the pulpit?

These questions are fundamental to any investigation of hermeneutics, as the answers that the individual gives to them will determine many of the methods employed in the interpretation of the Scripture. It will also determine the limit of the material that will be appealed to for the development of theological and doctrinal positions.

There are a series of other issues that must be addressed once the nature and limit of Scripture is determined. What is the authority of Scripture as compared with other possible sources of authority that may be appealed to when determining doctrine and practice for Christians? In this matter the Reformers asserted the sole authority of Scripture, while they accused their Catholic opponents of appealing at different times to the authority of popes, councils, schools, tradition, and reason as authoritative for determining the doctrine and practice of the church.

There was also a variety of opinion on the clarity of the Scripture. Was the meaning of the passage under discussion self-evident, plain, clear, and common sense as some demanded? Or was there need for the application of the older scholastic methods using the arts of the rhetorician, dialectician, and grammarian, as well as the well-known and tried four senses of Scripture? Or was there need for the application of the newer skills of the humanists in the languages of the Scripture, Hebrew and Greek; of philology; and historico-grammatical criticism of the text? In short, was Scripture not as clear and simple as some made it out to be, thus requiring skills and expertise beyond those of the untrained layperson?

A further consideration is the relationship of the Old Testament to the New. Is there a unity between the two, or does the New take precedence over the Old, and if so in what areas? Or does the Old take priority over the New? Was the Old Testament the "shadow" and the New Testament its "fulfillment" as seen in Christ? Does the concept of covenant, which became so important to the followers of Zwingli and later Calvin, act as the unifying link between the New and Old Testaments?

The role of the Holy Spirit in relation to Scripture is also a significant area of divergent views among theologians of the sixteenth century. Is the Holy Spirit necessarily involved in bringing understanding of Scripture to the individual and the church? Or does the Scripture have inherent in it the power to bring understanding of the truth, conviction of sin, and faith?

In conjunction with these issues, which relate primarily to the determination of Scripture, are the theories that the interpreter of Scripture employs to bring out the meaning of any given text or passage. The combination of exegesis and hermeneutics underpins the development of theology and doctrines. There are numerous formal principles for interpretation that are developed and then applied in the practice of hermeneutics. These often relate to rules of grammar and logic. There will also be displayed an attitude concerning the necessity for knowledge of languages, particularly of Hebrew, Greek, and Latin, for the interpretation of Scripture. The use or rejection of humanist tools of philology and textual criticism will help to determine the hermeneutical method of an individual, as will the use or rejection of the older scholastic interpretive method of the four senses of

Scripture: the literal, allegorical, tropological, and anagogical senses. Other issues that deal specifically with figures of speech may also play a part in determining hermeneutical method in some writers. Consideration or rejection of such figures of speech as typology, synecdoche, metaphor, and parables affected the hermeneutics of the different Reformers.

For some interpreters the attitude the reader brings Scripture is also determinative. Without the correct attitude the reader will not be able to ascertain the truth, understand the will of God, or be obedient to it. In this regard such issues as faith, humility, and obedience loom the largest.

It is also necessary to determine the presuppositions underlying a particular hermeneutic. Identifying a theologian's view of anthropology is among these crucial presuppositions. Does the interpreter follow a Platonic view of the dual nature of humanity; that is, body and spirit, or Origen's view of humanity being composed of body, soul, and spirit? Or is the view equivalent to Luther's; that is, the human being is to be considered as a whole and undivided? This discussion of anthropology leads to a discussion of how God interacts with people. Is it through infused grace without the aid of human beings; is it through infused grace with the aid of human beings via the soul, conscience, or an image of God that remains in human beings unaffected by the fall; is it imputed faith due to the merits of Christ's death on the cross?

Equally determinative for hermeneutics is the attitude the interpreter has towards the doctrine of the omnipotence of God. Has God limited his omnipotence so that he acts within an order that he has established and made plain in Scripture, or does God retain his right to act omnipotently at all times? Answers to these questions were often given in terms of the distinction between the ordained and absolute wills of God. The distinction was then applied to various texts of Scripture so that the unity of Scripture was not compromised by seeming contradictions.

Having established what the author's understanding of Scripture is and what method he has used to make clear the truth of Scripture, it remains to see how the author applies the theoretical model in practice, and to determine if the model is applied consistently. An analysis of a writer's use of Scripture can help to establish not only preferences for particular biblical writers and passages, but also the author's understanding of the relationship of the Old and New Testaments. The validity of an author's theoretical model can be tested by studying the particular use of texts chosen by an author. For example, does the author's use of parables comply with the theoretical model according to which parables cannot be used as the basis for the development of doctrines that are not plainly stated elsewhere in Scripture?

Sequences of texts can also provide information about how an author determines continuity across the Old and New Testament. This may be typological, or it may simply be the linking of a number of texts from a variety of different contexts by a word common to them all. A single meaning is attributed to that word, thus providing the continuity that the author understands exists between the Old and the New Testaments. Typical of this method of interpretation is Hubmaier's linking of all texts that mention "bridegroom" with the understanding that the bridegroom is Christ. All these questions provide parameters within which Hubmaier's hermeneutic can be defined and compared with those of other Reformers, Anabaptists, and Catholic theologians.

Each of Hubmaier's works will be analyzed in the light of this framework, though not every question will be asked in every instance. In order to trace development and change this analysis of Hubmaier's works will be undertaken according to the chronological order of the writing of his works.

The works will be divided into the following five periods:

1. Works written and published before his baptism at Easter 1525.

2. Works written at Waldshut and published between Easter 1525 and December 5, 1525.

3. Works written at Waldshut or Zurich and published at Nikolsburg after July 1526.

4. Works written and published at Nikolsburg from July 1526 to July 1527.

5. Works written during his final imprisonment in January 1528.

This periodization will also allow the influences of various opponents and supporters of Hubmaier to be recognized. In the first period, the influence of Luther and Zwingli can be seen positively in Hubmaier as he joined them in attacking the Catholic Church. In the second period, the positive influence of Zwingli wanes and the influence of the small Anabaptist group that had arisen in Zurich around Conrad Grebel and Felix Mantz became more important. It is also in this period that the Peasants' War occurred and may have exerted some influence on the development of Hubmaier's hermeneutic. The effects of the failure of the Waldshut Reform, and his imprisonment and torture in Zurich, are reflected in the writings of period three. Zwingli's role changes from ally to opponent, and as such his influence on Hubmaier can be seen negatively, as Hubmaier distances himself from Zwingli in both theology and hermeneutics. The writings of the fourth period reflect the growing complexity of opinion in the Nikolsburg Anabaptist church. Here Hubmaier has to meet the continued opposition of Zwingli and his supporters as well as meet the challenge of educated Lutherans and some fellow Anabaptists, such as Hut, who disagreed with him on the issues of free will, the magistracy, and eschatology. In the fifth period, Hubmaier is once more face-to-face with his Catholic opponents. In contrast to his 1523 experience, when he was Zwingli's ally and under the protection of the Zurich Council, Hubmaier is now the prisoner of the Catholic Austrian authorities and being examined for heretical beliefs and sedition. These writings thus reflect on theological concerns from within that specific framework, and need to be used cautiously in determining development and change in his hermeneutical principles and practices.

At the conclusion of the analysis of each group of works a summary will be given which will draw together Hubmaier's hermeneutic to that point. Developments and changes will be noted, as well as comparisons between Hubmaier's hermeneutic and the other Reformers who Hubmaier engaged in debate.

2

Biographical Sketch of Balthasar Hubmaier

IT IS NOT MY intention to provide anything more than a biographical sketch of Hubmaier's life. Torsten Bergsten produced the acclaimed "definitive" Hubmaier biography in German in 1961, with the slightly condensed and revised English translation of that text by William R. Estep being made available in 1978, to coincide with the 450th anniversary of Hubmaier's death in Vienna.[1] These two works have been drawn on extensively for the biographical content of the sections entitled "Settings" that precede the detailed analysis of each of Hubmaier's works. This biographical sketch intends only to provide a brief outline of Hubmaier's movements, and to note the various people that he had contact with or were influential in his life. Those who want to investigate Hubmaier's biography in more detail are directed to the work of Bergsten and the various books and articles that are identified in chapter 3, Balthasar Hubmaier: Anabaptist Enigma.

The notice of matriculation to the University of Freiburg on May 1, 1503, is the first record that survives of Hubmaier's life. Working from the information that Hubmaier was registered as a clerical student from Augsburg, it has been assumed that he gained his preliminary education in

---

1. *PY,* 16n 1; Bergsten, *Balthasar Hubmaier: Anabaptist Theologian,* Foreword. For a detailed discussion of the older works on Hubmaier see Bergsten's German work *Balthasar Hubmaier: Seine Stellung,* 1961. This work superseded the major works of Loserth, *Doctor Balthasar Hubmaier;* Vedder, *Balthasar Hubmaier* (Vedder provides a fascinating discussion on the nomenclature of Hubmaier's name, 66–68); Mau, *Balthasar Hubmaier;* and Sachsse, *Dr Balthasar Hubmaier als Theologe.*

Latin, possibly Greek, and in Catholic dogma and liturgy from the Cathedral School in Augsburg.[2] This early training in the liturgy of the Catholic Church found expression in Hubmaier's later life as a priest and pastor in Regensburg and Waldshut, where he was noted for his extravagant processions and for developments in the ceremonial life of the church.[3]

The date of Hubmaier's matriculation has also created some confusion as to the age he commenced his University studies. Estep and George Hunston Williams, following Johann Loserth, suggest that Hubmaier was born sometime between 1480 and 1481. He would therefore have been twenty-two or twenty-three at his matriculation.[4] Bergsten and Christof Windhorst are more conservative and suggest that Hubmaier was born sometime between 1480 and 1485.[5] Even taking the latest date, Hubmaier would have been eighteen years old at his matriculation, the same age as Luther, but some four years older than Zwingli.[6] He was therefore a "mature age" student when he commenced his formal studies at the University of Freiburg. He was the son of poor peasant farmers from Friedberg, some six miles east of Augsburg.

Johann Eck, Hubmaier's teacher and mentor at Freiburg, noted that Hubmaier's financial constraints forced him to interrupt his academic program in 1507 and move to Schaffhausen, where he was a schoolteacher.[7]

---

2. Bergsten, *Balthasar Hubmaier: Anabaptist Theologian*, 49; Windhorst, "Anfänge und Aspekte," 149: "Hier (Augsburg) lernte er Latein, vielleicht auch Griechisch. Sicher wurden ihm die zum Verständnis der Messe und der sonstigen Gottesdienste notwendigen Kenntnisse vermittelt. Vor allem aber wirde er in das gottesdienstlichen Leben der Kirche eingebübt. Die Schüler hatten an einer Fülle von Gebeten, Andachten, Messen, Prozessionen und Bittgängen teilzunehmen."

3. Bergsten, *Balthasar Hubmaier: Anabaptist Theologian*, 70.

4. Estep, *The Anabaptist Story*, 51; Williams, *The Radical Reformation*, 1992, 149. Vedder comments that Hubmaier was "past twenty years of age before he was ready for University, and past thirty before he took his baccalaureate degree." Vedder, *Balthasar Hubmaier*, 27.

5. Bergsten, *Balthasar Hubmaier: Anabaptist Theologian*, 48–49; Windhorst, "Professor, Preacher, Politician," 145.

6 Bainton, *Here I Stand*, "Chronology," 11–12; Potter, *Zwingli*, 11–12. According to Potter, Zwingli first matriculated to the university of Vienna in the autumn of 1498, and again in 1500. Parker suggests that the normal age for matriculation to university was fourteen. From the statement by Beza concerning Calvin's "extraordinaire memoire" and his "singulier esprit" he conjectures that Calvin first attended the University of Paris at the age of twelve or thirteen; that is, in 1520 or 1521. People matriculating to university after the age of fifteen he considers to be the "exceptions," the "older man." Parker, *John Calvin*, Appendix 1, 187–88.

7. Bergsten, *Balthasar Hubmaier: Anabaptist Theologian*, 49.

Hubmaier returned to Freiburg to succeed Eck as the rector of the "Pfauenburse" in the autumn of 1510, and then in 1512 followed Eck to Ingolstadt. On August 31, 1512, Hubmaier was promoted to "baccalaureus" and, according to the custom of the day, Eck eulogized his gifted student in a poem.[8] Three days later, he was granted his Doctor of Theology and responded with an extravagant eulogy of his teacher.[9] From this work by Eck it can be seen that Hubmaier was ordained as a priest and already had the reputation for "giving highly learned lectures to students, as well as useful sermons to the people."[10] He was appointed as Professor of Theology and Vicar of the Church of Our Dear Lady, the largest church in Ingolstadt. As Professor of Theology he would have given lectures on Peter Lombard's *Sentences* and on *via moderna* nominalist theology, probably mirroring his mentor Eck, with an eclectic mix from such authorities as Thomas Aquinas, Bonaventura, Duns Scotus, William of Occam, and Gabriel Biel. Later, Hubmaier was to name these teachers of the Catholic Church as the ones from whom he had learned his Catholic theology, his "hellish scriptures."[11] Hubmaier's academic career reached its pinnacle in the academic year 1515–16, when he was elected Prorector of the University of Ingolstadt. In this position he was responsible for the administration of the University, though the titular rector was the Margrave Friedrich van Brandenburg.[12]

---

8. Vedder, *Balthasar Hubmaier*, 28–29. Vedder provides a translation of the poem.

9. Bergsten, *Balthasar Hubmaier: Anabaptist Theologian*, 50. Loserth gives the date as September 29. Loserth, *Doctor Balthasar Hubmaier*, 16–17. "Balthasaris Hiebmaieris Pacimontani theologi, concionatoris Ratisponensis de suo Eckio:
O felix nimium felix Germania, quae nunc
Doctiloquos gignis multisciosque viros.
Haud Cleopatream priscus satis exulit umbram
Obicient doctum saecula nostra virum.
Eckius is meus est Germano sidere natus
Illo nimirum Theutona terra nitet.
Theologus rarus, iurus sophiaeque peritus
Saepius in populum semina sacra serit.
Nodosam logicen (si mavis) rhetoris arma
Quaeque mathematicus, astronomusque docent.
Quidquid habet rhetor, historia, culta poesis,
Dispeream si non singula solus habet."

10. Windhorst, "Professor, Preacher, Politician," 145.

11. Bergsten, *Balthasar Hubmaier: Anabaptist Theologian*, 51; Windhorst, "Anfänge und Aspekte," 150; *PY*, 343; *HS*, 309.

12. Bergsten, *Balthasar Hubmaier: Anabaptist Theologian*, 50.

Hubmaier did not complete his term as Prorector however, and left Ingolstadt in January 1516 for the city of Regensburg (also called Ratisbon) and an appointment as the Cathedral Preacher there. This sudden and unexplained departure is one of a number of occasions where he left a particular town or city without obvious reason. Henry Vedder proposes that Hubmaier's move to Regensburg removed him from the strong influence of Eck, and from that point on he became "independent, free to develop according to the laws of his own nature."[13]

In Regensburg Hubmaier soon became involved in the life of the city, particularly in the ongoing opposition to the Jews by the Regensburg City Council. Bergsten notes, "it seems that one of the responsibilities of the Cathedral Preacher in Regensburg was to preach against the Jews," and it soon became apparent that Hubmaier took up the task eagerly. Hubmaier's anti-Semitism brought him to the attention of the Emperor Maximilian I, not because he was anti-Semitic, but because he attacked people who were under the specific protection of the Emperor. By July 22, 1518, Hubmaier's opposition to the Jews of Regensburg saw him defending himself before the Emperor at the Diet of Augsburg. Two days later an Imperial envoy commanded the Regensburg Council to expel Hubmaier from his position as Cathedral Preacher, which they regretfully did. However, Hubmaier continued to receive support from the church authorities in Augsburg and he was permitted to retain his position, provided that he did not violate the Imperial authority concerning the Jews in Regensburg.[14] When Maximilian I died in January 1519, the people of Regensburg rose up against the Jews there, destroyed the synagogue on February 21, and by the end of the month had successfully expelled all Jews from the city.[15] Hubmaier then became involved in the pilgrimage movement that grew up around the Chapel to the Beautiful Mary (zur Schöne Maria), which was built on the site of the old synagogue. He preached at the consecration of the Chapel's altar, recorded the miracles that were supposed to have occurred there, and became its chaplain before September 1519.[16]

The success of the pilgrimage movement to Regensburg brought with it conflict as the City Council and the city's administrator struggled to gain control of the considerable financial resources that the pilgrimage

---

13. Vedder, *Balthasar Hubmaier*, 37. Williams also emphasizes the powerful influence of Eck over Hubmaier. Williams, *The Radical Reformation*, 3rd ed., 149.

14. Bergsten, *Balthasar Hubmaier: Anabaptist Theologian*, 58.

15. Ibid., 58–59.

16. Ibid., 62.

movement generated. Hubmaier was drawn into this debate in June 1520, but made no progress towards a settlement of the issue.[17] This dispute over the finances of the Chapel, coupled with the opposition of the Dominican monks of Regensburg; his doubts concerning the cult of Mary that he had helped ignite; and early contacts with the teaching of Luther, may all have contributed to Hubmaier leaving Regensburg in December 1520 and moving to the minor city of Waldshut on the Rhine.[18]

It may have been through the good offices of his friend and fellow student from Freiburg, Johann Fabri, now Vicar General to the Bishop of Constance, that Hubmaier acquired the position of priest of the upper parish of the town of Waldshut. Waldshut was a part of the Austrian Hapsburg territories, yet because of its geographical separation from the government in Innsbruck, and its special rights and privileges, it was not completely dominated by Hapsburg policy. The Swiss Canton of Bern did have some say in the appointment of the priests in Waldshut, via its relationship with the nuns at Königsfelden, who provided for the sustenance of the priests at Waldshut.[19] These connections with the Swiss were later to provide the people of Waldshut with a measure of hope that they might succeed in removing themselves from Hapsburg domination. They had sought to defy the Hapsburg attempt to reimpose the Catholic faith in Waldshut after they had accepted Hubmaier's reform of the church.

It was during his time in Waldshut that Hubmaier began to move away from his traditional Catholic understanding of theology and to be influenced by the works of humanists like Erasmus and by the works of Luther. Bergsten has shown that Hubmaier sought to develop a network of humanist correspondents with whom he not only discussed classical authors, but also the works of Luther. He particularly notes Hubmaier's relationship with Wolfgang Rychard of Ulm, who Hubmaier met on his way to Waldshut late in 1520. Rychard publicly acknowledged his pro-Lutheran leanings in January 1521, and was responsible for collecting and distributing evangelical literature. Bergsten argues that the meeting of Hubmaier and Rychard "cannot have been without significance" for Hubmaier's spiritual development, and that Hubmaier probably obtained a copy of Johnannes Oecolampad's *Judicium de doctore Martino Luthero*

---

17. Ibid., 63.

18. Estep, *The Anabaptist Story,* 53; Windhorst, "Professor, Preacher, Politician," 146. Williams goes so far as to suggest that the excess of the pilgrims "so distressed Hubmaier that he willingly accepted a call as priest in Waldshut." Williams, *The Radical Reformation,* 1992, 149.

19. Bergsten, *Balthasar Hubmaier: Anabaptist Theologian,* 69.

from Rychard, the same copy Hubmaier later sent to Beatus Rhenanus.[20] Windhorst is also convinced of the early influence of Luther on Hubmaier, arguing that this occurred between 1520 and 1522. Windhorst maintains that Hubmaier's early work, *Several Theses* (1524), provides an exact analysis of Luther's work *Sermon von dem hochwürdigen Sakrament des hl. wahren Leichnas Christi*.[21] This view of the early influence of Luther on Hubmaier's theological development is in sharp contrast to Joseph Loserth, who rejects such a claim, and Carl Sachsse, who acknowledges Luther's influence on Hubmaier only from 1522.[22]

The first two years of Hubmaier's residence at Waldshut were, according to Fabri, just as they should have been for a Catholic priest. Yet although Hubmaier seemed outwardly to conform to the expectations of his Catholic overlord, the Bishop of Constance, inwardly a transformation had begun that would irreversibly lead Hubmaier away from the Catholic Church.[23] Bergsten cites two extant letters of Hubmaier in 1521 that indicate that he had sought to establish contacts with leading humanists Beatus Rhenanus of Basel, Johannes Sapidus of Schlettstadt, and as mentioned above, Wolfgang Rychard of Ulm. From these letters is can be established that Hubmaier was not only studying the classical authors, but was influenced by the works of Erasmus and Luther, and showed a marked preference for Pauline theology as opposed to scholastic theology.[24] In a letter to Adelphi, a doctor and humanist at Schaffhausen, on June 23, 1522, Hubmaier reveals that he is involved in the study of the Pauline writings and has been reading some works of Luther and probably also of Philip Melanchthon. He also mentions that he has recently been to Basel and Freiburg. In Basel he met with Erasmus, Glarean, and Pelikan, and discussed with Erasmus the question of purgatory.[25] Hubmaier was by this time deeply influenced by the form of humanism represented by Erasmus, but was also giving careful consideration to the challenge of the Reformers, specifically Luther and Melanchthon.

20. Ibid., 71–72.

21. Windhorst, "Anfänge und Aspekte," 151.

22. Loserth, *Doctor Balthasar Hubmaier*, 25; Sachsse, *Dr Balthasar Hubmaier als Theologe*, 165.

23. Bergsten, *Balthasar Hubmaier: Anabaptist Theologian*, 70. Fabri's comments concerning Hubmaier's early years in Waldshut are taken from *Ursache*, the polemical work against Hubmaier that he wrote and published the day after Hubmaier's martyrdom in Vienna, March 10, 1528.

24. Bergsten, *Balthasar Hubmaier: Anabaptist Theologian*, 72–73.

25. Ibid., 73–74.

Biographical Sketch of Balthasar Hubmaier

Late in 1522, Hubmaier responded to a request from Regensburg to return to that city and take up the position of pilgrimage preacher at the Chapel of the Beautiful Mary. It was during this brief stay in Regensburg that Hubmaier made his position clear with regard to evangelical teaching.

On December 22, 1522, Hubmaier signed a contract with the Regensburg Council that committed him to sing three offices every week, to preach near or within the Chapel, to organize processions, and to examine and publicize the miracles that took place there. In short, the Council wanted Hubmaier to revitalize the flagging pilgrimage movement of their city. On January 17, 1523, Hubmaier wrote to his friend Rychard describing his intent to preach a series of sermons from Luke's gospel and continuing with another book of the Bible. He comments, "Christ was starting to sprout"[26] in him at that time, the process being assisted by his attendance at evangelical services held in the home of Laien Blabhans, a dyer. Blabhans had gathered together a group of artisans from Regensburg that followed Luther's evangelical doctrines, and it was in their company that Hubmaier took the step that put him on the side of the evangelical Reformation.[27] As in Ingolstadt, Hubmaier did not complete the full year of his contract, though in this instance the reason was clear. Having now publicly declared himself to follow evangelical teaching he found he could no longer fulfill the requirements of the contract and on March 1, 1523, Hubmaier again left Regensburg for Waldshut, taking up the pastorate from which he had not bothered to resign.[28]

On his return to Waldshut Hubmaier began to preach publicly against the Catholic Church, attacking priests as "murderers of men's souls and priests of Satan" who withheld the gospel.[29] He also sought contacts with the Reformation occurring in Switzerland. In late April 1523, Hubmaier preached at St Gallen, and found approval with the evangelical Reformer Joachim von Watt, known as Vadian. From there he travelled to Zurich where he met and held an informal discussion with Zwingli. They discussed among other things the issue of infant baptism, and Hubmaier was

---

26. Windhorst, "Professor, Preacher, Politician," 147.

27. Bergsten, *Balthasar Hubmaier: Anabaptist Theologian*, 76.

28. Estep, *The Anabaptist Story*, 54. Pike confuses this few months of evangelical preaching in Regensburg with the whole of Hubmaier's time in that city, "For about two years Regensburg receives purer doctrine from the preacher's lips than it has ever had before." Pike, *Story of the Anabaptists*, 44.

29. Bergsten, *Balthasar Hubmaier: Anabaptist Theologian*, 77. Bergsten dates an incident of this preaching as occurring on April 19, 1523.

later to state that at that time Zwingli and he agreed that infants should not be baptized until they had been instructed in the faith.[30]

Other trips into Switzerland followed as Hubmaier improved his contacts with the evangelical preachers. His support of the Swiss Reformers was most eloquently heard when Hubmaier gave his public support to Zwingli at the Second Zurich Disputation on October 26–28, 1523. The presence of such a famous preacher was acknowledged by Zwingli and the Zurich Council as Hubmaier was seated beside Zwingli throughout the disputation.[31] It was also at this meeting that Hubmaier made or renewed acquaintances with other evangelical Reformers such as Sebastian Hofmeister of Schaffhausen, Vadian, and Christopher Schappeler of St Gallen, and for the first time definitely came in contact with Conrad Grebel and Simon Strumpf.[32]

Hubmaier's stand for the evangelical cause of reform at Zurich in October 1523 brought a rapid response from his Austrian masters. On December 5, 1523, an Imperial delegation arrived at Waldshut demanding that Hubmaier be handed over to the Bishop of Constance. They accused him of joining the "Lutheran sect," of misinterpreting the Scriptures, and of misrepresenting himself as the representative of four Hapsburg cities in the Black Forest.[33] The council refused to accept that the accusations were correct and therefore rejected the Imperial demands. Over the course of the next ten months the Austrian pressure on Waldshut to dismiss Hubmaier steadily increased. Despite that pressure, Hubmaier went ahead with his program of reform for the little town on the Rhine, publishing his first work as a Reformer, *Eighteen Theses*, sometime in March 1524.[34] The Imperial government had demanded in April that Hubmaier be handed over to them, and gave the town a month to come to a decision. Hubmaier's *Eighteen Theses* appear to have been his attempt to win the clergy of the town and the surrounding area to his program of reform. The theses

---

30. Ibid. *PY,* 194–195; *HS* 186.

31. Bergsten, *Balthasar Hubmaier: Anabaptist Theologian,* 82.

32. Harder, *Sources of Swiss Anabaptism,* 234–50. Hubmaier did not, however, meet with Melchior Hoffman during 1523 as Pike asserts. Pike, *Story of the Anabaptists,* 43. Vedder suggests that Hubmaier was more in line with the Grebel group than with Zwingli at the Second Zurich Disputation, a view objected to by Bergsten. Vedder, *Balthasar Hubmaier,* 65; Bergsten, *Balthasar Hubmaier: Anabaptist Theologian,* 86.

33. Bergsten, *Balthasar Hubmaier: Anabaptist Theologian,* 91. Two years later to the day, Hubmaier was forced to flee Waldshut in the face of imminent Austrian military occupation of the town.

34. *PY,* 30.

themselves reflect Zwingli's *Sixty-Seven Articles* and the matters discussed at the Second Zurich Disputation.[35]

At Pentecost on May 15, 1524, the people of Waldshut were summoned to the Council House to discuss whether they should hand Hubmaier over to the Austrian authorities or continue to defy them. The inconclusive discussion of that day was continued the next day when the women of the town, partially armed, insisted that Hubmaier remain in the town. The council agreed and eight of the twelve priests of the town felt sufficiently insecure to leave.[36] This event marked Hubmaier's victory in his attempt to reform Waldshut. With the backing of the mayor and a majority of the Council and population Hubmaier now proceeded to undertake the reform of the church that he had outlined in his *Eighteen Theses*.

During the early months of 1524, Waldshut was able to utilize its close connections to Zurich as a deterrent to overt Imperial action to extradite Hubmaier forcefully from the town. However, Zurich's delicate position within the Confederation was highlighted during the Baden conference of the Confederation held between August 16 and 21 that year. The six Catholic Cantons agreed to hand over to Austria any of its subjects found in Switzerland, and the Austrians in turn agreed to hand over to the Swiss the two leaders of the group that had sacked the Carthusian monastery at Ittigen on July 18 of that year, and who were alleged to have found asylum in Waldshut.[37] Any possible support for Waldshut to defy the Austrians was thus put under extreme pressure.

However, in June 1524, Waldshut found other allies that help provide protection from Austrian intervention. The peasants of Stühlingen rebelled against their lord on June 23, 1524, and Waldshut, along with the other three Black Forest towns, participated in the negotiations. This resulted in a compromise agreement that there were to be no hostilities between the two groups until August 24. When the armistice ended both sides prepared for open conflict and the precarious protection of the rebellious peasants was put to the test. With an attack on Waldshut imminent, Hubmaier fled to Schaffhausen on August 29 where he stayed for two months, returning to Waldshut on October 27, 1524. In Hubmaier's absence Waldshut formally entered into an agreement of mutual protection with the peasants in early September 1524, but saw this agreement

---

35. Bergsten, *Balthasar Hubmaier: Anabaptist Theologian*, 99.
36. Ibid., 100.
37. Ibid, 107.

nullified when the peasants came to a negotiated agreement with their lord on September 10, 1524.[38] With the loss of peasant support, and with the evangelical majority of the Council regaining the initiative in Waldshut by the end of September, Waldshut actively looked to support from Zurich to protect the evangelical reform of the town. The appeal was successful and a group of Zurich volunteers came to Waldshut on October 3, 1524.[39]

In Schaffhausen, Hubmaier lived at the Benedictine Abbey of All Saints under the asylum offered there. It was from this relatively safe haven that Hubmaier wrote three works that further identified him with the evangelical cause. The first, *An Earnest Christian Appeal,* comprised Hubmaier's petitions to the Schaffhausen Council for asylum in that city and the opportunity to debate his theology with the Catholic pastors from Bremgarten and Schwyz.[40] It is also probable that while at Schaffhausen Hubmaier wrote *On Heretics*. In this pamphlet he wrote against the use of coercion to bring about obedience to the teaching of the church. It was specifically directed against the Dominican Cathedral Preacher of Constance, and was published in that city sometime after September 24, 1524. The third piece Hubmaier wrote at Schaffhausen was directed specifically against Eck, his former teacher. It was entitled *Axiomata*, and was translated from the Latin into German under the title *Theses Against Eck*. With this work Hubmaier joined Zwingli and Hofmeister in their attacks on Eck, who had attacked Zwingli's *Sixty-Seven Articles* at the Confederation's Diet at Baden in August 1524.[41] Hubmaier's *Theses Against Eck* focused on the issue of authority, the sole authority of Scripture as the judge in all matters of doctrine, and the role of the congregation in matters of discipline. This writing effectively brought into the open the breach between the two former colleagues, a breach that Eck had recognized a year earlier

---

38. Ibid., 109. Tom Scott has carried out a thorough reassessment of the relationship of Waldshut and the peasants, including Hubmaier's part in the whole incident. He concludes that Hubmaier's preaching made little impact on the peasants, and that Waldshut and the peasants joined together more for the settlement of common grievances against Catholic monasteries to whom they were both obliged to pay tithes. Scott, "Reformation Part 1."

39. Bergsten, *Balthasar Hubmaier: Anabaptist Theologian,* 116.

40. Ibid., 127–28 It was a great pleasure to learn from the Staatarchiv Schaffhausen that the original of the fourth and longest of Hubmaier's appeals to the Schaffhausen Council was rediscovered in 1984. The Archivist Dr Hans Lieb kindly made available copies of all four originals of Hubmaier's appeals.

41. Potter, *Zwingli,* 154–55.

when he was in Rome. While in Rome, Eck had placed Hubmaier and Zwingli under suspicion as being "Lutherans."[42]

Almost immediately upon Hubmaier's return to Waldshut, the pace of reform in the church increased. Unlike Zurich, where the removal of the images from the churches was directed by the City Council, in Waldshut the people took the lead in an iconoclastic outburst on All Saints Day 1524. Hubmaier followed up this iconoclasm with a modified form of the Mass on November 1, 1524.[43] The people of Waldshut no doubt felt secure from Austrian intervention because of the group of Zurich volunteers garrisoned in the town. These volunteers were not withdrawn until January 10, 1525, when the Zurich Council finally gave way to the pressure of the Catholic Cantons.[44] It was also through these Zurich volunteers in Waldshut that Hubmaier reestablished contacts with the Grebel circle in Zurich. In September 1524, this same group of young evangelicals had sent two letters to Thomas Müntzer, in which they outlined their pacifist and separatist view of the church. Müntzer himself came to the Klettgau sometime after November 10, 1524, a date too late for him to have influenced Hubmaier's reforms in late October, early November. However, it is possible that Müntzer's influence was apparent in both the Grebel circle and Hubmaier concerning the parallel development of their views on infant baptism.[45]

The military priority of the Hapsburgs at this time was France, and Waldshut benefited from this by being able to continue with its reformation of the church. By January 16, 1525, in a letter to Oecolampad, Hubmaier demonstrates his awareness of a difference of opinion between himself, Zwingli, and Leo Jud concerning infant baptism, and that discussions on the matter were taking place in Zurich between Zwingli and the Grebel circle.[46] Though he held to the same view as the Grebel circle concerning infant baptism, Hubmaier did not proceed to instituting believers' baptism as the Zurich group did on January 21, 1525.[47] Windhorst notes that the

---

42. Bergsten, *Balthasar Hubmaier: Anabaptist Theologian*, 78.

43. Ibid., 145–46.

44. Ibid., 154.

45. Ibid., 152.

46. *PY*, 69–70.

47. MacGregor, *Central European Synthesis*, 108, 141. MacGregor argues that Hubmaier had instituted believers' baptism by January 1523, and probably sometime in 1521, based on his view of Hubmaier's sacramental theology. However, he fails to take into account the lack of evidence for this position in Hubmaier's trial, where Fabri accepts Hubmaier initiated baptism in Waldshut only after Reublin baptized him in

"political situation was not conducive to radical church reforms. Besides, Hubmaier was more interested in agreement with Zwingli than in the separatist activity of the Zurich Anabaptists."[48] Bergsten also remarks that Hubmaier's delay in instituting believers' baptism was due to his continuing adoption of the method of preaching and teaching until all had come to agreement before instituting any new reform.[49]

Hubmaier was baptized by Wilhelm Reublin on Easter Saturday, April 15, 1525. From January to Easter 1525 Hubmaier had written *Several Theses* and *A Public Challenge*. The possible influence of Andreas Karlstadt is evident in the former work, as can be seen in his use of Karlstadt's interpretation of "This is my body" to signify the actual physical body of Christ present at the Last Supper.[50] He also held to the view of the Supper being a "memorial."

It was also during this time that Waldshut realized a degree of military protection against the Austrians. In February 1525, the peasants of Upper Swabia rose up against their overlords. The Black Forest peasants joined the revolt and Waldshut sided with the peasants. This partnership was made explicit on Easter Sunday, April 16, 1525, in a joint document signed by the mayor of Waldshut and Hans Müller, the leader of the Black Forest Peasant Army.[51] It was on this same day, Easter Sunday, that Hubmaier himself baptized a majority of the Council and some three hundred citizens of Waldshut. That the reform of both baptism and the Lord's Supper followed the practices of the Zurich Anabaptists is probably best attributed to the actual presence of Reublin in Waldshut at the time of these momentous events.[52] Several contacts between the Zurich and Zollikon Anabaptists and Hubmaier occurred between Easter and July 1525. However, Bergsten's assertion that "Hubmaier became a theological authority in the eyes of the Swiss Anabaptists" probably overestimates Hubmaier's position.[53] Certainly during this period Hubmaier wrote what was to be a fundamental statement of the Anabaptist position on baptism, *On the Christian Baptism*, which incorporated a slightly earlier work, *Summa*. However, Hubmaier's views on Christian government and the use of the

---

April 1525. Fabri, *Ursache*.

48. Windhorst, "Professor, Preacher, Politician," 149.
49. Bergsten, *Balthasar Hubmaier: Anabaptist Theologian*, 186.
50. *PY*, 75; *HS* 102. Bergsten, *Balthasar Hubmaier: Anabaptist Theologian*, 193.
51. Ibid., 212.
52. Ibid., 237.
53. Ibid., 242.

Biographical Sketch of Balthasar Hubmaier

sword, which were opposed to those of the Zurich Anabaptists, would have detracted from his position as a "theological authority" in all matters.

The security afforded Waldshut by the Peasant Army of the Black Forest was destroyed in early July 1525, when the peasants were forced to lift their siege of Radolfzell and then suffered defeat at the hands of an Austrian army the next day. It was only through the intervention of the Confederation on behalf of the Klettgau peasants that Waldshut, through its relationship with the peasants, was able to delay the intervention of Austria against the town and its famous preacher until late November 1525.

With the Anabaptist church of Waldshut now established, Hubmaier entered into a polemical confrontation in print with Zwingli over the issue of infant baptism. The intensity of the debate between these two is mirrored in the increasing pressure that the Zurich Council and the preachers of Zurich exerted upon the Anabaptists of Zurich and Zollikon. Zwingli was involved in a series of private and public debates with the Anabaptists concerning infant baptism,[54] as well as publishing a number of works in which he attacked them, namely *Those who give cause for Tumult* (*Wer Ursache gebe Aufruhr usw* December 28, 1524), *On Baptism, Rebaptism and Infant Baptism* (*Von der Taufe, von der Wiedertaufe und von der Kindertaufe*, May 27, 1525), and *On the Preaching Office* (*Von dem Predigtamt*, June 30, 1525). He specifically attacked Hubmaier's work *On the Christian Baptism of Believers* in his *Answer to Balthasar Hubmaier's Baptism Booklet* (*Antwort Über Balthasar Hubmaiers Taufbüchlein*, November 5, 1525). Though Hubmaier did not participate in any of the discussions concerning infant baptism in Zurich, he did write *On the Christian Baptism* (July 11, 1525) in preparation for a requested disputation with Zwingli and the preachers of Zurich. Zwingli in turn composed his *Answer to Hubmaier's Baptism Booklet* in preparation for the November 6 disputation with the imprisoned leaders of the Anabaptists.[55] It was Zwingli's attempt to counteract the influence of Hubmaier's work of July 11, 1525. Hubmaier also compiled a list of references to works of the church fathers as part of his preparations for debate with Zwingli, though these were not published until after July 1527, when he arrived in Nikolsburg (*Old and New Teachers*). Similarly, Hubmaier's response to Zwingli's *Antwort*, though drafted

---

54. Harder, *Sources of Swiss Anabaptism*, 334. Harder lists six Private Disputations: 1. Spring 1524; 2. 11 Aug 1524; 3. 6 Dec 1524; 4. 13 Dec 1524; 5. 7 Feb 1525; 6. 16 Mar 1525; and four Public Disputations: 1. 17 Jan 1525; 2. 20 Mar 1525; 3. 6 Nov 1525; 4. 5 Mar 1526.

55. Ibid., 432–33.

in Waldshut, was not published until after his arrival in Nikolsburg (*Dialogue*), as was also the case with his response to Oecolampad, (*On Infant Baptism*).

Hubmaier did try to reach Zurich for the November 6 Disputation, however the Austrian forces, which had won a victory over the Klettgau peasants on November 4, foiled his attempt.[56]

With the defeat of the Klettgau Peasant Army, the capitulation of Waldshut followed. On December 5, Hubmaier fled to Zurich, though this was not his first choice. He at first found refuge with Heinrich Aberli, who moved him to an inn called the Green Shield run by the widow Bluntschli.[57] His presence in Zurich was soon discovered, and he was placed under mild confinement on December 11.[58] Hubmaier was granted his opportunity to debate with Zwingli and the other evangelical pastors of Zurich. The outcome was Hubmaier's promise of recantation, which was to occur on December 29, 1525, in the Fraumünster. However, instead of a recantation of his view on infant baptism, the awaiting congregation heard from him a defense of believers' baptism. Hubmaier was immediately removed to the Wellenberg prison, tortured, and forced to confess his error and his obstinacy.[59] He was held in the Wellenberg prison until he made his formal recantations sometime between April 13 and 15, 1526, at the two principal churches in Zurich and at Gossau in Grüningen.[60] Hubmaier left Zurich secretly towards the end of April 1526 and made his way via Constance and Augsburg to the city of Nikolsburg in Moravia, where he arrived in July 1526.[61]

In Augsburg, Hubmaier met with Hans Denck and may have baptized him, and possibly also met with Hans Hut. The former may have influenced Hubmaier's views on free will, while the latter became the focus of a major dispute within the Anabaptist church in Nikolsburg.

In the relatively safe haven of Nikolsburg, Hubmaier worked at establishing his second Anabaptist church, which worked closely with the civil authorities. Hubmaier's abilities as a preacher and politician won to

---

56. Bergsten, *Balthasar Hubmaier: Anabaptist Theologian*, 266.
57. Vedder, *Balthasar Hubmaier*, 124–25.
58. Bergsten, *Balthasar Hubmaier: Anabaptist Theologian*, 300.
59. Ibid., 304–5.
60. Ibid., 307.
61. Pike appears to have erroneously included Hubmaier among the Anabaptist prisoners who escaped from the New Tower on 21 March 1526. Pike, *Story of the Anabaptism*, 45. Harder provides a translation of the Zurich Council's investigation of the event. Harder, *Sources of Swiss Anabaptism*, 450–52.

the Anabaptist faith the Lord of Nikolsburg, Leonhard von Liechtenstein, and a majority of the German speakers of the town. It also saw Nikolsburg become a haven for many Anabaptist refugees.

During the year Hubmaier lived in Nikolsburg he produced and published the majority of his writings as an Anabaptist. In the latter half of 1526 he wrote a series of tracts that defined the theology and practice of the Anabaptist church in Nikolsburg. These included two works that covered a wide range of issues, *A Brief Apologia* and *A Christian Catechism*; two on the Lord's Supper: *A Simple Instruction* and *Form for Christ's Supper*; two on baptism: *The Ground and Reason*, an enlarged version of the ten reasons for baptism he included in *On the Christian Baptism*, and *Form for Water Baptism*; and two on church discipline: *On Fraternal Admonition* and *On the Christian Ban*. This series of manuals for ordering the life of the Nikolsburg church was concluded by the end of December 1526.

By April 1527 Hubmaier had changed his emphasis in his writings. He now addressed the issues being raised by those opposed to his reform of the church who were within the church. Initially he dealt with those evangelicals who declared both verbally and by their life style that justification by faith is all they need. In response Hubmaier wrote two works on the issue of free will. After his disputation with Hans Hut (probably May 1527,)[62] Hubmaier wrote his last work from Nikolsburg, concerning the relationship of the Christian and the secular magistracy. In *On the Sword*, Hubmaier states in writing his position on Christian government, which he had also held earlier in Waldshut. Hubmaier is specifically refuting Anabaptists in his congregation who closely reflect the Swiss Brethren position on the separation of the church from all worldly government as stated in the *Schleitheim Brotherly Union*, more generally known as the *Schleitheim Articles*.[63]

The political position of Nikolsburg changed radically on October 23, 1526, when Ferdinand of Austria was elected King of Bohemia, and in November inherited the title Margrave of Moravia.[64] This placed Hubmaier's implacable foe in a position of authority over his patron and protector Leonhard von Liechtenstein. Sometime between June 24, 1527, when Hubmaier completed *On the Sword*, and July 22, 1527, when Ferdinand

---

62. Packull, *Mysticism*, 100.

63. Yoder, *Legacy of Michael Sattler*, 37–38.

64. Zeman, *Anabaptists and Czech Brethren*. Vedder notes that Louis II of Bohemia was killed at the battle of Mohacs on August 29, 1526, which made the way open for Ferdinand of Austria to occupy the position. Vedder, *Balthasar Hubmaier*, 149.

ordered his government, to gather information on Hubmaier for his trial, Hubmaier and his wife Elsbeth were arrested and imprisoned in Vienna. Exactly how this occurred is unclear.[65]

Hubmaier was held in the Kreuzenstein Castle, north of Vienna, and there he held discussions with his former friend and fellow student from Freiburg, Johann Fabri, as well as Marcus Beckh and Ambrosius Salzer.[66] The conversations did not obtain a satisfactory recantation from Hubmaier. Consequently Hubmaier was returned to Vienna, where he was questioned under torture. Fabri later asserted Hubmaier himself wrote a confession of guilt that was read publicly in the presence of some thousands of people. Hubmaier was then taken and burned at the stake outside the walls of Vienna on March 10, 1528. His wife Elsbeth was drowned in the Danube three days later.[67]

In his martyrdom at Vienna Hubmaier was shown to have stood by his convictions concerning baptism and the Lord's Supper in particular, whereas in Zurich he had succumbed to the fear of men and compromised the immortal truth for which he had so strenuously fought. For one who used as his motto "Truth is Immortal," martyrdom at Vienna rather than recantation at Zurich appears a more apposite ending.

---

65. Bergsten, *Balthasar Hubmaier: Anabaptist Theologian*, 377–78.
66. *PY*, 525; *HS* 460.
67. Bergsten, *Balthasar Hubmaier: Anabaptist Theologian*, 379.

3

Balthasar Hubmaier: Anabaptist Enigma

IN CURRENT ANABAPTIST HISTORIOGRAPHY, Balthasar Hubmaier is an enigma. Prior to 1944, Hubmaier was unequivocally considered by friend and foe alike to be an Anabaptist. By those who viewed Anabaptism negatively, as well as Free Church historians who viewed him positively, he was often considered a leader, if not the leader, of the Anabaptists. Among the heirs of sixteenth-century Anabaptism, his theology of baptism and his martyrdom confirmed his identity as an Anabaptist.

Among those who opposed the Anabaptists in the sixteenth century, Hubmaier was acknowledged as a leader of among the Anabaptists. His former Roman Catholic colleagues Johann Eck and Johann Fabri declared Hubmaier to be "the most dangerous leader of the Anabaptists"[1] and "the patron and first beginner" of Anabaptism.[2] By the time of the Council of Trent, Roman Catholic authorities identified Hubmaier as one of the Sacramentarians and Anabaptists that originated in Saxony. He was also included along with Luther, Zwingli, John Calvin, and Caspar Schwenckfeld in the list of "heresiarchs."[3]

Among his contemporaries, Hubmaier was also considered an Anabaptist. Zwingli is said to have considered Hubmaier "the greatest threat

---

1. Johann Eck, quoted in Loserth, *Doctor Balthasar Hubmaier*, 210.
2. Johann Fabri, quoted in Bergsten, *Balthasar Hubmaier: Seine Stellung*, 77–78.
3. Gonzalez, "Balthasar Hubmaier," 72n7.

among the Anabaptists to the Zurich Reformation."[4] In 1528, Luther wrote against Hubmaier "the Anabaptist" for misrepresenting his views on infant baptism as being the same as the Anabaptists.[5]

Among groups that claim continuity with sixteenth-century expressions of Anabaptism, Hubmaier is acknowledged as a part of Anabaptism. In their *Chronicle of the Hutterian Brethren* (1581) the Hutterites, a group that had once been part of Hubmaier's Nikolsburg congregation, only declare Hubmaier to be a "brother" after reporting his alleged acknowledgment that he had "unjustly opposed Hut on several points" and that "he was guilty of giving too much to worldly freedom in regard to retaining the sword." Only following the record of his declaration of repentance is Hubmaier's martyrdom recorded, and that of his unnamed wife.[6] Hubmaier's contribution is acknowledged, as are his powerful writings, in which he defended "true baptism and opposed infant baptism with proofs from Holy Scripture," and two songs he composed "that are still known in the church."[7] In the Dutch Mennonite Thieleman van Braght's *Bloody Theatre* (1660), Hubmaier does not appear with the likes of Conrad Grebel or Felix Mantz, but appears out of chronological sequence among the 1542 martyrs. Hubmaier is represented as one among many from the time of Zwingli who were "hated and persecuted by the world."[8] He is noted as a "learned and eloquent man" who after "manifold trials and long imprisonment . . . was burned to ashes, suffering it with great steadfastness." Hubmaier's unnamed wife, who was drowned for her steadfast commitment to her faith "received from God," is also included among the martyrs.[9] These comments by the Hutterites and Mennonites appear to accept grudgingly that Hubmaier was part of Anabaptism at its inception.

ORIGINS OF ANABAPTISM AND SWISS ANABAPTISM

This consensus that Hubmaier should be included among the Anabaptists was not challenged until 1944 with the publication of Harold S. Bender's paper "The Anabaptist Vision." In Bender's opinion, Hubmaier was "a transient aberration from original and authentic Anabaptism," worthy of

---

4. Ibid.
5. Luther, *Concerning Rebaptism*, 229.
6. Hutterian Brethren, *Chronicle of the Hutterian Brethren*, Vol 1, 48–49.
7. Ibid., 49.
8. Van Braght, *Bloody Theatre*, 465.
9. Ibid.

mention only as a footnote.[10] Normative or evangelical Anabaptism was represented by Conrad Grebel, Felix Mantz, and those other early supporters of Zwingli who become the Swiss Brethren.

John Howard Yoder, while following Bender's view that the Swiss Brethren constituted normative Anabaptism, softened Bender's totally negative assessment of Hubmaier. He argued that Hubmaier "played no essential part"[11] in the beginnings of Swiss Anabaptism since Hubmaier had no connection with Grebel prior to 1523. Yoder maintained that Hubmaier's questioning of infant baptism is "not an indication of direct contact between him and the Zurich circle of radicals."[12] In the formative years of the Swiss Brethren prior to 1523, Yoder argued that Hubmaier continued to follow the Reformers rather than the Brethren regarding the authority of the state to reform the church, resulting in the demand that Christians "disobey biblical injunctions (oath, armed defense, interest, defense of the property structure)."[13] Yoder concluded that prior to Easter 1525:

> In full awareness of the issues involved, Hubmaier refused to join the Brethren. He had not made the long pilgrimage in which they had been engaged since 1523. The rejection of state authority in matters of faith (October–December 1523); the understanding that the true church must be a persecuted minority (spring and summer of 1524); the rejection of Thomas Müntzer's gospel of revolution (September 1524); and the repeated unsuccessful attempts to carry on a conversation with Zwingli (ending in December 1524) had all gone on outside the realm of his interest and knowledge. This difference of orientation remained significant even after he finally had accepted believers' baptism. Precisely because he came to the problem of baptism as a trained thinker dealing with a theological problem as such, he was ever to remain distinct in his emphasis from the Swiss Brethren, for whom believers' baptism was only one expression of a whole new way of understanding faith and the church.[14]

While Yoder does not accept that Hubmaier played a part in the beginnings of Swiss Anabaptism, he does concede that Hubmaier contributed

---

10. Bender, "The Anabaptist Vision," 51. This is a reprint of Bender's original 1944 essay.
11. Yoder, "Beginnings of Swiss Anabaptism," 5.
12. Ibid., 6–7.
13. Ibid., 17.
14. Ibid., 7.

to wider Anabaptism through his tract *On the Christian Baptism*. Yoder declared Hubmaier's tract "a minor masterpiece" and opined that it had a "broader effect" than Zwingli's *Of Baptism*.[15]

About the time Yoder was reassessing the place of Hubmaier in the beginnings of the Swiss Brethren, a broader debate about classification of Anabaptists in the wider Reformation was taking place between Roland H. Bainton and George Hunston Williams. Bainton argued that Anabaptists were part of the "left wing of the Reformation" along with another distinct subgroup, the Free Spirits.[16] All the other Reformers were Protestants. Williams preferred to identify the groups as either Magisterial Reformers or Radical Reformers, with the Radical Reformers subdivided into Anabaptists, Spiritualists, and Evangelical Rationalists.[17] In both classifications, Hubmaier is included among the Anabaptists along with the likes of Conrad Grebel, Felix Mantz, and Michael Sattler. Williams's classification of Magisterial Reformers and Radical Reformers, together with its subgroupings, has dominated Reformation and Anabaptist scholarship.

Yoder's assessment of Hubmaier's place in the beginnings of Swiss Anabaptism in particular, and Anabaptism in general, did not go unchallenged. As "profane" historians explored Anabaptism from social and cultural perspectives, they challenged the conclusions of those "confessional" historians who continued to view Anabaptism primarily from a theological perspective.[18] The individual studies of James M. Stayer, Werner O. Packull, and Klaus Deppermann were synthesized in their 1975 essay "From Monogenesis to Polygenesis." They argued that Anabaptism did not have a single-source origin from the Swiss Brethren in Zurich but had multiple points of origin: the Swiss Brethren in Zurich; South German and Austrian Anabaptism, tracing its beginnings to the influence of Thomas Müntzer through the agency of Hans Denck and Hans Hut; and Central German and Dutch Anabaptism, whose principal early figure was the onetime Lutheran lay preacher Melchior Hofmann.[19] Stayer, in his 1972 work *Anabaptists and the Sword*, acknowledges that Hubmaier had associated

---

15. Ibid., 9, 11.

16. Bainton, "Left wing of the Reformation," 121.

17. Williams, *The Radical Reformation*, 1992, "Introduction to First Edition," xxiv.

18. This debate can be traced through the pages of the *Mennonite Quarterly Review*. Stayer, Packull, and Deppermann, "From Monogenesis to Polygenesis," 83–121; Goertz, "History and Theology," 177–88, and the various responses to that article in that edition of the MQR; Snyder, "Birth and Evolution of Swiss Anabaptism," 501–645 and the various responses to that article in the same edition of the MQR.

19. Stayer, Packull, and Deppermann, "From Monogenesis to Polygenesis," 83–121.

with the Swiss Brethren of Zurich but remained separate from them and closer to Zwingli's "realpolitical view" of the magistracy. Rather than being one of the founders of the Swiss Brethren, Stayer argued Hubmaier was one of the founders of the upper German Anabaptist sects, along with Denck and Hut.[20] Not having Hubmaier among the founders of the Swiss Brethren aligns Stayer with Yoder, at least on this point. Nevertheless, Stayer's definition of Anabaptism: "they are members of sects practicing baptism of believers and forming religious groups on that basis,"[21] includes Hubmaier as a genuine Anabaptist, while Yoder's definition excludes him.

However, the role of Hubmaier as a founder of South German-Austrian Anabaptism is predicated on his influence on Denck and Hut. Packull, in a 1973 article, challenged Hubmaier's role among the South German-Austrian Anabaptists by rejecting the proposition that Hubmaier baptized Denck, who in turn baptized Hut.[22] Gottfried Seebass's PhD on the work, life, and theology of Hut reinforced Packull's view when Seebass concluded that Hubmaier played no significant role in the development of Central German Anabaptism.[23]

In 1975, on the 450th anniversary of the beginnings of Anabaptism, Hans-Jürgen Goertz presented a compendium of essays representative of the tensions between the varieties of approaches then current in Anabaptist research.[24] In 1979, he summarized the key features of these tensions between profane historical research and confessional theological research, warning the theologians against presuming "a hermeneutical primacy of theology in the study of church history."[25] While Hubmaier is not mentioned in Goertz's article, he is identified in several of the responses to that article. Using either the methodology of social history or the modified theological methodology of the younger Mennonite historians, Hubmaier remained difficult to place in Anabaptism.[26]

The work of C. Arnold Snyder attempted to move forward the debate over the priority of history or theology in Anabaptist studies. In 1994,

---

20. Stayer, *Anabaptists and the Sword*, 141.
21. Ibid., 20.
22. Packull, "Denck's Alleged Baptism," 327–38.
23. Seebass, "Müntzers Erbe."
24. Goertz, *Umstrittenes Täufertum*.
25. Goertz, "History and Theology," 186.
26. Oyer, "Goertz's 'History and Theology,'" 195; Klassen, "History and Theology," 198; Davis, "Vision and Revision," 207; Stayer, "Let a Hundred Flowers Bloom," 215.

he contributed a chapter[27] to H. Wayne Walker Pipkin's *Essays in Anabaptist Theology*. This was expanded and published in 1995 as *Anabaptist History and Theology*.[28] His definition of Anabaptism is minimalist: "The principle we have followed for the inclusion or exclusion in 'Anabaptism' is simply whether or not the person in question believed that only adults (and not infants) should be baptized, following a mature confession of faith."[29] He confidently included Hubmaier among the Swiss Anabaptists, while explicitly separating the Swiss Anabaptists from the South German-Austrian Anabaptists on the basis that there is "no documented historical connections to the Swiss movement."[30] He agrees with Walter Klaassen that Anabaptism is neither Catholic nor Protestant, rather Anabaptism reflects a more conservative than radical approach to reformation of church and society.[31] He argues, "The origins of Anabaptism undoubtedly lie in large measure in the radical reformers who first articulated an alternative view of evangelical reform; but they also lie with the regenerationist and ascetic tradition of late medieval piety which conceived of salvation in terms of sanctification . . . the Anabaptist movement has a distinctive theological "shape" that is rooted in medieval piety and spiritual ideals."[32] His assessment of the early Swiss Anabaptists identifies Hubmaier as "an early Swiss Anabaptist leader of surpassing importance who has been unfairly marginalized by modern historians. Hubmaier did more to define an early theological core of Anabaptist teaching than did anyone else. His writings on baptism continue to be cited verbatim by Swiss Brethren into the seventeenth century."[33] He utilizes Hubmaier's *A Christian Catechism* as articulating the "theological core" of early Anabaptism.[34] Nevertheless, he admits, "Hubmaier presents one of the great ambiguities of Swiss Anabaptist beginnings."[35]

Snyder's confident identification of Hubmaier as the leading influential figure of Swiss Anabaptism is utterly rejected by Andrea Strübind.[36]

27. Snyder, "Beyond Polygenesis."
28. Snyder, *Anabaptist History and Theology*.
29. Ibid., 9.
30. Ibid., 6.
31. Ibid., 30.
32. Ibid., 91.
33. Ibid., 107.
34. Ibid., 143.
35. Ibid., 107.
36. Strübind, *Eifriger als Zwingli*.

She reads the origins of Swiss Anabaptism primarily as a theological narrative and rejects the revisionist approach of Stayer and others. The publication of her work led to a sharp exchange of views between her and Stayer in the April 2004 edition of the *Mennonite Quarterly Review*.[37] In 2006 Snyder reentered the debate in the *Mennonite Quarterly Review*.[38] He briefly reviewed the historiography of Hubmaier research before stating his own position: "Hubmaier did not learn 'Anabaptism' from these reformers (Zwingli, Oecolampadius, and Hofmeister) rather, Hubmaier's primary base of support for the institution of adult baptism was the group of Zurich radicals including Conrad Grebel, as an analysis of their continuing contact and his earliest writings make clear."[39] He maintains the close identification of Hubmaier and pre-Schleitheim Anabaptism by arguing that they shared a common ecclesiology in that they "are of one mind in excluding state intervention and coercion in the church itself, which is to be governed only by the Word of God and God's Spirit."[40] Demonstrating his synthesis of theological and social history methodologies, Snyder goes on to argue that "Hubmaier's state-affirming Anabaptism and the separatist Anabaptism of Schleitheim grew out of the same Swiss Anabaptist roots, but divergent anthropological and regenerationist principles eventually bore fruit in significantly different ecclesiologies, under the pressure of changing social and political circumstances."[41] In his response to Snyder's article, Geoffrey Dipple acknowledged that Synder's reevaluation of separatist ecclesiology and pacifism among the Zurich radicals "opens the door to a much greater role for Hubmaier in early Swiss Anabaptism."[42] Thomas Finger totally rejected Snyder's conclusion: "Only one early Anabaptist ecclesiology, so far as I can see, endorsed government and its sword, and it did not derive this principle from Anabaptist roots."[43] J. Denny Weaver argued "that the difference between the theology of the nonpacifist Hubmaier and pacifists such as Felix Mantz or those of Schleitheim is more than a matter of differing views of anthropology and regeneration," it is in the concept of "office."[44] By this he means, "Hubmaier

37. Stayer, "New Paradigm"; Strübind, "New Paradigm."
38. Snyder, "Birth and Evolution of Swiss Anabaptism."
39. Ibid., 558.
40. Ibid., 527.
41. Ibid., 627.
42. Dipple, "Response," 659.
43. Finger, "Response," 665.
44. Weaver, "Response," 689.

rules out in principle and in advance the possibility of living according to the example of Jesus,"[45] which he further defines as "to live out the nonviolent story of Jesus."[46] Ray Gingerich rejected Snyder's representation of Hubmaier's nonseparatist, nonpacifist Waldshut congregation as the "most important Anabaptist community of the time," suggesting rather it was "a most important aberration of Anabaptism until Nikolsburg and later Münster came along."[47] However, ecclesiology is not for him the crucial issue that separated Hubmaier from all the Swiss Anabaptists, it was Hubmaier's view of Jesus. He shares this opinion with Weaver. Gingerich argued that Hubmaier spoke of following Christ rather than Jesus. This view of discipleship "camouflaged . . . behavioral inconsistencies with the teaching and example of Jesus's that account for Hubmaier developing a nonseparatist, nonpacifist ecclesiology."[48]

In 2007, Stayer accepted Snyder's view that there was agreement between Conrad Grebel and Hubmaier regarding nonseparatist and nonpacifist ecclesiology prior to 1525.[49] However, Martin Rothkegel does not share their point of view, arguing that in Nikolsburg Hubmaier rejected "the separatist pacifism as upheld by the Swiss Anabaptists."[50]

Was Hubmaier an Anabaptist? Was he linked to the Swiss Brethren, influenced by the Swiss Brethren, or even a leader among the Swiss Brethren? Alternatively, was he linked to the South German-Austrian Anabaptists? Following these questions through the Anabaptist historiography leaves us with Hubmaier the enigma.

FREE CHURCH AND CONTEMPORARY RELEVANCE

While this broader debate about Anabaptism was occurring, two Baptist historians, Robert Macoskey (1956)[51] and Torsten Bergsten (1961),[52] were

---

45. Ibid.

46. Ibid., 690.

47. Gingerich, "Response," 673.

48. Ibid.

49. Stayer, "Introduction," xxiv.

50. Stayer, "Introduction," xxiv; Rothkegel, "Anabaptism in Moravia and Silesia," 172.

51. Macoskey, "Life and Thought." The essence of Macoskey's findings was made accessible to the wider public in his article "Contemporary Relevance," 99–122.

52. Bergsten, *Balthasar Hubmaier: Seine Stellung*. Later published in English translation as Bergsten, *Balthasar Hubmaier: Anabaptist Theologian*.

independently exploring Hubmaier's place in the world of the Reformation. While Macoskey identified Hubmaier as an Anabaptist, he concluded that Hubmaier was "an independent thinker who acted after his own inspiration and followed his own destiny."[53] He idealized Hubmaier as the forerunner of the modern Free Church movement.[54] For Macoskey, Hubmaier is the layman's theologian, one who refused to use the techniques he had learned studying theology under nominalist Scholasticism, rather only dealing with the plain text of Scripture, and the New Testament in particular.[55] The contemporary relevance of Hubmaier's ecclesiology for Macoskey is the challenge Hubmaier presents to the Free Churches in the United States that demand an "utterly free and autonomous church" in an "utterly free and individualistic society."[56] In Macoskey's opinion, the United States is no longer such a society and the Free Churches would do well to consider Hubmaier's theology of the church, which rejects individualism. Hubmaier's view of the particular church and the general church also provides opportunity for American Baptists to reassess the ecumenical movement in a more positive light.[57] While Macoskey noted the possible antecedents of Hubmaier's unique theological amalgam,[58] he did not explore those antecedents, as his focus was more on Hubmaier's contemporary relevance.

Torsten Bergsten investigated three relationships crucial to understanding Hubmaier's place in the Reformation: "1. Hubmaier's relationship to the Reformation and the Anabaptists; 2. Hubmaier and the German Peasants' War; 3. Hubmaier and the modern Free Church movement."[59] Bergsten removes the theological restrictions of Yoder's definition of Anabaptism, using the broad definition, "Anabaptists are only those who practiced or received believer's baptism . . . or adult baptism."[60] Not only is Hubmaier a genuine Anabaptist, Bergsten goes on to assert Hubmaier was the intellectual leader or theologian of the new Anabaptist movement. Nevertheless, he concluded that Hubmaier remained closer to the

---

53. Macoskey, "Contemporary Relevance," 102.
54. Ibid.
55. Ibid., 106.
56. Ibid., 120.
57. Ibid., 120–21.
58. Ibid., 108.
59. Bergsten, *Balthasar Hubmaier: Anabaptist Theologian*, 45–46.
60. Ibid., 22.

Zwinglian form of Reformation than to the more radical Swiss Brethren.[61] Bergsten does not exaggerate Hubmaier's role as a prototype of modern Baptists as does Macoskey. Bergsten also begins to look back to the various influences other than Scripture that shaped Hubmaier's theology and acknowledges continuing Roman Catholic features in Hubmaier's theology.

However, in his review of Bergsten's book, Robert Friedmann challenged the appellation of "theologian" of Anabaptism ascribed to Hubmaier, pointing out that the influence of Hubmaier among Anabaptists was restricted to a limited number of theological themes: baptism, the Lord's Supper, and free will. He argues that Hubmaier's writings were "studied and quoted from"[62] only with regard to this very restricted number of theological themes in the seventeenth century, themes that do not fully represent Anabaptism.

Macoskey and Bergsten are part of a long line of Baptist historians interested in Hubmaier as an early representative of the Free Church type of ecclesiology. William R. Estep, in his 1978 translation of Bergsten's biography of Hubmaier, lists the following Baptist historians who had interacted in some way with Hubmaier: Arthur H. Newman, Henry Vedder, Ernest Payne, Jarold Knox Zeman, William R. Estep, Wilhelm Wiswedel, Gunnar Westin, Robert Macoskey and Gerd Seewald.[63] H. Wayne Walker Pipkin updated this overview of Baptist engagement with Hubmaier in the 2006 Hughey Lectures at the International Baptist Theological Seminary, Prague.[64] Pipkin noted the differences of interpretation about Hubmaier among Baptists, especially noting the reticence of English Baptists in the generation after Ernest Payne to see any historical connection between the formation of English Baptists and Continental Anabaptists, including Hubmaier.[65] Nevertheless, there are among English Baptist historians a new generation willing to explore the contemporary relevance of Hubmaier for Baptist and baptistic churches both within the United Kingdom and worldwide.[66]

61. Ibid.
62. Friedmann, "Book Review," 358.
63. Bergsten, *Balthasar Hubmaier: Anabaptist Theologian*, 39–42.
64. Pipkin, *Scholar, Pastor, Martyr*, 22–31.
65. Ibid., 22.
66. Ibid., 22–23. See, for example, Jones, *A Believing Church*; Randall, *Communities of Conviction*.

McClendon introduced the idea of 'b' baptists for those churches that did not identify with the historic seventeenth-century Baptists but shared many of their perspectives. McClendon, *Systematic Theology: Ethics*, 23.

The English Baptist engagement with Hubmaier is, however, muted when compared to the "veritable revival" of Hubmaier research in North America. Pipkin identified six doctoral dissertations produced by North American Baptist scholars: Emir Caner,[67] Michael W McDill,[68] Samuel Beyung-Doo Nam,[69] Brian Brewer,[70] Kirk MacGregor,[71] and Darren Williamson.[72] In addition to the Baptist doctoral dissertations cited by Pipkin should be noted William McMullen's 2003 MA thesis[73] on the theme of discipline within Hubmaier's theology. This preempted the 2011 PhD dissertation on the same theme by Simon Victor Goncharenko, a Russian Baptist studying at Southwestern Baptist Theological Seminary.[74] Pipkin warned that "some interpreters write their own agenda onto Hubmaier."[75] There appears to be an agenda driving Hubmaier research originating from Southwestern Baptist Theological Seminary, an agenda that demonstrates the relevance of Hubmaier's ecclesiology to current Southern Baptist practices. Not only are there theses specifically focused on Hubmaier, there are also theses that trace Hubmaier's influence in themes current to Southern Baptists, such as Adam Harwood's *Spiritual Condition of Infants*.

Baptists and "baptists" are not the only Hubmaier researchers seeking to identify how Hubmaier can be relevant to the contemporary church. Younger Mennonite researchers acknowledge in their own church tradition an unhealthy emphasis on individualism. In Hubmaier, they have identified a more communal ecclesiology and are willing to overlook his aberrant status in Mennonite historiography. Tripp York explored the notion of the corporate ethical demands of discipleship inherent in Hubmaier's understanding of the Lord's Supper.[76] Ryan Klassen also explored the relevance of Hubmaier to social ethics, but from the perspective of the interconnection of ecclesiology and social ethics.[77] Gay Lynn Voth traced

---

67. Caner, "Truth is Unkillable."

68. McDill, "Doctrine of Human Free Will."

69. Nam, "A Comparative Study."

70. Brewer, "A Response to Grace."

71. MacGregor, "Sacramental Theology." This is now published as *Central European Synthesis*.

72. Williamson, "Erasmus of Rotterdam's Influence."

73. McMullen, "Church Discipline."

74. Goncharenko, "Importance of Church Discipline," and *Wounds that Heal*.

75. Pipkin, *Scholar, Pastor, Martyr*, 36.

76. York, "Martyrdom and Eating Jesus," 71–86.

77. Ryan Klassen, "Wielding Two Swords."

how reference to Hubmaier's liturgical writings, especially his writings on the Lord's Supper, enabled a major shift in the liturgical practices of a Mennonite congregation.[78] Hubmaier's writings are therefore proving to be a rich source for reflection for some Mennonites.

In addition to the Baptist dissertations on Hubmaier mentioned above, there are other doctoral dissertations exploring aspects of Hubmaier's life, work, and theology. Ernst Endres's 2003 Doctor of Divinity dissertation "The View of Balthasar Hubmaier of the Church," submitted to the University of Pretoria; Brian Cooper's 2006 PhD "Human Reason or Reasonable Humanity?" submitted to the University of St Michael College; Antonia Lucic Gonzalez's 2008 PhD "Balthasar Hubmaier and the Early Christian Tradition," submitted to Fuller Theological Seminary; and Andrew Klager's PhD "Hubmaier's Use of the Church Fathers," submitted to the University of Glasgow. While these dissertations occasionally allude to the contemporary relevance of Hubmaier's theology, in the main they follow another trajectory of Hubmaier research, the search for Anabaptist antecedents.

SEEKING ANABAPTIST ANTECEDENTS

Rollin Armour's *Anabaptist Baptism* is representative of the approach that looks to the contemporaries of various Anabaptists for the source of potential influence in the development of their ideas. He acknowledges Hubmaier's awareness of Luther's writing on the Mass. This alerted Hubmaier to the importance of faith in the recipient of the sacrament, though his understanding of faith is different to that of Luther.[79] He considers the possible influence of the Zwickau prophets as evidenced in Hubmaier's use of the Markan form of the Great Commission. He asserts that Hubmaier's understanding that corruption in the church stems from a misunderstanding of baptism was "likely" picked up from Müntzer, though this may have come through the Grebel group, or directly from Hubmaier's reading of Müntzer.[80] Erasmus "may have contributed to Hubmaier's distinction between external and internal baptism" and Karlstadt "was probably influential in Hubmaier's rejection of infant baptism."[81] In Armour's assessment, the most important influence on Hubmaier "was probably the

78. Voth, "Anabaptist Liturgical Spirituality," 3–14.
79. Armour, *Anabaptist Baptism*, 24.
80. Ibid., 25.
81. Ibid.

Zurich reformation, Zwingli first and then the Grebel faction."[82] Zwingli's influence was seen in Hubmaier's adoption of "a moderate spiritualism whereby the inner spiritual action of cleansing and regeneration was sharply distinguished, indeed separated, from outer baptism."[83] With regard to the influence of the Grebel group, Armour argued that Hubmaier represented the Grebel group on the third day of the October 1523 Disputation, and probably remained in communication with them late in 1524. Not only did Wilhelm Reublin baptize him but he also became their foremost spokesperson.[84] However, while there is evidence of connection, this does not demonstrate influence. Armour explored Hubmaier's understanding of faith, regeneration, and its association with baptism and concluded that while Hubmaier's theology displays continuity with many aspects of Catholic theology it is "illegitimate" to call Hubmaier's thought Catholic as Hubmaier had "wholly repudiated the Catholic sacramental theology."[85] At the same time, Hubmaier rejects the Protestant understanding of justification as a forensic declaration that leaves the sinner essentially unchanged.[86] Effectively, Armour declares Hubmaier as neither Catholic nor Protestant, a view of Anabaptism in general that was propagated by Walter Klaassen.[87]

Abraham Freisen commented on the influence of Erasmus on the Anabaptist interpretation of the Great Commission:

> In the last thirty years or so the theme of Erasmian influence on the early Swiss Anabaptist movement has grown exponentially, sometimes expressed in quite general terms,[88] at other times in more specific terms. Thus, it has been argued that the Anabaptists were dependent upon Erasmus for their views on the freedom of the will,[89] their pacifism,[90] their ethical sincerity,[91] and

---

82. Ibid.
83. Ibid., 26.
84. Ibid.
85. Ibid., 34.
86. Ibid.
87. Klaassen, *Anabaptism: Neither Catholic nor Protestant*.
88. Kreider, "Anabaptism and Humanism," 123–41.
89. Hall, "Possibilities of Erasmian Influence," 149–70.
90. Fast, "Dependence of the First Anabaptists," 110.
91. Davis, "Erasmus as Progenitor," 163–178 and *Anabaptism and Asceticism*, esp. ch. 5, 266–92.

> the spiritualism of a Hans Denck.[92] Whereas some Mennonite scholars, such as Harald [sic] S. Bender, have denied a direct influence,[93] a Catholic scholar of the stature of John P. Dolan has said: "There can be little doubt of the perduring influence of Erasmus of Rotterdam on the early development of Anabaptism and his efforts to interpret it as a religious rather than a social revolutionary movement. . . . As an independent movement originating in the immediate circle of Zwingli at Zurich, Anabaptism found its roots in the spiritualism of the Rotterdam priest."[94]
>
> Yet with the exception of direct Anabaptist dependence upon Erasmus in the area of free will,[95] the connections remain conveniently vague, lying too much in the nebulous realm of the "spirit of the times," of vague possibilities of influence, of tenuous connectedness.[96]

Friesen argued that in Zurich there was a broader understating of biblical inspiration than with Luther, and this was probably due to the influence of Erasmus. The Anabaptist followers of Zwingli probably acquired this understanding of biblical inspiration from Zwingli. Nevertheless, the Zurich Anabaptists also developed a strong sense of the "separation of the kingdom of God and the kingdom of the world" that "irreparably breached" Erasmus's Neoplatonic continuum between the shadows and the Ideal Forms.[97] Friesen uncritically includes Hubmaier among the Swiss Anabaptists, but only mentions him in passing when examining the influence of Erasmus on the Anabaptist understanding of the Great Commission. To include Hubmaier among the Anabaptists who separated the kingdom of God and the kingdom of the world is to misrepresent him. In his *On the Sword*, Hubmaier specifically argued against this view as expressed in the *Schleitheim Articles*.[98]

In his 2005 PhD dissertation, Darren Williamson accepts Friesen's judgment that much of the research exploring Erasmian influence on Anabaptism claims only vague possibilities of influence, including Friesen's

---

92. Dolan, "Review of I. B. Horst," 343.

93. Bender, *Conrad Grebel*. See also his "Pacifism of Sixteenth-Century Anabaptists," 119–51, and Friesen, *History and Renewal*, 139–40.

94. Dolan, "Review of I. B. Horst," 343.

95. Burger, "Erasmus and the Anabaptists." 43–204.

96. Friesen, *Erasmus*, 22.

97. Ibid., 37.

98. *PY*, 493.

own work on Anabaptism and the Great Commission.[99] Williamson used three criteria to prove the influence of Erasmus on Hubmaier: possible and verifiable contact; similarity of ideas, in this case using comparative exegesis of selected biblical texts; and source probability, which seeks to exclude all other possible sources for similarity of ideas between Erasmus and Hubmaier.[100] He selected the following biblical periscopes: Matt 28:19–20, the Great Commission; Matt 13:24–30, 36–43, the parable of the tares; and Matt 16:13–20, 18:13–20, concerning the power of the keys. He concluded that Erasmus influenced Hubmaier's understanding of the Great Commission and the parable of the tares, but not the power of the keys.[101] Hubmaier continues to exhibit an independence in his thinking that reinforces his enigmatic character among early Radical Reformers.

The exploration of Hubmaier's indebtedness to his Roman Catholic origins has also been a theme in Hubmaier research. In 1971, David Steinmetz argued that Hubmaier continued to utilize a number of nominalist motifs in his understanding of human free will; that God will give salvation to those who do what is naturally in them, the accompanying idea of merit, and the distinction between the absolute and ordained power of God.[102] In 1981, Walter Moore argued that these nominalist motifs in Hubmaier's theology arose from the teaching of John Eck, Hubmaier's teacher and patron prior to 1522.[103] With regard to the doctrine of free will, he concluded that Hubmaier was either semi-Pelagian or Pelagian in his understanding and remained closer to his Catholic teacher than to Erasmus and Denck, as Thor Hall had claimed in 1961.[104] James McClendon underscored the continuity of Hubmaier with his Catholic heritage when he argued that Hubmaier's "radicality is best understood in terms of his Catholic origins, education, and pastoral service prior to the radical turn of 1524–1525."[105] Nevertheless, Hubmaier fits McClendon's description of "baptists" and as such he classifies Hubmaier as a "Catholic baptist."[106] Christof Windhorst designated Hubmaier a "Reformed Catholic," acknowledging the continuity of understanding of free will with Erasmus, and of Luther in other

---

99. Williamson, "Erasmus of Rotterdam's Influence," 16n40.
100. Ibid., 19–22.
101. Ibid., 23.
102. Steinmetz, "Scholasticism and Radical Reform," 127–28.
103. Moore, "Catholic Teacher," 73–74.
104. Hall, "Possibilities of Erasmian Influence," 155–56.
105. McClendon, "Balthasar Hubmaier, Catholic Anabaptist." 21.
106. Ibid., 32.

"traditional elements" of his theology.[107] Kirk MacGregor has challenged these views as a "misclassification" of Hubmaier and explored Hubmaier's understanding of the sacraments based on his awareness of the teachings of Bernard of Clairvaux. MacGregor argues that Hubmaier "remained an evangelical reform theologian throughout the duration of his life who was convinced by Reublin to abandon none of his beliefs with the sole yet important exception of the validity of ordination."[108] For MacGregor Hubmaier is a "theological maverick,"[109] a Magisterial Radical. Following the theme of medieval Catholic antecedents, Hubmaier continues to confound simple classification.

The seminal work of Kenneth R. Davis, *Anabaptism and Asceticism* (1974), produced a trajectory in Anabaptist research along which the studies of Hans-Jürgen Goertz[110] and C. Arnold Snyder[111] also fall. Davis reviewed fourteenth- and fifteenth-century ascetic reform movements, identifying key features as "a desire for the elimination of institutional and administrative abuses," "a hope and call for 'a revival of fervor, charity, asceticism and discipline' in the masses of individual Christians," and the expectation that "when the renewal and general reform came, it would involve by divine impetus a cataclysmic, institutional upheaval."[112] While Luther's challenge to bring reform did see a "total repudiation of a papal hierarchy, monasticism, and a scholastic sacramental system," it failed to produce an increase in "general piety." The Anabaptists not only took up the theme of piety, but also linked it to the separation of church and state and the insistence on evidence of individual piety as essential to true Christianity.[113] Among the Grebel group in Zurich these ascetic themes found expression in three expectations:

> 1. They expected that any reformation that was truly divinely inspired would promote unquestioning obedience to the Word of God, without any compromise with existing institutions or traditions. 2. They expected and demanded a visible separation on moral grounds of church from nonchurch, the end of a morally mixed society called Christian but obviously not truly

107. Windhorst, "Anfänge und Aspekte," 168.
108. MacGregor, *Central European Synthesis*, 129.
109. Ibid., 10.
110. Goertz, *The Anabaptists*.
111. Snyder, *Anabaptist History and Theology*.
112. Davis, *Anabaptism and Asceticism*, 64.
113. Ibid.

Christian. In addition, they believed in the church as a *spiritual* entity, to be spiritually governed, with spiritual purposes. This is what led to the secondary notion that in its functional manifestation as churches it must be separated institutionally from "worldly" control whether papal or civil. 3. They expected the restoration of visible churches in which a spiritually vital and an ascetically holy Christian life would typify all members, individually and corporately.[114]

Davis argues that this view of the ascetically motivated church was fully formed among the Grebel group by the time of the first adult baptisms on January 21, 1525. However, Hubmaier's view evolved from being an evangelical view of reform closely aligned with Luther and Zwingli, to the adoption of the Grebel group's position by the time of his baptism on April 15, 1525.[115] Davis does note that Hubmaier differed from the Grebel group on the issue of the magistracy and the sword, but that Hubmaier's post-Easter 1525 view was closer to Grebel's initial proposal of 1524.[116] Hubmaier is therefore understood to be of the same mind as the Swiss Brethren in terms of the reform of the church being the expression of ascetic ideals of reform as mediated through the *via moderna*'s most persuasive exponent, Erasmus of Rotterdam. This view of Hubmaier's conversion to an ascetically motivated reformation of church and society is challenged by Werner O. Packull. Though Packull was investigating mysticism and early South German-Austrian Anabaptism, in which he concluded Hubmaier played no significant role, he does conclude that Hubmaier's position on the relationship between the magistrate and the church identifies Hubmaier's Anabaptism as substantially different from the Swiss Brethren.[117]

Hans-Jürgen Goertz agreed with Davis and Packull that Anabaptism drew much of its distinctiveness from medieval asceticism and mysticism. For Goertz this was expressed in anticlericalism: "Swiss Anabaptism was a child of anticlericalism." Hans Hut, expressing the influence of Thomas Müntzer, was even more strongly anticlerical than the Swiss Brethren.[118] For Goertz, "Anabaptist groups were connected neither loosely nor purely by accident with the anticlericalism of the Reformation period, but rather

---

114. Ibid., 83.
115. Ibid., 108.
116. Ibid., 107.
117. Packull, *Mysticism*, 104.
118. Goertz, *The Anabaptists*, 41.

actually grew out of it, from a reaction to abuses within the old church and in the course of actions geared towards the renewal of Christian life."[119]

One expression of the individualizing of anticlerical sentiment was the appropriation of the *sola scriptura* principle by the laity. Goertz contended that the Grebel group in Zurich had experienced "the explosive anticlericalism of the *sola scriptura* principle under the direction of the reformers,"[120] but it had only been applied to the level of individual salvation and piety. However, for the principle to be fully realized it needed to be applied to all areas of life; individual, ecclesiastical, and public. Goertz argued that the early Anabaptists in Zurich did not apply a "legalistic hermeneutic" but sought to subject the whole of a person's life to Scripture. This approach did not last long, as the Anabaptists soon adopted the position that "whatever was expressly ordered in Scriptures was legitimate and that everything else was forbidden," making the Bible a book of law.[121] Goertz asserts that the early Swiss Anabaptists possibly understood the relationship of the Spirit and the external Word in much the same way as Zwingli and Karlstadt.[122]

A second issue came to divide the Swiss Anabaptists and Zwingli, the relationship of the Old and New Testaments. Goertz argued that only during the course of the debate over baptism did the Grebel group come to oppose the New Testament and the commands of Christ to the Old Testament, and in the process develop a Christology different to that of Zwingli.[123]

A third feature of the early Swiss Anabaptists' critique of the Reformers' view of faith is also seen as an outcome of anticlericalism. A faith that claimed "salvation" yet was fruitless was denounced as "hypocrisy."[124]

Where does Goertz place Hubmaier in relation to the Swiss Anabaptists? He noted that Hubmaier shared their anticlerical attitudes as demonstrated when Hubmaier not only vented his anticlerical spleen against the Roman Catholic Church and Zwingli, but also against himself when he had acted as a priest for the old church.[125]

---

119. Ibid., 43.
120. Ibid., 50.
121. Ibid.
122. Ibid., 51.
123. Ibid., 52.
124. Ibid., 62.
125. Ibid., 39–40.

Goertz makes no specific comment about Hubmaier's view of the relationship between the two Testaments, but his silence may well be taken to mean he saw no difference between Hubmaier's position and that of the early Swiss Anabaptists.

Goertz cited the influence of Augustinian spiritualism as the basis of Hubmaier's understanding that "during the decisive phase of the process of salvation the work of the external word (*signum*) receded in favor of the internal activity of the Spirit (*res*),"[126] and it was the activity of the Spirit that was related to faith. He further noted that Hubmaier could not be "fundamentally separated" from the early Swiss Anabaptists on the matter of faith that leads to moral improvement, though he acknowledged that Hubmaier's theological reflections on the nature of faith "took him beyond Swiss Anabaptism."[127] Goertz, however, following the lead of Bergsten, argues for a "cautious approach to the mystical notion of a graded path to salvation," an approach to faith and salvation also seen in Denck.[128] However, Hubmaier's understanding of baptism is contrasted strongly with that of the mystic South German-Austrian Anabaptist Hans Hut. The two shared "a demand for faith-baptism on the basis of the commandment of Jesus . . . and a distinction between inner and outer baptism." However, in Hut "the baptism-commandment was stripped of its scriptural meaning and used to formulate a mystical doctrine of the knowledge of God, with which the process of salvation in man began."[129] Goertz concludes that Hubmaier, like the Zurich Anabaptists, was less influenced by mysticism than Hut. In Goertz's opinion, Hubmaier fits the pattern of anticlericalism expressed as early Swiss Anabaptism. The fit is less comfortable when mysticism is added as a criterion, or the date is shifted to after the production of the *Schleitheim Articles*.

In *Anabaptist History and Theology*, Snyder argued that Anabaptism reflected aspects of both anticlericalism and fervent lay piety. He listed six characteristics of medieval piety that the Anabaptists retained but that Luther wanted removed:

1. An ascetic understanding of salvation and the Christian life.

2. An idealization of the life of Christ as the model for pious Christians.

---

126. Ibid., 51.
127. Ibid., 62.
128. Ibid., 64.
129. Ibid., 77.

3. A more communal understanding of life, the cosmos, and salvation.

4. A linking of spiritual charisma to moral purity.

5. A view of the world that interpreted life as a struggle between the forces of good and evil, Christ and Satan.

6. A spiritualized view of the world that still considered the secular realm to be a place where Satan's power held sway.[130]

He argued that these ideas are essentially more conservative and readily accessible and understandable to "common people," whereas the ideas of the Reformers expressed the views of the literate elite of society.[131] Snyder contends that the Radical Reformers were able to articulate an alternative vision of reform to evangelical reform. It was a vision that resonated with the common people as it "expressed long-cherished medieval ideas, tenaciously maintained in a rapidly changing world,"[132] and that emphasized the "regenerationist and ascetic tradition of late medieval piety which conceived of salvation in terms of sanctification."[133] Snyder also specifically identified the "sacramentarian movement in the Netherlands," which denied that matter could be spiritualized, as there was an impassable gulf between the worlds of spirit and matter.[134] Given Luther's tenacious support of the connection of Christ with the physical elements of the Lord's Supper, it is surprising that Snyder would argue the "sacramentarians" were conservatives rather than radicals. In Snyder's estimation, Hubmaier is representative of early Swiss Anabaptism, since "early Swiss Anabaptism was not a sectarian movement of separation from the world," rather it was a "grass roots, alternative movement of popular reform."[135] He went on to claim that "early Swiss Anabaptism was democratic, open to the Spirit, hopeful of reforming church and society. It was an Anabaptism that had yet to resolve many questions."[136] While the publication of the *Schleitheim Articles* might be taken to represent the resolution of these questions for Anabaptism, especially separation of the church from the world and the demand for pacifism, Snyder argued

---

130. Snyder, *Anabaptist History and Theology*, 30.
131. Ibid., 91.
132. Ibid.
133. Ibid.
134. Ibid., 38.
135. Ibid., 109.
136. Ibid., 112.

that the debate simply shifted east to Nikolsburg.[137] Following this line of reasoning, Hubmaier can therefore be represented as the genuine expression of early Swiss Anabaptism, both at Waldshut and later at Nikolsburg. Snyder demonstrates this point of view by utilizing Hubmaier's *A Christian Catechism*, published in Nikolsburg, to illustrate what he describes as the core teachings of Anabaptism.[138] He goes on to argue that it was the disputes over the implications of the core teachings that led eventually to the definition of "rigid boundaries" that separated the identifiable "denominational expressions" within Anabaptism.[139] In his 2006 article "Birth and Evolution of Swiss Anabaptism," Snyder maintained his view of the origins of Anabaptism as expressed in *Anabaptist History and Theology*. He does, however, identify a separation between Conrad Grebel and Felix Mantz in their letter to Thomas Müntzer, which aligns Mantz with Michael Sattler and the *Schleitheim Articles*, and Grebel with Hubmaier's nonseparatist ecclesiology.[140]

Since 2002, a number of other tributaries of the Catholic antecedent stream have been explored: Hubmaier's sacramental theology;[141] Hubmaier's understanding and use of the church fathers;[142] Hubmaier and the role of catechization linked to baptism;[143] and the exploration of Hubmaier's relationship to Catholic natural law.[144]

Samuel Nam explored the theology of baptism in Augustine, Luther, Zwingli, and Hubmaier and concluded that Hubmaier avoided falling into either Augustinian sacramentalism or Zwinglian spiritualism.[145] While Hubmaier is represented as agreeing with Zwingli that "outward baptism" does not convey God's grace inwardly, he differentiates Hubmaier from Zwingli by noting that Hubmaier retained the connection of the outer and inner through the work of the Spirit in the heart of the believer.[146] While

---

137. Ibid., 117.

138. Ibid., 143.

139. Ibid., 164–66.

140. Snyder, "Birth and Evolution of Swiss Anabaptism," 526.

141. Nam, "A Comparative Study"; Brewer, "A Response to Grace"; MacGregor, "Sacramental Theology," *Central European Synthesis*.

142. Gonzalez, "Balthasar Hubmaier "; Klager, "'Truth is Immortal.'" The essential content of Klager's thesis is in "Hubmaier's Use of the Church Fathers."

143. Graffagnino, "Shaping." This followed up Snyder's initial work in "Modern Mennonite Reality."

144. Cooper, "Human Reason or Reasonable Humanity?"

145. Nam, "A Comparative Study," 263.

146. Ibid., 261–62.

this is not sacramentalism in Roman Catholic or Lutheran terms, Nam concludes, "Hubmaier moved from sacramentalism but reaffirmed the importance of the sacrament of baptism as the means of the making of the true church."[147] Brewer argued that Hubmaier "preserved something of his scholastic, medieval past by retaining its sense of sacramentalism, yet transposing the dispensation of grace from the symbol itself to the promise of the believer which the symbol represents and conveys."[148] This view is founded on Hubmaier's understanding of "sacrament" as "sworn pledge," especially as used in Hubmaier's liturgy of the Lord's Supper where it is expressed as the "pledge of love."[149] Brewer recognizes that Hubmaier and Zwingli arrive at the same Eucharistic conclusions, "differing only in their hermeneutical routes."[150] MacGregor questions whether Hubmaier should be considered among the Anabaptists. He suggests the following definition: "Anabaptists should be formally defined as that set of Radicals, or rebaptizers, who regarded baptism and the Lord's Supper as ordinances rather than sacraments."[151] Hubmaier does not fit that definition because his sacramental theology understood that baptism and the Lord's Supper both acted as "vehicles or channels of divine grace,"[152] *ex opera operato*.[153] Consequently, he should not be included among the Anabaptists.[154] In fact, Hubmaier is not only atypical of Anabaptists, he "created a unique theological synthesis" among the early sixteenth-century Reformers.[155] Nam utilizes the same definition of Anabaptism as MacGregor; that is, Anabaptists reject the term sacrament in favor of ordinance, though Nam does suggest an openness to Hubmaier using the term sacrament. Brewer asserts that Hubmaier has a sacramental theology, but continues to think of the necessity of faith preceding grace, independent of the enactment of the "pledge of love." MacGregor sees Hubmaier as continuing the medieval view of a sacrament via the influence of Bernard of Clairvaux, and allows for a "real presence" of Christ in the sacrament, not in the elements of water, bread, and wine, but in the gathered believing church. Can Hub-

---

147. Ibid., 266.
148. Brewer, "A Response to Grace," 109–10.
149. Ibid., 88.
150. Ibid., 98.
151. MacGregor, *Central European Synthesis*, 8.
152. Ibid., 265.
153. Ibid., 256.
154. Ibid., 264.
155. Ibid., 265–66

maier be unambiguously placed among the Anabaptists? It would seem not, if the lens of sacramental theology is applied.

Two scholars independently undertook studies on the continuity of Balthasar Hubmaier with early church tradition. Antonia Lucic Gonzalez submitted her doctoral thesis in 2008, and Andrew Klager submitted his doctoral thesis in 2011. While both undertake an investigation of the relationship of Hubmaier to early church traditions, they do so from very different perspectives. Gonzalez is concerned to place Hubmaier in Heiko Oberman's schema of Tradition I and Tradition II,[156] and McGrath's Tradition 0 in which he placed all Radical Reformers, and with which Gonzalez takes issue.[157] She concludes that on his appropriation of the church fathers, creeds, and councils Hubmaier should be included with the Reformers in Oberman's Tradition I, though not in the "center" of that category, and definitely not in McGrath's modified Tradition 0.[158] Not surprisingly, Klager in his thesis, which also explores Hubmaier's interaction with the church fathers, spends considerable time differentiating his approach to the topic from that of Gonzalez. His central argument is that Hubmaeir "viewed the church fathers as co-affiliates in the one, true *ecclesia universalis* by virtue of their fidelity to Scripture and witness to the preservation of credo-baptism beyond the apostolic era."[159]

Klager argues that the influence of Erasmus is crucial in Hubmaier's use of the church fathers, especially Erasmus's understanding of the decline of the church and the *restitutio* principle.[160] Klager observes that, for Hubmaier, church fathers who wrote prior to the point when the error of infant baptism corrupted the church are seen as Hubmaier's spiritual ancestors, and their exegesis of Scripture is cited as authoritative. Those who write after that point, like Augustine, are not cited as authorities.[161] The theses of Gonzalez and Klager are complementary, but Klager's more thorough examination of the immediate context in which Hubmaier lived and wrote and his more thorough examination of Hubmaier's corpus, provides better specific data on which to base a conclusion about Hubmaier's relationship to the church fathers, creeds, and councils. Nevertheless,

---

156. Gonzalez, "Balthasar Hubmaier," 39. See Oberman, *Harvest of Medieval Theology*, 365–93; McGrath, *Reformation Thought: An Introduction*, 96.

157. Ibid., 61–62.

158. Ibid., 307–8

159. Klager, "Hubmaier's Use of the Church Fathers," 19.

160. Ibid., 24.

161. Ibid., 27.

Klager and Gonzalez share the view that "when disputes about the correct scriptural interpretation came to an impasse" Hubmaier looked "for the way the Scriptures had traditionally been interpreted" by "trustworthy sources."[162] "This is the very move, from Scripture to a verified source of its interpretation and authoritative doctrinal content, that prompts the questioning of Hubmaier's placement on the scale of radical biblicism and his alleged radical rejection of Christian tradition."[163] Yet Gonzalez acknowledges that Hubmaier's citings of the church fathers, the creeds, and councils are predetermined: "He uses their pronouncements when they agreed with his theology and disregarded them when they did not."[164] Klager holds a similar view about Hubmaier's integrity in citing the church fathers. It would seem then that Hubmaier is not citing them as independent authorities, but as exegetes, from a period when the church was not yet corrupted by the error of infant baptism, who agreed with his exegesis of pertinent passages of Scripture.

Snyder brought to the attention of the scholarly community the role of Hubmaier's 1526 *A Christian Catechsim* in the development of Anabaptism. In his 2008 doctoral thesis, Jason Graffagnino traced the antecedents of Hubmaier's catechism to Erasmus's rediscovery of the role of prebaptism catechization in the early church and how this prebaptism catechization might find expression in the sixteenth-century church. Erasmus argued for a "rebaptism" of children after receiving catechetical instruction rather than confirmation, but Erasmus's views were rejected by Catholic scholars at the Sorbonne in 1526.[165] Graffagnino argues for Hubmaier's awareness of this view of catechism as prebaptismal instruction prior to faith, and his incorporation of this view into his own understanding of baptism in his 1526 catechism. However, this is not the only influence discovered in Hubmaier's catechism. Graffagnino identifies the catechism of the *Unitas fratrum* in Moravia as also playing a crucial part in the development of Hubmaier's catechism.[166] In turn, Hubmaier's cat-

---

162. Ibid., 20, cf. Gonzalez, "Balthasar Hubmaier," 29.

163. Gonzalez, "Balthasar Hubmaier," 29.

164. Ibid., 291.

165. Graffagnino, "Shaping," 54–57.

166. Ibid., 168. Graffagnino challenges Rothkegel's identification of Hubmaier's pre-baptismal catechetical practice with Latin Church Fathers, arguing it may have come from the Czech Brethren practices. He also rejects Zeman's view that there was no connection between Hubmaier's *Lehrtafel* and the *Kinderfragen* of the Czech Brethren, arguing it is plausible that Hubmaier both was aware of the document and used some of its language, concepts, and practices. "Shaping," 170. Klager is also at

echism is "mirrored" in the catechism of Leonard Scheimer,[167] whose work Graffagnino argues influenced the Hutterite education system.[168] In this work, the "multi-dimensional religious climate of Moravia," as described by Martin Rothkegel,[169] is seen as the crucial factor in the development of Hubmaier's catechism.[170] Hubmaier is characterized as an Anabaptist, with antecedents in Erasmian Christian humanism as well as the older dissenting Moravian groups that had their origins in the ecclesial revolution generated by Jan Huss in the fifteenth century.

Brian Cooper, in his 2006 doctoral dissertation, explored the possibility that the understanding of the relationship between church and state as expressed by Hubmaier, Pilgram Marpeck, and Menno Simons, had strong parallels to medieval Catholic natural law theology. For him, the appeal to governments to ameliorate the plight of their Anabaptist communities based on human moral awareness is enough to demonstrate the strong parallels between these Anabaptists and natural law theology.[171] Anabaptist scholars would demure at this conclusion, not least on methodological grounds that a parallel in ideas is insufficient to argue for reclassification of Anabaptist identity, but also based on a misrepresentation of the ecclesiology of these three representatives of Anabaptism.

In all of the above scholarship, the question of biblical interpretation is often raised. Sometimes it is given significant attention, at other times it is mentioned in passing. However, the question of hermeneutics is vital to any interpretation of Anabaptism, and it is to this stream of Anabaptist research we now turn.

HERMENEUTICS

Roland Bainton's 1963 article, "The Bible in the Reformation," provides a useful introduction to the study of the question of hermeneutics in the sixteenth century. He identified the major issue of the period that divided the Protestant and Catholic groups as the question of authority. He concluded

---

odds with MacGregor who argues Hubmaier first published his catechism in August 1524 and used it in the instruction of children, and later revised it in Nikolsburg. MacGregor, "Sacramental Theology," 107n62.

167. Ibid., 190.
168. Ibid., 203–4.
169. Rothkegel, "Anabaptism in Moravia and Silesia," 164.
170. Graffagnino, "Shaping" 2.
171. Cooper, "Human Reason or Reasonable Humanity?" 96.

that the principle of *sola scriptura* "was basic for all the Protestants," and distinguished them from Catholics.[172] Rupert E. Davies had previously extensively explored this problem of authority in 1946 with specific reference to Luther, Zwingli, and Calvin. He too acknowledges that all three of these Protestant Reformers believed that "the Bible was the repository of all religious truth."[173] Both Bainton and Davies go on to show that it is not enough simply to say that the Bible is the final source and authority to which appeals are to be made in matters of faith and life. There are questions raised as to the priority of the canon of Scripture vis-a-vis the church and its tradition; and what constitutes the text of Scripture, an issue that must be determined before the source of authority can be exactly defined.[174] Davies demonstrates the problems inherent in this external objectivization of the Bible as the Word of God by citing Luther's criteria of selection, "all that proclaims Christ." By imposing this presupposition on the text of Scripture Luther effectively reduced the canon of Scripture that he considered authoritative.[175] Similarly, Davies notes that defining the text of Scripture involves issues of translation. He maintains that "every translation is a surreptitious exegesis,"[176] implying that exegesis negates Scripture as an objective source of truth and thus its authority. Davies also applies these criticisms of Luther to Zwingli and Calvin, concluding that these Protestant Reformers failed to solve the problem of authority; that is, to demonstrate that there is an "accessible source of religious truth which is wholly authoritative."[177]

What Davies hints at, became explicit in Bainton and was forcefully stated by Alister McGrath: that the Reformation principle *sola scriptura* "is rendered either meaningless or unusable without a reliable hermeneutical program."[178] It was not enough to claim that the Word of God contained all that was necessary for faith and life, the words of Scripture had to be interpreted so that people understood what it was that God was saying to them. It is with these principles and presuppositions of interpretation that investigations in the area of hermeneutics are concerned.

---

172. Bainton, "The Bible in the Reformation," 4.
173. Davies, *The Problem of Authority*, 147.
174. Bainton, "The Bible in the Reformation," 6–21.
175. Davies, *The Problem of Authority*, 56.
176. Ibid., 57.
177. Ibid., 9, 154.
178. McGrath, *Intellectual Origins*, 152.

Robert M. Grant, while recognizing that some commentators propose a distinction between interpretation and exegesis, rejects that position and treats the two as equivalent.[179] Timothy George extends the discussion beyond *sola scriptura* by addressing what is at "the heart of Reformation hermeneutics," the Reformers' understanding of the clarity of Scripture.[180] In George's opinion, the Reformers not only viewed the Scripture as clear for all who had faith in matters relating to eternal salvation, but also saw the Scripture as a book different to all others: it was "alive" and it "interpreted" the reader.[181] Hermeneutics was therefore more than the application of "sound philological rules." It also required the development of a well-ordered ministry and program of rigorous theological education for the pastors and teachers who interpreted the Scripture to the congregation through the preached Word. Only through such a trained ministry could a harmony between the inner and external Word be achieved.[182] The emphasis on the preached Word as the process whereby the Holy Spirit brings about this reconciliation of the inner and outer Word is noted as axiomatic for Zwingli.[183] When tracing the influence of the Reformation, George includes a small section on Hubmaier, in which he notes a fundamental difference in hermeneutical approach between Zwingli and Hubmaier. For Zwingli, what is not forbidden in Scripture may continue to be practiced in accordance with the long traditions of the church; for Hubmaier, what is not explicitly commanded may not be practiced.[184]

The various Magisterial Reformers were themselves very aware of the importance of hermeneutics. Heinrich Bornkamm has shown that Luther, in his 1521 work *Lovaniensis scholae sophistis redditae Lutheriana confutatio*, demonstrated the intimate link between justification, hermeneutics, and philosophical considerations.[185]

Zwingli also shows his awareness of the hermeneutical issue in his writings *On Clarity* (1522) and *Sixty-Seven Articles* (1523). W. Peter Stephens claims that the series of rules that Zwingli enunciated for the interpretation of Scripture were developed in debate with various Catholic, Lutheran, and Anabaptist opponents. He maintains that most of the

---

179. Grant, *Short History*, 2–3.
180. George, *Reading Scripture*, 124.
181. Ibid., 127.
182. Ibid., 132–33.
183. Ibid., 131.
184. Ibid., 224.
185. Bornkamm, *Luther in Mid-Career*, 183–97.

developments in Zwingli's hermeneutic were present in his initial works, and that "little change" took place in these principles of interpretation.[186]

Heinrich Bullinger, Zwingli's successor, was also fully aware of the importance of the hermeneutical dispute, and wrote in a letter to the pastors of Bern specifically how to deal with Anabaptists when debating with them. His method was to challenge their interpretation of Scripture and insist on the Reformed understanding and method of interpretation, using firstly the unity of the Old and New Testaments, and secondly the rule of faith and love as the fundamental principles for interpreting Scripture.[187]

Calvin's *Institutes of the Christian Religion* is not only his "comprehensive summary" of theology, but included his hermeneutical principles so that his purpose "to prepare and qualify students of theology for the reading of the divine Word" could also be fulfilled.[188]

The Anabaptists also became involved in trying to define their own principles of interpretation. John Wenger translated and edited an early Anabaptist tract on hermeneutics that he attributed to Michael Sattler.[189] This tract begins by proposing to explain the principles for correct interpretation of Scripture, but does this more by way of a demonstration of a method than a description of the principles or presuppositions that guide the method.

This awareness of the importance of hermeneutics in the sixteenth century was reflected in Reformation studies from the late 1940s to the end of the 1980s. Various researchers investigated the link between Luther's theology and his hermeneutic. Gerhard Ebeling's *Evangelische Evangelienauslegung* pioneered this research and is, according to James Preus, foundational in understanding Luther's new hermeneutic.[190] Ebeling identified a shift in Luther's hermeneutic from the older four senses of Scripture and the method of the scholastics, to a historico-grammatical approach. He achieves this by conflating the three spiritual senses, the allegorical, tropological, and anagogical, into one, the *sensus literalis propheticus*. This resulted in Luther arguing that exegesis of Scripture involves only grasping the literal sense, which is understood as the tropological

---

186. Stephens, *Theology of Huldrych Zwingli*, 59.

187. Fast and Yoder, "How to Deal with Anabaptists," 84–88.

188. Preface to Calvin's *Institutes of the Christian Religion*, 18–19, cited in Forstmann, *Word and Spirit*, 22. Calvin's hermeneutics are not discussed at length as he played no part in the development of Hubmaier's hermeneutic.

189. Wenger, "An Early Anabaptist Tract," 26–44.

190. Preus, *From Shadow to Promise*, 148.

sense, where Christ is identified with faith.[191] McGrath does not accept the older view of the new hermeneutic being the cause of Luther's theological breakthrough, though he does concede that "Luther's hermeneutical and soteriological insights developed symbiotically, each dimension to his thought reinforcing and stimulating the other."[192]

Preus takes issue with Ebeling's view, arguing that to identify Christ and faith in the Old Testament does not adequately consider the way Luther deals with the Old Testament text. He proposes that a better understanding of Luther's hermeneutic is gained by considering how Luther developed the notion of promise. Luther broke with the older method of interpretation only when he ceased to use the tropological sense.[193] Darrell Reinke seeks to extend Preus's examination of Luther's hermeneutic by noting a move from allegory to metaphor in the way Luther used the Old Testament.[194] Siegfried Raeder has introduced the issue of Luther as translator into his discussion of Luther's hermeneutic.[195]

There have also been investigations into Luther's understanding of the term the "clarity of Scripture." Ernst Wolf has examined this topic by analyzing the debate between Luther and Erasmus on free will.[196] Erling Teigen approached the subject by analyzing the Lutheran confessions of faith.[197] Priscilla Hayden-Roy undertook a comparative study on the clarity of Scripture between Luther and Sebastian Frank.[198]

Some work was done on Zwingli's hermeneutic, though not as extensively as that done on Luther. Stephens, who undertakes an examination of Zwingli's use of the Bible, notes that the foundational work in this area was produced by Edwin Künzli in 1951 as a dissertation at Zurich University.[199] Fritz Busser noted that the lack of work on Zwingli's hermeneutic is

191. Ebeling, "The New Hermeneutic," 36–37.

192. McGrath, *Intellectual Origins*, 164.

193. Preus, "Old Testament Promissio," 161.

194. Reinke, "From Allegory to Metaphor," 338–39.

195. Raeder, "Exegetical and Hermeneutical Work," 363–406.

196. Wolf, "Uber 'Klarheit der Heiligen Schrift,'" 721–28. Hayden-Roy has also undertaken a similar discussion, comparing Luther with Sebastian Franck. Hayden-Roy, "Hermeneutica gloria," 50–67.

197. Teigen, "Clarity of Scripture," 147–66. Other works on Luther's hermeneutic include Franzmann, "Seven Theses," 337–50; Goldingay, "Luther and the Bible," 33–58; and Runia, "Hermeneutics of the Reformers," 121–52. Runia confines his comparison to Luther and Calvin.

198. Hayden-Roy, "Hermeneutica gloria."

199. Stephens, *Theology of Huldrych Zwingli*, 51n2. See also Künzli,

a "deplorable" gap in Zwinglian research. He addressed the issue in a brief article noting Zwingli's debt to Erasmus. He concludes that the detailed examination of the evidence that points to the early and sustained influence of Erasmus on Zwingli's hermeneutic gives "greater weight" to the view that Zwingli came to know the gospel independently of Luther.[200] Fulvio Ferrario has contributed to this area of research by investigating Zwinglian influences on the origins of Anabaptist hermeneutic in Zurich.[201] Christine Christ has contributed a significant article assessing the relationship between the hermeneutics of Zwingli and Erasmus in 1522. It provides an excellent foundation for further exploration in the development of Zwingli's hermeneutic in his dispute with the Anabaptists.[202]

The field of Erasmian hermeneutics has also occupied some researchers. It has received more attention than that given to Zwingli, but much less than to Luther. John W. Aldridge produced a study on this topic in 1966, which received very critical reviews.[203] John Payne, who was responsible for one of the negative reviews of Aldridge's work, presented his own brief assessment based on a wider selection of sources than those used by Aldridge. He rejects the view that Erasmus is the father of the modern historico-grammatical method of exegesis, and the view that Erasmus passed over the search for the literal sense of Scripture. He proposes an alternative view that the young Erasmus of the *Enchiridion Militis Christiani* (1503) followed the allegorical and tropological senses more than the older Erasmus who wrote the preface to the *Novum Testamentum* (1516). In the later work, Erasmus strongly advocates the historico-grammatical approach to the interpretation of Scripture. However, following his debates with Luther in *De libero arbitrio* (1524–25), Erasmus again shifts his position. He now gives greater weight in his hermeneutic to the tropological and allegorical senses compared to the literal sense derived through

---

"Quellenproblem Erster Teil," 185–207; Künzli, "Quellenproblem Zweiter Teil," 253–307; Marti's response to Künzli: "Mysticher Schriftsinn," 365–74; and Künzli's response to Marti: "Antwort an Paul Marti," 375–77.

200. Busser, "Zwingli the Exegete," 192.

201. Ferrario, "L'anabattismo," 383ff. He also has a chapter on the hermeneutics of Zwingli and Hubmaier in his PhD dissertation, which was presented to The University of Zurich in January 1992. He kindly made this chapter available to the author. He is in general agreement with the analysis of the hermeneutical relationship of Hubmaier and Zwingli as presented in this book, though he restricts himself to an examination of only Hubmaier's baptismal works. His PhD was later published as *La "Sacra ancora."*

202. Christ, "Das Schriftverständnis," 117–25.

203. Aldridge, *The Hermeneutics of Erasmus*.

the historico-grammatical method of exegesis.[204] Torrance holds a similar position recognizing, as does Payne, the distinctions between body and spirit, letter and spirit, which underlie all of Erasmus's hermeneutic.[205] These works on Erasmus's hermeneutic can be supplemented by referring to two sets of collected essays, *Essays on the Works of Erasmus,* edited by Richard L. DeMolen and *Erasmus,* edited by Thomas A. Dorey.

In 1984, Willard Swartley compiled *Essays on Biblical Interpretation.* The Select Bibliography shows that there was major interest in Anabaptist hermeneutics in the 1960s. Of the twenty-five articles cited that deal with sixteenth-century Anabaptist hermeneutics, sixteen come from the 1960s. The more general treatment of the topic before the 1960s was transformed into more specific studies of individuals and particular topics within the broader framework of hermeneutics. William Klassen wrote on Pilgram Marpeck, addressing the issues of letter and spirit, and the relationship of the Old and New Covenants.[206] Henry Poettcker investigated the hermeneutic of Menno Simons.[207] Walter Klaassen wrote on Word, Spirit and Scripture, as well as a brief article on the hermeneutic of Balthasar Hubmaier.[208] Wilhelm Wiswedel wrote on the theme of the "Inner and Outer Word," which included consideration of Hans Denck as the major contributor in this area.[209] This listing of materials on Anabaptist hermeneutics should be complemented by the addition of works on the hermeneutic of Peter Riedemann by Robert C. Holland and the hermeneutic of Dirk Philips in association with the theme of ecclesiology that Douglas H. Shantz addressed in 1986.[210]

In a short article for Volume 5 of the *Mennonite Encyclopedia,* Swartley identifies a number of principles on which both Protestants and Anabaptists agreed regarding interpretation of the Scriptures. These are: the final authority of the Scriptures; an emphasis on the literal-historical method of interpretation in contrast to the allegorical methods used since

---

204. Payne, "Towards the Hermeneutics of Erasmus," 13–49.

205. Torrance, "The Hermeneutics of Erasmus."

206. William Klassen, "Hermeneutics of Pilgram Marpeck." Also "Anabaptist Hermeneutics," 83–86 and *Covenant and Community.*

207. Poettcker, *Hermeneutics of Menno Simons.*

208. Walter Klaassen, "Word, Spirit, and Scripture." Also "Speaking in Simplicity" and "The Bern Debate."

209. Wiswedel, "The Inner and the Outer Word."

210. Holland, "Hermeneutics of Peter Riedemann"; Shantz, "Ecclesiological Focus." 115, 127.

the second century AD; and a christocentric emphasis.²¹¹ He further notes that the areas of disagreement included a difference in understanding the relationship between the two Testaments; the relation of the Word and the Spirit; the inner and outer word; the role of believers in the interpretation of the Scriptures; and in his opinion "perhaps most importantly of all, in the relation of discipleship and obedience to insight and knowledge."²¹² He goes on to suggest that there were "aberrations" to these stated Anabaptist hermeneutical presuppositions and principles, specifically identifying the Münster Anabaptists who did not hold to the superiority of the New Testament over the Old, and who shifted from nonviolence to violence. He attributes this shift to the eschatological views of Melchior Hofmann, which he asserts introduced a new hermeneutic.²¹³

Hubmaier's place in Swartley's Anabaptist hermeneutical family is not explored to any depth. For Swartley, Hubmaier is peripheral to Anabaptist hermeneutics. Swartley identifies a primary feature of Anabaptist hermeneutical principle as "communal hermeneutics." Pilgram Marpeck and Hans Denck provide the major sources from which Swartley draws material to describe this "communal hermeneutic." Hubmaier is noted as supporting this key principle, but only his *Theses against Eck* is cited in support of this view. Marpeck's *Testamentserleutterung* is cited as providing evidence of the way Anabaptists understood the Old Testament as preparatory to the New.²¹⁴ Hans Denck is cited to support the view that Anabaptists emphasized the inner Word, the inner illumination by the Holy Spirit that enables the believer to understand the Word of God. To balance Denck's emphasis on the Holy Spirit, Swartley cites Marpeck as an example of an Anabaptist who upheld the primacy of the written Word over the Spirit. Marpeck demonstrated his position in his debate on the issue with the spiritualist Caspar Schwenckfeld.²¹⁵ Finally, Denck is used as the example of one who stressed obedience as a hermeneutical principle, described by Irvin B. Horst as an "epistemological principle."²¹⁶

Research in Anabaptist hermeneutics virtually ceased in the 1990s, but was revived to some degree with Stuart Murray's 2000 publication of *Biblical Interpretation*. This work provided a general exploration of

211. Swartley, "Biblical Interpretation (Hermeneutics)," 80.
212. Ibid., 81.
213. Ibid., 82.
214. Ibid., 81.
215. Ibid.
216. Ibid.

sixteenth-century Anabaptists under what Murray identified as key themes. These key themes closely reflect the major issues current at that time in Anabaptist scholarship. We will return to Murray's work to examine where Hubmaier is located in this broad Anabaptist world of interpretation.

After Bender's attempt to define normative Anabaptism, research began that specifically focused on Hubmaier's hermeneutic. Walter Klaassen identifies Hubmaier as being like the Swiss Brethren in his general approach to the interpretation of the Bible.[217] He does acknowledge that Hubmaier differs from the Swiss Brethren in his view of the civil magistrate and that he does not make as definite distinction between the two Testaments as the Swiss Brethren.[218] Klaassen restricts his analysis to Hubmaier's works to those related to baptism. Hence it is hardly surprising that Hubmaier's method of interpretation seems very similar to that attributed to the Swiss Brethren, as they agreed with Hubmaier in his conclusions regarding baptism.

Klaassen maintained that Hubmaier and the Swiss Brethren shared a suspicion of learning that they believed was used to cloud the plain simple meaning of the Scripture.[219] Learning and knowledge of languages has a place when seeking the meaning of Scripture, but it is always supplementary to common sense (the literal sense) or natural reason.[220] This position was based on the presupposition that the Scriptures were essentially clear and understandable to even the simplest person, a position also held at various times by Erasmus, Luther, and Zwingli early in the Reformation.

Of a more technical nature was the principle that a command includes the prohibition of its opposite.[221] This was a principle that Zwingli had used in debate with his Catholic opponents to reject purgatory, and which Hubmaier also adopted. It was restated by Hubmaier as "everything not expressly commanded in Scripture [is] to be regarded as forbidden."[222] Hubmaier was later to qualify this by adding that it applied to those things that were to do with the honor of God and our salvation. This emphasis on the commands of Christ also led to the adoption of the principle of

---

217. Walter Klaassen, "Speaking in Simplicity," 139.
218. Ibid.
219. Ibid., 142.
220. Ibid., 144–45.
221. Ibid., 145.
222. Ibid.

obedience.[223] Where Christ gives a direct command, obedience is demanded of the disciple without fear of the consequences.

Hubmaier also subscribed to the generally accepted principle of the Reformers that Scripture interprets Scripture; the clear text being used to clarify the meaning of the obscure.[224] A supplementary rule states that the text must be interpreted in its context, the preceding and following text being taken into consideration.[225]

However, it is Klaassen's contention that Hubmaier did not consistently use his principles of interpretation, despite this being a fundamental principle of his hermeneutic.[226] As evidence of Hubmaier's failure to apply his own principle of consistency, Klaassen cites Hubmaier's work *On the Sword* (1527). In this work, Hubmaier argues against the Swiss Brethren's position concerning Christian magistracy and bearing the sword. Hubmaier maintains that it is not only possible for a Christian to be a magistrate, but that it is of greater benefit to the civil order if Christians are magistrates. Klaassen argues that the difference is the result of the inconsistent application of hermeneutical principles.[227] Although Klaassen has identified the difference in theological conclusions between the Swiss Brethren and Hubmaier concerning the magistracy, he has not provided the detailed analysis to prove his thesis that the difference is due to inconsistent application of hermeneutical principles. Klaassen's conclusions have been challenged by Snyder's position that early Swiss Anabaptism up to 1527 and the publication of the *Schleitheim Articles* was not sectarian, separatist, and pacifist.[228] Snyder used Hubmaier's *A Christian Catechism* of 1526 as the identifiable core of Anabaptist theology. While Snyder does not comment directly on the issue, he clearly implies that Hubmaier consistently applied his hermeneutic throughout his career. This conclusion is based on Snyder's redefinition of the theological core of Anabaptism, and the distinction between the Swiss Anabaptists before and after the publication of the *Schleitheim Articles*.

Stuart Murray's presentation of Hubmaier within the broader setting of Anabaptist hermeneutics represents the view of those researchers

---

223. Ibid., 146.
224. Ibid.
225. Ibid., 417.
226. Ibid., 145
227. Ibid., 147.
228. Snyder, *Anabaptist History and Theology*, 109.

who continue to see Hubmaier as "atypical" of Anabaptism.[229] On the one hand, Hubmaier is presented as sharing the hermeneutic of the Swiss Anabaptists, especially his understanding of the work of the Holy Spirit to "liberate reason from darkness to light."[230] On the other hand, Hubmaier's understanding of the relationship of the Word and the Spirit is different to the Swiss Anabaptists, allowing Hubmaier to be critical of their literalism that led to legalism.[231] Hubmaier also shared with the Swiss Anabaptists a view of the simplicity of Scripture and a suspicion of theological learning,[232] and an appeal to congregational hermeneutics, where the scholar aided the congregation to understand technical details but could not override the congregation's agreed understanding.[233] Murray notes Hubmaier urged that dark texts should be read in light of clear texts of Scripture and so avoid "half-truth."[234] This is Hubmaier's "cloven-hoof" hermeneutical principle, which was not used by the Swiss Anabaptists. However, Murray's analysis of Hubmaier's hermeneutic, like Klaassen's, is not based on a thorough assessment of all of Hubmaier's works, a task beyond the scope of what Murray was seeking to achieve.

The resurgence in Hubmaier studies since 2000 has not seen extensive commentary on his hermeneutics. Kirk MacGregor traces the development of Hubmaier's hermeneutic against the backdrop of Luther's hermeneutic of "*sola scriptura* plus faithful reason,"[235] but is more interested in tracing the influence of Bernard of Clairvaux on Hubmaier's sacramental theology. Gerald Biesecker-Mast does include a useful section on Hubmaier's "cloven-hoof" hermeneutical principle, which he sees as the individual reconciling apparently contradictory passages of Scripture. However, this fails to appreciate the congregational setting of Hubmaier's hermeneutic.[236] Emir Caner represents Hubmaier as at one with those who understand the Scriptures to be "the inerrant and infallible rule of faith."[237] Hubmaier's view of Scripture is complemented by his hermeneutic that he summarized in four premises: "Scripture must be read in its plain, simple

---

229. Murray, *Biblical Interpretation*, 29.

230. Ibid., 57.

231. Ibid., 126.

232. Ibid., 53.

233. Ibid., 163.

234. Ibid., 60.

235. MacGregor, *Central European Synthesis*, 98–100.

236. Biesecker-Mast, *Separation and the Sword*, 116–17.

237. Caner, "Balthasar Hübmaier," 32.

context unless otherwise indicated. . . . Scripture must be compared with other texts in order to confirm beliefs. . . . Ambiguous texts must be enlightened by clearer, more understandable texts. Scripture is unchanging and eternal, but humans can err in interpretation."[238] Caner sums up Hubmaier's hermeneutic as similar to the Swiss Brethren. Hubmaier teaches that the interpretation of Scripture should take place among the gathered body of believers, that correct understanding of Scripture brings about change in behavior, and that those who perform "tricks" with Scripture can "wreak havoc on the congregation."[239] However, Caner's interpretation is based exclusively on Hubmaier's *Theses Against Eck*, which is then erroneously represented as Hubmaier's hermeneutic for all his works.

Brian Brewer is representative of a number of other Hubmaier scholars who make passing reference to Hubmaier's use of Scripture or occasionally to his hermeneutic. Brewer acknowledged the contribution Luther made to Hubmaier's appreciation of *sola scriptura*, but did not systematically explore Hubmaier's hermeneutic.[240]

In 1981, John Oyer suggested the area of hermeneutics as a topic for further research in Anabaptist studies.[241] H. Wayne Walker Pipkin in 2006 decried that "some interpreters simply write their own agenda onto Hubmaier."[242] The research that follows seeks to allow Hubmaier to speak for himself, in his own words, and within his own historical context. By using the lens of the clarity of Scripture it is hoped to clarify the relationship of Hubmaier to the various sources of potential influence on the development of his hermeneutic. It is also hoped that by using the theme of the clarity of Scripture it will be possible to better determine Hubmaier's place in the Reformation as a whole. Finally, the careful assessment of Hubmaier's hermeneutic across the whole corpus of his work will provide a detailed basis on which future comparative studies between Hubmaier and his contemporary reformers: Magisterial, Radical and Anabaptist, may be undertaken.

---

238. Ibid., 33.
239. Ibid.,
240. Brewer, "A Response to Grace," 24.
241. Oyer, "Topics for Research," 381.
242. Pipkin, *Scholar, Pastor, Martyr*, 32.

4

The Plumb Line of Holy Scripture
(Writings from October 26–28, 1523, to February 2, 1524)

STATEMENTS AT THE SECOND ZURICH DISPUTATION

(October 26–28, 1523)[1]

Setting

HUBMAIER'S APPEARANCE AT THE Second Zurich Disputation (October 26–28, 1523) provided him with a public forum at which he unreservedly committed himself to the Reformation in its Zwinglian form. During the proceedings of this disputation, he made four statements on images and the Mass, providing the first records that can be analyzed to determine his hermeneutic.

Analysis

Hubmaier begins with an appeal to the words of Moses and Christ referring to rescuing an animal from a pit that he then applies to the greater

---

1. *PY,* 21–29.

need to rescue those in error in matters of salvation.[2] Such errors had indeed occurred with regard to images and the Mass. He asserts that settlement of the dispute concerning the images and the Mass "cannot take place more fittingly nor properly than through the proclamation of the clear Word of God as written in both Testaments. For all divisive questions and controversies only Scripture, canonized and sanctified by God himself, should and must be the judge, nothing else: or heaven and earth must fall."[3] He goes on to substantiate his claim that only Scripture is to be the judge in these matters by citing a series of Old and New Testament texts, giving prominence to the words of Christ, "Search the Scriptures. They give testimony of me" (John 5:39f). He goes on to add that this was also the usage of Christ, Paul, and the apostles when a controversial issue was to be judged.[4] He maintains that "holy Scripture alone is the true light and lantern through which all human argument, darkness, and objections can be recognized."[5] Again he links an Old Testament text with words of Christ to demonstrate that there is unity on this matter across the Old and New Testaments.[6] He concludes that the errors and abuses of making images and the Mass "shall be demonstrated only through the plumb line of the bright clear Word of God, thereby being recognized and moderated."[7]

Hubmaier's second recorded contribution to the disputation was to quote from Deut 27:15. He was responding to the objection of Jacob Edlibach, who argued that it was not wrong to make or paint images but only that they should not be worshipped.[8] This passage was accepted by all those present as a prohibition from God that images were not to be made or worshipped, and that it was still valid.

Towards the end of proceedings on the third day, Hubmaier returned to the theme of images to give a summation of his opinion. He supplies a sequence of Old Testament texts as the foundation for his argument for rejecting images: Exod 20:4–6; Deut 5:6–10; 7:25; 27:15. He argues that God had given in the first two texts a series of five distinct prohibitions against the making and worshipping of images, and in the final two texts commands for the destruction of idols and the cursing of those who make them.[9]

2. *PY*, 22–23.
3. *PY*, 23.
4. *PY*, 23.
5. *PY*, 23.
6. *PY*, 24.
7. *PY*, 24.
8. *PY*, 24.
9. *PY*, 25.

The Plumb Line of Holy Scripture

He then adds a "mosaic argument. . . . [E]ither it is commanded to possess images or it is not."[10] Here the emphasis falls on the necessity that a practice must be commanded by God if it is good; if it is not commanded then it is worthless, for "God alone is good, so everything that is good must come from God alone."[11] It follows from this that "everything which God has not taught us either with words or deeds is worthless and in vain."[12] He then links a command of God from Deut 12:32 with the words of Jesus from Matt 15:13 and a saying of Paul in Rom 14:23 to establish his principle that only those things commanded by God are to be done. In the process, Hubmaier also demonstrates that the Scripture is united in this matter.

There follows a second either/or argument about the usefulness of images. If they are useless what do you want with them; if they are useful then God is a liar because he has said in Isa 44:9 that they are useless. To say God is a liar is blasphemous, since God is not only good but also true in his nature.[13]

Hubmaier then addresses the practical problem of how the images in the churches are to be removed. He proposes that the "clear holy Word of God against the images and idols in Old and New Testament must be shown to the people earnestly and often with great care and diligence. This will exercise its authority and power and with time will drive all the images out."[14] He asserts that every Christian will come to recognize the truth of this position for himself through the preaching of the Word of God and that the parish congregation "will gather and decide unanimously without any disorder" that the images should be removed.[15] The removal of the images by the congregation is the demonstration that "the powerful Word

---

10. *PY*, 25.
11. *PY*, 25.
12. *PY*, 25.
13. *PY*, 26.
14. *PY*, 26.

15. *PY*, 26. Hubmaier shows that at this point in time he followed closely Zwingli's method of dealing with the removal of images. By way of contrast, the more radical members of the Zurich Reformers' supporters such as Conrad Grebel and Simon Strumpf did not want to wait on the weaker in the faith being instructed and convinced by the Word of God. Rather, they insisted that since the truth had been made evident it must be immediately acted upon. Strumpf placed the emphasis on the Holy Spirit as the source of revelation; Grebel placed the emphasis on Scripture. Harder, *Sources of Swiss Anabaptism*, 242, 247.

of God will have borne its fruit," something that the Word of God must do according to Hubmaier's understanding of Isa 55:10.[16]

Hubmaier's fourth comment occurred early on the third day of the disputation, in relation to the Mass and the numerous abuses that accompanied it. He wants the record to show that he is of the same opinion as Zwingli and Leo Jud that the Mass is not a sacrifice, rather it is a memorial or remembrance of Christ's suffering. By the outward sign and symbol of the Mass, "we are made completely certain of the forgiveness of our sins."[17] He cites a sequence of New Testament references that are the basis for his opinion: Matt 26:26–28; Luke 22:19ff; Mark 14:22–24; 1 Cor 11:23–26; Heb 7, 9. On the basis of this thesis that the Mass is not a sacrifice he proposes five further conclusions that argue for the necessity of faith in the participant for the Mass to be truly celebrated. Preaching also needs to accompany the celebration of the Mass and reading the Mass should be "in German to the Germans."[18] Finally, he states that those who celebrate the Mass must give it to others and not just themselves, and that both elements should be given to all.

Hubmaier concludes these remarks with an appeal to all those present to correct him if he has been in error, for being human it is possible that he could have erred. However, he will only accept correction based on the Scriptures.[19]

Even though the remarks Hubmaier made at the Second Zurich Disputation are not extensive, they do provide enough material to begin to define his hermeneutical principles. It can be seen that Hubmaier is in basic accord with Zwingli on most issues at this time. It is also possible to build a more complete picture of Zwingli's hermeneutical principles to this point as he has expressed himself clearly on the subject in a large number of sources and with more precision than Hubmaier in these four short comments.

With regard to his attitude to Scripture, Zwingli stresses the clarity of the Word of God. In his sermon *On Clarity* (July 1522), Zwingli is at pains to show that the Word of God is clear and certain and requires no human intervention for it to be understood.[20] This does not mean that the

---

16. *PY*, 26.

17. *PY*, 27.

18. *PY*, 28.

19. *PY*, 29. Luther is later to comment that this phrase has become a catchphrase for those who obstinately refuse to be corrected concerning their interpretation of Scripture. Luther, *On the Bondage of the Will*, 165.

20. Zwingli, *On Clarity*, 78–80.

The Plumb Line of Holy Scripture

Word of God can be understood by human reason alone, as he makes clear in his remarks at the First Zurich Disputation (January 1523) and in his *Sixty-Seven Articles* (July 1523). In these two works, greater emphasis is placed on the role of the Holy Spirit as the interpreter of Scripture and the means by which people gain an understanding of the truth as revealed in the Word of God.[21] In this regard, Zwingli moves from his earlier opinion in his work *On Clarity*, which indicated that the preached word was of itself clear and powerful enough to bring understanding of the truth of the gospel to people,[22] to his position in his short work *Of the Education of Youth* (August 1523). Here he states that though faith comes by hearing, and hearing by the Word of God, "this does not mean that very much can be accomplished by the preaching of the external word apart from the internal address and compulsion of the Spirit."[23]

Hubmaier supported this clarified position concerning the relationship of the preached word and the role of the Spirit at the Second Zurich Disputation.[24] For Hubmaier, the clarity of the Word of God is dependent on the interpretive function of the Holy Spirit.

Zwingli also modified his understanding of the power of the Word of God by the time he spoke at the Second Zurich Disputation. Whereas in his work *On Clarity* he had thought that "if God wills, all things are done the moment he speaks his Word,"[25] at the Second Zurich Disputation he is advising the gathered preachers to go back to their parishes and preach the Word of God. In due course, the people will, through the aid of the Holy Spirit, come to understand the truth concerning images and the Mass.[26]

While Hubmaier also emphasizes the clarity of the Word of God and the role of the Holy Spirit in bringing clarity, he does so without the extensive and explicit references found in Zwingli's writings of this period.

---

21. Zwingli, *Sixty-Seven Articles*, 56, 103, 106. See also Furcha, "In Defense of the Spirit" 51–52.

22. Zwingli, *On Clarity*, 68.

23. Zwingli, *Of the Education of Youth*, 104. It is this shift to the dominant role of the Spirit in the process of understanding Scripture that is reflected in Strumpf's outburst at the Second Zurich Disputation. When Zwingli suggested that the Zurich Council would decide how the Mass should be properly observed in their domains Strumpf responded: "Master Huldrych! You have no authority to place the decision in Milord's hands, for the decision is already made: the Spirit of God decides." Harder, *Sources of Swiss Anabaptism*, 242.

24. Harder, *Sources of Swiss Anabaptism*, 236, 240, 246.

25. Zwingli, *On Clarity*, 68.

26. Harder, *Sources of Swiss Anabaptism*, 246.

Hubmaier also stresses more strongly the importance of preaching than does Zwingli. Windhorst claims that this emphasis on the necessity of preaching the Word of God and the faith that follows from it finds its origin in Luther.[27]

Both Hubmaier and Zwingli insist on the sole authority of the Scripture to be the judge in matters of dispute in the church. Zwingli gives more detail as to which other possible authorities he has rejected. In his work *On Clarity,* church councils are the main target of his attack; while in his *Sixty-Seven Articles,* human reason, the popes, and the fathers are also rejected as authorities to whom one can appeal to obtain the meaning of Scripture.[28] Zwingli's opinion can best be summarized by the concluding statement in his *Sixty-Seven Articles,* "Scripture must be my judge as well as the judge of everyone else; but no person must ever be judge of the Word of God."[29]

With regard to the unity of the Scriptures, Hubmaier only implies that he accepts that there is a unity between the Old and the New Testaments when he notes the equal authority of the command of God through Moses and the words of Christ, and when he uses the formula "as written in both Testaments."[30] Zwingli uses similar methods when he notes that the Spirit speaks in the Psalms and Isaiah, and that Christ, Paul, and Peter are in agreement.[31] He also uses the formula as "written in both Testaments."[32]

In the matter of what constitutes Scripture, Zwingli is more definite than Hubmaier. Zwingli explicitly rejects both the Apocrypha and the Apocalypse; the first because it was not accepted by the Jews, the latter as it was not reckoned a sacred book by the early church.[33]

With regard to hermeneutical method, there are also similarities between the position of Hubmaier and Zwingli, as well as significant differences. Both emphasize the attitude of humility with which the reader must come to the Word of God. Any person who comes bringing their own understanding will, in Zwingli's opinion, inevitably twist the meaning

---

27. Windhorst, "Anfänge und Aspekte," 151.

28. Zwingli, *On Clarity,* 77, 79, 87; Zwingli, *Sixty-Seven Articles,* 10–11, 21, 35, 121, 168, 364.

29. Zwingli, *Sixty-Seven Articles,* 373.

30. *PY,* 23.

31. Zwingli, *On Clarity,* 62.

32. Zwingli, *Sixty-Seven Articles,* 162.

33. Zwingli, Ibid., 162, 166, 335.

of Scripture.[34] Zwingli spends a great deal of time in *On Clarity* dealing with the question, "How to prepare yourself to read Scripture?" His answer focuses on the attitude of humility and surrender to the Word of God. When he wrote *Of the Education of Youth*, he added the new dimension of the need for the interpreter of the Word of God to be equipped with three essential languages: Latin, Greek, and Hebrew. Without these languages Scripture cannot be understood correctly.[35] Like Hubmaier, he also stresses the need for the Mass to be read in the vernacular to the congregation. However, to this point Hubmaier had not declared himself on the issue of the need to read Greek and Hebrew as well as Latin to correctly understand the text of Scripture.

Both Hubmaier and Zwingli see the gathered congregation as having a role in determining the meaning of Scripture and implementing action to see that the church lives in conformity to the truth of Scripture. However, Hubmaier confines his opinion to the non-disruptive removal of images from the church following a unanimous decision by the gathered congregation.[36] Zwingli, on the other hand, extends the role of the congregation to making decisions, on the basis of Scripture, about the time and manner of distribution of the Lord's Supper.[37]

Hubmaier stated one formal principle of his hermeneutic in his comments at the Second Zurich Disputation; namely, "everything which God has not taught us either with words or deeds is worthless and vain."[38] Zwingli begins with the premise that God is the source of all good, and that all that God commands is good.[39] However, this does not lead Zwingli to demand that only those things that God commands are to be kept by the Christian as they alone are good, as is the case with Hubmaier. Rather, Zwingli goes on to expound his Article 28 to mean that "everything which God permits is not sin, but lawful" and "whatever he has not forbidden is lawful."[40]

---

34. Zwingli, *On Clarity*, 74.

35. Zwingli, *Of the Education of Youth*, 108–9.

36. *PY*, 26.

37. Zwingli, *Sixty-Seven Articles*, 236 and Harder, *Sources of Swiss Anabaptism*, 247–248.

38. *PY*, 25.

39. Zwingli, *Sixty-Seven Articles*, 184.

40. Ibid., 213.

Balthasar Hubmaier and the Clarity of Scripture

As will become apparent later, this is a significant difference and has far-reaching consequences in the debate concerning infant baptism between these two men.

There are a number of other formal principles that Zwingli has enunciated by this time, but which Hubmaier has not as yet addressed. This also applies to some other methods Zwingli used in establishing his hermeneutical model, principally to do with distinguishing between different literary styles and genre, and on that basis attributing to them differing levels of authority in the practice of interpreting Scripture. For example, Zwingli values parables and allegories only as "spice" in interpreting Scripture, for they can prove nothing unless the conclusion is clearly stated elsewhere in Scripture.[41] As Hubmaier comes to deal with these other areas of hermeneutics that Zwingli has already addressed, they will be introduced to aid the comparison between the two men.

Use of Scripture

Hubmaier's contribution to the disputation includes ten Old Testament references, with a further three quotations that do not have references supplied, and one allusion to an Old Testament text, giving a total of fourteen Old Testament quotations, references, and allusions. From the New Testament, Hubmaier gives eleven references, four quotations without references, and a further five allusions, a total of twenty New Testament references, quotations, and allusions. Of particular note is Hubmaier's method of citing a series of texts that begin with the Old Testament, then moving to the words of Christ in the gospels, followed by a reference to Paul or one of the other apostles. In this way, Hubmaier seeks to demonstrate that he is using the same method as Christ did when he used the Old Testament text, and that the apostles did the same thing. This is most clearly demonstrated in the sequence of texts Deut 12:32, Matt 15:13, Rom 14:23, where Hubmaier seeks to establish that only those things commanded by God are good and are to be obeyed by the Christian.

In the discussion regarding images, the majority of texts are taken from the Old Testament. Hubmaier is quite willing to use the Old Testament as a source of proof texts in this regard, as instanced in his use of Deut 27:15. He also demonstrates that he follows the general Reformation idea of a clearer text explaining a darker text, as for example when he declares that Deut 5:6–10 more clearly explains Exod 20:4–6.

---

41. Ibid., 319, 338.

Hubmaier's conviction that when the Word of God is preached it achieves what God has sent it out to accomplish is recognized in his allusion to Isa 55:10. In this use of Scripture, Hubmaier does not follow Zwingli exactly, as was explained above.

Summary

The above analysis provides a baseline for the hermeneutics of both Hubmaier and Zwingli and can be used to determine any development or change that might occur in them individually, as well as help to determine any divergence that might occur between their respective positions.

EIGHTEEN THESES CONCERNING THE CHRISTIAN LIFE

(March 1524)[42]

Setting

Having established himself as a supporter of Zwingli and in agreement with the process of reform that was taking place in Zurich, Hubmaier returned to Waldshut to institute the process of reform there. He too chose the method of the disputation to further the reform of the church, although it was not exactly the same process as that of the Zurich Reformers. The Zurich disputations had been called on the authority of the Zurich Council, which had extended invitations to outside theologians and opened them to the ecclesiastical and lay people of Zurich. It also acted as judge in the matters discussed, determining the implementation of those decisions. In Waldshut, the disputation was called by Hubmaier as part of the regular chapter meetings, and only those "to whom preaching God's Word has been commanded" were invited.[43] The civil authorities had no part in judging the issues discussed or in the implementation of such decisions as might be made.

---

42. *PY*, 30–34; *HS*, 69–74.
43. *PY*, 31; *HS*, 72.

Analysis

Sometime in March 1524, Hubmaier published *Eighteen Theses*, which was to form the basis of discussion at the next chapter meeting.[44] In the short preface to these theses, he once again places his emphasis on the "written divine Word" as the grounds to which any appeal is to be made in the discussions that are to take place, in contrast to wasting time on "human teachings, on our own opinions and fancies."[45]

A number of the theses echo themes of Zwingli's *Sixty-Seven Articles*. Although Hubmaier does not follow the same line of argument, he does arrive at the same conclusions as Zwingli as to what he considers to be no longer valid in the church. For example, Hubmaier's Thesis 4 concludes that "fish and flesh, cowl and tonsure" are condemned because "only those works are good which God has commanded, and only those are evil which he has forbidden us."[46] Zwingli concludes in his Article 26 that "vestments, insignia, tonsures, etc" are displeasing to God because they are practiced with hypocrisy; that is, they only "simulate goodness to human eyes."[47] In Article 24 Zwingli stated, "Every Christian is free of any of the works which God did not command and is allowed at all times to eat everything."[48] Zwingli specifies "dispensations concerning cheese and butter," two food types fundamental to sixteenth-century life in Switzerland, but his generalization covers equally well Hubmaier's examples of fish and flesh.

Behind Zwingli's conclusions lie more open principles, as previously explained, but for Hubmaier there is more emphasis on the commands and prohibitions of God; the commands to do good and the prohibitions forbidding evil. The other option of allowing the Christian to decide what to do concerning those things that God has not spoken directly about is not put forward as it is with Zwingli. Here is an indication that Hubmaier is more closely linked to the written word simply understood as the primary source for finding the answers to disputed matters, and therefore the will of God. For Zwingli the written word requires the interpretive role of the Holy Spirit, by which the believer experiences the gospel inwardly, thus verifying the will of God.

---

44. *PY*, 32; *HS*, 72.
45. *PY*, 32; *HS*, 72.
46. *PY*, 32; *HS*, 73.
47. Zwingli, *Sixty-Seven Articles*, 67, 202.
48. Ibid., 67, 197.

Hubmaier reinforces his stance on the primary function of the commands of God in Thesis 11 when he alludes to Matt 15:13, a passage already cited by him at the Second Zurich Disputation, "All teachings, which God himself did not plant, are in vain, interdicted, and shall be uprooted."[49] The conclusion he draws from this premise is that all human teaching that does not "spring forth from the Word of God" is useless. He names specifically, "Aristotle, scholastics like Thomas, Scotus, Bonaventure, and Occam" as human teachers whose opinion can be rejected. By so doing he becomes more specific in his rejection of interpreters of Scripture who were used as authorities to be appealed to by his Catholic opponents, than Zwingli had been to date.[50]

Hubmaier also expands on his view of the role of the congregation in the process of understanding Scripture. Based on the principle that every Christian "believes and is baptized for himself," he concludes that "every one should see and should judge by Scripture whether he is being rightly fed and watered by his shepherd" (Thesis 8).[51] This obligation of the individual member of the congregation to test the teaching being given by the priest is based on the conviction that the lay member of the congregation is capable of understanding the Scripture. Hubmaier thus underscores his view that Scripture is essentially simple to understand.

His understanding of the role of the congregation is further clarified in Thesis 13, where he uses the unusual term "kirchgenossen" to define church members. Pipkin and Yoder note that the term "points to a concept of membership involving rights and obligations" different from those of other parish congregations.[52] The obligations are seen in the provision of food, clothing, and protection for those who "exposit to them the pure, clear, and unmixed Word of God."[53] The rights of the congregation are

---

49. *PY*, 33; *HS*, 73.

50. Zwingli usually gives a very general term when referring to popes, councils, and other interpreters to whom his Catholic opponents appealed as authoritative interpreters of Scripture. The church father that Zwingli names most frequently is Jerome. Like the early Erasmus, Zwingli notes his indebtedness to Jerome as an interpreter of Scripture. However, Zwingli maintains that even Jerome's opinion is to be rejected if he does not support it with Holy Scripture. In Zwingli's opinion, such was the case with Jerome's opinion concerning the intercession of the saints in his *Contra Vigilantium*. Zwingli, *Sixty-Seven Articles*, 67, 168.

51. *PY*, 33; *HS*, 73.
52. *PY*, 33n11.
53. *PY*, 34; *HS*, 74.

those contained in Thesis 8, the right to test the validity of what the priest teaches them on the basis of Scripture.

The theses primarily focus on the abuses of the Mass and the need to do away with the wide variety of masses and pilgrimages then current in the church. They are to be replaced by a memorial of Christ's death that must be accompanied by preaching (Theses 10 and 12) in the language of the local people. Theses 15 and 16 relate to the need for a married priesthood, while Thesis 14 refers to purgatory, though only as the doctrine on which certain priests based their desire for wealth.[54]

Use of Scripture

There are no scriptural references given by Hubmaier in these theses, a little surprising given his insistence that the ensuing discussion should take place only with reference to Scripture. However, four Old Testament allusions and ten New Testament allusions have been identified. Hubmaier alludes to a number of texts he had used at the Second Zurich Disputation, namely, Matt 15:13; 19:17; Deut 12:32, to establish that only those things God has commanded are good and are therefore to be obeyed. He also demonstrates his willingness to use texts of Scripture in a polemical way (Phil 3:19; Jer 23:25–32; Deut 34:6). There is also an example of Hubmaier interpreting a literal text in a tropological sense in Thesis 15. Here he likens forbidding marriage to the priests and then tolerating their carnal immorality to freeing Barabbas and killing Christ.

Summary

This short work reinforces Hubmaier's position that the Word of God provides the basis for all discussion on the reform of the church, and that it is primarily the commands of God that supply the substance on which to base reform.

---

54. *PY,* 34; *HS,* 74.

AN EARNEST CHRISTIAN APPEAL TO SCHAFFHAUSEN
(September–October 1524)[55]

Setting

The process of reform that Hubmaier instigated through the debate of his *Eighteen Theses* brought with it the opposition of the Austrian authorities, who exercised sovereignty over the town of Waldshut. When the impact of the Peasants' War began to be felt in the immediate area of Waldshut the town sided with the peasants, causing even greater tension between it and its Austrian overlord. In late August, Hubmaier fled Waldshut for Schaffhausen to seek refuge from the demand of the Austrians that he should be handed over to them for trial. While in Schaffhausen Hubmaier wrote three appeals and a final covering letter to that city's Council arguing against extradition and for religious toleration. Later in 1524, these four letters were printed as a unit in Basel.[56]

Analysis

The first appeal demonstrates Hubmaier's basic attitude toward the magistrates. He is willing to have the matter settled before them, trusting in their justice. His fear is that they will wrongly imprison him, believing the words of those who falsely malign him.[57] There are no scriptural references or allusions contained in this very short first appeal.

The second appeal is also very short. In it, Hubmaier extends his appeal from just the Schaffhausen City Council to "Milords the confederates." It also advances our understanding of the accusations against Hubmaier in that he nominates as the main charge against him his erroneous teaching of the Word of God. In this matter, he notes that his opponents are the pastors at Lucerne, Apozell, Vri, and Baden, and he issues a challenge to debate the accusation with them, using the Word of God as the basis of the debate. He is confident that the Word of God "would itself be

---

55. *PY*, 35–48; *HS*, 75–84. I gratefully acknowledge the assistance of Dr Hans Lieb of the Staatsarchiv Schaffhausen who made available to me the original handwritten copies of Hubmaier's appeals to the Schaffhausen City Council. Dr Lieb also informed me that the fourth and longest of Hubmaier's appeals was rediscovered in 1984 (*Staatsarchiv Schaffhausen*, AA, 73, 4, 42).

56. *PY*, 37.

57. *PY*, 40; *HS*, 78.

the judge" in the matter, and that the truth of what he expounds from the Scripture will be self-evident so that every "pious Christian will not only hear but will also see, and grasp it in faith."[58]

Hubmaier also expounds an attitude to his opponents that becomes characteristic of the Swiss Brethren. If he should be found guilty then he will accept punishment. However, if his opponents are in error, he desires only "that they may be led to recognize their error and not be punished afterwards."[59]

Again there are no Scripture references cited, nor allusions to texts of Scripture. The appeal Hubmaier is making is based on the famed justice of the Swiss Confederacy.

The third appeal is by far the longest. Hubmaier again extends the range of those whom he desires to hear his case, this time including the Bishop of Constance.[60] Hubmaier establishes his argument for having a fair and just hearing of his case on a detailed exposition of Deut 1:16–18. This passage provides the first insight into the way Hubmaier deals with Scripture as an exegete. By developing his understanding of the word "hear," he argues that God has commanded through Moses that all authorities are always to hear both sides of a case if they are to judge correctly. Not only is it God's will, it is also "required by nature and fraternal love."[61] He continues that for the authorities to judge justly requires that they have "God and his Word before their eyes," as the kings of Israel were commanded so to do in Deut 17:19–20. They were given no latitude; they were to deviate neither to the right nor to the left. On this basis Hubmaier then concludes that "all old practices, customs, origins, ancestors, fathers, councils, and scholastics, if they depart to the right or to the left and do not straightway follow the divine Word" must fall away.[62]

Hubmaier then develops his understanding of the section of Deut 1:16 that deals with judgments between "every man and his brother or the sojourner." He argues the word "brother" is an inclusive term; in it "the judge, the native, and the foreigner shall come together and be as one."[63] It is invalid

---

58. *PY*, 41; *HS*, 79.

59. *PY*, 41; *HS*, 79. The Swiss Brethren also followed this course of declaring they would accept punishment if they were proved wrong from Scripture, while protecting their opponents from any punishment should they admit that they were wrong and the Anabaptists right. Harder, *Sources of Swiss Anabaptism*, 349.

60. *PY*, 43; *HS*, 80.

61. *PY*, 43; *HS*, 80.

62. *PY*, 43; *HS*, 81.

63. *PY*, 44; *HS*, 81. This is an example of synecdoche which Zwingli would have

to ignore justice to the foreigner simply because he is a foreigner, for judges are not to be respecters of persons (Deut 1:17). In this Hubmaier is arguing for his own position as a foreigner in the city of Schaffhausen.

Thirdly, he draws the conclusion that the judge should also not be intimidated by "anyone's person," for judgment is God's. All judgment must be in accordance with the will of God that can be learned only from the Word of God. To judge other than by the Word of God is to steal what is God's, namely His judgment. Hubmaier then links this Old Testament understanding of the magistracy with Paul's view as expressed in Rom 13:4, where judges are called "servants of God." This does not give the magistracy unlimited authority, nor are they to be obeyed in all they command, for if "anything should be commanded or forbidden which is against God's command" then the Christian is to say with Moses, "Judgment is God's" (Deut 1:17), and with the apostles, "We must obey God more than man" (Acts 5:29).[64] In this regard, Hubmaier holds similar views to the young Luther in his 1520 works *To the Christian Nobility* and *On Good Works*.[65]

Hubmaier then quotes from Deut 1:17, "But if a case should be too difficult for you, let it be brought before Moses." The difficult cases are those that concern the soul. The magistrate has nothing to do with making judgments in these matters. Rather the judge is to be Moses. Hubmaier describes this text as "einer figur,"[66] Moses being a symbol for his five books. He maintains that the same thing is taught in Ezek 44:23-24, which he quotes in part: "that the people be taught the difference between the holy and the common and between the clean and the unclean. But if a controversy should arise, men should judge according to God's judgments."[67] Here is an interesting example of Hubmaier paraphrasing a text to suit his position. The text emphasizes the role of the priests serving as judges, deciding the case in accordance with the ordinances of God, rather than emphasizing the Scripture as the sole judge.

Hubmaier goes on to link these Old Testament texts to the sayings of Jesus in Luke 6:29; John 5:39; 12:47-48. The effect of these texts is, on

---

been likely to use.

64. *PY*, 44; *HS*, 82.

65. Luther, *To the Christian Nobility*, 130, 183; "But, if as often happens, the temporal power and authorities . . . would compel a subject to do something contrary to the command of God, or hinder him from doing what God commands, obedience ends and the obligation ceases." *Treatise On Good Works*, 100.

66. *HS*, 82; *PY*, 44. Bergsten gives the word as "symbol." Pipkin and Yoder translate it as "parable."

67. *PY*, 45; *HS*, 82.

the one hand, to strengthen the unity that Hubmaier understands exists between the Old and New Testament in this matter of the magistracy and the sole authority of Scripture to judge in matters of the soul. On the other hand, Hubmaier refers to John 12:47–48 to elevate the sayings of Jesus to be equal to the commands of God.[68] He concludes that it is "great folly" for his opponents to try to establish any other judge over Scripture.

At this point he expands on his understanding by drawing attention to the role of the gathered congregation as he understood both Paul and Jesus to have described it (1 Cor 14:29–37; Matt 18:18–20), which allowed it to "judge from the divine Word which one is a true or a false prophet."[69] Then in statements very reminiscent of Zwingli he says, "the living Word of God cannot suffer a judge."[70] This concludes his appeal to Scripture as his judge in matters of his teachings that are being attacked by his opponents, who denounce him as "a seducer of the people, seditionary, a Lutheran, a heretic, and similar epithets."[71]

Once again, Hubmaier states that he may be in error but that he cannot be a heretic as he desires to receive instruction, though only from the Word of God. He claims that all he has taught for the past two years was wholly founded on the Word of God, and that the only thing he has been guilty of is sparing the weak in faith by having not "expressed everything as perfectly" as he knew.[72]

He also goes on to expand his previous thoughts on the treatment of his opponents if they are found to be in error. Not only are they to be brought to recognize their error, they must also "cease such words of disgrace and shame, improve their teachings and life, and henceforth walk before the people with right Christian teaching in which alone souls can live."[73]

The final letter, which acted as a covering note for the preceding three letters, is in the main an appeal to the tradition of justice on which the city of Schaffhausen prided itself. Hubmaier closes the letter with reference to

---

68. *PY,* 45; *HS,* 82.

69. *PY,* 45; *HS,* 82.

70. *PY,* 45; *HS,* 82. Cf. Zwingli, *Sixty-Seven Articles.*

71. *PY,* 45; *HS,* 82.

72. *PY,* 46; *HS,* 83. Hubmaier's method of dealing with those weak in the faith is different from that of Zwingli. Zwingli states he proclaims the full message but delays implementation of the reform until all are agreed or no disturbance to the peace and unity of the church will ensue from the implementation of the reform. Harder, *Sources of Swiss* Anabaptism, 246.

73. *PY,* 47; *HS,* 84.

the fact that the city had for several years "listened with joy to the clear divine Word." Within Hubmaier's hermeneutical framework, such preaching of the Word of God must have had some effect in the city, as the Word of God is powerful enough to achieve that for which God sent it forth. However, Hubmaier declares that God is in fact putting them to the test to see what the Word had affected in them, "what fruit it is bringing forth."[74] The fruit that Hubmaier has in mind is the willingness to suffer, to carry the cross of Christ. Schaffhausen could demonstrate this fruit by resisting the demands of the Catholic Cantons of the Swiss Confederation and the Austrian authorities that were demanding his extradition.

Use of Scripture

In the main, Hubmaier presents quotations and partial quotations of Scripture in this work, with only two references to biblical texts in the entire work (Deut 17:19–20; Ezek 44:23–24). Hubmaier demonstrates his continuing method of using the words of Jesus as the interpretive authority for the Old Testament. He achieves this by taking statements from Deut 1:17; Ezek 44:23–24 and defining Moses and the judgments of God as the words of Jesus (Luke 16:29; John 5:39; 12:47–48) since Jesus uses these words. In this sequence of verses, Hubmaier demonstrates how a "clearer text" of Scripture can interpret a "darker text." However, in this instance the Old Testament texts are considered darker because they are considered parables that need clarification.

Summary

Essentially, Hubmaier maintains his position of adhering to the commands of God as they are defined in Scripture. He makes more explicit his view that the commands of God can be reinterpreted to mean the words of Jesus. Thus, by his use of Scripture he demonstrates a christocentric approach to the interpretation of Scripture that is akin to Zwingli and Luther.

---

74. *PY*, 39; *HS*, 77.

Balthasar Hubmaier and the Clarity of Scripture

THESES AGAINST ECK

(September 1524)[75]

Setting

While in Schaffhausen, Hubmaier took part in a polemical exchange between Eck and Zwingli, producing a series of twenty-six theses in Latin challenging Eck to hold a disputation. A German translation of the theses was produced, probably not by Hubmaier but, as Bergsten maintains on the basis of linguistic analysis of the German text, a Swiss German.[76] The title page of the Latin text is more provocative than the German, referring to Eck as an elephant, while Hubmaier refers to himself as a mouse, though both texts conclude with the same derogatory remark that Eck, the Hercules of Ingolstadt, was seized "by Herculean disease," a reference to the legend that Hercules was at times insane.[77]

Analysis

These theses provide evidence not only of Hubmaier's irreversible break with Eck, his former teacher and patron, but also the closeness of the allegiance Hubmaier felt towards Zwingli, who he terms his brother in Christ in the Latin text.[78]

The focus of the theses is clearly stated in the title page, "In a conflict of faith, where two are in disagreement, then who should be the proper judge?"[79] Throughout the theses Hubmaier outlines his basic hermeneutical principles as well as defining procedures that help determine the correct understanding of Scripture. There are a number of theses that expand on themes he has already addressed in his comments at the Second Zurich Disputation and in his *Eighteen Theses* and *An Earnest Christian Appeal*. Foremost in this group of expanded ideas is the role of the gathered congregation.

Thesis 5 is the first thesis that goes beyond simply conflating a series of biblical texts into a thesis. He states: "Further, the decision which of

---

75. *PY*, 49–57; *HS*, 85–94.
76. *HS*, 85.
77. *PY*, 57; *HS*, 90, 94.
78. *HS*, 87.
79. *PY*, 49; *HS*, 87.

two understands it more correctly is conceived in the church by the Word of God and born out of faith. When you come together, etc., the others should judge" (1 Cor 14:26).[80] In this thesis, Hubmaier joins "faith," which has been the focus of the previous thesis, to the role of the church as the body that determines who understands the Word of God more correctly. Faith is necessary for understanding, but that faith is bound to the Word of God. The metaphor of conception and birth highlights the primary role of the Word of God, out of which comes faith, and the two combined bring understanding concerning the correct or false interpretation of Scripture within the gathered congregation.

In Thesis 6, Hubmaier for the first time recognizes the need for arbiters, so that discussion can take place in an orderly fashion. He insists that these arbiters are not judges "over the truth of the Word," rather they are to judge "which party comes closest to the intent of the divine Word or deviates from it."[81] This reference to the intent of Scripture is reminiscent of Zwingli, who uses it as a hermeneutical device to attribute to the words of Christ the meaning that he considers the true meaning of a passage.[82] It may also indicate that Hubmaier's loose paraphrasing of texts is the outward expression of this principle that the actual words of the text are not as important as the intention of the speaker.

Later, in Theses 14 and 15, Hubmaier describes the procedural function of these three or four arbiters that the church is to appoint. It is their function to ensure that an orderly discussion takes place, each speaker taking it in turns, and to moderate and record the conclusions of the congregation, not to impose on the church any particular conclusion. When there is silence in the gathered church, that silence confirms the unanimity of the church on the matter and therefore that the interpretation is correct.[83]

---

80. *PY,* 51. My adjustment of Pipkin and Yoder's biblical reference.

81. *PY,* 52; *HS,* 88.

82. Two examples of Zwingli's use of the intention of Christ's words are found in Zwingli's *Sixty-Seven Articles.* Dealing with Matt 16:13–19 and John 20:20–23, Zwingli insists that the meaning of the keys is not authority but the preaching of the gospel that has been entrusted to Peter and the other apostles. Zwingli, *Sixty-Seven Articles,* 305, 309. Against those who argue for purgatory from Matt 12:32; 5:25, he argues that Christ's intention is clearer in Luke 12:57–59; Matt 18:34. He rejects the Catholic word linkage of "prison" with "purgatory," and suggests instead that Christ's intention is simply the general principle of forgiveness. Zwingli, *Sixty-Seven Articles,* 336–38.

83. *PY,* 54; *HS,* 89.

Balthasar Hubmaier and the Clarity of Scripture

The qualities of the arbiters are outlined in Thesis 24. They are to be theologians ("theologi" or "gotzglernig"), though not of the old order; that is, neither monks nor doctors of theology. Rather theologians are those who have been instructed by God himself. Learning is to be based on the reading of Scripture, as demonstrated by the example of Josiah (2 Kgs 22; 2 Chron 34). Hubmaier does not totally negate learning, as he states in Thesis 25 that the "learned ones are still to be listened to,"[84] though they are not to direct the proceedings nor dictate its decisions. Those who do not read the Book of the Law and the Prophets are not to be arbiters in matters that concern the faith.[85] Although Hubmaier has a place for learning in his congregational hermeneutic, it is not developed to the same degree as Zwingli, who makes knowledge of the three biblical languages mandatory for the correct understanding of Scripture.[86]

There is in these theses an emphasis on Christ as central to understanding Scripture. In Thesis 8, there is a typical reference to judgment being given according to the "plumb line of Holy Scripture." The example of Christ is then put forward as an illustration of Scripture interpreting Scripture, "Christ . . . ruled on the heads of grain plucked by the apostles according to Scripture."[87] Hubmaier continues to focus on Christ as the exemplar of interpretation when he demands that truth is to be found in the Scriptures in the words of Christ "for it is the discourse which Christ spoke which shall judge all things."[88] This consideration of the example of how Christ used Scripture and the authority of the words of Christ culminates in Thesis 12 where Hubmaier defines what he means by "searching the Scriptures." Here he states a formal principle of his hermeneutic. Searching the Scriptures takes place "by illuminating the darker texts of Scripture with the clearer."[89] Again the example of Christ is used to authenticate this principle, but this time it is the occasion of Jesus explaining the meaning of "Levirate marriage by reference to the Scripture on resurrection."[90]

---

84. *PY,* 56; *HS,* 90.
85. *PY,* 56–57; *HS,* 90.
86. Zwingli, *Of the Education of Youth,* 108–9.
87. *PY,* 52; *HS,* 88.
88. *PY,* 53; *HS,* 88.
89. *PY,* 53; *HS,* 89.

90. *PY,* 54; *HS,* 89. Hubmaier gives as Scripture references in the margin of the text Deut 25; Matt 22; Mark 12; Luke 20. The verse references for these texts should be: Deut 25:5ff.; Matt 22:23ff.; Mark 12:18ff.; Luke 20:27ff.

The Plumb Line of Holy Scripture

In Thesis 11, Hubmaier comments on the attitude with which the judges should come to Scripture, "opening the Bible with a prayerful spirit, searching the Scriptures like the noble Thessalonians to see whether things are so."[91] This prayerful approach to reading Scripture is reminiscent of Zwingli's advice in *On Clarity:* "Before I say anything or listen to the teaching of man, I will first consult the mind of the Spirit of God . . . Then you should reverently ask God for his grace that he may give you his mind and Spirit so that you will not lay hold of your own opinion."[92] The attitude of the one who reads Scripture is therefore of prime importance in discerning who correctly understands Scripture. For Hubmaier, the prayerful attitude is demonstrated in the willingness of the reader to submit "without any speculation or disputation" to what is plainly said in Scripture. For Zwingli, the prayerful attitude is the first step that ensures that the reader is not coming to the Scripture with preconceived ideas that may cause him to force Scripture into an erroneous understanding.[93]

With the publication of the *Theses Against Eck,* Hubmaier has described his hermeneutic in greater detail. He has added the formal principle of the clearer text explaining the darker texts, and has clarified the role of the congregation in seeking to understand the Word of God in a series of theses. He has also outlined some of the prerequisites for correctly understanding Scripture. Firstly, he maintains that it is impossible to understand the Word of God without faith. Secondly, to the prerequisite attitude of humility he adds prayerfulness and obedience to the commands of God. Finally, he states it is necessary to accept the plain or literal meaning of the text.

However, there is little extended prose material in *Theses Against Eck* to test the application of his hermeneutical model. The twenty-six theses that make up *Theses Against Eck* do not develop his argument at length, as is to be expected. The theses were to be the basis for a debate, and their

---

91. *PY,* 53; *HS,* 88. Hubmaier incorrectly refers to the Thessalonians, since it was the Bereans who "searched the Scriptures."

92. Zwingli, *On Clarity,* 88–89. Zwingli also gives a list of twelve instructions on how to come to Scripture, which begin with a prayer that God would kill off the old man. Zwingli, *On Clarity,* 93–95.

93. *PY,* 53; *HS,* 89. Zwingli, *On Clarity,* 88. "Here we come upon the canker at the heart of all human systems. And it is this: We want to find support in Scripture for our own view, and so we take that view to Scripture and if we find a text which, however artificially, we can relate it to it, we do so, and in that way we wrest Scripture in order to make it say what we want it to say."

development would have occurred in the debate or in a written exposition of the theses, as was the case with Zwingli's *Sixty-Seven Articles*.

Use of Scripture

Fortunately, Hubmaier did give extensive biblical references as supporting texts for his various theses and these allow some exploration of Hubmaier's attitude to, and use of, the Scriptures.

Hubmaier's adherence to his expressed principle that only Scripture is to be appealed to as the judge in disputed matters is well demonstrated in his eighty-three references to Scripture, only one of which is a reference to a book of the Apocrypha. However, these figures are slightly inflated when it is considered that all four references to Mark and two of the eight references to Luke are simply synoptic parallels for references given in the first instance from Matthew. Similarly, there are two Old Testament references that are simply citing Old Testament passages Jesus was quoting in the New Testament text previously cited. Hubmaier also provides one instance of citing a parallel text in the Old Testament.

Of the total of twenty Old Testament citations, nine refer to characters of the Old Testament who display attitudes that Hubmaier has noted as either positive (five instances, one being duplicated by a parallel reference), or negative (four references); examples that are to be followed or avoided respectively. Three references are simply quotations or part quotations of texts that Hubmaier is using as the basis for doctrinal statements, with a further two supportive texts. Two references simply identify the Old Testament texts that Jesus was quoting. One text, Deut 18:15, "The Lord your God will raise up for you a prophet like me from among your own brothers. You must listen to him," is interpreted christologically. Hubmaier identifies Christ as the prophet that God would raise after Moses by linking the Old Testament text with a series of New Testament texts where God says, "This is my son . . . listen to him" (Luke 9:35; Matt 3:17; Mark 1:11).[94]

There are four references whose function is uncertain. Thesis 11 contains as a final reference Deut 33. The thesis deals with the attitude with which those who would be judges of Scripture should come to Scripture. The example of Mary who sat at the feet of Jesus is used as the model to be

---

94. *PY,* 57; *HS,* 90. Neither Pipkin and Yoder nor Bergsten supply verses for the Matthew and Mark references. However, the word linkage "listen to him" provides adequate justification for choosing Matt 3:17 and Mark 1:11.

followed. The link phrase to Deut 33 appears to be "at the feet," a variant of which is found in verse three of Deut 33, "at your feet they all bow down, and from you receive instruction." Two other references to Deuteronomy are included in these uncertain usages. Both occur in Thesis 16 and relate to the concept of the rule of Scripture. Hubmaier first refers to Matt 18:15ff, then supports this New Testament text with the two references to Deuteronomy. Both chapters in Deuteronomy contain verses that refer to not adding to the commands of God (Deut 4:2; 12:32). Given that Hubmaier places great emphasis on the commands and prohibitions of God it is likely that he referred to these verses. The reference to Joel in Thesis 22 is another example of Hubmaier using a text from the Old Testament to support a New Testament practice. However, the description in Joel 2 of gathering the people does not specifically mention that the women are to be silent during the meeting and are to learn from their husbands at home.

The last of the twenty Old Testament references to be considered occurs in Thesis 24. In this thesis, Hubmaier is concerned to show that those who would be judges in disputed matters of faith are to be instructed in divine teaching by God himself. He uses the example of the breast plate of Aaron to depict how these judges are to be taught by God himself, giving Exod 28 as the reference. Exodus 28:15ff. describes the pattern for building the breast plate of Aaron and concludes that it is to contain the Urim and Thummim, the "means of making decisions for the Israelites" (Exod 28:30). The breast plate of Aaron is thus a figure or symbol of God's control of all judgment, just as he controlled the Urim and Thummim.

The Apocryphal book of Ecclesiasticus provides the only reference to the Apocrypha, and its usage is uncertain.

Over half of the sixty-two New Testament references are used as statements upon which doctrinal principles are built as either proof texts or supporting texts of the proof text. Particular verses are quoted in part and combined with other verses to make up the thesis for which Hubmaier argues. For example, Hubmaier gives Matt 7:15; 24:4; 1 John 4:1ff; Rom 16:17–18 as scriptural support for Thesis 19. His construction of Thesis 19 is compared with verses from the NIV as follows:

Hubmaier: Protect yourselves against false prophets.

NIV: Watch out for false prophets (Matt 7:15).

Watch that no one seduces you.

NIV: Watch out that no one deceives (seduces) you (Matt 24:4).

Test the spirits, whether they are from God,

NIV: Test the spirits, to see whether they are from God (1 John 4:1).

and give attention to those who cause contention and offence outside the doctrine which you have learned. Avoid the same, for they serve not Christ but their own belly. Through sweet talk and speech they seduce the heart of the innocent

NIV: Watch out for those who cause divisions and put obstacles in your way that are contrary to the teaching you have learned. Keep away from them. For such people are not serving our Lord Christ, but their own appetites. By smooth talk and flattery they deceive the minds of naive people (Rom 16:17–18).

in order to receive twelve hundred ducats from the pope.[95]

This is typical of Hubmaier's use of scriptural texts when composing theses for debate. It demonstrates both his desire to build all of his argument upon the Scriptures, yet at the same time not be a slave to the letter of the printed text but seek to convey the intent of the text.

Eight of his New Testament references reflect an attitude to Scripture that holds Scripture to be normative for establishing procedures within the church as well as for establishing doctrine. Five of the eight are from the section in 1 Corinthians that deals with orderly worship within the church. The remaining three relate to the so-called Jerusalem Council of Acts 15.

There are nine uses of the New Testament as historical example: six from Acts, two from Luke and one from Matthew. Three of these historical uses display a degree of carelessness in Hubmaier's handling of Scripture. These references occur in Thesis 23 where Hubmaier is making the point that women may speak in the gathered assembly only when the "men are afraid and have become women."[96] He begins with the example of the Old Testament women Deborah and Hulda. He then seeks to show that what is true in the Old is also true in the New by citing the examples of Anna and the four daughters of Philip the Evangelist (Luke 2:36ff; Acts 21:9). The problem with these New Testament examples is that there are men available to speak and have spoken at the same time as the women have spoken. This is especially true of the four prophetess daughters of Philip.

There are nine references that demonstrate Jesus's use of the Old Testament; however, Hubmaier only makes explicit reference to two Old Testament texts. All nine references come from the gospels, and reinforce

---

95. PY, 55; HS, 89.
96. PY, 56; HS, 90.

The Plumb Line of Holy Scripture

Hubmaier's principle that the example of Christ's usage of Scripture should be normative for the interpreter of Scripture.[97] One reference, John 6:45, which is taken from Isa 54:13, is repeated in two different theses, while four of the other references are synoptic parallels of verses first cited from Matthew.

There remain two marginal references, Luke 12 and Matt 15, that have uncertain usages. It is possible that the Matt 15 reference is to verse 13 as Pipkin and Yoder suggest.[98]

The above analysis of Hubmaier's use of Scripture shows that Scripture is his only source of authority from which both doctrine and practice is to be derived. It also demonstrates a marked preference for the New Testament as the principal source to which he appeals; yet he also demonstrates that the Old Testament is still authoritative as he emulates the practice of Christ, who used the Old Testament as the source of authority in his debates with the religious authorities of his day. It also demonstrates that Hubmaier practices his hermeneutical theory that gives priority to the example and the words of Christ (the clearer texts of Scripture illuminating the darker texts).

It should also be noted that the Old Testament does have a role in establishing doctrine in its own right, though this occurs only in four instances and in all of them the Old Testament texts are simply quoted in a combined form to establish a doctrinal principle.

Summary

In this work, Hubmaier has made more specific his understanding of the role of the congregation in the resolution of both doctrinal disputes and the direction of the life of the believers. In this process, the Word of God remains central as the source of faith. He also makes plain that it is the intention of the words, not the words interpreted literally, which is of major importance. In this regard, Hubmaier approaches Zwingli's position on the need for the Spirit to interpret the literal word. However, Hubmaier does not cite Zwingli's proof text for this position, John 6:63.

In these theses, Hubmaier also clearly indicates his christocentric hermeneutic, in that it is both the words of Christ and the method of Christ in handling the Old Testament that provides Hubmaier with his

---

97. *PY,* 52; *HS,* 88.
98. *PY,* 53.

model for interpreting the Old Testament. He enunciates this method in Reformation terms of the clearer text interpreting the darker text.

Hubmaier also demonstrates in this work the need for humility in the person who comes to read Scripture. Without a humble heart, a clear understanding of Scripture cannot be obtained.

ON HERETICS AND THOSE WHO BURN THEM

(September–October 1524)[99]

Setting

During his stay in Schaffhausen in September and October 1524, Hubmaier compiled a series of thirty-six articles under the title *On Heretics*. In them, he expands some of the ideas he previously expressed in his appeals to the Schaffhausen Council, declaring himself in favor of toleration of those who hold to unorthodox doctrinal positions. Heretics are not to be forced by violence to recant, nor are they to be handed over to the temporal authority to be put to death. In Hubmaier's opinion, the heretic can harm neither body nor soul.[100]

That heretics were handed over for execution to the temporal authorities led Hubmaier to discuss the topic of the authority of the magistracy. Hubmaier maintains that the magistracy was established by God and is to be obeyed in all matters that relate to temporal things. It has also been established by God for the punishment of evildoers. However, evildoers are considered to be only those who cause physical harm to others. Therefore, heretics who do not cause physical harm are excluded from the sphere of temporal authority.[101]

Hubmaier presents a case that defends his own situation in Schaffhausen. He is not an evildoer, and as such is not liable to punishment by the civil authorities. Nor is he a heretic, as he does not believe he has deliberately misrepresented the Word of God. He has also made it plain that he is willing to receive further instruction from the Word of God. This teachable attitude also demonstrates that he is no heretic. It could be argued

---

99. *PY*, 5: 58–66; *HS*, 4: 95–100.
100. *PY*, 64; *HS*, 99 (Article 24).
101. *PY*, 63; *HS*, 99 (Article 22); *PY*, 64; *HS*, 99 (Article 24).

that Hubmaier's statements on liberty of conscience in this work primarily represent special pleading by him on his own behalf.

Analysis

There is little in these articles to add to the hermeneutical position that Hubmaier has already established in the preceding four works. Articles 8, 9, and 11 all relate to the parable of the wheat and the tares (Matt 13:29ff.) and demonstrate the hermeneutical device whereby Hubmaier declares the meaning of the text as he interprets it to be the intention of Christ.[102]

Article 13 again recalls the teaching and example of Jesus as normative for the correct understanding of Scripture, "The inquisitors are the greatest heretics of all, because counter to the teaching and example of Jesus they condemn heretics to fire."[103]

Articles 22 and 23 demonstrate Hubmaier's use of the principle that the clearer text illuminates the darker text of Scripture. Hubmaier uses the words of Jesus in Matt 10:28, "Do not fear those who kill the body but are unable to kill the soul" to clarify the teaching of Paul in Rom 13:4, "It is fitting that secular authority puts to death the wicked."[104] The point that Hubmaier is making is that the wicked are those who cause physical harm to others, while the unbeliever does not cause such harm. Therefore, the unbeliever does not come under that mandate of the secular authority, which can only kill the body, but comes under the authority of God alone.

The role of "the light of nature," or natural reason, is dealt with in Article 30. Hubmaier maintains that all things that "have been begged from the light of nature . . . are lethal errors, when they are not led and directed according to Scripture."[105] Natural reason is therefore not to be appealed to in matters of faith and practice in the church. This statement strengthens Hubmaier's opinion that only Scripture may be appealed to by the church as its sole authority in matters of faith and practice.

There is also a brief mention in Article 2 that adds to the definition of a heretic already given in Article 1; that is, heretics are "those who wantonly resist the Holy Scripture." Hubmaier adds that a heretic blinds Scripture by expounding it "otherwise than the Holy Spirit demands."[106] He then

---

102. *PY,* 61; *HS,* 97.
103. *PY,* 62; *HS,* 98.
104. *PY,* 63; *HS,* 99.
105. *PY,* 65; *HS,* 100.
106. *PY,* 59; *HS,* 96. This emphasis on the Spirit's role in interpretation is rare in

gives four examples of how his Catholic opponents blind Scripture in this way: interpreting "'a wife' as a prebend, 'pasturing' as ruling, 'a stone' as the rock, 'church' as Rome."[107] They are like the devil who was the first to do this, when he contradicted God's words to Adam and Eve, suggesting they would not die if they ate of the fruit of the tree of knowledge of good and evil.[108] Hubmaier is emphasizing that the simple literal meaning of the words have been denied and twisted so that they are no longer the truth.

Use of Scripture

The Scripture references included in the body of the text in these articles are not as extensive as in *Theses Against Eck*. Four of the eight Old Testament references simply use the texts as historical examples. There are two references to Job of uncertain usage, though a case can be made to show they depend on specific words linking Hubmaier's thought in the particular article under consideration.

For example, Hubmaier states in Article 17: "If we act otherwise God will consider our sword as chaff and our fire mockery" (Job 41:19).[109]

His reference to Job 41 makes sense only if we understand God to be equated with Leviathan. In Job 41, Leviathan mocks the attempt of man to capture him with sword, spears, and arrows, which he treats like chaff and rotten wood (v. 26). However, the fire that is mentioned issues from Leviathan, not from those who seek to capture him (vv. 18–21). Yet it seems that for Hubmaier it is enough that fire and sword are mentioned in the text, as these are the two elements combined for the execution of most heretics. Thus, through finding a text in Scripture that uses the words in a way that partially supports his basic point, he demonstrates his desire to be totally dependent on Scripture. However, at the same time he shows that he also is just as capable of twisting the text of Scripture to gain support for his position as were his Catholic opponents.

The second reference to Job is even more tenuous in its application to the point under discussion. In articles 33 and 34, he deals with those who unwisely reject God's Word, citing the example of Jehoiakim who

---

Hubmaier's work. In this early work, where he still saw himself as a brother of Zwingli, it is probably a reflection of his proximity to Zwingli's reliance on the Spirit as the interpreter of Scripture.

107. *PY*, 59–60; *HS*, 96.
108. *PY*, 59; *HS*, 96.
109. *PY*, 62; *HS*, 98.

burnt the scroll of Jeremiah (Jer 36). Hubmaier concludes by saying, "Thus it shall proceed so that on those who fear the frost, a cold snow will fall" (Job 6:16).[110] The reference to Job does have the words ice and snow in it; however, in the context of the passage Job is talking about the unreliability of his friends, and not the greater severity of God punishing those who have rejected his Word. Again Hubmaier is using a text to support an idea that has nothing but the words to link it with the point under discussion. It may well be that Hubmaier is seeking scriptural support for a common local saying.

The remaining two Old Testament references are linked together in Article 12, declaring, "Blessed is the man who stands watch before the bridal chamber" (Prov 8:34) "and neither sleeps nor sits in the seat of mockers" (Ps 1:1). The contrast is with the negligent bishops in Article 11 who slept while enemies sowed tares among the wheat (Matt 13:25). The two Old Testament references have in common the idea of being blessed by God. In the Proverbs reference, those are blessed "who listen to me [wisdom], watching daily at my doors, waiting at my doorway" (NIV). In Ps 1:1, the person is blessed "who does not walk in the counsel of the wicked or stand in the way of sinners or sit in the seat of mockers" (NIV). Hubmaier conflates these two references to support his view that God requires of both the bishops and the people watchfulness and avoidance of error due to human interpretations.[111] Whatever comes from human intention and not from Scripture is error and to be avoided (Articles 30 & 31).

There are sixteen references to the New Testament given by Hubmaier, with an additional reference to Matt 15:14 noted by Pipkin and Yoder. Six of the nine references to the gospels are drawn from Matthew, two from John and one from Luke.

The reference to Matt 15:14 is given twice, once identified by Hubmaier, on the other occasion simply being quoted without the reference. It is a comment Hubmaier also used at the Second Zurich Disputation referring to the errors of the Catholic priests: the blind will lead the blind and both will fall into the pit.

Two references to Matt 13 relate to Jesus's parable of the wheat and tares, which Hubmaier uses to support his contention that heretics are

---

110. *PY,* 65; *HS,* 100. "But my brothers are as undependable as intermittent streams, as the streams that overflow when darkened by thawing ice and swollen with melting snow, but that cease to flow in the dry season, and in the heat vanish from their channels" Job 6:16 (NIV).

111. *PY,* 61; *HS,* 97.

not to be judged by anyone other than Christ and then only at the coming of Christ. Between these two references he cites Paul's comment, "There must be divisions so that the trustworthy among you may be manifest" (1 Cor 11:19). Here the words of Christ and Paul are juxtaposed to demonstrate the unity that exists between them.

The reference to Matt 10:28 again demonstrates Hubmaier's conviction that Paul and Jesus speak with one voice. In this case, he quotes Paul from Rom 13:4. Hubmaier interprets this text to mean that secular authority can put the wicked to death (Article 22). He goes on in Thesis 23, "Christ said the same thing clearly: 'do not fear those who kill the body but are unable to kill the soul'" (Matt 10:28).[112]

The two references from John's gospel demonstrate two usages that Hubmaier makes of Scripture. The first, from John 10:10 simply provides the words that become part of the thesis that Hubmaier is proposing. In this instance, Hubmaier takes the words of Jesus concerning the thief who comes to steal, kill, and destroy, and applies them to Christ in the negative, "For Christ did not come to slaughter, kill, burn," and then continues with a paraphrase of the words of Christ, "but so that those who live should live yet more abundantly."[113]

The other reference is to John 19:11 where Hubmaier alludes to the historical example of Jesus, who was handed over to a secular authority to be executed. Here both the historical example and the words of Jesus are important, for Jesus says that "the one who handed me over to you is guilty of a greater sin" (NIV). Thus, both the words of Jesus and the historical example of the Jewish teachers of the law handing Jesus over to secular authority correspond to the Dominicans handing over heretics to secular authorities. Hubmaier concludes that on the authority of the words of Jesus the Dominicans are the ones that Jesus is accusing of the greater sin.

With the reference to Luke 9:54, Hubmaier introduces an example of those who misuse Scripture. Here the Dominicans "shamelessly distort the Word of God" by shouting, "Into the fire!"[114] This phrase Hubmaier alleges is linked to the reference in Luke he has cited, a passage where the disciples of Jesus want him to call down fire from heaven to destroy the Samaritan town that did not welcome him. In Article 2, Hubmaier had previously cited four examples of those who "blind the Scripture, and

---

112. PY, 63; HS, 99.
113. PY, 62; HS, 98.
114. PY, 63; HS, 98.

The Plumb Line of Holy Scripture

exposit it otherwise than the Holy Spirit demands."[115] Unfortunately, he does not give references to the passages in Scripture that his opponents are citing. Rather, he assumes that the examples cited are so well known they require no further identification.

There are two references to Titus, the first linked with a reference to Revelation in Thesis 5. Here Hubmaier is establishing a procedure for dealing with heretics. From Titus 3:10 he takes the principle to avoid them, and adds to it the idea of the consequence that the heretics' wanton rejection of the gospel will bring; that is, they will become yet more filthy.[116] The other reference to Titus draws on the linking concept of those whose actions deny their claim to know God. The particular action he has in mind is the burning of heretics. Hubmaier modifies the Titus reference by equating knowing God with confessing Christ (Article 28).[117]

Article 21 contains a reference to the sword that the Christian does have to use against the godless, namely the Word of God. Ephesians 6:17 is cited as a supporting text for this statement. Hubmaier goes on to argue that the Christian does not have a sword to use against the "evildoers."[118] That sword rightfully belongs to the secular magistrate to whom God has entrusted it.

The final New Testament reference is to Acts 19:19. Here the historical example of the burning of unchristian books at Ephesus is cited to support the view that the burning of books is legitimate (Article 35).[119] Hubmaier here expands his views on dealing with heretics as previously expressed in his *An Earnest Christian Appeal*. The toleration he advocates is not total. The heretic may retain his unchristian views but he is not allowed to propagate them through the written word.

---

115. *PY*, 59; *HS*, 96.

116. *PY*, 60; *HS*, 97.

117. *PY*, 64; *HS*, 99.

118. *PY*, 63: *HS*, 98. The two swords relate to the two spheres of the spiritual and secular authorities respectively. For Hubmaier, the Christian continues to live in both of these spheres simultaneously. He does not demand the total withdrawal of the church from the secular world, as eventually happens with the Swiss Brethren. Hubmaier also makes a distinction between the evildoer, who causes bodily and or material harm to others, and the heretic, whose thoughts he asserts can harm neither body nor soul.

119. *PY*, 65; *HS*, 100.

Balthasar Hubmaier and the Clarity of Scripture

Summary

Though there is little in this work to add to Hubmaier's hermeneutic, he does address briefly two issues that are of interest. Firstly, Hubmaier objects to the "light of nature" as a source from which to develop doctrine or practices for the church. In this regard, Hubmaier takes up a position that is similar to Zwingli and Luther and opposed to Erasmus, as will become evident in the later discussion on freedom of the will.

Hubmaier also makes explicit the dependence of correct interpretation of Scripture on the role of the Holy Spirit. While his comment on this matter is all too brief, it nevertheless indicates that Hubmaier was in general agreement with Zwingli on this point at that time.

Otherwise, this work simply underscores Hubmaier's attitude to the authority of Scripture as the only source of appeal for faith and practice, as well as his method of using the intention of the speaker in a clearer text of Scripture to interpret a darker text.

A LETTER TO OECOLAMPAD

(January 16, 1525)[120]

Setting

Hubmaier returned from Schaffhausen via Zurich, reaching Waldshut on October 27, 1524. In Zurich, he held a discussion with Zwingli on the subject of baptism that he referred to in a letter he later addressed to Zwingli.[121] Soon after his arrival, on All Saints Day 1524, Hubmaier saw the implementation of radical reforms concerning images and the Mass. Iconoclasm resulting from Hubmaier's preaching saw the removal of images and other church articles, and the Mass was performed in German, with the people receiving the elements in both kinds.[122]

The people and pastor of Waldshut felt confident to undertake these reforms at that time because the town was then receiving support from Zurich, Schaffhausen, and Basel, and a contingent of volunteers from

---

120. *PY*, 6: 67–72.
121. Bergsten, *Balthasar Hubmaier: Anabaptist Theologian*, 156–57.
122. Ibid., 145–146.

Zurich had arrived in Waldshut to defend the town from any threatened Austrian aggression.[123]

The issue of baptism was also at that time hotly debated in Zurich between Zwingli and the Grebel group. Hubmaier may have reestablished contact with the Grebel group through Heinrich Aberli, a member of the group who was also part of the Zurich volunteers in Waldshut.[124] Perhaps it was through this contact that Grebel knew of Hubmaier's differences with Zwingli. Grebel implied that Hubmaier would not be present at the first public discussion on baptism in Zurich because of these differences, while some others thought Hubmaier would be invited.[125] Hubmaier makes known to Oecolampad his differences with Zwingli on baptism in this letter, and of his knowledge of the foreshadowed discussion.[126]

Analysis

On January 16, 1525, Hubmaier wrote to "his Christian colleague" and "dearly beloved brother in Christ," Oecolampad of Basel.[127] The letter deals with the topics of the Lord's Supper and the baptism of infants. With regard to the first topic, Hubmaier notes that "there was no difference of view" between them and also that Oecolampad had agreed with the views on the Lord's Supper as just published by Karlstadt.[128]

On the topic of infant baptism, Hubmaier notes that in Zurich there is to be a comparison of Scripture texts on that day, but that he disagrees with the conclusions of Zwingli and Jud on the matter.[129] The major part of the letter is given over to the discussion of this topic, and provides a demonstration of how Hubmaier goes about dealing with Scripture.

---

123. Ibid., 153–154.
124. Ibid., 153.
125. Harder, *Sources of Swiss Anabaptism*, 332.
126. *PY,* 69–70.
127. *PY,* 68.
128. *PY,* 68.
129. *PY,* 69. The disputation was called by the Zurich Council on January 17, 1525. It was not as open as the first two Zurich disputations, which established both the process of reform in Zurich and the manner of implementation of that reform. For a list of the six private and four public disputations held on the subject of infant baptism at Zurich see Harder, *Sources of Swiss Anabaptism*, 334. Bromiley is incorrect when he states there were two conferences on January 10 and 17 and that Hubmaier was present as a representative of the Anabaptists. Bromiley, *Zwingli and Bullinger*, 120.

Hubmaier states that baptism is an ordinance instituted by Christ in the words of Matt 28:19. He does not elaborate on this text, but simply leaves the word order to demonstrate how baptism is to be performed; teaching precedes baptism. It is not possible for the very young child to receive teaching, therefore baptism is not appropriate for infants. He then deals with the objection that it is disruptive to dispute so fiercely over a "naked sign" as Zwingli had called baptism. His answer again shows his focus on the words of Jesus as fundamental to his interpretative framework. Though the thing signified is of greater value than the sign itself; that is, the binding of oneself to God unto death for the sake of faith and in hope of the resurrection to eternal life, nevertheless, to weaken the sign or abuse it "gives offense to the words with which Jesus inaugurated the sign."[130]

He goes on to suggest that the bond with God signified in the Lord's Supper is like that of baptism; in the Lord's Supper the communicants commit themselves to lay down "body and blood for his (Christ's) sake, as Christ did" for them.[131] He summarizes this bond as the fulfillment of "the laws and the prophets," perhaps a reference to Jesus's words in Matthew 7:12, "In everything, do to others what you would have them do to you, for this sums up the Law and the Prophets" (NIV).

There follows a plea if he is in error to be "instructed otherwise" by Oecolampad and others "who come instructed by the Word of God."[132] That instruction requires that God enlighten them all "with his Spirit." If the instruction is not forthcoming then Hubmaier will maintain his position on infant baptism, for he has been "driven to this view by Christ's institution, by the Word, by faith and truth, by judgment, and by conscience."[133]

This list provides significant insight into the sources of authority that Hubmaier relied on, at least in this case, to come to his theological conclusions. The evidence from this work and the preceding works supports the opinion that the order of these items is significant for Hubmaier. It is the words of Christ that take priority in establishing true doctrine, followed by the rest of the words of Scripture, which Hubmaier demonstrates equate to the words of Christ or the intention of Christ as he perceives it. Faith and truth derive from the words of Christ and the Scripture, while judgment concerns the application of reason and grammatical rules that

130. *PY*, 70.
131. *PY*, 70.
132. *PY*, 71.
133. *PY*, 71.

are valid only when the conclusions concur with the simple meaning of Scripture. Finally, conscience is called on to check that what is proposed does not bring a troubled conscience. If it did, it would not be the truth. Hubermaier has not previously mentioned this aspect of determining the truth of doctrine, but as will be seen later, it becomes of major significance in holding to the truth once it has been grasped by faith.

Hubmaier then identifies a particular verse that is a source of controversy, "Suffer the little children to come unto me" (Matt 19:14). The disputed point is whether the "promise" of this verse applies only to children; that is, "for them," as Zwingli insisted, or whether "the Word of Christ" supports Hubmaier's view that the promise is "for such as them."[134] Hubmaier thus demonstrates his awareness of the need to determine the correct text of Scripture upon which to build a true interpretation.

He also outlines at the end of the letter a ceremony of child naming that he has instituted at Waldshut in place of infant baptism. However, he notes that if the parents of a sickly child insist on baptizing the child he will do so, being for a time weak like the child. "But as for interpreting the Word, I do not give ground in the least respect."[135] There is a tension here between correctly interpreting the Word of God and delaying its application locally because of the weak in faith. The question of forbearance was an issue that helped hasten the division between Zwingli and those who became Anabaptists in Zurich. Hubmaier thus identifies himself as following the more liberal method of Zwingli at this time. Hubmaier had earlier made the same point concerning formal writings. It had not been politically expedient to come out openly with what had been "whispered only among ourselves."[136] But now God has provided "this new atmosphere of freedom" in which to speak, and with receptive hearers who will not create a disturbance.

---

134. *PY*, 71. Hubmaier picks up this point again in his work *On the Christian Baptism*, declaring that "the child washers" are wrong to apply it only to children, *PY*, 141. Although he does not identify Zwingli as his opponent in that work it would seem that he does have Zwingli in mind, particularly as Zwingli has used this translation of Matt 19:14 in his book *Of Baptism* (May 27, 1525) that in turn grew out of his dispute with the Zurich Anabaptists on January 17, 1525.

135. *PY*, 72.

136. *PY*, 69.

Use of Scripture

In this short letter, Hubmaier does not make extensive use of Scripture. The three references that he makes to specific texts are given either to obtain Oecolampad's interpretation or to provide his own. This also applies to the allusion to 1 John 5:8.

Three of the remaining allusions are in essence one as they are the synoptic parallels of the one event; that is, the calming of the storm by Jesus. It is not unreasonable to include all the synoptic references, as Hubmaier more frequently than not follows this practice where he gives references to accounts drawn from the Synoptic Gospels. The final allusion is to Matt 7:12 and was discussed above.

Summary

This short letter demonstrates how Hubmaier was using his hermeneutical method in developing his doctrinal position. It shows how Hubmaier looks to the words of Jesus as the primary source of authority in Scripture to which the interpreter appeals to obtain a correct understanding of the Word of God. It introduces the new concept of "conscience" as part of the process of identifying and holding to the truth. It also demonstrates Hubmaier's awareness of the need to clarify the text of Scripture before a clear understanding of the truth of the text can be established.

SEVERAL THESES CONCERNING THE MASS

(Between January and April 1525)[137]

Setting

This short work is probably a reworking of the twenty theses on the Mass Hubmaier mentioned in his January letter to Oecolampad. It provides evidence of Hubmaier's teaching on the Mass that accompanied his reform of that sacrament in Waldshut in November 1524. The content demonstrates a close affinity with the teaching of Zwingli and Karlstadt on the subject.[138]

---

137. *PY,* 7: 73–77; *HS,* 5: 101–4.

138. *PY,* 73–74. Westerburg had arrived in Zurich early in October 1524 with eight manuscripts written by Karlstadt on baptism and the Lord's Supper. With the help of

Analysis

In this work, Hubmaier expands his brief thoughts on the Mass that he had shared with Oecolampad in his letter of January 16. The emphasis falls on the idea of the Lord's Supper being the outward sign or symbol of the inward commitment of the Christian to obediently follow Christ. As Christ loved and suffered for us, so Christians are obligated to love and give themselves for their neighbor. In this way, the Lord's Supper moves beyond the individual's relationship to Christ, to be an essential part of the communal expression of the church. The Lord's Supper is termed a commemoration *(wider gedechtnuss)* of the suffering of Christ's mortal body *(seinen streblichen leyb)*.[139] The bread and wine do not suffer for us and are therefore not the mortal body of Christ. As well as the commemoration of Christ's death in the Supper, there must also be the proclamation of his death, if the Supper is to be celebrated according to the instructions in Scripture.

Hubmaier reiterates his position regarding signs and symbols when he states, "One should always pay more attention and that more seriously to the things signified by the word symbols than to the symbols themselves."[140] He prefaces this statement with a demonstration of the method he employs to discover what is signified by the word symbols. It is an application of the principle that the clearer text explains the darker.

Beginning with the debated text "Take, eat, this is my body given for you" (Luke 22:19), Hubmaier asserts that the phrase "my body" means Christ's "mortal body." He does so on the basis that Christ was using the same "manner of speaking" at the Lord's Supper as he did when he said to Peter, "You are Peter and on this rock," meaning Christ himself, "I will build my church." Hubmaier can safely assert that the rock being spoken of is Christ for Paul says this in 1 Cor 10:4, "And the rock was Christ."[141] In the example of the rock being Christ, Hubmaier has a specific text of Scripture to support him in his contention that the word symbol signifies Christ. He states that the same use of language is intended by Christ in the words of institution. What he has not shown is that it is the mortal body of Christ that is signified.

Mantz, printing of all except the work on baptism was accomplished at Basel. Mantz returned to Zurich with copies of the works and distributed them in the area. Harder, *Sources of Swiss Anabaptism*, 295, 571.

139. *PY*, 74–75; *HS*, 102.
140. *PY*, 75; *HS*, 103.
141. *PY*, 75; *HS*, 103.

At this point Hubmaier introduces the role of the Holy Spirit in soteriology. The Holy Spirit is the one who "makes us alive, and the Spirit comes with the Word."[142] Although this statement does not explicitly define the role of the Spirit, it does point to Hubmaier's awareness of the linking of the Spirit and the Word. The Word on its own is not sufficient to bring either spiritual understanding or assurance of eternal life; for that the Spirit is necessary.

There is also in this work an emphasis on the example of Christ that the believer is to follow. This example is chiefly one of suffering for our neighbor. Hubmaier adds an interesting variation on this theme in his closing statement of this work. Having again stated his willingness to have his understanding corrected "with Scripture" he goes on to state, "I will wholeheartedly follow him with great thanksgiving as he follows Christ."[143] Here is expressed the idea that correct understanding of Scripture will be verified by the life of the one who interprets Scripture. The key to verification is whether or not the interpreter follows Christ. This concept of *nachfolge* became common among the Swiss Brethren as a hermeneutical principle. Christ is again the focus of Hubmaier's hermeneutic.

One other minor point can be ascertained from this work. In part, Hubmaier declares himself against the Mass because it is "an invented name without any basis in Scripture."[144] This example points to a possible new hermeneutical principle: that only those words that are in Scripture are to be considered; that is, their meanings, or what they signify. Instead of "Mass" Hubmaier uses "Supper of Christ" (*Nachmal Christi*). If nothing else, this rejection of the Mass simply because the word is not specifically mentioned in Scripture indicates that Hubmaier was willing to insist on the letter of Scripture where it suited him. This possible principle will be remembered in the course of the following analysis of Hubmaier's works.

Use of Scripture

In this work, Hubmaier only gives three Scripture references, one from Matthew and two from 1 Cor 10. The Matthew and 1 Cor 10:4 reference have already been discussed above. Hubermaier uses the remaining

---

142. *PY*, 75; *HS*, 103.

143. *PY*, 76; *HS*, 104. *Nachfolge* is a common Anabaptist term translated as "discipleship." Hubmaier uses *nachuolgen*, a more literal sense of "following after." *HS*, 104, 129; *PY*, 75.

144. *PY*, 76; *HS*, 102.

reference, 1 Cor 10:16, to support his idea that the Supper involves an obligation of the participants to bind themselves to one another. He maintains that Paul calls this obligation "a communion or fellowship" (*ain gmainschafft oder geselschafft*). Here Hubmaier has translated the Greek *koinonia* literally, and understood it in that sense, rather than as a "participation" in the body and blood of Christ.[145]

Apart from these three stated references, there is the quotation of the words of institution taken from Luke 22:19, and four allusions to verses from 1 Cor 10, 11. Consideration of the Luke reference has been given above in connection with Hubmaier's application of the principle that the clearer texts of Scripture explains the darker.

Two of the allusions to 1 Cor 11 both relate to procedural aspects of participating in the Lord's Supper. The first is an allusion to "drinking unworthily" (1 Cor 11:27), the second to testing oneself before eating from the table of the Lord (1 Cor 11:28). Both are used in the context of the obligation of the participants to share with others in the Lord's Supper.[146] Hubmaier also alludes to 1 Cor 11:26b when he refers to "proclaiming the Lord's death." Hubmaier says, "in the Christ meal one should proclaim the death of Christ." From this statement, it is not clear whether or not Hubmaier is insisting on the preaching of the gospel as an integral part of the Lord's Supper. However, his previous statements in the *Eighteen Theses*, Theses 6 and 12, do insist on preaching in the vernacular accompanying the celebration of the Lord's Supper.[147] There is a second reference to 1 Cor 11:26, but this time to the first part of the verse, which Hubmaier quotes and Pipkin and Yoder identify.[148] On the basis of this text, "As often as you eat of this bread and drink from this cup," Hubmaier asserts that Masses for the dead are an abuse, as the dead cannot share in eating and drinking. Participation in the Lord's Supper therefore defines the members of the church.

There remains one other allusion to consider: 1 Cor 10:17, "Because there is one loaf, we who are many, are one body, for we all partake of the one loaf" (NIV). Hubmaier renders this, "We all are one bread and one body," and uses it to supports his view that the Christian is to be Christ to his neighbor because of their unity in Christ.[149]

145. *PY*, 75; *HS*, 102.
146. *PY*, 75–76; *HS*, 103.
147. *PY*, 33; *HS*, 73.
148. *PY*, 76; *HS*, 104.
149. *PY*, 75; *HS*, 103.

Hubmaier's discussion of the Lord's Supper is therefore focused on the way the Supper is to be understood within the practice of the church, rather than about the theological dispute over the real presence of Christ.

Summary

There is little new in this work with regard to hermeneutics, with the exception of Hubmaier's statement concerning the word "Mass" being rejected as unscriptural. Otherwise, the work simply supplies further examples of how Hubmaier applies his basic hermeneutical principles, this time on the topic of the Mass.

A PUBLIC CHALLENGE

(February 2, 1525)[150]

Setting

Wilhelm Reublin, the Zurich Anabaptist, visited Waldshut between January 29 and 31, 1525, probably bringing Hubmaier the first news of the adult baptisms that had occurred in Zurich on January 21, 1525. Perhaps in response to that news, but certainly in an attempt to continue the reform process in Waldshut, Hubmaier issued a public challenge to debate the topic of infant baptism on February 2, 1525. However, the challenge did not contain a time or venue for the debate. Pipkin and Yoder speculate that Hubmaier, by virtue of issuing the challenge, would, "certify his right to move on in the direction indicated."[151] However, Hubmaier was slow to move in the direction of adult baptism, as it was not until Easter Saturday, April 15, 1525, that Hubmaier submitted himself to baptism at the hands of Reublin.[152]

---

150. *PY*, 8: 78–80; *HS*, 6: 105–7.
151. *PY*, 79.
152. Bergsten, *Balthasar Hubmaier: Anabaptist Theologian*, 230.

Analysis

This one-page text has not survived on its own, but is only found bound with Hubmaier's *On Christian Baptism*.[153] It is a public challenge to those who advocate infant baptism to prove their assertions using "German, plain, clear, and unambiguous Scriptures."[154] Hubmaier proposes that a Bible "fifty or one hundred years old, as the right, proper, and true arbiter be placed between these two positions. Let it be opened and read aloud with imploring, humble spirit."

There is in this challenge an emphasis on the use of German as the proper language for debate. This is in marked contrast to Zwingli's insistence on the use of Latin, Greek, and Hebrew if the correct understanding of Scripture is to be obtained. There is also the assumption that the text of Scripture being read with the right attitude and in the language of all those present will of necessity cause those present to arrive at the correct understanding of the texts under discussion. What is not clear from this short leaflet is who makes up the audience to the dispute; only the learned doctors who continue to advocate infant baptism and those who advocate the baptism of believers, or the whole congregation of the church?

A Public Challenge contains no references to Scripture, or specific biblical allusions.

Summary

This short work is valuable for the discussion of the development of Hubmaier's hermeneutic in that it demonstrates a widening of the gap between Hubmaier and Zwingli on the issue of the necessity of competence in the biblical languages for the correct understanding of Scripture. It also shows that Hubmaier continues to insist that it is the Bible, God's Word, that is to be the sole judge in matters of doctrine, and that the Word can be understood when read in the vernacular by those who come with imploring and humble spirits.

---

153. *HS*, 105. "An keinem dieser drei Orte (St Gallen, Augsburg and Vienna) hat man aber einen solchen Einzeldruck nachweisen können, auch sonst befragte Biblitheken besitzen kein Exemplar davon. Dagegen exisiert die 'Öffentliche Erbietung' als Anhang zu Hubmaiers 'Von der christlichen tauf der Gläubigen.'"

154. *PY*, 80; *HS*, 107.

Balthasar Hubmaier and the Clarity of Scripture

SUMMARY OF WRITINGS FROM OCTOBER 26–28, 1523, TO FEBRUARY 2, 1524

From the above analysis it is clear that for Hubmaier the Word of God equates, in the main, with the text of Scripture. He has demonstrated this attitude at the Second Zurich Disputation, in his *Eighteen Theses,* and in his *An Earnest Christian Appeal.* The Scriptures that he appeals to are those of both the Old and New Testaments, though he does make one reference to the Apocryphal book, *Ecclesiasticus.* The authority of Scripture lies in its being "canonized and sanctified" by God himself.

The Word of God is of itself powerful, and can effect change in those who hear it. At this point Hubmaier identifies preaching as the proclamation of the Word of God, implying that the Word of God is wider than just the letter of Scripture. However, it is not until his booklet *On Heretics* that Hubmaier gives any indication of the role of the Holy Spirit as the interpreter of Scripture and of preaching so that the hearer understands what God is saying. This emphasis on the role of the Holy Spirit is strengthened by further references to the Spirit in his *Letter to Oecolampad* and *Several Theses.* In the latter, he maintains that the Spirit is the agent by which eternal life and assurance are given, but that the Spirit is not independent of the Word that is Scripture.[155]

Like Zwingli and Luther, Hubmaier appeals to Scripture as the sole authority and judge in matters of dispute concerning doctrine and practices in the church. In this respect, he maintains a position that is in the main stream of Reformation understanding.

For Hubmaier the relationship between the two Testaments can be described as one of unity. That unity is to be found in Christ. Beginning at the Second Zurich Disputation Hubmaier makes it plain in the way he handles the text of Scripture that the words of Christ are of fundamental importance. His key text is John 5:39, "Search the Scriptures for they speak of me." The prophets of the Old Testament and the apostles of the New are shown to agree with the intention of the words of Christ. Later in *Theses Against Eck,* Thesis 9, this usage becomes a formal principle of his hermeneutic. He again begins with John 5:39 as the foundation of the principles: "Search in Scripture, not in papal law, not councils, not fathers, not schools; for it is the discourse which Christ spoke which shall judge

---

155. *PY,* 75; *HS,* 103. In this close link between the proclaimed Word and the interpretive function of the Spirit, Hubmaier is closer to Luther than to Zwingli.

all things. He is the truth, the plantation, and the vine" (John 5:39; 12:48; 14:6; 15:1; Matt 15).[156]

In these works, Hubmaier also describes several other formal principles of his hermeneutic. The commands and prohibitions of God form a fundamental principle in his hermeneutic. He first states his position at the Second Zurich Disputation, and commits himself to it in writing in his *Eighteen Theses*, Number 4, "Only those works are good which God has commanded, and only those are evil which he has forbidden us."[157]

As noted above this rule is tied more to the actual words contained in Scripture than the more liberal view held by Zwingli on the subject.

In *Theses Against Eck*, Thesis 12, Hubmaier adds a further formal principle that again reflects his general acceptance of Reformation thinking in this area: "Searching the Scriptures does not take place with unspiritual chatter about innovations, nor with wordy warfare fighting until one is hoarse, but rather by illuminating the darker texts of Scripture with the clearer."[158]

He then uses the example of Jesus explaining Levirate marriage with reference to the resurrection to demonstrate his meaning. Again the words and example of Christ become the focus for correct interpretation of Scripture.

The role of the congregation forms another aspect of Hubmaier's hermeneutic to this point. Again he first states his position briefly at the Second Zurich Disputation and expands on it in *Theses Against Eck*. Like Zwingli, Hubmaier urges that the local congregation should be unanimous in their decisions agreeing to reform of the church so that disturbance is avoided. For Zwingli, however, the congregation only comes to recognize that their priests have presented the correct understanding of Scripture, while for Hubmaier the members of the congregation take an active part in determining the true interpretation of Scripture. Here Zwingli lays greater authority on the learning and linguistic expertise of the priests, while Hubmaier insists that the Scripture is essentially simple and can be correctly understood by lay people who read it and hear it in the vernacular. For Hubmaier, the learned ones have their part to play in helping the congregation come to the correct understanding of Scripture, but they do not dictate that understanding.

---

156. *PY*, 53; *HS*, 88.
157. *PY*, 32; *HS*, 73.
158. *PY*, 53; *HS*, 89.

Balthasar Hubmaier and the Clarity of Scripture

For Hubmaier, as for Zwingli, the attitude of the one who comes to Scripture is all important. Those who come prayerfully with humility will be the ones to whom God will reveal his truth. For Zwingli, the role of the Holy Spirit as both the illuminator and giver of inward assurance of the truth is stressed more strongly than for Hubmaier.

As a university-trained theologian and teacher Hubmaier would have been aware of the rules of grammar and logic, and of the various current theories of signification. He gives limited attention to the place of logic and reason in interpreting Scripture, but where he does he is always critical. Where reason does not lead to the same conclusion as Scripture it is to be regarded as leading into error. His most forceful condemnation comes in Thesis 30 in *On Heretics*.

The greatest deception of the people is the kind of zeal for God that is invested without Scripture in the interest of the salvation of souls, the honor of the church, the love for the truth, good intentions, usages or custom, episcopal decrees, and the indications of reason, all of which have been begged from the light of nature. These are lethal errors when they are not led and directed according to Scripture.[159]

Hubmaier also spends some time in *Several Theses* dealing with the issue of word symbols and what they signify. It is what the word symbol signifies that is of importance, not the sign or symbol itself. The two examples that Hubmaier provides both focus on Christ as the thing signified. Hubmaier is here using the language of the theory of signification that developed from Boethius and became a science under the influence of Aristotle.[160] However, there is not enough material to this point in Hubmaier's work to determine whether he was following a specific theory of signification or whether he was simply using a term familiar to him from his university training, but in a way independent from that formal understanding.

Hubmaier also acknowledges his interpretive use of a "figure." In *An Earnest Christain Appeal*, he equates the person Moses with his five books of the law. He then clarifies that the five books of the law are all the Scriptures, basing his claim on the authority of the words of Christ.[161] He uses literary devices such as figure, parable, metaphor, and allegory far less as an interpretive tool than Zwingli. Hubmaier is concerned to demonstrate the simple meaning of the text, whereas Zwingli moves from the literal

---

159. *PY*, 64–65; *HS*.
160. Evans, *Language and Logic*, 75.
161. *PY*, 44–45; *HS*, 82.

sense to a spiritual sense by applying such literary devices to a text so that it reinforces a point he has made from a clear text of Scripture.

Hubmaier also employs a method of linking various texts by key words, and attributing to the key word the meaning that best aids his argument. In general, the links are obvious and continuity of thought exists between the texts. However, there are occasions when the link words are the only thing common between the idea Hubmaier is seeking to support by his reference to the text and the text itself. In this Hubmaier shows a fine disregard for the context of his text. The few examples of this practice in his works to date do not relate to the main argument of the text.

There is also a tendency in Hubmaier to inflate the number of references he makes to Scripture by citing parallel texts, both from the gospels and from the Old Testament. While on the one hand this demonstrates Hubmaier's intention to appeal only to Scripture for support of his views, it also shows a willingness to pad out his case so that it appears stronger than it is.

There are also cases in these works where Hubmaier has paraphrased a particular text so that it suits his argument, whereas the text as it stands in Scripture does not. Generally, he does so on the grounds that the "intention of Christ" is such as to legitimize the paraphrase. However, in general Hubmaier faithfully applies his hermeneutical principles in his handling of the Scripture.

5

The Bright and Clear Word of God
(Writings at Waldshut from Easter 1525 to December 5, 1525)

SUMMA OF THE ENTIRE CHRISTIAN LIFE

(July 1, 1525)[1]

Setting

As has been seen in his *Letter to Oecolampad* and *A Public Challenge*, Hubmaier was beginning to promote theological opinions opposed to those of Zwingli, particularly regarding infant baptism, and more in keeping with the young Zurich radicals Conrad Grebel and Felix Mantz. These young radicals had made their formal break with Zwingli on January 21, 1525, when they had moved beyond their rejection of infant baptism to the institution of the baptism of believers on confession of faith in Christ, probably at the home of Mantz.[2] Despite contact with members of this group in the intervening months,[3] Hubmaier did not take the step of

---

1. *PY*, 9: 83–89; *HS*, 7: 108–15.
2. Harder, *Sources of Swiss Anabaptism*, 338–42; 706–10.
3. Bergsten, *Balthasar Hubmaier: Anabaptist Theologian*, 229; Harder, *Sources of Swiss Anabaptism*, 350–51, 359. Hubmaier is known to have had contact with Reublin, Johannes Brötli, and Grebel in Waldshut before Easter 1525.

himself being baptized until Easter Saturday, April 15, 1525. At that time, Wilhelm Reublin baptized him in his own church at Waldshut, along with some sixty other adult believers from his congregation.[4] He himself baptized some three hundred Waldshut citizens over the intervening period of the Easter Festival.[5]

Hubmaier's formal adherence to Anabaptism can be dated from this time, as can his influence as a writer and theologian for Anabaptism. His first writing as an Anabaptist, entitled *Summa,* was published on July 1, 1525. It is dedicated to the councils and citizens of Regensburg, Ingolstadt, and Friedberg. Friedberg was the town of his birth, while he had served as priest in both Ingolstadt and Regensburg. He thus showed his desire to correct the errors of the Catholic faith in the towns where he had personally been involved in propagating that faith.

Analysis

In the words of the dedication, Hubmaier notes that he not only lived a life "contrary to the teaching of Christ," but that as their priest he "instructed, fed, and tended [them] outside the Word of God."[6] What he had taught them were the deceptions of the "red whore of Babylon . . . her school teachings, laws, and fables" that had also deceived him. He urged them to "test and examine the prophets and preachers as to whether they go before [them] with God's teaching or not."[7] He exhorted them to search the Scriptures, for in them they will see the testimony of Christ and the Christian life.[8] He concluded his dedication with a familiar reference to Christ's words of the blind leading the blind, except that in this instance the truth of the saying is attributed to the "authority of the Word of Christ."

The *Summa* itself is composed of five sections. Section 1 begins with Hubmaier's paraphrase of Mark 1:15, "repent or change your lives, and believe the gospel."[9] This text provides the framework for sections one, two, and three of the *Summa.* Prior to repentance, Hubmaier argues that people need to look into their hearts and recognize what they are by nature; that is, conceived and born in sin, and unable to help themselves to

---

4. Bergsten, *Balthasar Hubmaier: Anabaptist Theologian,* 230.
5. Ibid., 231.
6. *PY,* 83; *HS,* 110.
7. *PY,* 83; *HS,* 110.
8. *PY,* 83–84; *HS,* 110.
9. *PY,* 84; *HS,* 110.

either do that which God has commanded or to leave undone what God has forbidden.

Here Hubmaier applies the basic formal hermeneutical principle that he first proposed at the Second Zurich Disputation and continued to promote in his *Eighteen Theses* and *Theses Against Eck*. To be justified before God requires that people do what God commands and leave undone that which he forbids. To do otherwise is to sin and to face the just condemnation of God. People who recognize their sinfulness before God and their helplessness in that situation despair and "lose heart like the man who had fallen among the killers."[10]

With his reference to this parable, generally known as the parable of the Good Samaritan, Hubmaier moves to section two. Following a typical medieval allegorical interpretation, Hubmaier describes salvation as Christ bringing medicine and comfort to the wounded man. The wine brings the sinner to repentance and sorrow for sin; the oil brings comfort by driving the pain away. He identifies the oil with the gospel, the message Christ brings to sinners, that he is the "only giver of mercy, reconciler, intercessor, mediator, and peacemaker toward God, our father, so that whoever believes in [him] will not be damned but have eternal life."[11] To believe the words of the gospel enlivens the sinner, yet Hubmaier is at pains to make it clear that it is not within the capacity of the sinner to respond in faith to the message of the gospel.

He goes on to state that the words of the physician before they are believed "are letter and they kill."[12] It is only by faith that the Spirit of God makes the words of the gospel alive, that they begin to live and produce fruit. The second section describes the inward response of the sinner to the message of the gospel, a response of faith and surrender to Christ.

Section three goes on to describe the outward response that follows the inward response of faith. The outward response requires the public oral confession of the person, noting recognition of sin, repentance, faith, and intention to then live in accordance with the Rule of Christ. This public confession is followed by water baptism and acknowledgment that the

---

10. *PY*, 84; *HS*, 110–11.

11. *PY*, 84; *HS*, 111. Timothy George has noted that prior to 1518, Luther had used the parable of the Good Samaritan in the same medieval way, describing sin as a weakness or illness that is overcome through the impartation or infusion of grace. It was a gradual healing process. Luther moved his imagery from the infirmary to the courtroom, from impartation to imputation of grace, speaking of an "alien righteousness" being imputed to man. George, *Theology of the Reformers*, 69.

12. *PY*, 85; *HS*, 111.

person in included in the visible Christian church. It also involves submission to brotherly discipline.[13]

Section four describes what for Hubmaier are the inevitable consequences of faith in Christ and living under His rule, "the person bursts into word and deed, proclaims and magnifies the name and praise of Christ, so that also through us others may be healed and saved."[14] Accompanying praise and preaching, Hubmaier notes the inevitability of persecution. He maintains that suffering follows as a direct consequence of proclaiming the gospel since the world opposes the gospel, the simple Rule of Christ, substituting its own rules and wisdom.[15] This outward opposition is paralleled with an inner struggle in the Christian, which he describes as the old Adam fighting against the Spirit in the person. To overcome the old Adam requires a daily killing of the flesh, which is achieved through the assistance of the Spirit of Christ, resulting in the person bringing forth "good fruits which give testimony of a good tree."[16] This implies that there has been an ontological change in the believer, for prior to trusting in Christ the person is a "bad tree," incapable of bring forth anything but bad fruit.

The outward pledge and promises that are made by the believer prior to baptism are not made out of human capacity but in the grace and power of God. Only in God's grace and with His power can the believer make and live by the pledge and promise involved in baptism.

At the end of section four is a short summary of Hubmaier's position: "a whole Christian life . . . begins in the Word of God. From this follows knowledge of sin and forgiveness of the same in faith. Faith is not idle but is industrious in all good Christian works. But only those are good works which God himself has commanded us and of which he will demand a reckoning from us at the last day."[17]

Section five deals with the Lord's Supper, which Hubmaier says has been instituted by Christ so that we will remember God's great goodness to us for not sparing his only Son, but giving him up to death so that sinners may be saved. By emphasizing the words of Christ, "do this in remembrance of me," Hubmaier focuses on the memorial aspect of the Supper. He refers to Paul's words in 1 Cor 11:26, "until he comes," reasoning

---

13. *PY,* 85–86; *HS,* 111–12.
14. *PY,* 86; *HS,* 112.
15. *PY,* 86; *HS,* 112–13.
16. *PY,* 87; *HS,* 113.
17. *PY,* 87; *HS,* 113.

that Christ is not bodily present and consequently that the bread is only bread and not his body, and similarly with the wine.

Hubmaier goes on to suggest that those who participate in the Supper and contemplate Christ's goodness to us through his self-sacrifice for us, will surrender their wills to Christ, and in the same way as Christ gave himself unreservedly, will do the same for their neighbors. This giving of oneself also requires the grace and strength of God.

Use of Scripture

Although Hubmaier only makes four references to specific passages of Scripture, there are six quotations or paraphrases of various texts, as well as a further nineteen recognizable allusions to identifiable texts, giving a total of twenty-nine quotations, references, and allusions. All four Old Testament references in this work are allusions. Three of the four are grouped in one line of his work. All describe the lament of Old Testament characters who state that they have been conceived and born in sin.[18] The other allusion to those who fear the frost being threatened with eternal snow had previously been provided with a reference, Job 6:16, in his work *On Heretics*.[19]

The New Testament references and allusions provide a variety of examples of how Hubmaier deals with the text of Scripture. Hubmaier expands the text of John 3:16 by inserting part of Phil 2:8 so as to emphasize the shameful nature of the death of Christ.[20] Similarly, in his final words of warning to his readers he takes the text of Matt 10:28, 32–33 to support the point he is making that his readers should not fear those who can harm them in body and goods. By confessing faith in Christ they have no need to fear God, who can harm body and soul. However, in doing so he reverses the order of the verses and adds an allusion to Matt 6:25 to expand the word "body" from Matt 10:28, so that his wording is, "do not fear those who take the body from you, which is more than earthly goods, but fear him who can take both body and soul."[21] In both these examples, the intention of the passage of Scripture is made clearer to the reader by inserting other words from Scripture.

18. *PY*, 84; *HS*, 110. He later provides references for these allusions: Job 3:3; Ps 51:5; Jer 20:14.
19. *PY*, 89, 65; *HS*, 114–15, 100.
20. *PY*, 87; *HS*, 113.
21. *PY*, 89; *HS*, 115.

The Bright and Clear Word of God

Hubmaier also demonstrates an aspect of his method of interpretation that he has not yet formally stated. This can be seen in the way he deals with the "words of institution" of the Lord's Supper. Hubmaier takes a wider selection of verses as the context for interpretation than Luther was to do later. For Luther, "this is my body" was the clear Word of God that was to be literally understood and believed. Erling R. Teigen has shown that Luther saw the works of the sacramentarians, Zwingli and Andreas Karlstadt, as attempts to "harmonize or reconcile empirical reality with revelation," and this was illegitimate.[22] Luther asserted that clear Scripture would be perverted by the importation of "foreign categories" such as mystic visions and Aristotelian-Thomist categories. All that is required are the normal rules of grammar, syntax, and vocabulary.[23]

This objection of Luther's certainly challenges Zwingli's hermeneutical method, which relies heavily upon identifying particular passages of Scripture as belonging to specific literary types, and interpreting the texts in accordance with those literary types.

What Hubmaier has done is to demonstrate that the normal rules of grammar, syntax, and vocabulary are the basic method for exegesis and interpretation of a text, but that any text is always within an associated context and that the context must also be carefully considered if its true meaning is to be clearly understood. Hence, it is not enough to quote, "this is my body" without also considering the wider immediate context that goes on to include the phrase, "do this in remembrance of me."[24] Similarly, 1 Cor 11:26 includes the phrase "until he comes," from which Hubmaier concluded that Christ is not present bodily in the elements of the Lord's Supper but "will come only at the hour of the last judgment."[25]

It was previously noted that Hubmaier used allegorical interpretation of the parable of the Good Samaritan to describe his soteriology. This clearly shows that he still used medieval methods of interpretation on occasion.

Hubmaier's other allusions to the New Testament demonstrate that he lived constantly with the Scriptures, since he uses images and words as either illustrations or proof texts to support his arguments. The use of these texts as proof texts assumes that the reader will also accept the statements as self-evidently true. Hubmaier evidently does not find it necessary

---

22. Teigen, "Clarity of Scripture," 156.
23. Ibid., 158.
24. *PY,* 87; *HS,* 113–14.
25. *PY,* 88; *HS,* 114.

to argue for the truth of the statements he uses as proof texts, as for example his statement that people are conceived and born in sin.[26] Later, the doctrine of original sin was to exercise Zwingli's theological ingenuity. His debate with the Anabaptists over baptism lead him to reject the traditional view that original sin was damning. He maintained that it was a *präst*, a defect or weakness that attaches no guilt to the individual. Sin requires the person to choose to do wrong.[27] Hubmaier was later to challenge Zwingli on this point, as did Urbanus Rhegius and Luther.

Summary

From this first work of the Anabaptist Hubmaier we can see the consolidation of the hermeneutical method and principles that he was developing after the Second Zurich Disputation.

The basic principles for interpreting Scripture are now well in place in Hubmaier's framework. The Word of God, which is here equated with the Word of Christ, is the locus for faith. Yet this Word is not of itself sufficient to bring salvation. The work of the Spirit is required to enliven the Word of God and to elicit the response of faith to effect the healing of the sinner. There is also the unmistakable emphasis on the need of the grace and power of God to be at work in the sinner if there is to be an ontological change, making a good tree from a bad tree so that it may produce good fruit. In this area of his theology Hubmaier has strengthened the link between the Word of God and the Spirit, the Spirit seeming to be the major partner. However, from Hubmaier's allegorical interpretation of the parable of the Good Samaritan it remains unclear as to where faith originates. The wounded person surrenders to the will of the physician "as much as it is possible for a wounded person" to do.[28]

By this time Hubmaier has in place his theology on baptism that separated him from Zwingli, and his view of the Lord's Supper that puts him closer to Zwingli and opposed to Luther. Although Hubmaier's soteriology cannot be said to unequivocally follow Luther or Zwingli, with their strong emphasis on the grace of God that excludes free will in man, he does appear to be struggling to integrate Luther's ideas with his older Catholic position.

---

26. *PY*, 84; *HS*, 110.
27. Stephens, *Theology of Huldrych Zwingli*, 149. Cf. Zwingli, *Antwort*, 588.
28. *PY*, 85; *HS*, 111.

The Bright and Clear Word of God

LETTER TO THE ZURICH COUNCIL

(July 10, 1525)[29]

Setting

After completing his *Summa* on July 1, 1525, Hubmaier obtained and read Zwingli's work *Of Baptism*, first printed on May 27, 1525.[30] Having failed to attend the disputations on infant baptism that had been held in Zurich between Zwingli and the group led by Grebel and Mantz, Hubmaier wrote this letter to the Zurich Council. In it he requested a safe conduct to enable him to come to Zurich and debate the issue of baptism with Zwingli and his supporters, who he names as Leo Jud, Oswald Myconius, and Konrad Schmid, the Commander of Küssnach.[31] He was later to meet with these people, but in a setting much less convivial from that which a safe conduct would have provided.

Analysis

He states that if he can be shown from the Word of God to be in error he would gladly recant and support Zwingli in his view. However, should he prove to Zwingli the error of his position, as he is sure he can, then Zwingli should recant his error and feel no shame in having been wrong. In what may be an attempt to placate Zwingli in this regard, Hubmaier cites from Gal 2:11 how even Peter failed and was rebuked for his error by Paul. Nevertheless, Hubmaier sincerely believes that a reconciliation between himself and Zwingli is possible and that such a reconciliation will reestablish peace in the church.

Hubmaier also notes that he has commenced his own work on baptism and hopes to have it completed the following day, July 11, 1525, which in fact he did.[32]

---

29. *PY,* 10: 90–92.
30. *PY,* 90. Cf. Zwingli, *Of Baptism, 120.*
31. *PY,* 91.
32. From the sources we have it can be shown that Hubmaier wrote his work *On the Christian Baptism of Believers* in five days.

Summary

The letter confirms Hubmaier's ongoing conviction that the "bright and clear Word of God" is to be appealed to as the sole judge in this matter and that conversation between the parties will lead to agreement as to the meaning of the Scripture regarding baptism. Hubmaier still considers himself to be Zwingli's brother at this time and that such a conversation between them is not only possible but can lead to an agreed position that will avoid unrest in the church.

ON THE CHRISTIAN BAPTISM OF BELIEVERS

(July 11, 1525)[33]

Setting

The description of the setting given for Hubmaier's *Summa* provides the background for this present work as well. There is, however, an additional element in Hubmaier's preface to this work that is lacking in the *Summa*; that is, the vehement attack on Zwingli's insistence on the knowledge of the biblical languages for the correct understanding of Scripture. C. Arnold Snyder has shown convincingly that Zwingli had not only encouraged lay reading and interpretation of the Bible through bible reading groups such as the one lead by Andreas Castleberger, but had sought to gain the support of the laity for his reform program by maintaining that everyone could read and correctly interpret Scripture through the guidance of the Holy Spirit. He also did not discourage the disruption of Catholic preaching in the early days of his struggle against the Catholic Church in Zurich.[34] However, when these same lay people challenged his reform program and began to disrupt evangelical preaching, Zwingli acted in two ways to regain control of the reform process. On June 30, 1525, he published a booklet entitled *The Preaching Office* in which he argued that only duly authorized preachers should occupy the pulpits of Zurich and its surrounding area. He also claimed that only those who knew the biblical languages, particularly Hebrew, were qualified to interpret Scripture.[35]

---

33. *PY*, 11: 95–149; *HS*, 8: 116–63.
34. Snyder, "Word and Power," 268, 270.
35. Zwingli, "The Preaching Office," 158–59.

The second action was to establish the school known as the Prophecy on June 30, 1525, the same day *The Preaching Office* was completed. Here the Scripture was interpreted by those learned in the original languages, with a vernacular sermon preached to those assembled by one of the preachers.[36] The Zurich Council also prohibited unauthorized public preaching and bible reading, prescribing death by drowning for those who undertook such activities.[37] In this way Zwingli reasserted the control of the authorized pastors of Zurich over the interpretation of Scripture, something Hubmaier likened to the establishment of a new papacy.

Analysis

With the publication of *On the Christian Baptism*, Hubmaier commits himself to a position opposed to that of Zwingli and the other preachers in Zurich on the question of infant baptism. Although this work contains detailed criticisms of Zwingli's arguments in *Of Baptism*, Hubmaier does not name his opponent. However, Zwingli considered it to be a personal attack, since he identified Hubmaier's disparaging reference to the "Züngler" (language artists), as a thinly disguised form of his own name "Zuingli."[38] Hubmaier charged that a new papacy would be established if the interpretation of Scripture had to wait for those who were learned in the languages of the Biblical text, that is, Hebrew, Greek, and Latin.[39]

Hubmaier also included such epitaphs as "Scripture rippers" to refer to those who supported infant baptism, and berated those who introduced "invented, sophistic glosses and additions" for misleading and confusing the simple people.[40] His strongest condemnation comes in response to the assertion that Christ did not institute and command water baptism: "There has never been on earth a Christian so impertinent, godless, and proud who would say that water baptism is not a command and institution of Christ. . . . [H]e who dissolves baptism is cursed and damned by

---

36. Stephens, *Theology of Huldrych Zwingli*, 39–40, 307n104.

37. Snyder, "Word and Power," 281; Harder, *Sources of Swiss Anabaptism*, 338.

38. *PY*, 142; *HS*, 155. Zwingli picks up Hubmaier's use of Züngler in a marginal note, "Züngler ist nach by Zuingli." Zwingli, *Antwort*, 601. Cf. Windhorst, *Täuferisches Taufverständnis*, 45, n.51.

39. This was in fact the outcome of the Reformation in both its Lutheran and Reformed expression.

40. *PY*, 113–14; *HS*, 133.

the power of the Word of Christ."[41] Zwingli had noted that on this matter the Anabaptists and the papists were agreed against him that baptism was instituted by Christ after the resurrection with the words of Matt 28:18ff. Nevertheless, for the sake of the truth as he knew it "in the strong and invincible Word of God," Zwingli boldly continued to affirm that baptism was instituted by John the Baptist.[42]

However, Hubmaier's invective, though restrained by Reformation standards, leaves the impression that he felt the possibility of reaching agreement between himself and Zwingli, though not impossible, was diminishing. At one point he includes an oblique reference to his request for an interview with Zwingli made in his letter to the Zurich Council, "if these people were not too learned for me to be allowed to talk to them."[43] This may indicate that Zwingli did not desire to respond to Hubmaier's request, or that the Zurich Council had rejected it. Either way, the possibility of reaching agreement through dialogue had been effectively impeded at that time.

Nevertheless, there were good reasons for Hubmaier to continue to hope that a reconciliation of views was possible since there were a number of areas on which he and Zwingli agreed. They agreed that those who say they can live without sin after baptism are in error and should be stopped teaching such a falsehood. Both men use the same reference to 1 John 1:8 to support their argument.[44] It follows from this that as long as a person remains alive he or she is never without sin, and that the Christian continues to bring forth both good and bad fruit.[45]

They also agree that government does have a legitimate place and that it is to be obeyed. Hubmaier qualifies this obedience with the phrase, "in all things that are not contrary to God."[46] Zwingli presents the view that the Council of Zurich and those who "teach and watch at Zurich" are in partnership in preventing the disruption of the peace of the Church

---

41. *PY*, 125; *HS*, 143.

42. Zwingli, *Of Baptism*, 161.

43. *PY*, 120; *HS*, 139.

44. Harder, *Sources of Swiss Anabaptism*, 364; Zwingli, *Of Baptism*, 139; *PY*, 98; *HS*, 120.

45. Harder, *Sources of Swiss Anabaptism*, 374; *PY*, 146–47; *HS*, 161. This is part of the *Summa* that Hubmaier repeats here virtually unchanged.

46. *PY*, 98; *HS*, 120.

through the rebellion and partisanship of the rebaptizers over the issue of infant baptism.[47]

Christof Windhorst sees Hubmaier as writing this work in response to three charges that Zwingli had brought against the Anabaptists: 1. the Anabaptists by their rebaptism establish conspiracies and sects, 2. they reject authority, 3. that following baptism they sin no more.[48] He argues that Hubmaier is able to distance himself from the Zurich Anabaptists by demonstrating his unity with Zwingli on two of the matters.[49] With regard to the remaining charge, the accusation of sect formation, Hubmaier replies that the Anabaptists are falsely accused as were Christ, Jeremiah, Paul, and others before them and that they, as Christ's disciples, are no greater than their master.[50] He argues that it is impossible for them to form a sect as in the matter of baptism under discussion they handle the Word of God correctly, and do not obscure the "clear, bright, and plain baptismal Scriptures" as do their opponents.[51] In this regard Hubmaier stands with the Zurich Anabaptists.

There are, however, other specific accusations that Zwingli makes against the Anabaptists to which Hubmaier responds in the body of the text and not just in the foreword where Windhorst has gathered his three points. Zwingli paraphrases an Anabaptist argument that infant baptism is no baptism at all, an argument he had heard in the private and public disputations, "either we have previously been baptized in the pope's baptism or we do not know whether we have been baptized at all."[52] Hubmaier acknowledges Zwingli's charge in his foreword but does not rebut it there.[53] He dedicates question 2 in chapter 6 to this issue, though he does not specify Pope Nicolas II as the instigator of infant baptism.[54] Zwingli asserts that the Zurich Anabaptists held Pope Nicolas II to be the instigator of infant baptism. Zwingli appears to have taken great pleasure in writing of the humiliation of an Anabaptist opponent on this point. Firstly, he shows

---

47. Harder, *Sources of Swiss Anabaptism*, 364.

48. Windhorst, *Täuferisches Taufverständnis*, 41, citing Zwingli: "1. dass die Taufer durch die sogenannte Wiedertaufe 'Rotten vnnd Secten' aufrichten; 2. dass sie die Obrigkeit ablehnen und 3. dass nach der Taufe keine Sunden mehr geschehen."

49. Ibid., 44.

50. *PY*, 97; *HS*, 119. The allusion is to John 13:15 or 15:20.

51. *PY*, 98; *HS*, 120.

52. Harder, *Sources of Swiss Anabaptism*, 368.

53. *PY*, 97; *HS*, 119.

54. Harder, *Sources of Swiss Anabaptism*, 368.

that Augustine was aware of and practiced infant baptism more than six hundred years before Nicolas II. Secondly, he presses his opponent as to where he had read of the Pope's institution of infant baptism. His opponent replies that he had read it in "the papal book." Zwingli seizes on this and asks if he could read Latin, which he could not. In fact, Zwingli tells us, he could read only simple German. As the "papal book" had not been translated into German, the Anabaptist "blushed with embarrassment," though he refused to withdraw his opinion.

Hubmaier rephrases Zwingli's question as follows: "Have people not always, from apostolic times until today, baptized infants, or has it not always been like that?" To this he replies, "even if it had always been like that, it would still not be right, because a wrong is always a wrong."[55] He goes on to demonstrate from canon law, citing his source with care and in Latin, that infant baptism was not always practiced by the church fathers. He leaves his most stinging attack until the end, when he implicitly acknowledges Augustine's support of infant baptism, by citing his chapter *Firmissime* (Most firmly) in the letter to Diaconus. Caustically Hubmaier comments, "Would to God that he had said *Impiissime* [Most impiously] for that, then he would have spoken the truth."[56] In this way, Hubmaier supports the Zurich Anabaptists by continuing the line that infant baptism has not always been practiced as it was in his day, and stating that the evidence is to be found in "the books of the pope" and those of the church fathers.

Hubmaier addresses the first point under the theme of rebaptism, echoing Zwingli's words in his answer, "it has not been proven to us whether or not we have been baptized."[57] He argues that as infant baptism has "no basis in Scripture" it is not a baptism, and therefore the "present baptism is not rebaptism but a baptism."[58] For Hubmaier, there is nevertheless such a thing as rebaptism, a possibility Zwingli denies. The debate centers around the disciples of John the Baptist that Paul encountered at Ephesus (Acts 19:1ff). For Zwingli these disciples never received water baptism at the hands of John the Baptist, so that when they were baptized by Paul it was their first baptism and therefore not a rebaptism.[59] Zwingli comes to this conclusion by insisting that the word baptism used in the

---

55. *PY*, 137; *HS*, 153.
56. *PY*, 139; *HS*, 154.
57. *PY*, 97; *HS*, 119.
58. *PY*, 121; *HS*, 140.
59. Zwingli, *Of Baptism*, 169–75.

passage should be understood to mean teaching. These men therefore only knew the teaching of John the Baptist that called people to repentance. For Zwingli, repentance is John the Baptist's call for people to "believe on him which should come after him."[60] This Zwingli describes as being the whole gospel, and in this way equates the preaching of John the Baptist with the gospel Christ preached. Therefore, the baptism of John is equal to the baptism of Christ. Zwingli overcomes the problem that these disciples needed to hear the gospel again through Paul by asserting that the teaching of Apollos was incomplete. Therefore, though these disciples had heard the preaching of John through Apollos they did not know the full gospel.[61]

Hubmaier rejects Zwingli's arguments that baptism must be taken to mean teaching, and that the preaching of John was the same as the preaching of Christ. He argues that the disciples in Ephesus had received the water baptism of John as the simple understanding of the text implies, but that they had not followed John's preaching to go to Christ for the forgiveness of sin. Paul therefore preached Christ to them and the forgiveness of sins through faith in Christ. "When they heard that, they believed without a doubt and let themselves be baptized in the name, that is, in the grace and power of the Lord Jesus Christ; and they testified publicly that they fully believe the remission of their sins."[62] Hubmaier concludes that there is a true distinction between the baptisms of John and Christ, and that this is an instance of true rebaptism. Earlier he had also argued that John's preaching was "the harsh and frightful law, the letter, sin, and death, just as the other preachers of the law and the prophets."[63] For Hubmaier the gospel differs essentially from the preaching of John in that pardon or forgiveness of sins is presently available in the person of Christ, or guaranteed to all believers in the disciples during the time of Christ's bodily absence, for they had received after the resurrection the authority to declare sins forgiven as Christ had while bodily present on earth.[64]

For Hubmaier, "believed forgiveness of sins is the true gospel."[65] John is only able to declare the law and lead "downward into hell,"[66] while in Christ the work of the Spirit causes the dead letter to be made alive, and

---

60. Ibid., 172.
61. Zwingli, *Of Baptism*, 173.
62. *PY*, 113; *HS*, 132.
63. *PY*, 102; *HS*, 123.
64. *PY*, 103, 116; *HS*, 125, 135.
65. *PY*, 106; *HS*, 127.
66. *PY*, 106; *HS*, 127.

leads up into heaven. Hubmaier had combined the images of the Good Samaritan and the physician to describe the response of faith in the believer in his earlier work the *Summa,* and continues to use these images in this work. He describes the sequence of hearing and believing with the illustration: "It is just as if one were to tell a sick person for a long time about a good physician. He still is sick until he comes to the physician who heals him."[67] From this passage it would seem that faith is dependent on the action of the believer and on the necessity of the preached word. In chapter 7 of the work under consideration, Hubmaier included an extended version of his previous work the *Summa,* in which he spells out more clearly the relationship of faith and forgiveness of sins. The wounded one hears of his guilt through preaching of repentance, recognizes his total inability to help himself, and calls on the physician for healing. Hubmaier explains the allegory of the Good Samaritan as follows:

> He confesses himself guilty and desires grace, with the firm faith that God will not hold him to account for such weakness and sickness to eternal damnation because he has surrendered himself to this physician Jesus and has committed his sickness to him to be healed. Now, if God wanted to be angry and were to demand health from the wounded person and say: "I created you in my own image, healthy, pure, and perfect; thus I want you to be or I shall condemn you"—here now the physician steps forth, to whom you have entrusted yourself in faith. He pleads for you before God his Father with faithful intercession, that he may abstain from his anger, and also be gracious and favorable to you through the grace and favor which he has towards Christ. Here then the Father neither wants nor can deny anything to his most beloved Son but he grants him his request and thus forgives you your sin through Jesus Christ, our Lord.[68]

Roland Armour has correctly concluded that for Hubmaier faith is the individual's spontaneous commitment to Christ and as such a precondition for spiritual regeneration carried out by the Holy Spirit. Baptism follows as a sign of faith and regeneration.[69] This conception of faith is distinctly different from that of Zwingli, who sees faith as the result of God's action "implanting" it in the believer.[70] This faith is also independent of all

---

67. *PY,* 105; *HS,* 126.
68. *PY,* 145; *HS,* 159.
69. Armour, *Anabaptist Baptism,* 31.
70. Zwingli, *Of Baptism,* 137.

external things, which includes the Scriptures and teaching. For Zwingli, baptism as an initiatory sign does not require a personal response of faith to demonstrate the presence of the Holy Spirit. Therefore, baptism is available to all people, including children. He uses this as an argument against the Anabaptists who demand that only those who have the Holy Spirit may be baptized. He goes on to assert that the Anabaptists are wrong to state that infants do not have the Holy Spirit, citing the cases of Jeremiah and John the Baptist to demonstrate that God can give his Holy Spirit to children. In this way, Zwingli can argue that infants are also possible subjects to receive baptism.[71] Hubmaier counters Zwingli's argument by objecting that, while infusing faith is possible with God as demonstrated in the specific cases of John the Baptists and Jeremiah, he cannot accept as "theology" that it happens to all people generally: "but that he is doing the same also to others—about that I have no Scripture."[72]

Behind this argument is a very significant basic difference between Zwingli and Hubmaier. From the beginning of his work, Zwingli is at pains to argue that there is no cleansing in any external ceremony. He bases this on his understanding of Heb 9:9–10.[73] It is only the Spirit that brings this cleansing, and it is only God who gives this baptism of the Spirit, God himself doing the drawing and implanting of the faith necessary for salvation.[74] In the context of his later analysis of John 3:5–6, he challenges those who have misunderstood Augustine, for they argue that the spoken word with the water constitutes the sacrament of baptism, which effects salvation. Zwingli comments: "It is still the case that a spoken or material word has no greater power than that of the water. For none can remit sin but God alone."[75] Zwingli's presupposition is then that the omnipotence of God is not to be hindered or made dependent on anything, including the material word of Scripture.

Hubmaier, on the other hand, uses as the basis of his understanding of faith Rom 10:13, "faith comes through preaching, preaching, however through the Word of God."[76] God has not only revealed his will to man in his Word, but the order in which faith is made possible is also clearly

---

71. Ibid., 149.

72. *PY,* 142; *HS,* 156.

73. Zwingli, *Of Baptism,* 130. Zwingli goes on to state that the two ceremonies that Christ has left for us are a "concession to our frailty," 131.

74. Ibid., 130–31, 138.

75. Ibid., 154.

76. *PY,* 116; *HS,* 135.

Balthasar Hubmaier and the Clarity of Scripture

discernible. Here faith is the result of preaching that is based on the Word of God. Through preaching, God calls for a response from man, a response of faith. "This confidence and sincere trust in God through Jesus Christ, that is, through the favor, grace, and good will which God the Father has for his most-beloved Son Jesus Christ, is exactly true faith."[77] Hubmaier's use of Scripture demonstrates that he believes that God has chosen to limit his sovereignty, restricting himself to the concept of order as revealed in Scripture. This dependence on the principle of order underlines all his exegesis of the baptismal texts of the New Testament, particularly those Scriptures on the baptism of Christ. Hubmaier provides very little exegetical comment on these texts. Instead he simply commends his readers "to observe the following order, both in regard to the words and the meaning: (1) word, (2) hearing, (3) faith, (4) baptism, (5) work."[78]

In contrast, Zwingli rejects the contention that the order of the words in the text of Scripture has any significance. Rather, it can in fact be misleading. Using the texts John 1:29 and 1:31, Zwingli argues that dependence on the word order would mislead since John says in verse 29, "behold the Lamb of God" and in verse 31, "and I knew him not." He means by this that John is saying in the first verse he knew Christ and then two verses later that he does not know Christ.[79] His second example, from Rom 10:9–10, demonstrates his presupposition that salvation can in no way be dependent on external things. Outward confession cannot be allowed to take precedence over faith.[80] Hence he concludes: "Therefore I do not place too great importance upon the literal wording. We are to study the literal sense, but with moderation. We must not allow the letter to kill us, for the letter of the Gospel kills no less surely than the letter of the Law."[81] Thus, he counters the insistence of the Anabaptists on the order of the words in Matt 28:18ff.

---

77. *PY*, 116; *HS*, 135.

78. *PY*, 129; *HS*, 146. He makes similar statements regarding order with regard to the texts he uses for the baptism of John and the apostles. *PY*, 106, 129; *HS*, 127–28, 146.

79. Interestingly, Zwingli does not note the distinction between the present tense that governs "Behold the lamb of God" and the pluperfect "I knew." If this is noted there is no possible error through accepting the word order as it exists in the text. Hubmaier also uses John 1:29–31, but to support his contention that the preaching of Christ and John differ on the crucial point that forgiveness only comes in the person of Christ. *PY*, 105; *HS*, 126–27.

80. Zwingli, *Of Baptism*, 143.

81. Ibid., 142.

The Bright and Clear Word of God

It is at this point that there are further observable differences between Hubmaier and Zwingli. For Hubmaier the texts are clear and understandable to all people. It requires nothing other than simply to read them and believe the plain meaning as it is seen there. For these clear passages of Scripture there is no need to resort to rhetorical devises, such as synecdoche.[82] Zwingli specifically notes his use of synecdoche as part of his argument to prove that children were included in the multitude that went out to John at the Jordan.[83] It is also the basis for his claim that children are included in the "household" of Stephanas (Acts 16). Hubmaier ridicules Zwingli on this point, saying that Caiaphas, Annas, and Pilate would also be included in those who went to be baptized by John if synecdoche were a valid method of interpretation.[84] It is also wrong to insist on the use of Greek, Hebrew, and Latin for the correct understanding of these texts.[85] Languages should be used for the edifying of the church, not for obscuring what is clear and thus confusing simple people, as he alleges these theologians are doing.[86] Nor will he accept Zwingli's assertion that the gift of tongues; that is, knowledge of foreign languages, is restricted to a few people.[87] Rather, knowing what God is saying is a general gift to all who have the Spirit.[88] The simple German text is sufficient for people to read or hear and understand both the law and the gospel.

Both Hubmaier and Zwingli demand a clear word of Scripture from the other with regard to baptism. Hubmaier restricts himself to New Testament texts, as only in the New Testament is baptism described. He rejects Zwingli's identification of circumcision with baptism since he has a clear word that Noah's ark, mentioned in 1 Pet 3:20, is the only figure used in the Old Testament for baptism.[89] He dismisses Zwingli's use of Rom 6:3-4 and Col 2:12 as erroneous, since he believes that Zwingli has

---

82. *PY*, 98, 141; *HS*, 120, 155.

83. Zwingli, *Of Baptism*, 147. Two years later Zwingli included a lengthy defense of the use of synecdoche that took as its focus the text 1 Cor 10:1, "All our fathers were under the cloud." This text became the center of the debate over baptism between Hubmaier and Zwingli in December 1525 when Hubmaier was imprisoned in Zurich. Zwingli, *Refutation of the Tricks*, 159ff.

84. *PY*, 108; *HS*, 129.

85. *PY*, 99; *HS*, 120. Hubmaier does accept that for the dark passages of Scripture these languages are valuable.

86. *PY*, 142; *HS*, 156.

87. Zwingli, *Of Baptism*, 137.

88. *PY*, 113; *HS*, 132.

89. *PY*, 134; *HS*, 150.

confused internal baptism, to which he believes these texts refer, with external baptism.[90] Zwingli, on the other hand, insists that he has a "clear word" in Scripture that circumcision in the Old Testament is an analogy for, or better, is what baptism is in the New Testament. He refers to Gen 17:23–27 where Abraham dedicates his child to God.[91] This use of an Old Testament text as a clear word had been foreshadowed by Zwingli in his work *Those Who Give Cause*, in which he argued that as there is no clear word in the New Testament that either commands or forbids the baptism of infants, the practice of circumcision should be taken as the sign that foreshadowed baptism.[92]

In *On the Christian Baptism*, Hubmaier continues to apply his basic principle that Christians only do that which God has commanded. In this instance God commands only that those who believe are to be baptized. For Hubmaier, the positive command includes the prohibition. Baptism of believers necessarily precludes baptizing all who do not believe, and that includes children.[93] Similarly, the command to preach the gospel precludes preaching "human teachings, laws, dreams, and legends." This is the position that both Hubmaier and Zwingli took at the Second Zurich Disputation with regard to images and the Mass, as has been shown in chapter 1. In his discussion of this principle Hubmaier alludes to the Second Zurich Disputation and puts it to Zwingli that permitting what is not explicitly prohibited would set up again "a nice double popery" in such matters "which concern God and the souls."[94] Zwingli should beware that he adds nothing to the Testament of Christ.

Zwingli for his part accuses the Anabaptists of adding to the Word of God: "It does no good to say in reference to things which should be forbidden, 'Add nothing to my Word,' but only to the things that should be considered sin; for they must show a prohibiting law. Now if infant baptism is not forbidden with a law, it is no sin."[95] For Zwingli, baptism is an external ceremony that is continued as a concession to the frailty of humanity; it cannot affect salvation one way or another and it is not a matter of sin as there is no law prohibiting it. It is in fact to be considered in the same category as eating meat; that is, as a matter of indifference

---

90. *PY*, 135–36; *HS*, 151. Cf. Zwingli, *Of Baptism*, 151.
91. Harder, *Sources of Swiss Anabaptism*, 366.
92. Ibid., 319.
93. *PY*, 136; *HS*, 152.
94. *PY*, 136; *HS*, 152.
95. Harder, *Sources of Swiss Anabaptism*, 366.

or *adiaphora*. However, the rebaptism that he accuses the Anabaptists of practicing is adding to the Word of God, is causing others to stumble, and should therefore cease.[96]

It can be seen from the preceding discussion that Hubmaier and Zwingli not only arrive at different conclusions about infant baptism and rebaptism, but that they have very different presuppositions from which they begin their exegesis of Scripture. Zwingli had declared himself fully on the side of those who begin with the sovereignty of God, attributing both the grace and faith necessary for salvation to be solely the work of God.[97] It follows for Zwingli that faith cannot be dependent on the response of man to the offer of salvation God has made available in Christ. Rather, God implants the necessary faith in the believer. This activity he describes as the internal baptism of the Spirit, which is different from the external baptism in water. The first brings salvation, the second acts as an initiatory sign, declaring those who receive it as set apart to live in accordance with the Word of God. The two baptisms are not necessarily concurrent, and it is possible to be saved without external baptism. Zwingli also identifies the water baptism of John with the baptism of the apostles and of Christ.

Hubmaier begins with the presupposition that God has revealed an order of salvation in Scripture: hearing; response in faith; regeneration through the work of the Holy Spirit; public confession of faith followed by public baptism to witness to the event of regeneration. This order is self evident in Scripture, and though he admits that salvation is possible without outward baptism in water, he warns that those who believe in Christ for salvation are under obligation to receive water baptism where water and a baptizer are available, for Christ has instituted baptism with an earnest command.[98] This follows from his formal principle that the commands of God are to be obeyed. It is also evident that people are in some way responsible for the response they make to the message of the gospel that must be preached if they are to hear of salvation in Christ. Although Hubmaier goes to some lengths to describe that people do not have the ability in themselves to respond, and that the word is enlivened in them by

---

96. Zwingli, *Of Baptism*, 159.

97. Harder, *Sources of Swiss Anabaptism*, 318. Zwingli proposes the scenario of a debate between two people over the issue of free will. Both produce clear words from Scripture, yet have contradictory conclusions. Zwingli's criterion for judging who has understood Scripture correctly is to identify "who gives God the honor and ascribes to him all deeds, glory, and honor."

98. *PY*, 121–22; *HS*, 139–40.

the Holy Spirit; nevertheless, people do still respond in faith to the message of the gospel, as much as a wounded person is capable of doing.

Personal faith as a response to Christ is a prerequisite to baptism in Hubmaier's understanding, while for Zwingli that faith may be the faith of parents or the faith God implants in the child.

There is also an obvious tension between Hubmaier and Zwingli over the clarity of Scripture. Hubmaier considers the baptismal texts of the New Testament to be clear and self evident, requiring no special skill in languages such as Greek, Hebrew, and Latin, nor in rhetorical and grammatical techniques. Hubmaier is arguing that the common man, the simple people, are able to read or hear the Word of God, understand it, and validly interpret Scripture. He goes so far as to suggest that if interpretation of Scripture requires special skills in languages, rhetoric, and grammar, a new papacy of evangelical academics will replace the recently overthrown Roman papacy and its official teaching offices. The use of languages, rhetorical devices, and grammatical argument that Zwingli employs against the Anabaptists only serves to obscure and confuse the clear Word of God. This does not mean that Hubmaier has no place for languages and the other skills mentioned, for he clearly states that they can serve in interpretation of dark passages. However, with regard to these baptismal texts, one needs only place the clear texts beside the dark text to be assured of the correct interpretation.[99]

There is a further distinction that the two Reformers make, but it is not developed in these works. Hubmaier outlines his understanding of the apostle's office, which consists of three commands: preaching, faith, and outward baptism. Preaching consists in proclaiming the same message as did Moses, the promise of the coming of Christ, "He died on account of our sin and rose again for the sake of our justification, so that all who believe in him should not be lost but have eternal life."[100] This is the message that Christ himself gave through the prophets, specifically referring to Isa 43:24ff. However, the forgiveness of sin is not possible until Christ the Word has become flesh. While Christ was on earth bodily, the disciples pointed to him and people believed in him for the forgiveness of their sins. After the resurrection, the authority to announce and guarantee forgiveness of sins has been given to the apostles and after them to the church.[101] There is then a distinction between the promise of the gospel as

99. *PY,* 109; *HS,* 130.
100. *PY,* 115; *HS,* 134.
101. *PY,* 116; *HS,* 134.

The Bright and Clear Word of God

given in the Old Testament and in the preaching of John the Baptist, and the fulfillment of the promise with the coming of Christ. Hubmaier uses the preaching of the apostles recorded in the book of Acts as the basis for this distinction between promise and fulfillment. The apostles themselves repeatedly emphasized the nature of the Old Testament promise by citing texts from the Old Testament and then declaring that these words find their fulfillment in Christ.[102]

Zwingli, on the other hand, sees the sovereignty of God working through both Old and New Testaments. God gives saving faith to whom he will. There is one covenant that God has made and one way that people are to be saved.[103] The historical coming of Christ does not act as a fulcrum in the history of salvation as it appears to do for Hubmaier. However, at this time in the development of Hubmaier's theology and hermeneutic, he has not spelt out the full implications of this distinction between promise and fulfillment.

Use of Scripture

It remains to examine Hubmaier's use of Scripture in this work. Hubmaier provides twenty-one Old Testament references, seventeen linked with quotations and recognizable allusions. In the remaining four references it is not immediately obvious which verses Hubmaier intends to refer to in the chapter cited. There are a further nine allusions that are identifiable but do not have a reference supplied. Of the total thirty uses of the Old Testament in this work only two are in common with Zwingli's *Of Baptism*. Both are allusions without references. Hubmaier alludes to circumcision as the "foolish command that on the eighth day of their life the little boys should have the little foreskin of their penis cut off."[104] It is one of a sequence of four commands that God has given that are to be obeyed even though they appear foolish. Baptism has been said to be of no consequence by Zwingli, but Hubmaier stresses that a command, no matter how foolish it might appear, is to be obeyed. Zwingli had alluded to the same passage as his "clear word" that circumcision is the Old Testament equivalent of baptism.[105] Zwingli also insists that the command should be obeyed, but that its place is now taken by baptism. The second reference is

---

102. *PY*, 115; *HS*, 134.
103. Zwingli, *Of Baptism*, 138–39.
104. *PY*, 126; *HS*, 144.
105. Harder, *Sources of Swiss Anabaptism*, 366.

to the sanctification of an infant in the womb, specifically Jeremiah. As has been noted above Zwingli argues for the possibility of a general application of the passage to all children, while Hubmaier denies that is a valid extrapolation.

With regard to the New Testament references Hubmaier provides one hundred fifty-six references either with quotations (fifty-four), or with allusions (seventy-three), or standing free of either quotations or allusions (twenty-nine). A further eighteen quotations and forty-two allusions are identifiable that have no reference. Extended quotations of specified texts account for the majority of chapter 3, "The Passages on the Baptism of John," and chapter 5, "Scriptures on the Baptism of Christ." Hubmaier prefaces each chapter by stressing the importance of noting the order in which particular ideas occur in the individual passages. He thus demonstrates two aspects of his hermeneutic. Firstly, that there is an order in God's revelation of his will in Scripture that is to be heeded, and secondly, that the context of a given text is to be carefully considered. He comments on Matt 21:25–26 that the "simple meaning" of the texts should stand "as long as neither the preceding nor the succeeding words compel or lead us differently."[106] Zwingli had used this text to equate baptism with teaching, demanding that the context required this interpretation, for the Pharisees that questioned Jesus could not have been worried about external baptism with water, since the Jews already had many other washings.[107] Hubmaier brings into play his other principal rule for interpreting Scripture in this exchange, claiming that the clear texts are to be brought beside the darker texts so that the meaning is made plain. If this is done it will do away with strange glosses. His clear text is John 1:26 where John specifically calls his baptism a baptism of water.[108] Hubmaier also uses this principle of the clear text making understandable the darker text in his comments on Mark 1:1–5. Zwingli had insisted that if the word order did have to be observed, which he states is misleading, then it followed that baptism preceded preaching, a claim he also made with regard to Matt 28:18ff.[109] Hubmaier notes that the Mark 1 reference does have the order baptize then preach, but claims that the fuller description of this event that is recorded in Luke 3 shows that baptism followed the preaching. He concludes that John preached and led people to recognition of their sins. He

---

106. *PY*, 114; *HS*, 133–34.
107. Zwingli, *Of Baptism*, 134.
108. *PY*, 109–10; *HS*, 130.
109. Zwingli, *Of Baptism*, 147, 141, 143.

then baptized with water those who made a public declaration of their repentance. Then he preached to them again, pointing them to Christ for the forgiveness of sins. John the Baptist therefore preached both before and after baptism.[110]

Reference has already been made to the debate between Zwingli and Hubmaier over Acts 19:1ff. Hubmaier adds to his criticism of Zwingli's interpretation of this text a subtle jibe at Zwingli's choice of the vernacular translation he used. Zwingli chose Luther's translation above the new Zurich translation, since Luther's translation supports his view that verse 3 should read "unto what" or "into what," rather than "in what" were you baptized.[111] Hubmaier notes that the old Latin and the new German translations agree with his view that the verse should be "in what you were baptized."

Of the twelve texts Hubmaier quotes at length and provides references to in the chapter on the "Baptism of Jesus," seven are also used by Zwingli. Analysis of Matt 28:18ff occupies a major part of Zwingli's attack on the Anabaptists. First, Zwingli objects to their insistence on the order that preaching and confession of faith must precede baptism; second, that with the words of Matt 28:18ff Christ instituted baptism; and finally, that the Anabaptists reject baptism in the name of the Trinity as a valid baptism.[112] Throughout his work, Hubmaier picks up these points and rebuts them all, insisting that the order must stand, that Christ did institute baptism with these words, and that it is not enough to simply say the Trinitarian formula and pour water on the candidate for baptism to be valid.[113] In this rebuttal of Zwingli Hubmaier frequently couples Mark 16:16 with Matt 28:18ff. Hubmaier's treatment of Acts 10:44ff, 19:1ff has been previously noted.

Hubmaier cites 1 Cor 1:13ff, which includes the reference to "the household of Stephanas" (v16). Zwingli had used this to suggest the possibility that children were included among those baptized by Paul.[114] He refutes Zwingli's allegation that children were also baptized by referring

---

110. *PY*, 109–10; *HS*, 30.

111. Zwingli, *Of Baptism*, 171n106. In the footnote Bromiley notes that the new translation that Zwingli refers to is Luther's 1522 New Testament, "*Warauff seyt yhr den toufft?*" Cf. the new Zurich translation of 1524, "Worinn sind ir den toufft?"

112. Zwingli, *Of Baptism*, 141, 143 and 142, 160; Harder, *Sources of Swiss Anabaptism*, 366, 373.

113. *PY*, word order: 110, 120, 129; Christ instituted baptism: 104, 114, 118, 121–22; Trinitarian formula 142; 130, 139, 146; 125, 134, 137, 140; 156.

114. *PY*, 133–34; *HS*, 149; Harder, *Sources of Swiss Anabaptism*, 320.

to his principle that personal confession of faith must precede baptism. He also challenges Zwingli to prove that children were there. Here again Hubmaier challenges Zwingli's use of inclusive speech.

With regard to 1 Pet 3:20–21, an interesting divergence of exegetical method becomes apparent between Hubmaier and Zwingli. Hubmaier takes the literal sense of the passage as determinative. For Hubmaier, when Peter speaks of water it is literally physical water. He understands that water baptism, which is preceded by faith, gives knowledge of a good conscience before God: "Water baptism does not wash away sin, nor does it save us, but only the certain knowledge of a good conscience toward God through the resurrection of Christ Jesus. This knowledge is nothing but the faith, in which we are sure and certain that we have a gracious and favorable Father in heaven."[115] For Hubmaier the focus is on faith. From this passage he argues that Noah's ark is the only legitimate Old Testament figure or type of baptism and not circumcision.[116] Zwingli, on the other hand, while he begins with the literal sense of the text, moves to a spiritual sense that allows him to equate water with Christ. He states: "We may see clearly that in this passage Peter commits us to the view that although baptism may wash the body—and that is all that water-baptism can do—it cannot take away sin. Sin is taken away only when we have a good conscience before God."[117] He proceeds to redefine the word "water." By using passages of John's Gospel where Jesus refers to himself as the water, and also the bread, he transforms the literal sense of the word "water" into the spiritual meaning "Christ." In this way, Peter is seen to be referring not to physical water but to the gospel, which is Christ. By this method Zwingli can also demonstrate that Christ is preached in the Old Testament, as for example in his use of the text Isa 55, "Ho, everyone that thirsteth, come ye to the waters."[118]

Here it becomes apparent that the literal sense controls Hubmaier's hermeneutic more than that of Zwingli, a fact Zwingli himself noted in his dispute with the Anabaptists in Zurich, suggesting that Hubmaier is at this point closer to the Zurich Anabaptists. It also provides further evidence that Zwingli holds the two Testaments together through finding the gospel proclaimed in its fullness in both the Old and the New Testaments. Thus,

---

115. *PY*, 134; *HS*, 150.

116. *PY*, 134–35; *HS*, 149–50.

117. Zwingli, *Of Baptism*, 154. Similarly, he writes, "For neither as water nor as external teaching does baptism save us, but faith."

118. Zwingli, *Of Baptism*, 154–55.

The Bright and Clear Word of God

the letter of the word in either the Old or the New Testament can kill. Hubmaier holds a different position. The gospel is located in the words of Christ, which are enlivened by the Holy Spirit and responded to by the hearer; Word and Spirit working in conjunction to bring about faith. Zwingli, on the other hand, describes the process of salvation as entirely the work of God through the Spirit, working independently of the external word, whether written or preached.

The remainder of Hubmaier's New Testament references and allusions demonstrate that Hubmaier continues to use Scripture as he had previously in the works discussed in chapter 4.

SUMMARY OF WRITINGS FROM EASTER 1525 TO DECEMBER 5, 1525

The assessment of Hubmaier's hermeneutic for *On Christian Baptism* will serve as a summary for these three works. From the analysis of Hubmaier's debate with Zwingli concerning baptism, certain presuppositions behind Hubmaier's hermeneutic have been identified. They can be discussed under four broad ideas: 1. Sovereignty of God; 2. The clarity of Scripture and the role of the biblical languages; 3. Promise and gospel; 4. Obedience to the commands of God.

A fundamental presupposition behind Zwingli's hermeneutic is his belief in the unlimited sovereignty of God. No material thing, be it Scripture or the material substances of the sacraments, can limit the activity of God to impute grace and faith to whom he will. Therefore, the Spirit acts independently of Scripture, giving faith in a way that is independent of Scripture.

For Hubmaier, God has chosen to limit his sovereignty by establishing a particular order by which people obtain faith. Once this order has been established and revealed to people through Scripture, God always acts in accordance with that order. A literal reading of Rom 10:13 gives that order; faith comes through hearing the Word of God. The Holy Spirit is inextricably linked to the preached Word, making it alive and fruitful in the believer. People who hear the Word are held responsible before God for their responses, either believing or rejecting the offer of salvation.

The concept of order acts as the basis for a second dispute between the two. Hubmaier insists that the actual order of the words in Scripture is significant and dictates the literal understanding of the text. For example, Scripture indicates that the order of salvation is word, hearing, faith, baptism, work. Zwingli, on the other hand, maintains that to base doctrine on word order is wrong as this is sometimes misleading. Hubmaier is therefore closer to the Zurich Anabaptists at this time when he insists on the literal sense of the text as the basis for the correct interpretation of that text.

The second matter of debate focused on the idea of the clarity of Scripture. Hubmaier insists that the Scriptures are clear and simple to understand on the matter of baptism. There is no need to introduce the requirement of interpretation by reading Scripture in the original languages, as Zwingli does. Biblical languages have their place, but it is not a dominant place, nor can knowledge of the biblical languages be demanded as a prerequisite for biblical interpretation. Though the original languages are useful for those texts that do remain dark in Scripture, it does not apply to the baptismal texts. In Hubmaier's opinion they are clear, bright, and pure, and can be simply understood by anyone. Nor is there any need to introduce rhetorical categories, such as synecdoche, and glosses based on interpretation of figures and analogies. Such categories and glosses only serve to confuse and darken what is clear and plain.

The third difference concerns the promises of God and the gospel. Zwingli understands the gospel to be present in the promises of God in the Old Testament. There is therefore a continuity between the Testaments based on the continuity between promise and the gospel. Hubmaier on the other hand sees salvation being effected only after the incarnation. The promise does not convey the same salvific effects as the gospel, for Christ has not yet preached the gospel of forgiveness. The gospel is linked to the preached Word of God in a way reminiscent of Luther's emphasis on the necessity of preaching the Word of God.

The final dispute concerns obedience to the commands of God. Hubmaier insists that all the commands of God that relate to salvation and the honor of God are to be obeyed, even the seemingly trivial commands. This is particularly true of the commands of Christ, which have been given with serious and earnest words. Zwingli makes his definition of the commands of God narrower when he argues that those things which God has not forbidden are permitted. This allows him to argue for the practice of infant baptism, as it is nowhere specifically forbidden in Scripture. Hubmaier, on the other hand, argues that the command contains the prohibition of its negative. Thus, to command the preaching of the gospel automatically excludes preaching human teachings. Similarly, to command the baptism of believers automatically forbids the baptism of infants, for they have not heard the gospel and therefore cannot believe.

Hubmaier also applies a number of hermeneutical principles in this work. In a number of instances, he demonstrates the rule that the clearer text illumines the darker text. He also consistently applies the rule that unless the context of a passage requires differently, the simple, literal meaning of the text is the correct meaning. The overwhelming hermeneutical principle in this work is the priority given to the literal meaning of the text and to the words of Christ in the New Testament.

In this work, Hubmaier shows himself to be very close to the Swiss Brethren in his hermeneutic. He also reflects something of Luther's insistence on the preaching of the Word of God and the accompanying work of the Holy Spirit to make the dead letter of Scripture alive in the hearer. He is most distant from Zwingli on the issue of the clarity of Scripture.

6

Against Those who Mutilate the Word of God
(Writings at Waldshut or Zurich, late 1525 to July 1526, published 1526–27)

DIALOGUE WITH ZWINGLI'S BAPTISM BOOK

(November 30, 1525–late 1526)[1]

Setting

Between the completion of *On the Christian Baptism* (July 11, 1525) and the writing of this work, which Hubmaier indicates in its preface to have occurred "about St Andrew's Day, 1525" (November 30, 1525), a great many significant changes had occurred for Hubmaier and the Anabaptist church at Waldshut.[2] By that date, both Hubmaier and the town had been effectively isolated from any significant help to stave off the imminent military and consequent religious assault that the Catholic Austrian authorities were preparing to launch.

From a military point of view, Waldshut had lost its last source of support when the troops of Count von Sulz and the Archduke Ferdinand

---

1. *PY*, 14: 166–233; *HS*, 9: 164–214.
2. *PY*, 175; *HS*, 164.

had defeated Waldshut's allies, the Klettgau peasants, at Griessen on November 4, 1525. It should be noted that the so-called Peasants' War in South Germany had virtually been brought to an end by late June 1525. The Christian Union of Upper Swabia had been destroyed or disbanded by July 1525, the Alsace uprising had been crushed on May 16, and the Klettgau peasants had, through the good offices of Zurich and Schaffhausen, negotiated an armistice from the end of June until September 1, 1525. It was only because the Swiss had a limited jurisdiction in the Klettgau that they had intervened on behalf of the peasants, and it was only because of the threat of Swiss defense of the peasants that the Austrian authorities restrained from direct military action against the Klettgau peasants and their ally Waldshut. However, after further fruitless negotiations in October between the Klettgau peasants and their overlord Count von Sulz, the Swiss withdrew their support and the peasants and Waldshut were left open to attack. The decisive engagement occurred on November 4, 1525.[3]

In a different, but equally significant way, Hubmaier himself had been isolated from former friends and allies. Oecolampad's first face-to-face confrontation with Anabaptists took place in Basel in early August 1525. The private disputation that he and several other evangelical preachers of Basel had undertaken with the small group of Anabaptists served to reinforce for him Zwingli's estimation of Anabaptists as obstinate people who would not surrender their view on baptism even when shown with clear Scriptures that they were wrong. As a result of the released Anabaptists spreading the rumor that they had defeated the preachers of Basel, Oecolampad produced a short account of the disputation, which he published under the title *A Dialogue of Several Preachers at Basel, Held with Several Confessors of Rebaptism*.[4] This work came to the attention of Hubmaier, who produced his own response to it. A manuscript copy of Hubmaier's response was in Oecolampad's hands by December 1525.[5] However, Hubmaier's final response was not published until early in 1527 at Nikolsburg. On October 2, 1525, Oecolampad wrote to Zwingli, enclosing a copy of Hubmaier's *On the Christian Baptism*, which he noted as being extremely dangerous.[6] Any support in the theological debate on the topic of infant baptism that Hubmaier may have hoped for from Oecolampad would now not materialize.

3. Bergsten, *Balthasar Hubmaier: Anabaptist Theologian*, 265.
4. Ibid., 256.
5. Ibid., 257.
6. Ibid., 257–58.

A closer theological ally of Hubmaier's was Hofmeister of Schaffhausen. Hofmeister's preaching on the Mass, infant baptism, and images closely paralleled that of Hubmaier's, and is considered to have contributed to the uprising of the vinedressers in Schaffhausen on August 9, 1525.[7] The Town Council suppressed that revolt and the next day dismissed Hofmeister, sending him to Basel to have his evangelical orthodoxy verified by Oecolompad and the evangelical preachers of the city.[8] However, Hofmeister arrived at the time Oecolampad and the City Council in Basel were preoccupied with the threat of Anabaptism in their midst. Without a hearing, Hofmeister was expelled on August 14, and therefore could not return to Schaffhausen. As Bergsten has shown, he visited Hubmaier at Waldshut on August 15, and in a conversation it became apparent that Hofmeister and Hubmaier had begun to differ over key points in the interpretation of Scriptures related to baptism.[9] Hofmeister moved to Zurich, and with Zwingli's support, became the preacher at the Fraumünster. Later he played a leading role defending infant baptism in the Third Public Disputation on baptism held in Zurich on November 6–8, 1525.[10]

Capito, a former fellow student of Hubmaier's, had already rejected Hubmaier's new understanding of baptism in a letter to Oecolampad in January 1525. By October 8 of that year he was calling Hubmaier that "vain man," completing his separation from him.[11]

Further isolation for Hubmaier took place in the days immediately after the defeat of the Klettgau peasants. At the instigation of the Grüningen Magistrates, the Third Public Baptismal Disputation was held in Zurich on November 6–8, 1525. Zwingli completed his *Answer to Doctor Balthasar's Booklet on Baptism (Antwort)* on November 5, possibly as the basis for the forthcoming disputation and a direct refutation of Hubmaier's *On the Christian Baptism*.[12] With the publication of this work (November 14, 1525), Zwingli hoped he could counter the positive effect Hubmaier's work had produced for the Anabaptist cause in the region of Zurich and Grüningen.[13]

7. Ibid., 259.
8. Ibid., 258.
9. Ibid., 260–61.
10. Ibid., 265.
11. Ibid., 261–62.
12. Ibid., 264.
13. Ibid., 262.

Hubmaier had attempted to attend this November 6–8 disputation, but was forced to return to the security of Waldshut under threat of arrest by the Emperor's agents.[14] The disputation was considered to prove the validity of Zwingli's view of infant baptism and the Zurich Town Council issued its harshest mandates yet against those who continued to hold to their erroneous view of believers' baptism: life imprisonment on bread and water.[15] This was not merely a theoretical mandate, as those Anabaptists who had taken part in the disputation, both men and women, were returned to their prison cells where the mandate was enforced.[16] An open letter containing an outline of the mandate was sent to the Grüningen Magistrates on St Andrew's Day 1525. It detailed the penalties the Zurich Council had imposed and planned to adhere to in all future cases dealing with Anabaptists.[17]

As Bergsten has commented: "The third Baptismal Disputation in Zurich and the publication of Zwingli's polemic against Hubmaier had dealt the Anabaptists a severe blow. A further result was that the attitude of Zwingli and Zurich towards the Anabaptists became a model for other Swiss reformers."[18]

---

14. Harder, *Sources of Swiss Anabaptism*, 432.

15. Ibid., 442.

16. Ibid., 422. The Zurich Anabaptists Grebel, Manz, and Hottinger, with Blaurock, were again imprisoned, while Teck of Waldshut, Lingg of Schaffhausen, and Sattler of Stauffen were banished on oath never to return.

17. Ibid., 443.

18. Bergsten, *Balthasar Hubmaier: Anabaptist Theologian*, 265. Much has been written about the turning point or lack of one in the Zwinglian Reformation, the chief protagonists being Yoder and Walton. Yoder has argued that Zwingli's acquiescence to the authority of the Zurich Council marked the turning point for the Zurich radicals, Grebel, Mantz, and Strumpf. Walton however argues the Zwingli had always understood that the reform of the church in Zurich would take place with the cooperation of the Council and under its authority. Walton, *Zwingli's Theocracy*, 181. Williams concedes that Zwingli's acceptance of the Council's directive concerning the delay of the reform of the Mass on December 19 "may have been a fundamental shift" in Zwingli's understanding of the relationship of the authority of the council and the congregation. However, it need not be seen as such as Zwingli's view of "canton, town, commune, and congregation (*Gemeinde*) could also be considered interchangeable." Williams, *The Radical Reformation*, 1992, 187. However, Hubmaier in his *Dialogue* is not so much concerned with the shift in understandings of the relationship between the congregation and the magistracy, but with Zwingli's hermeneutical shift.

Analysis

Since Hubmaier's *Dialogue* follows very closely the structure of Zwingli's *Of Baptism*, and not that of Zwingli's *Antwort*, it would appear that Hubmaier became aware of the *Antwort* only after he had completed the body of the text of the *Dialogue* about 30 November, 1525, a mere five days before he himself was forced to flee Waldshut.

In the midst of this disintegration of support Hubmaier wrote the body of the text of *Dialogue*, adding a stinging preface and a final diatribe against Zwingli from Nikolsburg in 1526. Bergsten has speculated that Hubmaier wrote this work as a response to his failure to participate in the third Zurich Baptismal Disputation.[19] Pipkin and Yoder repeat Bergsten's suggestion that Hubmaier wrote the *Dialogue* "apparently without having read Zwingli's Answer."[20] That this is so follows from an analysis of the three references Hubmaier makes to a book of Zwingli's in the *Dialogue*. The first two occur in the preface that Hubmaier added to the *Dialogue* after his arrival in Nikolsburg in July 1526.[21] The third is in the postscript that can also be shown to have been added after Hubmaier's own experience of imprisonment and torture in Zurich. The postscript must have been added after March 7, 1526, since it refers to "drowning" as part of the harsh judgment of the Zurich Council.[22] Drowning was first included in the Zurich Council Mandates against the Anabaptists on March 7, 1526, at the resentencing of a large group of Anabaptists, including Hubmaier. The mandate was made public on the following Sunday in the three parishes of Zurich.[23] The first two references are also linked to this harsh "drowning" sentence of the Zurich Council. The only other reference to the harsh measures being used against the Anabaptists in Zurich in the body of the text does not include this reference to "drowning."[24]

As has been demonstrated in the preceding analysis of *On the Christian Baptism*, Hubmaier wrote his work in response to Zwingli's arguments as expressed in *Of Baptism*. In *On the Christian Baptism* Hubmaier creatively rearranged Zwingli's themes and composed a genuinely independent and positive statement on the topic of baptism. In the *Dialogue*

---

19. Bergsten, *Balthasar Hubmaier: Anabaptist Theologian*, 270.
20. *PY*, 167.
21. *PY*, 171, 174; *HS*, 168, 170.
22. *PY*, 232; *HS*, 213.
23. Harder, *Sources of Swiss Anabaptism*, 447–48.
24. *PY*, 183; *HS*, 177–78.

the independence and creativity are lost as Hubmaier restricted himself to following closely not only the arrangement of Zwingli's arguments but also the texts that Zwingli used in support of his view of infant baptism. An analysis of the biblical references used by the two protagonists provides evidence of this. Of the thirty-one Old Testament references that Zwingli used in *Of Baptism,* only three of Hubmaier's twenty-one Old Testament references are common to both works. In Hubmaier's *Dialogue* the number of common texts increases to thirteen out of forty-seven. New Testament references are thirty-nine of 156 in common in *On the Christian Baptism,* while it is forty-five of 132 individual texts cited in the *Dialogue.* In the *Dialogue* the creativity and independence exhibited in *On the Christian Baptism* is stifled as Hubmaier slavishly follows not only the structure of Zwingli's argument but also seeks to deal with specific texts Zwingli uses.

There are a number of sections of Zwingli's work that Hubmaier ignores completely, some that he dismisses in perfunctory manner, and one section where he refers the reader back to his previous work for a more detailed explanation. He completely ignores those sections that deal with the humiliation of particular Anabaptists at the Second Public Baptismal Disputation,[25] as well as any reference to the outward manifestation of baptism of the Spirit, the gift of "tongues" that Zwingli argued was necessary for the correct understanding of Scripture.[26] This issue had been addressed by Hubmaier in his previous work.[27] He also ignores an extensive section where Zwingli deals with the topic of original sin.[28]

Of greater importance is Hubmaier's failure to deal with two aspects of Zwingli's argument that the baptism of John is the same as the baptism of Christ. Zwingli had argued that Christ has left us a perfect example to follow. Since Christ received the baptism of John, his example would not be perfect if the baptism of John were not the same as that used by Christ's disciples.[29] Zwingli also argued that when John made the statement, "Behold the Lamb of God that takes away the sins of the world," he was making essentially the same confession as Peter, "You are the Christ the Son of the living God." Jesus confirmed Peter's confession concerning his person, then stated, "on this rock I will build my church." Zwingli

---

25. Harder, *Sources of Swiss Anabaptism,* 368f, 373.
26. Zwingli, *Of Baptism,* 137.
27. *PY,* 98–99; *HS,* 120.
28. Zwingli, *Von der Taufe* 307: 16ff.
29. Harder, *Sources of Swiss Anabaptism,* 307f.

Balthasar Hubmaier and the Clarity of Scripture

argued that since the two confessions are the same they must grant access to the same church.[30]

Hubmaier also fails to deal with Zwingli's use of Mark 1:2–4, which gives the order of events as baptize and preach. He had previously addressed this text in his work *On the Christian Baptism,* proposing that it was reconciled to the other texts that gave the order of hearing, repentance, baptism when it was placed beside the clearer texts, "as one must do for the interpretation of the Scriptures."[31] It would appear that Hubmaier therefore considered this text irrelevant to any future debate on the topic of baptism.

Hubmaier curtly dismisses all Zwingli's references to circumcision, the sign of God's covenant with Abraham, as being the equivalent of the new covenant sign of baptism, with the comment: "I also beseech you here, for the sake of the last judgment, drop your circuitous argument on circumcision out of the Old Testament. For you well know that circumcision is not a figure of water baptism. You have no Scripture about that."[32] The only valid Old Testament figure of baptism that Hubmaier will accept is that of Noah and the ark that Peter mentions in 1 Pet 3:20f. In this way, Hubmaier countered Zwingli's use of God's covenant with Abraham expressed through circumcision, but he does not deal with another Old Testament figure that Zwingli used, namely that of Moses and the people of Israel during the escape from Egypt. Zwingli finds this figure mentioned by Paul in 1 Cor 10:1–5. He argues that as the people of Israel were baptized into Moses before the giving of the Spirit, it follows that infants can be baptized before they have the Spirit.[33] This directly challenges Hubmaier's position of baptism at two points. Firstly, Noah is not the only Old Testament figure used for baptism, a fundamental presupposition in Hubmaier's understanding of the relationship between the two Testaments. Secondly, Zwingli challenges Hubmaier's understanding of faith. It is Hubmaier's contention that only after hearing the Word of God preached, and having that Word illuminated to them inwardly by the Holy Spirit, can people respond in faith.

---

30. Zwingli, *Of Baptism,* 161.
31. *PY,* 109; *HS,* 130.
32. *PY,* 180; *HS,* 175.
33. Zwingli, *Von der Taufe,* 326:18ff.

Hubmaier also summarily deals with the text of Col 2:11ff. He maintains that the text refers only to inward baptism, which is not performed by any human agency, and not to outward water baptism.[34]

With reference to the texts John 3:22; 4:2, which Zwingli had used to show that baptism must be taken here for teaching, Hubmaier facetiously uses Zwingli's own argument to prove that Christ did not teach. The reader is then referred back to Hubmaier's *On the Christian Baptism* for the "right simple meaning of this Scripture."[35]

As a work that might further the debate on baptism, Hubmaier's *Dialogue* adds very little new material. However, it does provide some new material on other topics. For the first time in his written works, Hubmaier addresses the topic of community of goods: "I have ever and always spoken thus of the community of goods: that one person should always look out for the other, so that the hungry are fed, the thirsty given drink, the naked clothed, etc. For we are not lords of our goods, but stewards and distributors. There are certainly none who say that one should take what belongs to the other and make it common. Rather, much more that one should give the coat besides the mantle" (Matt 5:40).[36]

He also reinforces his basic idea that the individual local congregation is competent to judge in matters of innovation. However, when challenged by Zwingli that it is the church that must be consulted prior to any change being instituted, Hubmaier makes the very strong statement that "one should ask the Scriptures and not the church, for God wants to have from us only his law and his will, not our stubborn heads or opinions."[37] This statement reflects the attitude Grebel displayed towards Scripture at the Second Zurich Disputation (October 26–28, 1523).[38] By September 5, 1524, in his letter to Müntzer, Grebel refers to the delay in bringing about changes in the Mass as "the unchristian forbearance, which the very learned foremost evangelical preachers established as an actual idol and planted throughout the world." He continues, "It is far better that a few be correctly instructed through the Word of God and believe and live right in virtues and practices than that many believe deceitfully out of adulterated false doctrine."[39] It is Scripture and not the majority of the church that is

34. *PY*, 186; *HS*, 180.
35. *PY*, 190; *HS*, 183.
36. *PY*, 183; *HS*, 178.
37. *PY*, 181; *HS*, 176.
38. Harder, *Sources of Swiss Anabaptism*, 247f.
39. Ibid., 288.

to be adhered to. Hubmaier himself makes this point against Zwingli in the *Dialogue*. Zwingli had earlier contended that at the time of Augustine infant baptism was permitted, since the majority of the church baptized infants. Hubmaier also adds church councils and traditions to his list of things subject to the primacy of Scripture.[40]

A major alteration occurs in Hubmaier's enumeration of the different kinds of baptism and their meanings as he recognized them in the New Testament. In *On the Christian Baptism* Hubmaier had listed five kinds of baptism:

> 1. Baptism in water.
>
> 2. Baptism in water, for or unto change of life.
>
> 3. Baptism in the Spirit and fire.
>
> 4. To be reborn out of water and Spirit.
>
> 5. Baptism in water in the name of the Father, Son, and Holy Spirit, or in the name of our Lord Jesus Christ.[41]

However, in the *Dialogue*, having ridiculed Zwingli's fourfold division, Hubmaier revises his own division into three categories:

> 1. The internal baptism of the Spirit, John 3:5–6.
>
> 2. Outward water baptism, Matt 28:19.
>
> 3. The subsequent suffering, Luke 12:50.[42]

It can be seen that Hubmaier has contracted his previous categories 3 (baptism in the Spirit and fire) and 4 (to be reborn out of water and Spirit) into his new category 1, (the inner baptism of the Spirit); while the previous categories 1, 2, and 5 become the new category 2, (outward water baptism). He adds a new category, that of subsequent suffering, which he later identifies in his *A Christian Catechism* as baptism in blood.[43] This new category reflects his own experience, and that of other Anabaptists, in and around Zurich. Imprisonment of Anabaptists in Zurich increased after July 1525, culminating in the arrest of their leaders Grebel and

40. *PY*, 225; *HS*, 207–8.

41. *PY*, 99; *HS*, 121.

42. *PY*, 189; *HS*, 182.

43. *PY*, 189; *HS*, 182 Cf. *PY*, 349f; *HS*, 313. Although Hubmaier keeps the same threefold division in *A Christian Catechism*, baptism in blood shifts to "daily mortification of the flesh until death," whereas in the *Dialogue* the emphasis is more on the physical suffering that the Anabaptists experienced at the hands of the Zurich evangelicals.

Against Those who Mutilate the Word of God

Blaurock on October 8, 1525, at Grüningen. Then followed the arrest of Mantz and Sattler. All of these men were brought to the Third Public Baptismal Disputation, October 6–8. Grebel, Mantz, and Blaurock were incarcerated in the New Tower, while Margaret Hottinger was imprisoned in the Wellenberg prison, and all received life sentences on bread and water. Teck, Lingg, and Sattler were released under oath never again to return to the territory of the Zurich Council.[44]

At the end of this section dealing with the three kinds of baptism, Hubmaier uses the phrase "patchwork" (*flickwerk*) to describe those who divide the unity of Scripture incorrectly. This is a new description, and will feature strongly in his later works.[45] Throughout the work, he continues to inveigh against those who do violence to and destroy the Scriptures[46] and ask frivolous and arbitrary serpent questions.[47] He makes derisive comments about Zwingli's "foreign glosses,"[48] and "tricks" and sophistries.[49] He also accuses Zwingli of setting up a new papacy.[50] Yet this designation "patchwork" points to a new emphasis in Hubmaier's attack against Zwingli. In the first exchange of the *Dialogue*, Hubmaier responds to Zwingli's argument that salvation cannot be connected to external things. He accepts that salvation is not dependent on the external ceremonies that are still valid in the New Testament; that is, baptism and the Lord's Supper. Nevertheless, public confession is required, and water baptism is the obligation of the believer, since Christ himself instituted it. This order of salvation revealed in Scripture is foundational for Hubmaier's hermeneutic. He then writes: "Whoever now destroys his Word and institutions, whether they be outward or internal, should after sufficient instruction be properly esteemed as a destroyer of the indivisible cloak of Christ."[51]

Later in the work he attacks Zwingli's translation of Mark 10:13f with the comment: "You know, Zwingle, that the Holy Scripture is such a whole, consistent, genuine, infallible, eternal, immortal Word that cannot

---

44. Harder, *Sources of Swiss Anabaptism*, 429, 442.

45. *PY*, 189; *HS*, 182.

46. *PY*, 192, 199, 211, 229; *HS*, 184, 189–90, 197, 211.

47. *PY*, 203, 219; *HS*, 192, 203. By asserting that Zwingli asks such questions Hubmaier implies that Zwingli is using the old discredited scholastic method of exegesis that focused more on the resolution of difficult questions through dialectic, rather than seeking the truth from the literal meaning of the text.

48. *PY*, 192, 221, 231; *HS*, 186, 205, 212.

49. *PY*, 211, 230; *HS*, 197, 211.

50. *PY*, 187, 215; *HS*, 180, 200.

51. *PY*, 179; *HS*, 174.

wear away nor can the smallest letter or the smallest point be changed.... Cursed is he who adds to or detracts from it.... However, disregarding all this you make one, Zwingle, and say publicly in print.... 'Of theirs is the kingdom of God.' That is directly against the clear word, sense, and understanding of Christ, as well as hinders and discards his teaching."[52]

In this comment, Hubmaier again emphasizes the unity of Scripture, with the added criticism of those who change the text of Scripture even by one letter. He had earlier in the work made the same point describing Zwingli's new German translation as a "false New Testament," commenting that "we would have to learn a new faith as often as you let a New Testament be published."[53]

Not only does Hubmaier begin with the presupposition that Scripture is a unity, he also implies by his negative response to Zwingli's new translation, especially his translation of Luke 21:33, that there is a set text of Scripture. Paraphrasing the words of Jesus, Hubmaier insists that not the smallest letter or smallest point of the Scripture can be changed. This might be interpreted as indicating that for Hubmaier the actual text of Scripture has been fixed in a particular text, possibly the Vulgate. Like Erasmus, Hubmaier has a very high opinion of Jerome, and valued his Vulgate translation.[54] Yet he also notes with approval Erasmus's new translation, the Latin translation that was accompanied by a Greek text.[55] However, Hubmaier's own paraphrasing of Scripture to clarify the intention of the original authors argues against him viewing the text as fixed. This use of Jesus's words from Matt 5:18 is therefore a polemical attack on Zwingli and not a comment on Hubmaier's attitude to the fixed nature of the text of Scripture.

The most obvious difference between the *Dialogue* and *On the Christian Baptism* is Hubmaier's explicit references to the First Zurich Disputation, in particular to Johann Fabri and his argument in favor of traditions. Zwingli refused to accept anything Fabri said if it did not have a clear Word of Scripture to support it.[56] In *On the Christian Baptism* Hubmaier

---

52. *PY*, 229; *HS*, 211.

53. *PY*, 182; *HS*, 177.

54. *PY*, 225; *HS*, 208. "Zwingli: We read the words of Augustine to the opponents of baptism. Nevertheless, they have told everyone that infant baptism is popish. Balthasar: Whether it is popish or abbotish it is still not Christian. Read to us the word of Christ, not of Augustine. Or we read to you the above-mentioned word of Jerome on the last chapter of Matthew." *PY*, 222f; *HS*, 206.

55. *PY*, 132; *HS*, 148.

56. *PY*, 213; *HS*, 199. "Be still, be still my Zwingle. Fabri of Constance hears it. That

uses the same objection against Zwingli, referring to Matt 15:13; Isa 29 as Zwingli himself had done. He concludes that it is not necessary for the Anabaptists to supply a prohibition as Zwingli demands in *Of Baptism*.[57] The burden of proof falls to Zwingli as the common law of justice requires: "Affirmanti incumbit probatio. Tu affirmas baptisma infantium, ergo, etc" (The burden of proof falls to the affirming. You affirm infant baptism; therefore, etc). The Anabaptists remain free in all things that God has not commanded, the view Zwingli himself intimated he held in his discussion on purgatory at the Second Zurich Disputation.[58] He therefore demands that Zwingli give a clear passage of Scripture where Christ commands the baptism of infants or, to be consistent, that he show a prohibitory law concerning purgatory.[59]

Zwingli contends that "it does not help, concerning things which should be forbidden, to say: 'Do not add anything to my word.' But, as to what is supposed to be sin, one must point out a prohibitory law." In response Hubmaier draws a number of illustrations from the Ten Commandments to show that the "the prohibitions are also included in the commandments."[60] Hubmaier proposes that by following Zwingli's argument it would be no sin to "throw father and mother by their hair down the stairs."[61] However, should Zwingli declare that such action is prohibited by the law "honor your father and your mother," then Hubmaier has shown that the prohibition is included in the affirmative command. However, he weakens his argument when he tries to prove that chastity is required by the commandment against adultery, acts of mercy are included in the commandment not to steal,[62] or restitution is commanded where stealing is forbidden.[63]

Hubmaier in turn accuses Zwingli of adding to the Scriptures. As has been noted above, he attacks Zwingli's new translation of Mark 10:13f, "of theirs is the kingdom of God." He also attacked Zwingli's new baptismal service, which Zwingli had added to the end of his booklet *Of Baptism*.

---

was also his opinion at Zurich during the dialogue, but you would not let him have it. You required clear Scriptures from him and not without reason."

57. Harder, *Sources of Swiss Anabaptism*, 366.
58. *PY,* 184–85; *HS,* 178–79.
59. *PY,* 184; *HS,* 178–79.
60. *PY,* 185; *HS,* 179.
61. *PY,* 185; *HS,* 179.
62. *PY,* 185; *HS,* 179.
63. *PY,* 226; *HS,* 208.

Zwingli insists that there is nothing in the service that is not grounded in the Word of God.[64] However, Hubmaier notes that neither godparents (*die gottinen*), nor the baptismal shirt (*wosterhembd*) are mentioned in those Scriptures that deal with water baptism.[65] That being the case, Hubmaier asserts it is Zwingli that is adding to Scripture.

Although this matter of adding to Scripture had been addressed in *On the Christian Baptism*, there is a new vehemence in Hubmaier's tone. In addition, the frequent explicit references to Zwingli's use of the same interpretive principle Fabri used at the First Zurich Disputation, which Zwingli himself had later so forcefully rejected, was intended to embarrass Zwingli and force him to admit his change of mind. Hubmaier would also demonstrate that he alone was consistently following the hermeneutical principles Zwingli had at first championed.[66]

It was mentioned above that Hubmaier respected the opinion of Jerome above that of Augustine. He refers to Jerome as "the holy teacher,"[67] while he says of Augustine, with respect to the eternal torment of infants who die without baptism, that "he says this without any basis; therefore we do not believe him in this matter."[68] In this work, Hubmaier increases his number of references to the church fathers. Though their opinions do not have the authority of Scripture, they do nevertheless have some supportive role in argument. Zwingli had used references to Augustine in *Of Baptism* to support his contention that infant baptism was practiced by a majority of the church in Augustine's time. Zwingli was only seeking to prove that infant baptism was not first introduced by Pope Nicolas II in contrast with the Zurich Anabaptists who he insisted taught that infant baptism was

---

64. Zwingli, *Von der Taufe*, 334.12–14. "Ietz volgt die form des touffs, wie man die yetz ze Zurich brucht, und sind alle zusatz, die in gottes wort nit grund haben, underlassen."

65. *PY*, 196, 226–27; *HS*, 187, 209. Cf. Zwingli, *Von der Taufe*, 334, 336. "Zu dem wosterhembd: Gott verlich dir, das, wie du yetz mit dem wyssen kleid liplich angezogen wirst, also am jungsten tag mit reiner unvermassgoter conscientz vor imm erschinist. Amen."

66. *PY*, 232; *HS*, 213. "Look to yourself, my dear Zwingli, for the sake of the last judgment, confess that you are guilty, leave off your word battles, give glory to God, confess the truth. . . . Your fall has happened for the best, for you and for us all, so that you may not raise yourself up so high, so that we do not look onto the person, yea, and that we humble ourselves under the powerful Word of God and not go forth any more according to our own brain."

67. *PY*, 222; *HS*, 206.

68. *PY*, 224–25; *HS*, 207.

Against Those who Mutilate the Word of God

instituted by that Pope.[69] As we have seen above, Hubmaier also rejects the contention that infant baptism began with Pope Nicolas II, but goes beyond that point of the argument to insist that it does not matter with whom the practice began; it is contrary to Scripture, and as such must be discontinued.[70]

Hubmaier does not state the presuppositions that underpin his use of the church fathers, yet it becomes clear from the way that he uses them that their authority is dependent on their agreement with Hubmaier's interpretation of Scripture. He cites Eusebius, Cyril, Origen, Chrysostom, and Jerome, all with reference to specific texts of Scripture, showing that they support his interpretation of the text.[71] He also cites some of the new teachers, specifically Erasmus and Zwingli himself, as two recent writers who also support his view.[72] Hubmaier in fact uses the same phrase that Zwingli used in *Of Baptism*, "old and new teachers," in his own work, using it with the same sense, that the old and new teachers support his view. Later Hubmaier produced two editions of a book of references to the writings of the church fathers and to contemporary theologians, the old and new teachers, whose views on baptism he presented as supporting his own view of the baptism of believers. These references in the *Dialogue* form the nucleus of that work and seem to indicate that Hubmaier was gathering them when he was writing this work in November 1525.

Zwingli's exegesis of Mark 10:13f acts as the focus for another issue to which Hubmaier draws Zwingli's attention, that of the use of parables in exegesis. Hubmaier consistently speaks of a parable (*ein gleichnuss*) as a physical or bodily thing that Christ takes and gives a spiritual meaning (*ainen Geistlicheb verstand gezogen*).[73] In this instance Hubmaier cites as "parables" examples which Christ used; the well of Jacob (John 4:13ff) and the five barley loaves (John 6:26ff). He concludes that Christ, through the parable of the children, "has taught us humility," and not that the kingdom of heaven is of such as these children.[74] This simple understanding of

---

69. Harder, *Sources of Swiss Anabaptism*, 368f.

70. *PY*, 225; *HS*, 208.

71. *PY*, 193, 197; *HS*, 185, 188 (Esebius); *PY*, 210; *HS*, 197(Cyril); *PY*, 210, 217; *HS*, 197, 202 (Origen); *PY*, 210; *HS*, 197(Chrysostom); *PY*, 210, 222, 225, 227; *HS*, 197, 206, 208, 209 (Jerome). This attitude parallels Luther's attitude to the Church fathers as he stated it in *On the Bondage of the Will*, 153. He attributes value only to those statements of the fathers that deny free choice.

72. *PY*, 227; *HS*, 209.

73. *PY*, 216f; *HS*, 210f.

74. *PY*, 217; *HS*, 201.

parables contrasts strongly with Zwingli's use of the same passages in support of his exegesis of John 3:5. Zwingli argues that the water referred to in that text was not material water, but the "word." The "word which saves the soul is not the word outwardly spoken, but the word inwardly understood and believed."[75] He achieves this by citing John 7:37f and 4:13f, passages where Jesus refers to water. Zwingli identifies this water as the gospel. John 6:27 refers to bread, which Zwingli similarly equates with the proclamation of the gospel. The reference to water in John 3:5 is therefore "simply a proclamation of the Gospel." Having identified water and bread as the proclamation of the gospel, it is possible for Zwingli to identify the gospel in the Old Testament, as he illustrates by his references to food and drink in Isa 55:1f and water in Zech 14:8.[76]

Hubmaier challenges this use of parables, or similitudes, by demonstrating that "to be like children" does not guarantee a place in the kingdom of God, as Zwingli had claimed through his exegesis of Mark 10:13f. To do this Hubmaier contrasts Eph 4:14 and 1 Cor 14:20 with Mark 10:13f to show that Scripture explicitly states that we are not to be like children or God will "close his kingdom before us."[77]

Hubmaier concludes: "Therefore it is necessary that one is careful about what is written in a parable, to use it according to the purpose of the parable and not further, for all parables limp. Or it would also come to that afterward that we also had to ride on sticks like children if we wanted to enter the kingdom of God."[78]

Zwingli interprets Mark 10:14 as follows: "Whoever does not receive the kingdom of God like a child does not enter it. For we must first become like children or we are not receptive to the kingdom of God, for the kingdom of God belongs much more to children." In response, Hubmaier interprets Matt 17:20 and Luke 17:6 using Zwingli's method: "Truly I say to you . . . if you will have faith like a mustard seed. . . . Therefore, much more is the mustard seed faithful, like which we must first become," which is obviously ludicrous. Hubmaier thus seeks to dismiss Zwingli's argument that baptism is applicable to infants.[79]

---

75. Zwingli, *Of Baptism*, 154.

76. Ibid., 155.

77. *PY*, 217; *HS*, 202. The comparison of contradictory texts becomes a dominant method of interpreting Scripture for Hubmaier after 1526.

78. *PY*, 217; *HS*, 202.

79. *PY*, 218; *HS*, 202–3.

Zwingli himself had cautioned about the use of parables and figures, stating that they were not suitable as the foundation for the development of doctrine that could not be shown with clear Scripture elsewhere,[80] although God had chosen to use figures to "provoke" us to search out the hidden meanings.[81] However, he appears to be doing just what he cautioned against, in order to strengthen his position on infant baptism by finding the gospel in the Old Testament.

An interesting exchange occurs between Zwingli and Hubmaier over references to "faith" in Acts 8:13. Zwingli cited the text as additional proof that external baptism was sometimes administered without prior inward faith. The text states that Simon (Magus) believed. For Zwingli, with his view of predestination and election, "believe" could not be understood in the same way as "faith," which God grants to bring about the salvation of sinners, for "shortly afterwards it became clear he did not believe."[82] In this context faith must therefore be understood to mean "he listened" or "he counted himself among the believers." Zwingli vaguely refers to Augustine for support, as he alleges that Augustine also understood the reference to Simon in this manner.[83]

The contrast with Hubmaier could not be stronger: "Whoever understands 'faith' here differently than that he believed destroys the Scripture and violates it against their own understanding, whether it be Zwingli or Augustine."[84] Hubmaier understands the word "faith" is used uniformly throughout Scripture. "Faith" describes the individual's response of accepting that the gospel message is true and trusting that in Christ the Christian has a merciful Father in heaven. That Simon sinned after confessing his faith is not strange, for "such happens to us all."

Here the difference between Hubmaier and Zwingli concerning salvation once more comes to light. For Zwingli, the faith that God gives, saves, and does so perfectly. For Hubmaier, the confession of faith declares the sure confidence of the sinner that he or she shares forgiveness of sins through the mercy God the Father has shown to his Son. Good works follow as the outward manifestation of the confession of inward faith. However, these works of faith are never perfect, which means for Hubmaier

---

80. Zwingli, *Sixty-Seven Articles*, Article 9, 49.

81. Zwingli, *On Clarity*, 73. This is the same attitude that Ersasmus had regarding parables.

82. Zwingli, *Of Baptism*, 135.

83. *PY*, 192; *HS*, 184.

84. *PY*, 192; *HS*, 184.

that the Christian cannot say that they live without sin. It remains ambiguous in Hubmaier's theology at this point whether it is possible for the Christian to fall from grace and lose their salvation. For Zwingli, there is no such ambiguity; the elect cannot lose that which is wholly dependent on God.

Use of Scripture

It remains to examine Hubmaier's use of Scripture in this work. The raw statistics are as follows: Old Testament references with quotations, none; references with recognizable allusions, twenty-eight; references alone, nineteen; allusions without references, eight; and quotations without references, three; a total of fifty-eight identifiable Old Testament references and a further forty-seven Old Testament references supplied by Hubmaier. For the New Testament the figures are forty-eight quotations, one hundred five references with recognizable allusions, twenty-nine references and six allusions without references, giving totals of 188 identifiable New Testament references and a further 253 New Testament references supplied by Hubmaier.

These New Testament figures are inflated by Hubmaier's use of references to Matt 28:19 and Mark 16:16, and references to the apostles' practice of baptism in the book of Acts. The former texts are used as proof texts for the order of events leading to baptism; that is, preaching of the word, believing, and water baptism. The later references occur in long sequences added in the margin to support this argument concerning the order leading to baptism. These references to Acts account for eighty-nine of the total 277 New Testament references.

Further inflation of the number of references occurs through use of synoptic parallels. There are three references to the sequence referring to Christ blessing the children, focusing on Mark 10:13f. One sequence refers to faith and the mustard seed, Matt 17:20, Luke 17:6; and one sequence refers to Christ's statement that not the least part of Scripture shall pass away, Matt 5:18 and Luke 16:17.

Hubmaier also inflates the figures by citing the Old Testament references of texts that occur in the New Testament. He does this five times: Ps 118:22 cited in 1 Pet 2:7 is given twice; Isa 40:13 cited in Rom 11:3; Isa 40:3ff cited in John 1:23, and possibly in the synoptic parallels Matt 3:3f and Luke 3:4ff; and Gen 8:1ff alluded to in 1 Pet 3:20.

Against Those who Mutilate the Word of God

In this work, the analysis of Hubmaier's use of Scripture is complicated by the nature of the dialogue, in which some of the references are used by Zwingli, (forty-two references), and some of these references attributed to Zwingli are in fact Anabaptist references that Zwingli is citing so that he can argue against them (five references). One example of Zwingli's use of Anabaptist texts occurs at an early stage in the work. Zwingli cites the sequence of texts Deut 4:2; 12:30; Gal 3:15; Prov 30:6,[85] which he states the Anabaptists use to prove to the "simple people" that infant baptism is an addition to the Word of God.[86] The Anabaptists argued God did not say that infants should be baptized, therefore infants should never be baptized. Zwingli accepts these texts as proof texts for the thesis that nothing is to be added to the Word of God. His response is to prove that it is the Anabaptists that add to the word and not him. He proposes that Scripture does not say anywhere that infants should never be baptized, therefore the Anabaptists are adding to Scripture if they say infants should not be baptized. Secondly, that "add nothing to my Word" only refers to those things that are considered sin "for they must show a prohibiting law." He quotes Rom 4:15 as his proof text, "for where there is no law, there is no transgression."[87]

For Hubmaier, the texts concerning adding to the Word of God are also taken as proof texts. His dispute with Zwingli centers on the argument of determining what is an addition. He chides Zwingli that he has learned his argument from Fabri, who had argued on the basis of his proof text Luke 9:50, "whoever is not against you is with you," that as the customs and the laws of the church are not against God, they are permitted.[88] Hubmaier in turn reiterates Zwingli's argument against Fabri, which he based on Matt 15:1–13 and Isa 29:13. The argument hinges on the phrase, "all plants which my heavenly Father has not planted should be uprooted" (Matt 15:13). As there is no clear institution of infant baptism, Hubmaier demands that Zwingli "uproot" it if he is to be consistent. He adds to this the common rule of justice, "the burden of proof falls to the affirming,"[89] and a reference to Zwingli's twenty-four theses where he writes "every Christian is free of the works which God has not commanded."[90]

---

85. *PY*, 183; *HS*, 178.
86. Harder, *Sources of Swiss Anabaptism*, 366.
87. Ibid.
88. *PY*, 184; *HS*, 178.
89. *PY*, 184; *HS*, 179.
90. Not verses 24 and 30 as in *PY*, 229.

Hubmaier uses specific cases from the Ten Commandments to counter Zwingli's second objection that a prohibiting law should be stated. The first, which refers to honoring parents, is linked to the reference in Matt 15:1ff, showing that an affirming commandment contains a prohibitory law. Therefore, it is not necessary to have a clear law forbidding infant baptism.

These references to Deut 4:2; 12:32; Gal 3:5 are used a second time by Hubmaier, but this time in relation to Zwingli's new translation of Mark 10:13f, where Zwingli substituted "of theirs" for "of such." The list of references is expanded by adding Luke 21:33; Heb 12:29; Rev 22:18f.[91] The reference to Prov 30:6 is dropped. In this sequence of verses Hubmaier focuses on the unity and unchanging nature of Scripture, the Word of God. Christ "dwells, lives and rests" in the Scripture, and His word will never fade away (Luke 21:33). By taking the reference to a "human testament" (Gal 3:15) and joining it with an argument from the lesser to the greater, he goes on to assert that Scripture, which is "Christ's testament. . . . confirmed . . . with his bitter death," should be held in greater honor than a human testament. The reference to Heb 12:29 is used to add a polemical note, "our God is a consuming fire," as is the reference to Rev 22:18f, which Hubmaier paraphrases as "cursed is he who adds to or detracts from it."[92] The curse of Rev 22:18 that Hubmaier does not expand on has a very sharp polemical tone; the plagues described in the book will be added to those who add to Scripture, and to those who take away from the book, their share in the tree of life will be taken from them.

Hubmaier concludes this short exposition of these texts with a comment on the nature of Scripture. Scripture is the beautiful friend of God (an allusion to Rom 10:15) "in which Christ dwells, lives, and rests; and there is no flaw in it."[93] Yet in the words that follow, Hubmaier makes it clear that it is the meaning and the understanding of Christ's speech that is determinative, not the particular letter of the text, an attitude that he has in common with Zwingli. For both of them, it is the intention of Scripture that matters. For Zwingli, it is the Word of Christ that is in all the Scripture; for Hubmaier, it is the Word of Christ as stated in the New Testament, and those sections of the Old Testament that Christ uses, which gives those Old Testament passages equal authority to His own words. This difference in approach allows Hubmaier to dismiss the Old Testament commands

---

91. *PY,* 229; *HS,* 211.
92. *PY,* 229; *HS,* 211.
93. *PY,* 229; *HS,* 211.

Against Those who Mutilate the Word of God

that Christ has not endorsed, while insisting that the Christian should obey only that which God commands.

It also gives Hubmaier a more limited understanding of the gospel as compared to Zwingli. For Zwingli, the gospel, which proclaims God's election of the faithful, is to be found with equal force in the Old Testament as in the New, though in the Old it is found under figures, parables, and types. He demonstrates this method when interpreting Christ's references to water and bread in John's Gospel as being the proclamation of the whole gospel. He then argues that passages in Isaiah that refer to water also contain the gospel. For Hubmaier, the gospel cannot be proclaimed prior to the manifestation of Christ in history, since only after his death and resurrection is it possible for sinners to receive forgiveness of sins. This point is crucial in the debate between the two protagonists concerning the baptism of John and that of Christ.

The reduced extent of quotations is one noticeable feature that distinguishes this work from Hubmaier's *On the Christian Baptism*. In that work, Hubmaier produced many lengthy quotations, to which he added very little commentary and sometimes none at all, as he seems to have considered the texts self-evident to prove the point he was making. In the *Dialogue* there are no extended quotations at all, and texts that are quoted are provided with exposition to counter Zwingli's use of them, or to support his own view.

It would appear that Hubmaier's confidence in the clear Word of Scripture to convince opponents and to be easily understood by simple people has been severely reduced by the impact of Zwingli's *Of Baptism* and the result of the Third Public Baptismal Disputation. Nevertheless, throughout the work he appeals repeatedly to the reader and to the congregation that they should judge who is correctly interpreting Scripture. He adds that it is the "preached" or "read and heard" Word of God that is required if Scripture is to be correctly understood and interpreted.[94] Zwingli, on the other hand, repeatedly asserts in his introduction to *Of Baptism* that the Anabaptists mislead the simple people in their interpretation of Scripture.[95] There is then a battle going on in this work for the support of the simple people. Zwingli proclaims the truth of the gospel to the simple people, insisting that they accept it and reject the errors of the Anabaptists. His teaching is given political support by the mandates of the

---

94. Harder, *Sources of Swiss Anabaptism*, 365f.
95. Ibid., 443.

Zurich Council against those who refused to have their children baptized and continue to practice baptism of believers.[96]

Hubmaier, on the other hand, insists that the simple people can understand the clear Scriptures as they are read and heard, and that the congregation is still competent to judge in all matters of interpretation of the Scripture.

Summary

Of major importance in this work is the debate between Hubmaier and Zwingli concerning prohibitions. Zwingli argues that the Anabaptists must produce a clear command of God forbidding infant baptism. Hubmaier counters that Zwingli has become inconsistent, as Zwingli argued during the First Zurich Disputation that purgatory was forbidden since it was nowhere clearly stated. Following the same line of argument, Hubmaier asserts the onus is on Zwingli to show a clear command for the baptism of infants, which he believes he cannot do. It is precisely at this point that Zwingli has moved away from Hubmaier and the Zurich radicals and become more flexible in his understanding of what is permitted for Christians, while Hubmaier and the Zurich radicals maintain a more literal interpretation of the idea that only those things God commands are good and are therefore to be obeyed.

Hubmaier also introduces a phrase "patchwork of Scripture," which will feature more consistently in his later works from Nikolsburg. At this time, Hubmaier uses the phrase simply to emphasize his understanding of the unity of Scripture and to contrast that unity with the fragmenting of the Scriptures he believes Zwingli is causing. This is particularly so when Hubmaier debates Zwingli's use of parables, for Hubmaier claims that Zwingli is introducing glosses, tricks, and sophistries that only destroy the simple meaning of the text. However, the simple meaning of the text of a parable does not mean that it is literalistically applied. Hubmaier expressly denies that to become as little children means people should play childish games and ride on sticks, an action that did in fact occur in some Anabaptist groups. Hubmaier is also vehement in his opposition to Zwingli's translation of Mark 10:13ff, which he views as adding to the Scriptures, an action that will bring the curse of God upon the perpetrator.

---

96. *PY*, 173; *HS*, 169–70. Harder, *Sources of Swiss Anabaptism*, 443. This mandate was made public through the open letter sent to the Grüningen Magistrates on November 30, 1525.

In this work, Hubmaier also for the first time demonstrates his attitude towards the church fathers. By the use he makes of the church fathers, Hubmaier shows that they have value in theological debate, but only where they can provide evidence to support his particular interpretation of Scripture.

There is also a recognizable similarity in thought between Hubmaier and the Zurich radicals concerning the majority view and truth. Hubmaier maintains that it is not the voice of the majority that endorses a view as correct, but simply the Word of God. The Zurich radicals hold to the same opinion, but take this view further by arguing that once the truth is plainly known there should be no waiting. The truth should be implemented despite the reluctance of the majority. However, Hubmaier does not hold to this view of forbearance at this time.

Hubmaier's dependence on the literal sense of Scripture is further underscored by his enumeration of the order of salvation. He does not argue for this order as he believes it is plainly evident from the order in which it is written in the text of Scripture.

Although there may not be a significant increase in the material presented for the discussion of infant baptism, Hubmaier's *Dialogue* does make an important contribution in tracking the development of his hermeneutic.

THE TWELVE ARTICLES IN PRAYER FORM

(December 11, 1525–April 1526)[97]

Setting

The historical setting for this work also provides the context for Hubmaier's *A Brief "Our Father," Recantation at Zurich*, and *Interrogation and Release*. All these works were either written by Hubmaier or are surviving records of interviews that took place while he was in Zurich.

As stated above, Hubmaier was forced to flee Waldshut on December 5, 1525. At the time of his flight he was, according to his own statements, an ill man, having "greatly swollen" feet.[98] He had to leave all his personal goods behind. These were later disposed of by the Austrian authorities,

---

97. *PY*, 234–40; *HS*, 215–20.
98. *PY*, 161.

including his clothing, some of which was sold at auction.[99] He escaped with only the shirt on his back, not even having a coat to wear,[100] and took with him "6 gulden worth of batzen in a neck purse" to sustain him in his flight.[101]

His first thoughts were to escape to Basel or Strasbourg, but the roads to these places were sealed against him by the presence of Austrian troops. He therefore crossed the Rhine and came to Zurich where he stayed first with Aberli and then moved to the widow Widerker's house. His intention was to rest for a few days and to change his clothing so that he would not be so easily recognized.[102] However, when news of Hubmaier's presence in Zurich became known to the city authorities, on December 11, 1525, they arrested him and placed him under "house arrest" in the Council Hall.[103] The Zurich Council feared that Hubmaier, who they considered was held in such high regard by the Anabaptists, would foment an uprising against them if he were allowed to freely mix with the citizens of Zurich and the Zurich Oberland.[104]

On his arrest, Hubmaier again requested an interview with Zwingli, having previously done so in his letter to the Zurich Council on July 10, 1525. The discussion took place on December 19, with Zwingli, Jud, Myconius, Hofmeister, four councilors, and a Zurich schoolteacher named Binder. Prior to the interview Hubmaier was aware that the Austrian authorities had made a formal written request (December 14) and a verbal request (December 19) to the Zurich Council to hand him over to them.[105] As a result of this discussion Hubmaier recanted his Anabaptist views. Bergsten rejects Yoder's suggestion that Hubmaier recanted in order to secure for himself a preaching position in Zurich[106] and proposes instead that the recantation was the price Hubmaier had to pay for a safe refuge.[107]

The recantation was read before some of the councilors on December 22, and was to be publicly made in the three principal churches of Zurich

---

99. *PY*, 164.

100. *PY*, 152.

101. *PY*, 164.

102. *PY*, 161.

103. Bergsten, *Balthasar Hubmaier: Anabaptist Theologian*, 300. Pipkin and Yoder dates his arrest as December 19. *PY*, 150.

104. Bergsten, *Balthasar Hubmaier: Anabaptist Theologian*, 300.

105. Ibid., 303.

106. Ibid., 302–3.

107. Ibid., 304.

on December 29.[108] However, Hubmaier did not proceed with his recantation as planned. Instead, he began a defense of believers' baptism. He was hastily removed to the Wellenberg prison and subjected to torture on the rack, where he "anathematized the 'error and obstinacy of the Anti-Baptists.'"[109] He was kept in the "*Wasserturm*," as he called the Wellenberg prison, until early in April 1526, when he was released after Zwingli intervened on his behalf, and later secretly escorted from Zurich's territory.[110]

A further interrogation of Hubmaier took place on March 5, as part of a series of interrogations of the eighteen Anabaptists then in Zurich prisons.[111] Hubmaier agreed to "let baptism drop" and asked permission to write on government, interest, tithes, and community of goods, assuring the Council that he would "acquit himself to such a degree that they would be compelled to see that he had been treated unjustly."[112] On March 7, at the conclusion of this retrial, the Council issued its harshest mandate to date, confirming the life sentences of the prisoners, and declaring: "Whoever henceforth baptizes another will be seized by Our Lords and, according to this present explicit decree, drowned without any mercy."[113] Hubmaier was returned to his solitary confinement in the Wellenberg, while the others were returned to the Heretics' Tower "located on the city wall between the two gates, Neumarkt and Niederdorf."[114]

Following his agreement to drop baptism, a month passed before Hubmaier was released from the Wellenberg on April 6, according to Councilor Bluntschli.[115] On April 11, the Council demanded that Hubmaier recant as he had agreed to the previous December.[116] Zwingli states that Hubmaier produced a new recantation,[117] which Hubmaier read sometime between April 13 and 15, 1526, first in the Fraumünster, then the Grossmünster, and finally in Gossau in Grüningen. Zwingli insisted on the

---

108. Ibid., 304. Pipkin and Yoder date the Fraumünster incident as occurring the next Sunday, January 5, 1526.

109. Bergsten, *Balthasar Hubmaier: Anabaptist Theologian*, 305.

110. Ibid., 306–7.

111. Harder, *Sources of Swiss Anabaptism*, 443ff.

112. Ibid., 445.

113. Ibid, 448.

114. Ibid., 741n74. The prisoners in the Heretics Tower managed to escape on March 21, 1526. Ibid., 450ff.

115. Bergsten, *Balthasar Hubmaier: Anabaptist Theologian*, 307.

116. Bergsten, *Balthasar Hubmaier: Seine Stellung*, 392. In the translation the date is given as April 16.

117. *PY*, 158.

recantation being read in the Grüningen area, since the Anabaptists had been particularly successful there and Hubmaier was much admired.[118]

In his letter to Gynoräus on August 31, 1526, Zwingli depicted himself as going out of his way on Hubmaier's behalf, requesting that the Council not expel Hubmaier immediately he had recanted because of the "grave peril" facing him from "our Swiss and Caesar." The Council agreed and some time elapsed before Hubmaier and his wife were escorted by a member of the Council out of Zurich's territory.[119]

Analysis

It was during this period of imprisonment in the Wellenberg that Hubmaier wrote *Twelve Articles*. Hubmaier used the Apostles' Creed as the basis for his personal confession of faith in the form of a prayer. Under the twelve headings of the Creed, Hubmaier briefly outlines his understanding of the faith. He uses the first statement, "I believe in God, the Almighty Father, Creator of the heavens and the earth," as a starting point for depicting his understanding of man as he was in his created state before the fall. People before the fall were all children of God, lords, and heirs who would have remained so for eternity but for the "disobedience of Adam."[120] Yet the fall is no source of harm for those who place all their "consolation, hope, and confidence" in the "gracious Father."

The atonement is the focus of the discussion that flows from the second statement of the Creed, "I also believe in Jesus Christ, his only Son our Lord." Christ by his obedience has not only made peace between the Father and the sinner, but has also won back the inheritance lost at the fall. Further, through the "holy Word which he sent," he grants power to the sinner "to become thy child in faith."[121] It is the "saving and consoling name of Jesus" that sustains the sinner in faith and redeems him from sin.[122]

The work of the Holy Spirit in the conception of Christ acts as a link for Hubmaier to outline the new birth the believer experiences. Hubmaier declares: "I believe and trust that the Holy Spirit has come into me, and that the power of the most high God has overshadowed my soul like that

---

118. Bergsten, *Balthasar Hubmaier: Anabaptist Theologian*, 307.
119. *PY*, 159.
120. *PY*, 235; *HS*, 216.
121. *PY*, 235; *HS*, 216.
122. *PY*, 235–36; *HS*, 216.

of Mary, so that I might be conceived a new man and be born again in thy living, indestructible Word."[123] A statement such as this might well have given Zwingli support in his accusation that the Anabaptists considered themselves sinless, and capable of living a sinless life after baptism, a contention we have seen that Hubmaier strenuously rejects.

Christ's suffering and death under Pontius Pilate gives Hubmaier cause for thanks, as through these acts Christ has demonstrated the "greatest and highest love towards us" in that he died for our sins. Yet Christ's death also effects a transformation in the believer; it transforms "thy heavy cross into an easy yoke, thy bitter suffering into imperishable joy, and thy grim death into eternal life."[124]

Statement Five of the Creed, which deals with the descensus, demonstrates Hubmaier's understanding of the extent of the atonement. He claims that the "holy patriarchs" received the "new and joyous message" of the gospel when Christ preached to them in the Spirit. Not only did Christ rise on the third day, having reunited "spirit, soul, and body in the grave," but he also led the patriarchs "mightily out of captivity."[125] The theme of the resurrection also finds its application in the life of the believer. Christ is the victor over death, hell, and the devil, and those who believe in him "should also overcome sin, death, hell, and the devil, and might also attain to eternal life, as thy brothers and fellow heirs with thee."[126]

The reference to the ascension in statement six provided Hubmaier with the opportunity to once again insist that because Christ sits at the right hand of the Father he cannot be worshipped "either here or there, yea neither in bread nor in wine."[127] He also includes his views on Christ as the "sole intercessor, mediator, and advocate before the Father."

The second coming of Christ provides the background for Hubmaier to develop his understanding that Christ will bring to an end the carnal life of the believer and therefore the ongoing effects of sin. Christ will also recompense them for the works they have done. He provides a long quotation from Matt 25:34–36, 40 to demonstrate the type of works that Christ expects of believers.[128] He also includes a dire warning describing the fate of those who do not carry out the works that Christ has commanded

123. *PY*, 236; *HS*, 216.
124. *PY*, 236; *HS*, 217.
125. *PY*, 236; *HS*, 217.
126. *PY*, 237; *HS*, 217.
127. *PY*, 237; *HS*, 217.
128. *PY*, 237–38; *HS*, 218.

them to do. Hubmaier alludes to Rev 21:8, which he uses as the basis of an expanded list of those who will "fall into the lake which burns with fire and brimstone."[129]

The statement, "I also believe in the Holy Spirit" elicits a short exposition on the work of the Holy Spirit, not in the process of bringing about salvation, but in sustaining the believer and kindling "genuine, unadulterated, and Christian love toward God and my neighbor."[130] Here Hubmaier alludes to the necessity of the believer demonstrating his love of God in praise and thanksgiving and love of neighbor in works of brotherly love. Hubmaier considers both of these responses to be linked to baptism and the Lord's Supper.

This link with the two sacraments that Christ left to his church becomes explicit in the next section of the Creed that deals with the "one holy universal Christian church." It was Hubmaier's conviction that "unless these two elements are again established and practiced according to thy institution and ordering, there is among us neither faith, love, church covenant, fraternal admonition, ban, nor exclusion, without which it can never again be well with thy church."[131] It is through baptism and the Lord's Supper, the two keys that Christ has left to his church, that the bride of Christ is to be kept "fully beautiful, without blemish, infallible, pure, without wrinkle, and blameless."[132] Though Hubmaier is speaking of the universal church in this statement, his reference to the actual practice of baptism and the Lord's Supper would suggest that he also had the particular local gathering of believers in mind. Again he has left ambiguous his understanding of the perfection of the saints by allowing the perfection of the universal church to be attributed to the particular local gathering.

It is in this section on the church that Hubmaier once again declares his most fundamental position on the understanding of Scripture. The universal church is "gathered, established, and governed on earth by the one living divine Word." This living word is Christ himself who has sanctified the church through his "rose-red blood," and will remain with her to the end of the world. Yet the practice and doctrine of the church is to be found in the word; that is, the Scriptures. Hubmaier writes, "May we in concord with her believe, teach, and hold all that thou dost command us through thy Word, and also root out everything contrary that thou

129. *PY*, 238; *HS*, 218.
130. *PY*, 238; *HS*, 218.
131. *PY*, 239; *HS*, 219.
132. *PY*, 238; *HS*, 218.

hast not planted."¹³³ This is Hubmaier's common hermeneutical principle, which we have seen develop in his debates with both Catholic opponents and Zwingli. He also warns against "any kind of respect of persons, human dogmas, or doctrine of the ancient fathers, popes, councils, universities, or old customs" that might lead into error.[134] Here again is the strong contrast between Scripture as the sole source of authority for faith and practice in the church and all other sources of authority.

Remission of sins is linked to the power of the keys that Christ has granted to his church. This power is for the readmission of repentant sinners who demonstrate their remorse, and for the exclusion of those who, having received the threefold fraternal admonition required by a literal interpretation of Matt 18:15ff, are unwilling to abandon their sin, and henceforth live according to the rule of Christ. This exclusion from the visible church of gathered saints has eternal implications, as Hubmaier explicitly states, "The same also stands bound before God in heaven and excluded from the universal Christian church (outside which there is no salvation)."[135]

Hubmaier's own desperate situation in the Wellenberg Tower is reflected in his comments on the theme of the resurrection of the body. He contrasts the very real prospect of death by starvation or on the heretics' pyre, and the loss of all personal possessions and honor; with the imperishable possessions, and the impassable, transfigured, immortal body, and eternal life that await those who persevere in the faith. The day of resurrection is joyous only for those who remain in the universal church, and Hubmaier gives heartfelt expression to his concern to continue in the faith in his closing prayer: "I pray thee faithfully, wilt thou preserve me therein graciously [i.e. the faith] until my end. And if through human fear and weakness, through tyranny, torture, sword, fire, or water I should be driven away from it, even so I herewith appeal to thee, O my merciful Father, restore me again with the grace of thy Holy Spirit and let me not depart in death without this faith."[136]

Section twelve of the Creed allows Hubmaier to continue his contemplation on the blessed state of "believers and elect ones" who will certainly contemplate with joy the divine countenance, and have all their desires satisfied. Such bliss as is in store for the faithful cannot be expressed in

---

133. *PY,* 238; *HS,* 219.
134. *PY,* 238–39; *HS,* 219.
135. *PY,* 239; *HS,* 219.
136. *PY,* 240; *HS,* 220.

words. He therefore chooses to echo Paul's paraphrase of Isa 66:4 as found in 1 Cor 2:9, "for no eye has seen, no ear has heard, and it has never entered into the heart of man, what God has prepared for those who love him."[137]

There is little new in the doctrinal content of this prayer, except the reference to the salvation of the patriarchs. What is new is the identification Hubmaier makes between his own situation and that of people in the Scriptures. This becomes an additional method for interpreting Scripture so that it is immediately applicable to the life of the believer. Hubmaier also maintains his formal hermeneutic of obedience to the commands of God and the eradication of all that God has not specifically commanded.

Use of Scripture

Although he does not once provide a reference to a passage of Scripture in the entire work, there are nevertheless three identifiable quotations and some thirty-three allusions in this text.

The quotations are from Matt 25:34ff; Rev 21:8; 1 Cor 2:9. The Matthew reference is used in a standard way as a supporting text. Hubmaier contends that Christ will recompense those who do the works that he commands them to do, and uses this reference to provide illustration of the works that are commanded.

Revelation 21:8 is used in a polemical way, warning those who are fearful and unbelieving that they will face eternal damnation if they continue in that way. This reflects the Anabaptists' preoccupation with the theme of undue respect being given to men, such as Zwingli and Luther, which diminishes the sole authority of Scripture. The warning is for those both inside and outside the church. It is their opinion that to follow man instead of obeying the commands of God leads to exclusion from the universal church and thus exclusion from salvation.

The 1 Cor 2:9 reference demonstrates Hubmaier's use of a text in this new method of experiential identification. The text incorporates an Old Testament passage in it, thus granting to the Old Testament text equal status for the life of the believer.

The discussion of articles 1 and 2 of the Creed includes a number of allusions to Rom 5:1ff, 12ff, 19; 8:17; John 1:12, 14; Matt 16:16. Here Hubmaier focuses on the contrast that exists between the disobedience of Adam and the obedience of Christ. The obedience of Christ enables sinners to regain their inheritance through faith in Christ, the sent word,

137. *PY*, 240; *HS*, 220.

when they make the confession of faith, "you are the Christ." Hubmaier continues to emphasise his basic view of the contrast between obedience and disobedience. However, the context of Rom 8:17 is important in that it provides a possible reason for Hubmaier's focus on salvation as the regaining of a lost inheritance.

Paul states: "The Spirit himself testifies with our spirit that we are God's children. Now if we are children, then we are heirs—heirs of God and co-heirs with Christ, if indeed we share in his sufferings in order that we may also share in his glory" Rom 8:16–17 (NIV).

Although Hubmaier does not specifically identify this theme of sharing in the sufferings of Christ as part of the process of salvation, his use of scriptural allusions in this work linked to his own suffering suggests that he was conscious that suffering has a role in salvation.

This is best shown by looking at the allusions Hubmaier makes to 1 Peter, a pastoral letter addressed to Christians who were encouraged to persevere in the face of the suffering they were experiencing.

Of the thirty-three allusions in this work five are identifiable as allusions to 1 Peter. They are as follows: 1 Pet 1:3–7, the restoration of the believers' inheritance; 1:10–11, salvation foretold by the prophets; 1:23, being born again of imperishable seed through the Living Word of God; 3:19, Christ proclaims the gospel in the Spirit to the patriarchs in prison; 3:22, Christ is seated at the right hand of the Father with authority.[138] There are also a number of other themes that Hubmaier uses in this work that are to be found in 1 Peter as well as other New Testament writings, such as the second coming of Christ, judgment according to the works done, stirring up love of God and neighbor, placing all of one's trust in God alone, and the final inexpressible joy that awaits those who persevere in the faith to the end.

It is possible that Hubmaier has used 1 Peter to provide an interpretative structure for the Creed. Consistent with a method of interpreting Scripture he has previously used, Hubmaier identifies a theme and then expands on it by reference to a clearer text of Scripture. Hence the theme that Christ will come and judge all people according to the works they have done, though mentioned in 1 Pet 2:12, 4:5ff, is in Hubmaier's view explained more clearly by referring to Matt 25:34ff, where the works that are required are clearly spelt out. Other themes identifiable in 1 Peter are dealt with in a similar way in this work of personal confession.

---

138. *PY*, 235, 236; *HS*, 216, 217.

A further issue strongly links this work of Hubmaier's to 1 Peter. In his previous writings Hubmaier has consistently identified the necessary part the preached Word of God has in the process of salvation. In this work, the Word of God is spoken of specifically as the "living, indestructible Word," which echoes 1 Pet 2:23 "the living and abiding Word of God" by which believers are "born again." And it is this word that was preached to them. Here Hubmaier's theme of the necessity of preaching the Word of God is also to be found in 1 Peter in a way that complements his use of Rom 10:9ff, yet has the new setting of sharing in the sufferings of Christ.

Hubmaier appears to have identified himself and his sufferings in the Zurich prison with those to whom the letter of 1 Peter was addressed, particularly his loss of honor and possessions, and the threat of death by fire or through starvation and disease. This describes a subjective hermeneutic of personal identification that does not rely on grammatical or historical exegesis of the text. Nor is it necessary to seek a spiritual sense of the text by interpreting it in any of the other three spiritual senses.

Summary

The most significant addition to Hubmaier's hermeneutic identified from this work is his technique of personal identification with the various experiences of people mentioned in Scripture. This identification is particularly made with the experiences of suffering. The mark of suffering with and for Christ is seen to confirm the truth of the gospel for which Hubmaier and the Zurich Anabaptists had been imprisoned. While at this time suffering had not yet become a formal principle in Hubmaier's concept of discipleship, the hermeneutic of personal identification of the believer with the experiences of people as described in Scripture provided the basis for this later development.

Hubmaier also reveals that he does not consider the work of Christ to have been effective in the period of the Old Testament, for only after Christ has preached to the patriarchs are they released from their prison. Yet Hubmaier also identifies Christ as the Living Word of God, a designation that could be understood to mean that Christ as the Word of God could have been preached in the time of the Old Testament.

There is a discussion on the power of the keys that comes to light in this work, a discussion that emphasizes the need for fraternal admonition and "the ban" to be practiced within the church, if the church is to be kept pure. At this time Hubmaier considers the correct restoration of baptism

Against Those who Mutilate the Word of God

and the Lord's Supper will bring about the implementation of true faith and love, fraternal admonition, and the ban. Later, the practice of church discipline will be raised to the same level as baptism and the Lord's Supper. Only in a church where all three are truly practiced will there be a true church.

By now, Hubmaier's understanding of doing only that which God commands and uprooting all that God has not planted has become fundamental to his hermeneutic, and these themes recur in this work.

A BRIEF "OUR FATHER"

(December 11, 1525–April 1526)[139]

Analysis and Use of Scripture

This work appears to have been written during the same period as *Twelve Articles*. Bergsten has shown that the distress Hubmaier expressed in his *Recantation at Zurich* with reference to his physical plight finds a strong echo in the section of this work under the heading "lead us not into temptation."[140] The strong expressions of remorse contained in this work, as compared to *Twelve Articles*, suggests that this work was composed closer to Hubmaier's experience of forced recantation due to torture on the rack.[141]

---

139. *PY*, 241–44; *HS*, 221–23.

140. *HS*, 221.

141. *PY*, 242; *HS*, 222: "We confess that we have often and frequently dishonored thy holy name in word and in deeds. . . . Forgive us, Father, and henceforth give us grace that we may not speak thy name in vain, that we might set aside all blasphemy and swearing, so that thy holy name might be exalted, magnified, and praised eternally."; *PY*, 243; *HS*, 223: "We again confess ourselves guilty, that we have sinned much with words, works, and evil thoughts, so that we do not even know the number, the measure, nor the size of our sins. O Father, forgive us and give us strength henceforth to improve our lives."; "*But deliver us from evil*. From sin, from the devil, from our own body, which is our greatest enemy." Cf. Zwingli's letter to Capito, January 1, 1526, which states that after Hubmaier's withdrawal of his recantation in the Fraumünster "he was thrust back into prison and tortured. It is clear that the man had become a sport for demons, so that he recanted not frankly as he had promised, nay he said that he entertained no other opinions than those taught by me, execrated the error and obstinacy of the Catabaptists, repeated this three times when stretched on the rack, and bewailed his misery and the wrath of God which in this affair was so unkind." *PY*, 156.

It is a short work that takes as its structure the prayer Jesus taught his disciples in Matt 6:9–13 that was used as part of the church's liturgy. The first five statements of the prayer focus on the Father, and Hubmaier consistently contrasts the positive aspect of God that is referred to with the negative aspect of the human condition. Hence, considering God as Father leads Hubmaier to declare that people are not children of God but of the father of liars. He does not finish his meditation there, but goes on to pray for pardon and to be made a child of faith.[142] The same pattern is to be found in his consideration of the other four phrases. Heaven is contrasted to this "miserable valley of suffering," with the concluding plea that God take his "miserable children" to him in heaven.[143] The hallowing of God's name is contrasted with the dishonoring that has taken place in word and deed, with a request for grace so that such blasphemy and swearing will be avoided in the future and God's name will be "exalted, magnified, and praised eternally."[144] The kingdom of God is contrasted with the kingdom of sin, the devil, hell, and eternal death, of which those who pray are captives. The final plea is for God to come and help, for without his help "we are completely miserable, troubled, and forsaken."[145] The will of any human being is "fully and completely in contradiction to thy divine will." The prayer is that God will send the Holy Spirit to work in them "genuine faith, constant hope, and fervent love" so that they might do the will of the Father.[146]

The pattern of exposition changes when the phrases of the prayer that make requests of God on behalf of those who pray are considered.

Hubmaier uses the phrase "give us today our daily bread" as a springboard to interpret the bread as "thy holy Word." He alludes to passages from Matt 4:4 and John 6:32–35 to achieve this understanding of the bread as Scripture. He does not suggest, as Zwingli did in his *Of Baptism*, that the bread is Christ or the gospel.[147] This concentration on the Word of God is further developed as Hubmaier prays that it be brought "to life in our soul, that it might burgeon, grow up, and bear fruit for eternal life."[148] He does not say here how the Word of God is brought to life, though he

---

142. *PY*, 241; *HS*, 222.
143. *PY*, 241–42, *HS*, 222.
144. *PY*, 242; *HS*, 222.
145. *PY*, 242; *HS*, 222.
146. *PY*, 242; *HS*, 222.
147. Zwingli, *Of Baptism*, 155.
148. *PY*, 243, *HS*, 222

does identify the Holy Spirit in the *Summa* as that agent who through faith brings the word to life so that it bears fruit.[149] He also alludes to 2 Tim 2:15 in his prayer that God provide "industrious workers" to divide the Word "pure, clear, and undefiled and distribute it faithfully." Here Hubmaier again underlines his conviction that the word is clear, though now he acknowledges that it does require some interpretation.

The centrality of the Word of God to understanding and doing the will of God is emphasized in the final statement of this section. The "Christian and industrious workers" are necessary if God's will is to be known, for it "can be known only from thy word," and it is the preacher who rightly divides the Word.[150] The process of interpretation therefore appears to be focused more in the preacher of the Word of God than in the congregation as it was earlier in Hubmaier's writings.

The reference to "temptation" gives rise to Hubmaier's reflection on his miserable condition on earth. The request is that God would not abandon him to pain and suffering. He fears that if he were, he might be overcome and "fall away from thy holy word." As part of the prayer he alludes to 1 Cor 10:13, where Paul promises that the believer will not have to endure temptation that is beyond their capacity to bear.[151]

The evil from which Hubmaier pleads to be delivered is identified as sin, the devil, and his own body, his "greatest enemy."[152]

In a final prayer the various requests that have been made are presented to God, relying on his "fatherly good pleasure. . . . the multitude of thy mercifulness, and . . . thy gracious promise."[153] This gracious promise has been repeated through Moses, the prophets, and the apostles, but especially in the words of Christ in John 16:23–24, to which Hubmaier now alludes, and which he quotes in part on the title page of this work.[154]

There is also in this work a strong personal identification of Hubmaier with the crucifixion of Christ. Twice he uses quotations of the words of Christ from the cross as his own: "Father forgive them; they know not what they do" (NIV Luke 23:34),[155] "Father; into thy hands I commit my

---

149. *PY*, 85; *HS*, 111.
150. *PY*, 243; *HS*, 222.
151. *PY*, 243; *HS*, 223.
152. *PY*, 243; *HS*, 223.
153. *PY*, 243; *HS*, 223.
154. *PY*, 241, 244; *HS*, 221, 223. "Ask and you will receive."
155. *PY*, 243; *HS*, 223.

spirit" (NIV Luke 23:46).[156] This latter reference shows Hubmaier continuing a practice with which we have become familiar. He expands this quotation by adding his own words, "we commend our body, life, honor, goods, soul, and spirit." This is the first reference to a tripartite anthropology that Hubmaier makes, an aspect of his theology that plays a central role in his later writings on the freedom of the will.

The final allusion that Hubmaier uses in this work refers to Job 1:21, "thou dost give and thou dost take, may thy name be praised."[157] This attitude of resigned reliance on the mercy of God was also present in his *Twelve Articles*.

Summary

In this work Hubmaier continues to demonstrate his new hermeneutic of personal identification. This method relies on the readers of Scripture identifying themselves with the events and people of Scripture without exegetical considerations of the historical or grammatical contexts. Rather, where the emotions of the reader find a response in the words of Scripture, the text becomes personally applicable, and considered as the Word of God for them. Hubmaier also continues to demonstrate his dependence on the Word of God as the sole source available to people from which they can discern the will of God. He maintains his position that the word, read or preached, is not effective without the work of the Holy Spirit to enliven it. He has now added the view that the Word of God also requires the interpretative work of people who will rightly "divide" it so that it will remain pure and clear. What is not clear is whether these "teachers" of the word continue to function as equals within the gathered community of the church, assisting the whole church to arrive at a clear interpretation of the word, or whether they are considered to be superior to others of the community and bring to it the clear Word of God.

---

156. *PY,* 244; *HS,* 223.
157. *PY,* 244; *HS,* 223.

Against Those who Mutilate the Word of God

RECANTATION AT ZURICH AND INTERROGATION AND RELEASE

(December 1525)[158]

Setting

Pipkin and Yoder have added these works to the collection edited by Westin and Bergsten. By doing so they have provided material on the life of Hubmaier which was not previously readily accessible.

The *Recantation at Zurich* is believed to be the statement that Hubmaier composed after his first interview with Zwingli and the other preachers of Zurich. Bergsten identifies it as the Statement of Recantation that Hubmaier was to have read out in the Fraumünster on December 29, 1525.[159] Pipkin and Yoder place the dating of events one week later than Bergsten, giving the date of the events in the Fraumünster as January 5, 1526.[160] This seems highly unlikely, given that Zwingli wrote to Capito on January 1, 1526, and described Hubmaier's "most explicit and unconstrained withdrawal."[161]

Analysis

The content of the recantation shows that Hubmaier was led to reverse his position on infant baptism because Zwingli had shown him that the covenant sign of circumcision had been replaced by baptism, and that "love is to be the judge and referee in all the Scriptures," a position that he was shown by Jud, Hofmeister, and Myconius.[162]

He goes on to deny the accusations that he rejects Christian government, the practice of community of goods, any special feeling that may accompany baptism, the possibility of being sinless, and living a sinless life. All these denials are to be found in *On the Christian Baptism*, and

---

158. *PY*, 150–65.
159. Bergsten, *Balthasar Hubmaier: Anabaptist Theologian*, 304.
160. *PY*, 150.
161. *PY*, 156.
162. *PY*, 151.

later in the *Dialogue*, which he had only recently completed in draft form in Waldshut before he had to flee.[163]

The third point he makes appears to be a plea of mitigation. He states that "since Augustine and many others since his time, also in our time, have been wrong about baptism," he also should be treated mercifully and forgiven for any offence he has caused.[164]

He concludes by referring to his "great sickness, tribulation, banishment, and poverty," a theme reflected in both his *Twelve Articles* and *A Brief Our Father,* and his fear of being handed over to his enemies, which he identifies in his later interrogation by the Emperor's agents.

The process whereby Hubmaier arrived at his recantation is described by Zwingli in a letter written on August 31, 1526, to Gynoräus in Constance. Zwingli was writing in response to a report from Gynoräus that Hubmaier had been maligning Zwingli to the pastors of that city, and setting them against him. The general chronology of events as described in Zwingli's letter corresponds to the information available through the official records of interrogation. There is however in Zwingli's letter the additional information of his intercession on Hubmaier's behalf for merciful treatment from the City Council, and that Hubmaier be allowed to leave Zurich secretly so as to avoid capture by the Emperor's agents.[165]

What is significant to note in this investigation of the development of Hubmaier's hermeneutic is Zwingli's description of the interview that was held between himself, Jud, Hofmeister, Myconius, and Hubmaier. Zwingli describes how he sought to convince Hubmaier of the "perpetual covenant," which he failed to do. He then moved his argument to a discussion of Acts 2, "from which I proved that the children of Christians were in the beginning reckoned as of the church." Hubmaier is said to have stubbornly refused to acknowledge this as true, and Zwingli moved on to the text of 1 Cor 10:2, "All our fathers were baptized unto Moses." This text in Zwingli's view would compel Hubmaier to acknowledge that the children are included, though not expressly mentioned. Hubmaier continued to refuse to say whether children were included or not and Zwingli reports "that I went for the man rather vigorously," not over the issue of baptism but the consequences of Hubmaier's actions in Waldshut, by which "he had drawn many wretched citizens into a revolt in which they had perished."[166]

---

163. *PY,* 152.
164. *PY,* 152.
165. *PY,* 158–59.
166. *PY,* 157. Zwingli incorrectly gives the reference as 1 Cor 2.

It is significant that it was this very passage from 1 Corinthians that Hubmaier failed to take up in the *Dialogue*. The debate in Zurich had centered on the admissibility of the Old Testament as providing a sign for New Testament water baptism. On the basis of his hermeneutical principles Hubmaier would only accept the sign of Noah, yet by applying the same principles Zwingli had confronted him with another Old Testament example.

Yet it was probably not the verbal tirade to which Zwingli subjected Hubmaier that brought about a recantation. Hubmaier also had a private conversation with Jud, Hofmeister, and Myconius that gave him a possible way of overriding his principle that infant baptism was permitted only if a clear text of Scripture commanding it could be cited. Hubmaier suggests that these men persuaded him to modify his principle of only doing that which God had clearly commanded in Scripture and rooting out all that God had not commanded, by imposing a prior interpretive principle, the principle of love. Essentially, it meant that disputed matters that caused division to the unity of the church should be dropped for the sake of that unity.

In Zwingli's opinion, Hubmaier's admission to having been shown the validity of the sign of baptism replacing that of circumcision was more contrived than sincere.[167]

This discussion also shows in embryo a pattern that was later developed by Bullinger for all Reformed pastors to follow in debates with Anabaptists. It focused on the different view the two groups held concerning the Old Testament. Bullinger accepts as primary to any discussion that both the Old and New Testaments are to be considered equally authoritative for determining the correct interpretation of Scripture.[168] He appeals to the use of synecdoche, metalipsi, and other tropes to demonstrate that a literal interpretation of Scripture is not possible.[169] Zwingli had appealed to and developed these literary tropes in his debates with Hubmaier. Further, Bullinger appeals to the use of the Old Testament in the New to demonstrate the continuity between the two and the authority it held for Jesus and the apostles.[170]

---

167. *PY*, 159. "After the recantation, which he pretended he made heartily, whereas there could have been nothing less hearty."

168. Fast and Yoder, "How to deal with Anabaptists," 84. "When tensions and conflicts arise between Christians concerning matters of faith, they should be decided and clarified with the Holy Scripture of Old and New Testaments."

169. Ibid., 86.

170. Ibid., 86–87

Balthasar Hubmaier and the Clarity of Scripture

Bullinger's second major thesis is that "Scripture shall not be interpreted according to the judgment and spirit of men but by and through itself, with the rule of faith and love."[171] He then outlines the procedure for interpreting the text of Scripture; an obscure text must be interpreted by a clearer text, with consideration of its context, and faith and love. "From this it follows already that whatever is affirmed in Scripture is also clarified and exposited by Scripture. Thus everything is straightened out by the rule of faith and love; the lesser by the greater, the obscure by the evident."[172]

He goes on to cite how the rule of faith and love are to be applied in specific cases: "The texts by means of which we intend to interpret a given contested passage must either be clearer than the one which is the object of contention, or else they must be contrary to it, so that everyone can see by the contrast that the contested text must have another meaning than the one yielded by the words themselves. In the former case, whenever the sense should be sharpened, follow the context; in the latter, follow faith and love."[173]

Fast and Yoder define "faith" as "the whole body of orthodox Christian belief, assumed identical with the whole of Scripture, symbolized and summarized in the Apostles Creed," while "love" is "whatever serves the interest of social order and peace in the Christian society of the sixteenth century."[174]

Zwingli's debate with Hubmaier in Zurich shows evidence of this method of interpretation coming into being. This is evidenced by Zwingli's attempt to convince Hubmaier of the validity of the Old Testament in matters of baptism, and by his use of literary tropes to allow his interpretation of "dark passages" to conform with orthodox interpretations of Scripture, as he had determined them to be orthodox. It is also seen in the emphasis of Jud, Hofmeister, and Myconius on the "rule of love," by which they provided Hubmaier with an opportunity to override his formal principles of interpretation so that he could accept an interpretation that was contrary to his own view. All these aspects of the interview with Hubmaier are precursors of Bullinger's method for dealing with Anabaptists.

---

171. Ibid., 88.
172. Ibid., 90.
173. Ibid.
174. Ibid., 95.

Use of Scripture

The *Recantation at Zurich* provides five allusions to now familiar texts. In his defense against the charge of practicing community of goods Hubmaier incorporates an allusion to Matt 25:35ff, where true community of goods is described as responding to the needs of others when they are seen to be hungry, naked, thirsty, and imprisoned.[175]

As he has done in *On the Christian Baptism,* he rejects the charge of sinlessness and alludes to the sequence of verses Ps 51:7; Job 3:3; Jer 20:14, references he cites in the *Dialogue,* to prove that all people are conceived and born in sin.[176]

His final allusion to Scripture involves Hubmaier's hermeneutic of identification. He makes his own part of the Lord's Prayer and paraphrases it as, "forgive me as we ask that God should forgive our sins."[177] This method of interpretation of the Lord's Prayer was demonstrated earlier in his *A Brief "Our Father."*

The *Interrogation and Release* provides a wealth of material on the biographical detail of Hubmaier's life, both in Waldshut as the Anabaptist leader of that town and for his previous work in Regensburg. However, there are no references or allusions to Scripture and they add nothing to our understanding of the development of Hubmaier's hermeneutic.[178]

Summary

The conflict of the hermeneutic of faith and love one the one hand, and the hermeneutic of truth on the other, dominates these two works. It is by adopting the hermeneutic of faith and love, which Hofmeister, Jud, and Myconius offered Hubmaier in their discussions, that Hubmaier is able to abandon his views on baptism. The hermeneutic of love permits Hubmaier to allow a practice which is not specifically commanded in Scripture.

During the interview before his recantation, Hubmaier came to apply the same hermeneutic as Zwingli, with the same result that water baptism of believers became a matter of indifference.

---

175. *PY,* 152.
176. *PY,* 152.
177. *PY,* 152.
178. *PY,* 160–65.

Balthasar Hubmaier and the Clarity of Scripture

OLD AND NEW TEACHERS ON BELIEVERS' BAPTISM

(July 1525 to July 21, 1526)[179]

Setting

This collection of citations of various church fathers, canon law, and contemporary theologians by Hubmaier is difficult to place in the chronological sequence of the writing of his works. There is some dispute between authors over where and when it was compiled. Bergsten cautiously states that Hubmaier began the work in Waldshut and completed it after his arrival in Nikolsburg.[180] He suggests this in contrast to Sachsse's assertion that Hubmaier collected most of the citations on his way to Nikolsburg, in Augsburg, and other places. Armour generally supports Sachsse, while Windhorst is more positive than Bergsten and asserts that Hubmaier gathered most of the material in Waldshut and took it with him to Nikolsburg.[181]

Although this discussion demonstrates the problem of dating material in this text, an analysis of the material itself does not greatly affect the discussion of Hubmaier's hermeneutic. We can however, for the present, leave out of our considerations the preface, as it was written after Hubmaier's arrival in Nikolsburg. Its content relates to the development of his hermeneutic more than the body of the work.

Analysis

Pipkin and Yoder suggest that Hubmaier had three purposes in mind when he compiled this work: firstly, to demonstrate that believers' baptism was the practice of the early church; secondly, that the dispute among contemporary theologians proved that the practice of believers' baptism did not automatically mean the creation of sects and schism; and finally, that his contemporaries, who had stated that infant baptism had no clear text in Scripture on which it was based, had failed to act in accordance with their belief through either inconsistency, stubbornness, or failure of nerve.[182]

---

179. *PY*, 245–74; *HS*, 224–40.

180. *HS*, 225.

181. Armour, *Anabaptist Baptism*, 52. Cf. Windhorst, *Täuferisches Taufverständnis*, 108.

182. *PY*, 245.

Armour has divided Hubmaier's use of the citations into four groups according to their purpose. He suggests that Hubmaier used some texts to demonstrate believers' baptism as the practice of the early church; some to support his own theological views; a third group to support his view of the distinction between the baptisms of John and Christ; and one citation by Origen to support his exposition of the verse "of such is the kingdom of God" as teaching an example of humility.[183]

Only once in the body of the work does Hubmaier refer to his basic hermeneutical principle concerning the rooting out of that which God has not commanded.[184] He attacks the current practice of infant baptism as practiced by the Roman Catholic Church, with particular reference to the presence of godparents, and the use of salt, oil, dirt, and spittle. As usual the text he used to support this view was Matt 15:13, though he only alluded to the text in this instance.

Use of Scripture

Hubmaier's selection of church fathers appears to relate to his finding favorable remarks by them on his key proof texts concerning believers' baptism. Of the seventy-eight references, allusions, and quotations from the New Testament that are contained in this work, fifty refer to the key texts Matt 28:18–19; Mark 16:15–16; Rom 6:3–4; 1 Pet 3:20–21, the sequence of references in the Acts to the practice of baptism by the apostles, and his principle hermeneutical text, Matt 15:13. The citations from Origen, Basil the Great, Jerome, and Theophylact, and those from Erasmus, Oecolampad, and Hegendorf all relate to selections of the above texts and show that his interpretation of them is supported by these theologians.

In a number of other cases, Hubmaier cites a comment of a church father or canon law that he agrees with and then adds one of his proof texts in an attempt to have the comment appear as an exposition of the text so that it agrees with his exposition of the text.

In both these ways, Hubmaier tries to maintain his earlier view that the church fathers have no authority of their own in judging Scripture, but

---

183. Armour, *Anabaptist Baptism*, 50–51. This use of Luke 14:11 by Origen is in Hubmaier's *Dialogue* and not in *Old and New Teachers*. *PY,* 217; *HS,* 202. Armour refers to Origen's *Commentaria in Evangelium secundum Matthaeum* as the location for this reference. Pipkin and Yoder suggest the source is his *On First Principles*.

184. *PY,* 255; *HS,* 232. He also cites Zwingli with approval: "Every Christian is unbound toward those works which God has not commanded." *PY,* 257–58; *HS,* 235.

Scripture judges them. They are to be believed only as far as they are shown to be in agreement with Scripture. His argument is weakened by his biased selection of evidence from the church fathers and his contemporaries. Armour has shown that Hubmaier cited passages from Origen that did not relate to baptism in any way, and that he took these citations from passages where Origen specifically affirms the practice of infant baptism.[185]

Pipkin and Yoder demonstrate that the same practice occurs in his selection of evidence from his contemporaries, particularly Luther, Zwingli, and Oecolampad. From Luther, Hubmaier adduces support for his view that without prior faith baptism and the Lord's Supper are meaningless. What Luther had in fact said was that every promise of God required the Word and the sign, not faith.[186] Similarly, when Hubmaier cites Zwingli and Oecolampad as saying that infant baptism has no clear word in Scripture, he fails to add that they also said that there is no clear prohibition.[187]

Summary

Hubmaier is wholly consistent with his previously declared hermeneutic in this work. He has demonstrated a further use of Scripture in the way he juxtaposes his proof texts with the opinion of the church fathers to show that the church fathers were to be accepted because they were in agreement with the Scripture. Hubmaier was in reality using the comments of the fathers to confirm his own exposition of these texts of Scripture. This is particularly clear in his use of Origen. Though not explicit in *Old and New Teachers*, in the *Dialogue*, he explicitly represents Origen as affirming his interpretation of Matt 19:13 "Let the humble come to me, for of such is the kingdom of God."[188]

---

185. Armour, *Anabaptist Baptism*, 50.
186. *PY*, 256n43.
187. *PY*, 256n44; 258n51.
188. *PY*, 217; *HS*, 202.

ON INFANT BAPTISM AGAINST OECOLAMPAD
(After September 1525 to early 1527)[189]

Setting

In the preface to the *Dialogue*, dated 1526, Hubmaier noted that he had four works ready for printing: "The first is a catechism or a textbook which teaches what a person should know before being baptized in water. Next is an order of the Christian church, then what Christian water baptism is, and finally, an answer to the derisive dialogue of several preachers held at Basel."[190] It is known that this work underwent revision before it appeared in its final form early in 1527. Oecolampad had written to Zwingli on December 1, 1525, saying he had obtained a manuscript copy, a "gloss," of a writing of Hubmaier's against himself and the other preachers at Basel.[191] This was probably a draft of the present work under discussion. Sachsse suggests that the work was completed by the summer of 1526 at the latest in Nikolsburg.[192] However, Bergsten has shown that this is not possible as Hubmaier makes reference in this work to Zwingli's work on *Original Sin*, which was written in response to Rhegius. Zwingli's work was not published until September 1526, in Zurich. From this Bergsten concludes that the work obtained its final form during October and December 1526 and was published at Nikolsburg early in 1527.[193]

Analysis

Bergsten has noted the similarity in form and in the use of dialogue between this work and the *Dialogue*, and also similarities of content between these two and *Old and New Teachers*. In terms of content Bergsten cites references to first Zwingli and then Oecolampad as "stumbling blocks" to the debate concerning the institution of baptism by Christ. Hubmaier asserts in the *Dialogue* that the debate over baptism began six years previously and in *On Infant Baptism* seven years previously.[194] These examples

---

189. *PY*, 275–95; *HS*, 256–69.
190. *PY*, 175–76; *HS*, 172.
191. Bergsten, *Balthasar Hubmaier: Anabaptist Theologian*, 257.
192. *HS*, 257.
193. *HS*, 257.
194. *HS*, 258. *PY*, 171; *HS*, 168, Cf. *PY*, 294; *HS*, 269 and *PY*, 177; *HS*, 173, Cf. *PY*,

are taken from the preface of the *Dialogue*, not from the body of the text, and *On Infant Baptism*. This could imply that the preface to the *Dialogue* and the text of *On Infant Baptism* were written nearer to one another than the body of the *Dialogue* and the text of *On Infant Baptism*.

Bergsten's illustrations of common usage between *On Infant Baptism* and *Old and New Teachers* all relate to the citation of the church fathers and to Oecolampad's work.[195] What should also be noted is the variation of Hubmaier's fundamental hermeneutical principle concerning obedience to the commands of God. This modification of his principle occurs in *On Infant Baptism* and the preface to *Old and New Teachers*, the latter completed by July 21, 1526. This similarity of content again suggests that *On Infant Baptism* was revised in its final form after Hubmaier's arrival in Nikolsburg.

Hubmaier writes in *On Infant Baptism*, "What is not commanded in Scripture is already forbidden in those matters concerning the honor of God and the salvation of our souls."[196] This very closely resembles the statement in the preface to *Old and New Teachers*, "Whatever Christ has not commanded in those things which concern the honor of God and salvation is already forbidden.[197] It also echoes an earlier passage from *On the Christian Baptism:* "For it is not prohibited anywhere in explicit words that we do these things [i.e. baptize a dog or donkey, circumcise little girls, mumble prayers, hold vigils for the dead etc]. Realize what a nice double popery we would set up again if it were acceptable to juggle outside the Word of God in those matters which concern God and the souls."[198]

In contrast to his previous statements concerning the commands and prohibitions of God that had no restrictions, this phrase limits this principle for his hermeneutic only to those matters that relate to salvation and the honor of God. The context in which Hubmaier makes this statement is in response to Oecolampad's introduction of Augustine's dispute with the Pelagians. Marshalling together a collection of texts with which to support this principle, Hubmaier argues that the commands of Scripture that are to be observed are those things that God has planted (Matt 15:13), which

---

279; *HS*, 260.

195. *HS*, 257.

196. *PY*, 280. "Was nit gebotten ist in der schrift, ist schon verbotten in den dingen, so die eer Gottes vnd vnser seel selikait betreffen." *HS*, 261.

197. *PY*, 248. "Was Christus nit geboten hat in denen dingen, so die eer Gottes vnd seligkayt antreffen, das selb ist schon verbotten." *HS*, 229.

198. *PY*, 136. Cf. *HS*, 152.

he equates with the gospel. All those things not contained in the gospel are a curse, as Paul says (Gal 1:8), and those who teach them are the lying masters Peter speaks of (2 Pet 2:1) who face the apocalyptic plagues (Rev 22:18) if they teach anything other than those things that Christ commands (Matt 28:20). He challenges Oecolampad, "Either you must point out with a clear Scripture where God has instituted infant baptism or it must be rooted out."[199]

Here in succinct form are the two governing principles that drive Hubmaier's hermeneutic: 1) that a clear Word of Scripture is required if a work is to be considered good and 2) that what is not commanded in the gospel is forbidden.

Hubmaier adds to these a further limitation with regard to water baptism. Since water baptism is a New Testament ceremony, he rejects outright any attempt to use Old Testament illustrations as symbols of this ceremony: "Water baptism is a ceremony of the New Testament. Therefore I demand of you a clear word out of the New Testament with which you bring to us this infant baptism."[200] This marks a further distancing from the Old Testament that was seen developing in his *Dialogue*. There the division between the two Testaments was seen in the manner of his use of the New Testament texts and his rejection of all Old Testament allusions to circumcision as the forerunner of baptism as "shadows." Any Old Testament illustrations used for baptism other than Noah and the ark, which has a specific New Testament text to support it, are erroneous. Hubmaier now considers a text relevant to the debate over infant baptism only if it comes from the New Testament.

He goes on to ridicule Oecolampad's constant citation of the church fathers instead of Scripture, and then demands that Oecolampad gather together Scriptures on infant baptism, as Hubmaier did with the Scriptures on believers' baptism in *On the Christian Baptism*, "then we will both consider them against each other and will soon agree."[201] This comparison of texts is a fundamental method of Hubmaier's hermeneutic. For the first time however, Hubmaier makes it clear that there are conditions for the choice of texts that are to be compared.

Underlying this challenge is Hubmaier's continuing confidence that the Scriptures correctly preached are clear and that both the individual and local congregation will judge that he has correctly interpreted them.

199. *PY*, 280; *HS*, 261.
200. *PY*, 288; *HS*, 265.
201. *PY*, 291; *HS*, 267.

We find this attitude reflected in his closing statement of *Old and New Teachers*: "And if the churches are instructed rightly in the Word and thoroughly, they will themselves beseech and desire that everything be uprooted and abolished that is against God and which he has not planted."[202] Infant baptism is one such practice God has not planted.

These developments in Hubmaier's thought do not, however, see him develop new arguments rejecting infant baptism. In this respect Bergsten is correct to say that there are "hardly any new arguments" in *On Infant Baptism*.[203] However, there is one area of argument that Hubmaier does develop. It was only mentioned in passing in his *Recantation at Zurich*, but here, in response to Oecolampad's arguments, Hubmaier gives greater attention to the proposition that faith and love must act as the final interpreters of Scripture.

Oecolampad used the themes of faith and love to attack Hubmaier for rejecting infant baptism. He argued that by rejecting infant baptism Hubmaier was teaching schism, and this was plainly against love and faith.[204] Hubmaier had indicated that he was persuaded by this argument at Zurich when it was presented to him by Jud, Myconius, and Hofmeister, consequently dropping his insistence on believers' baptism.[205] From the safety of Nikolsburg he now totally rejects this argument. The unity of the church is not the primary consideration as Oecolampad would insist through this method of interpretation. Rather it is truth that is all important. In this renewed emphasis on the truth Hubmaier again reflects the foundational principle of the Swiss Brethren as it was stated by Grebel.[206]

Hubmaier demonstrates this primary concern for truth in his response to Oecolampad's first challenge that Hubmaier's teaching is against true love. He employs a form of syllogism to demonstrate that water baptism is not against love. He argues that if the Scriptures show "that water baptism was instituted for the instructed and believers and not for cradle babies, then it is the truth." He uses 1 Cor 13:6 as a proof text, "love

---

202. *PY*, 263; *HS*, 240.

203. *HS*, 257.

204. *PY*, 278, 281; *HS*, 259, 262.

205. *PY*, 151.

206. Harder, *Sources of Swiss Anabaptism*, 288. Grebel wrote to Thomas Müntzer: "Pay no attention to the apostasy or to the unchristian forbearance, which the very learned foremost evangelical preachers established as an actual idol and planted throughout the world. It is far better that a few be correctly instructed through the Word of God and believe and live tight in virtues and practices than that many believe deceitfully out of adulterated false doctrine."

rejoices in the truth," and concludes, "how now is truth against love?"[207] He goes on to assert that the love Oecolampad refers to must be "worldly love, which cannot suffer divine love, for its works are evil. Therefore it hates the light."

Oecolampad's second application of this principle of faith and love is directed against the schism that results from teaching believers' baptism.[208] Here Hubmaier counters that to teach baptism and the Lord's Supper correctly is to correctly teach faith and love. He appeals to "the baptismal vow and pledge of love;" that is, to the faith that precedes water baptism and the pledge of love for all other Christians. This understanding of love is integral to Hubmaier's teaching on the Lord's Supper. To strengthen his case Hubmaier then focuses on faith. Using Rom 14:23 as his proof text, that "works that do not flow out of faith are sin," he then proposes that infant baptism is a work without faith, for faith flows from the Word of God (Rom 10:17).[209] He leaves unstated in this instance what he has said plainly many times before, that infants are incapable of receiving instruction from the Word of God and therefore cannot have the prerequisite faith for water baptism.

Later in the work, he responds to Weissenburger who appeals to the faith of the church as the prerequisite faith that infants have. Hubmaier rejects this outright, declaring it to be an appeal to a foreign faith. Any appeal to a foreign faith would mean that "people would be saved by the faith of another."[210] To prove the necessity of each individual believing, Hubmaier cites the sequence of texts Hab 2:4; Rom 1:17; Mark 16:16; Matt 16:18. Faith is the response of the individual who confesses Jesus is Lord, and it is on this confession of faith that the church is built. Faith is not built on the church. In the preface to *Old and New Teachers*, we find the same theme expanded by references to 1 Cor 3:11–12; John 1:1,14. Here Hubmaier identifies the foundation as the gospel, which is to be orally confessed by the believer.

Though his arguments are not new, they do have a new focus for their attack, and this is important to note as it demonstrates that Hubmaier had given further thought to the place of love and faith as a means for interpreting Scripture, and had rejected them for his hermeneutic. What is also

---

207. *PY*, 278; *HS*, 259.
208. *PY*, 281; *HS*, 262.
209. *PY*, 282; *HS*, 262.
210. *PY*, 290; *HS*, 266.

Balthasar Hubmaier and the Clarity of Scripture

important to observe in this sharp exchange is Hubmaier's willingness to pursue truth at the expense of unity and peace in the church.

Previously, Hubmaier has simply maintained that his teaching on believers' baptism does not bring about schism and sectarianism. For the first time, he gathers together Scripture to demonstrate that there must be divisions so that the truth can be identified. His collection of references makes the point that when Christ came he brought a sword and not peace and that contention and division in one household followed (Luke 2:34; Matt 10:34; Luke 12:52f). Divisions are not due to the truth, but rather to the fault of our own wickedness. To illustrate this he cites the case of Herod and the infant Jesus. It was Herod who was guilty of the murder of the innocent children, not the new born Christ (Matt 2:16ff).[211]

Later he chastises Oecolampad for accusing the Anabaptists of "grafting" themselves "to the devil." "If you look to the only master in the heavens and to truth itself with a gentle and eager-to-learn heart, then you will avoid such scolding and shameful words."[212] Here the focus on the paramount importance of the truth is linked to the attitude of heart with which one seeks it. This echoes Zwingli's statements in *On Clarity* regarding the attitude of the heart that is required of those who are to read Scripture aright. The inevitable triumph of the truth is expressed by Hubmaier in his use of his famous epitaph "truth is immortal" in his first response of the dialogue with Oecolampad.[213]

There is a short section in this work where Hubmaier responds to Oecolampad's assertion that children do not first need to be instructed in the Word of God before baptism because they are "without all sin and unspotted."[214] Here Hubmaier has significantly altered what Oecolampad said, replacing "own sin" with "all sin." In this way he can accuse Oecolampad of being seduced by Zwingli and having fallen into the same error as the Zurich reformer on the subject of original sin. Hubmaier does nothing more than cite his usual texts Job 3:3; Ps 51:7; Jer 20:14, with the added support of Eph 2:3; 1 Cor 15:22, to prove that children are subject to the effects of original sin.[215] He goes on to charge that Zwingli "fights for godless infant baptism with pen, teaching, and executioner against

---

211. *PY*, 278; *HS*, 260.
212. *PY*, 281; *HS*, 262.
213. *PY*, 277; *HS*, 259.
214. *PY*, 284; *HS*, 263.
215. *PY*, 284; *HS*, 263.

recognized truth."²¹⁶ From this initial error, Hubmaier claims that Zwingli subsequently falls into three others: that original sin is no sin, that Paul did not speak with careful rhetoric about sin, and that Eve was a most unhappy symbol.²¹⁷ These intolerable errors Zwingli has published in his letter to Rhegius, and that "scholarly doctor" has shown Zwingli his errors.

This polemical attack on Zwingli must have been written after September 1526 when Zwingli's reply to Rhegius was published. It does not further the discussion on baptism, nor does it add anything new to Hubmaier's understanding of the place of children in relation to salvation. Nevertheless, it does demonstrate the late completion of this work. However, the bulk of the work may well have been completed by the time Hubmaier wrote the preface to the *Old and New Teachers*, as there are a number of significant new phrases in this work that are reproduced almost exactly in the preface of that work dated July 21, 1526.

This work is also significant for the emphasis that Hubmaier places on the simplicity and clarity of his speech, compared to the complexity and darkening effect of the speech of his opponents. His final words in this work relate to this theme: "I acknowledge all of you are highly educated, but I have spoken in simplicity. My speech should always be so because the carpenter's Son, who never went to any school, has commanded me to speak in this way and to write such things with the pen he himself cut with his carpenter's axe."²¹⁸ Here the conflict between the educated interpreter of Scripture and those who claim to read and understand simply what the text has to say is clearly described. He remarks that Christ himself went to no school, one example from the life of Christ that Hubmaier could not emulate as he was a Doctor of Theology.²¹⁹ Rather than seeking to legitimize his own educational status by this example from the life of Christ, Hubmaier seeks to support the simple interpretation of Scripture. This reinforces Hubmaier's hermeneutical focus on the words and actions of Christ as normative for the interpreter of Scripture.

---

216. *PY*, 285; *HS*, 263. The reference to the executioner probably indicates that Hubmaier had in mind his own treatment at the hands of the Zurich reformer.

217. No doubt Hubmaier's reference to Paul not using "careful rhetoric" would have drawn from Luther the same stinging rebuke as he gave to Erasmus's use of this phrase.

218. *HS*, 269. My own translation. Cf. *PY*, 294–95.

219. It may also reflect a subtly different application of the text that Christ has chosen to make his mysteries known to the simple and not the wise (Matt 11:25), a text used by Zwingli in his earlier dispute with the Catholic authorities, and in turn used against him by the Zurich Anabaptists. Snyder, "Word and Power," 269.

On Infant Baptism is then a transitional text in Hubmaier's development showing clear links with works he wrote in Waldshut; reflections on his time of captivity in Zurich; and his arrival in Nikolsburg, which provided him with security to write boldly again on the issue of infant baptism.

Use of Scripture

His usage of Scripture and interpretation of texts remain consistent with his previous works. There are a total of twelve Old Testament quotations and references. One is a general reference to Exod 8 in relation to Origen's use of this passage as previously cited in *Old and New Teachers,* and two references to Oecolampad's use of Exod 19:8 and 24:6–8 to provide an Old Testament image of baptism, which Hubmaier rejects out of hand. He also rejects Zwingli's reference to Gen 41:2–3 where he argues that *est* should be replaced by *significat* in the Lord's Supper. There occur the now familiar proof texts to support the concept of original sin (Job 3:3; Ps 51:7; Jer 20:14f), along with Deut 1:39 which indicates that infants know neither good nor evil. He cites Exod 20:23ff and its parallel in Deut 5:7ff as supporting texts in his defense that the debate over baptism is not about water but about the earnest command of God, just as making idols is not about wood and stone, but idolatry, which is against the earnest command of God.

He inflates his Old Testament references by giving the origin of Paul's statement in Rom 1:17; that is, Hab 2:4, though he glosses that quotation by adding that the righteous will live by his own faith. The final Old Testament reference is to Isa 30:1 which is a warning of woe to those who take counsel but not of their God. This he links with a reference to Matt 15:13, using it as a supporting text and warning to those who would do that which God has not commanded; in this instance, baptize infants.

There are sixty-six references to New Testament texts that stand on their own or accompany quotations or allusions. There are a further twelve quotations and allusions that Hubmaier uses without references. The book most often cited is Acts. Of the twenty-six references to Acts, eighteen are associated with long sequences of texts by which Hubmaier seeks to provide clear evidence for the practice of believers' baptism by the apostles. In this work Hubmaier uses for the first time references to the baptism of Paul, Acts 9:18 and 22:16. He also introduces a reference to Acts 8:1–4 in association with the familiar text Acts 16:15, to prove that women were mentioned by name as having been baptized. He does this in response to Geyerfalk's claim that women who were baptized were not mentioned by name in the Scriptures.[220] The text in Acts 8 does not however specifically name Samaritan women, though it can be inferred. The other references to Acts that appear for the first time are those that are used as historical examples to support Hubmaier's contention that the Word of Christ has long been challenged as something new and spoken against (Acts 17:18; 28:22).

Texts taken from Mark relate to either 16:16, Hubmaier's foundational proof text for faith followed by baptism, or 10:13f, where he challenges Zwingli's new translation of the text, "of theirs is the kingdom of heaven." However, Habermaier uses one reference to Mark 1:27 to identify his own treatment at the hands of the religious authorities with the treatment Christ received.

Unexpectedly, only three of the fourteen references to Matthew refer to Matt 28:18–20. Three citations are to Matt 15:13, his other foundational text that describes what is commanded by God and therefore to be obeyed. Two references to Matt 16:18 describe the confession of faith on which the church is built. One reference, Matt 5:19, is the synoptic parallel of Mark 10:14. The remaining citations are used to support Hubmaier's new insistence on the divisions that preaching the gospel brings. Here he paraphrases Matt 12:30 so that it reads: "for what is not with the Scripture is against the Scripture," to counter Oecolampad's claim that papal abuses and infant baptism are two different things. He also links Christ's comment that he came to bring a sword not peace with the historical example of Herod, who killed the innocents while seeking to destroy the infant Jesus (Matt 10:34; 2:16).

This is not a new method in Hubmaier's hermeneutic, rather a new selection of texts demonstrating that he has become convinced that the unity of the church that the Basel and Zurich reformers urged was built on a false hermeneutic of faith and love. For him truth is the focus, truth that is clearly stated in Scripture through the words of Christ who speaks on behalf of his Father in heaven. This is clearly demonstrated by the way Hubmaier links the familiar verse Matt 15:13 with Matt 17:5, where the Father directs the disciples to listen to his Son.

There is also a continuing use of texts as polemical warnings against those who reject his interpretation of the baptismal texts. In this case he uses the words of Jesus from the Sermon on the Mount, Matt 5:19,

---

220. *PY*, 284; *HS*, 263. Geyerfalk was the Novice Master of the Augustinian Order at Basel.

"whoever loosens the smallest commandment will be called the smallest in the kingdom of God."[221] Again Hubmaier demonstrates his preoccupation with the commands of God that are to be obeyed.

The three references Hubmaier cites from John provide no new material or usages; however, two of the three allusions that have been identified do demonstrate his new interest in acknowledging that preaching the gospel brings false accusations and unjust treatment. Here he focuses on the questioning of Christ by the high priest. Jesus is portrayed as teaching a new gospel and suffers unjustly for it (John 18:22–23). Hubmaier identifies the Anabaptists with Christ in this unjust suffering for the truth, once again using his hermeneutic of personal identification. The other allusion is to John 5:39, a standard proof text that the reformers all used to direct their opponents to search the Scriptures in which people will find Christ.

All the other references and allusions or quotations reflect earlier usages of texts, or simply add newly discovered texts to bolster his arguments for believers' baptism.

Summary

Hubermaier sharply challenges the hermeneutic of faith and love in this work. He categorically rejects Oecolampad's view that faith and love protect the unity of the church. Instead, Hubmaier for the first time insists that pursuit of the truth, despite the consequences to the outward unity of the church, is what matters.

Hubmaier also explicitly modifies his appeal to obedience to the commands of God as fundamental to his hermeneutic. Obedience to the command of God is now required in all those matters that concern the honor of God and the salvation of souls. Practices of the church may well be considered matters outside these parameters, and therefore open to speculation.

The attack on Zwingli concerning the doctrine of original sin does not develop Hubmaier's hermeneutic, though it does supply some evidence of the hostility Hubmaier felt towards Zwingli after his experience of torture in Zurich.

The strong appeal of this work is to simplicity of speech and understanding of the Scriptures. Hubmaier contrasts his own desire to speak with simplicity so that every person can hear and understand the Word of

---

221. *PY*, 292; *HS*, 268.

Against Those who Mutilate the Word of God

God, with the learning of his opponents, who use their learning to gloss the Scripture and obscure the simple clear meaning of the text of Scripture.

SUMMARY OF WRITINGS FROM LATE 1525 TO JULY 1526, PUBLISHED 1526–27

The above analysis demonstrates that the development in Hubmaier's hermeneutic at this time occurred principally in response to the debate he entered into over infant baptism. There is also evidence of the effect his imprisonment in Zurich after the fall of Waldshut to the Austrian authorities had on some aspects of his hermeneutic.

Of primary importance is Hubmaier's reiteration of his foundational principle that only what God commands is to be obeyed and that the negative of the command is included in the command as a prohibition. This point is made repeatedly in his *Dialogue* and in *On Infant Baptism,* being qualified in the latter by the inclusion of the phrase, "in those matters concerning the honor of God and the salvation of our souls."[222] In both works Hubmaier contrasts this interpretive presupposition with the position to which Zwingli has moved. Hubmaier asserts Zwingli has learned his new position from Fabri at the First Zurich Disputation, and that Oecolampad has learned from Zwingli. Zwingli now defends the position that those things that are not forbidden are permitted, an argument that Fabri employed to justify traditions and ceremonies in January 1523.

By focusing on the commands of God, Hubmaier comes to a more literalistic interpretation of Scripture. If there is no specific command for infant baptism, then to practice it is adding to the Word of God, and that is judged by God as sinful. However, this emphasis on the commands of God does not lead to a literalism similar to that of Grebel and the Swiss Brethren. Grebel had shown his literalism at the Second Zurich Disputation when he had insisted that ordinary bread be used at the Lord's Supper and not wafers, that water not be added to the wine, and that each participant should take the bread individually, and not have it placed in their mouth, as in the Mass.[223] Zwingli's responses show that he clearly felt these things fell into the category of *adiaphora,* and could be dealt with at the discretion of individual congregations.

Hubmaier does not show any tendency to the Swiss Brethren's narrow type of literalism. Nevertheless, he does engage Zwingli in the debate

222. *PY, 280; HS,* 261.
223. Harder, *Sources of Swiss Anabaptism,* 247.

about *adiaphorism,* agreeing that water in itself is of no significance, but arguing that to reject the command of Christ to baptize with water those who confess their faith is to despise the Word of God.

We also see Hubmaier develop his hermeneutic by considering the role of faith and love in the process of interpretation. At Zurich during his imprisonment he undertakes a recantation of his position of infant baptism partly on the strength of the argument that love must take precedence as an interpretative consideration so that the unity of the church can be maintained. However, in his writing against Oecolampad he specifically rejects the appeal to faith and love as hermeneutical rules that override the demand to demonstrate infant baptism with a clear command in Scripture. Hubmaier maintains that truth is the crucial issue, and that disunity is not the consequence of the truth being proclaimed, but of the sinful nature of humanity.

In the debate over infant baptism Hubmaier can be seen to ascribe to the New Testament a greater authority than the Old Testament. This attitude, which is implicit in his use of the Old and New Testaments, becomes explicit in *On Infant Baptism* when he challenges Oecolampad to provide New Testament texts for infant baptism as baptism is a New Testament ceremony.[224] This would appear to give greater authority to the New Testament and the words of Jesus than to the sayings of Moses and the prophets in the Old Testament. If this distinction between the two Testaments was considered a general rule in Hubmaier's hermeneutic it would misrepresent him, for he specifies this only with regard to infant baptism. He also makes it plain that Christ speaks through Moses and the prophets, thus giving the Old Testament equal authority to the New through this christocentric understanding of the Word of God.

He maintains his position with regard to the authority of the church fathers, councils, popes, and canon law. These are to be listened to only insofar as they conform to the clear Word of Scripture. What he makes clear by the way he uses passages from the church fathers, popes, and canon law, is that the clear Word of God equals his interpretation of the text under consideration, and that the church fathers cited support his interpretation. He also demonstrates carelessness in his choice of citations from the church fathers, as he often ignores the context from which he takes a passage. This context often contains information that contradicts the point he is seeking to support.

224. *PY,* 288; *HS,* 265.

The clarity of the Word of God continues to feature as a fundamental presupposition in his writings. Not only is the Word of God clear, it is also simply understood. This emphasis on simplicity is placed in opposition to Zwingli's attitude that the Word is complex and requires the work of trained interpreters if the common person is to understand it correctly. Hubmaier maintains his position that the work of the Holy Spirit is necessary for the Word of God to be made alive in the individual believer, a position that Zwingli also held. They differ on how the Holy Spirit makes the Word alive. For Hubmaier, the public proclamation of the Word leads to faith, while for Zwingli, the Spirit can and does act independently of the preached word.

While Hubmaier had maintained that the Word of God was to be interpreted and understood in the context of the congregation, where those educated in theology played an equal part in the process, his position on this point has become less certain. There is now a qualification added to this general proposition, namely that the preacher of the Word divide it to the hearers "pure, clear, and undefiled and distribute it faithfully" so that God's will, which can only be known from Scripture, can be done.[225] The role of the preacher is given greater emphasis than previously as he is now depicted as feeding the congregation. The congregation appears to be more passive than previously depicted in the process of understanding and interpreting the clear Word of God. This attitude to the role of the preacher that Hubmaier exhibits in his writing from prison in Zurich must be balanced against his continuing insistence that the congregation will judge correctly over the issue of baptism if the clear baptismal texts are read and heard by them. Nevertheless, he does begin to give the interpretative role of the preacher more weight than he has done previously.

With regard to the other rules Hubmaier has stated for the correct interpretation of Scripture, they remain unaltered. He still argues for the darker text of Scripture to be interpreted by the clearer text. His use of Scripture shows that the clearer text is frequently the fuller text. He continues to apply the principle of comparing texts of Scripture and considering their context. He does not, however, simply collect texts together and allow them to stand alone without interpretation as he had done in *On the Christian Baptism*. As he does not specifically discuss the role of the original languages in these works it would appear that he continues to allow a role for them in the interpretation of the darker texts of Scripture. He does maintain that the texts on water baptism do not require any language

---

225. *PY*, 243; *HS*, 222.

other than German to be used for their meaning to be clearly understood by his German-speaking congregation.

In the debate with Zwingli he does raise the issue of translations of the Bible. He chastises Zwingli for "ripping apart the seamless robe of Christ," that is Scripture, by his new translation of the Bible. He cites Zwingli's new translation of Mark 10:14, "of theirs is the kingdom of heaven," which he claims should be "of such is the kingdom of heaven." By references Hubmaier makes in these works to various translations of Scripture it is apparent that he generally prefers the old Latin text to the newer Wittenberg and Zurich translations.[226]

From his usage of Scripture Hubmaier demonstrates a consistency with his preceding works. He only occasionally uses parables and typology in his arguments. The most striking example of this occurs in his *A Brief "Our Father,"* where he uses the phrase "give us today our daily bread" to facilitate interpreting the bread come down from heaven as being the Word of God, that is Scripture and not Christ, that must be rightly divided if the will of God is to be done.

In his arguments with Zwingli and Oecolampad in which Hubermaier uses syllogisms, the major or minor proposition of the syllogism is a text of Scripture. He assumes the truth of the text is self-evident. This proof-text approach to Scripture is used not only by Hubmaier but also by the Reformed pastors and the Swiss Brethren. Among the Swiss Brethren it is almost the only way that Scripture is used, demonstrating that they understood Scripture to be clear and its truth self-evident. With Zwingli and the other Reformed pastors, using verses of Scripture as proof texts was only one of a wide variety of uses of Scripture. Zwingli urged consideration of the differing literary genre of Scripture. This allowed him to interpret Scripture by describing particular texts of Scripture as belonging to different literary categories. Thus, by identifying synecdoche as a legitimate literary trope in Scripture he could argue that all those texts of Scripture that spoke of households or families included children. If Scripture said that the members of a household were baptized, then the children must also have been baptized, even though they were not specifically mentioned. Hubmaier does not reject outright the consideration of literary categories. However, he does not allow them to override his fundamental hermeneutical principle that a clear word or command of God in Scripture is required if some action is to be taken. Thus, he rejects Zwingli's use of synecdoche when he applies it to baptism, for in Hubmaier's opinion

---

226. *PY*, 242; *HS*, 222.

Against Those who Mutilate the Word of God

God has given a clear command for water baptism, and Zwingli is only making dark to the common man what is already clear and simple.

Hubmaier introduces for the first time in these works his hermeneutic of personal identification. This is best seen in his works written from the Wellenberg Tower, where he identifies the emotions and suffering of himself and the other Anabaptist prisoners with those of Christ and the first-century Christians. Scripture is thus applied to the life of the contemporary Christian without seeking either the literal sense of the text through grammatical and historical considerations, or by applying any of the other three medieval senses of Scripture.

There is also a sharper polemical tone in his work, which reflects the treatment he experienced at Zurich. This is reflected in the selection of particular texts of Scripture that focus on dire warnings and the wrath of God against His enemies, which Hubmaier applies to his opponents. There are other instances where Hubmaier takes a text in which the opponents of the gospel are castigated and uses it against his own opponents, for example, 2 Pet 2:1: they are "lying teachers."

It also becomes evident in the above analysis that Hubmaier has by this stage gathered together a concordance of scriptural references that are the basis for his interpretation of Scripture.

Fundamental to his hermeneutic are those references that relate to faith and the commands of God. His proof text for faith proceeding from the preached Word is Rom 10:10–11, while the necessity of oral confession of faith that Jesus is the Christ is supported by reference to Peter's confession in Matt 16:18.

In his argument to establish that only what God commands is to be obeyed, and that the command includes the prohibition, he links together the following series of texts: Matt 15:13; 17:5; John 14:6; Deut 5:32; Isa 29:13. He juxtaposes this topic with consideration of the error of adding to Scripture, something which is anathema. For scriptural support of his position he refers to Deut 4:2; 12:32; Isa 30:1–2; Matt 5:17ff; Gal 3:15; Heb 12:29; and as a warning of the consequences such actions would incur he refers to Matt 5:19; Rev 22:18.

The sole authority of Scripture to judge in matters of faith and practice is supported by references to John 5:39 (the key text), in association with Rom 15:4; 2 Tim 3:15; John 2:12.

With regard to the topic of water baptism Hubmaier uses as his proof texts Matt 28:18–20; Mark 16:15–16; Rom 6:3–4; 1 Pet 3:20–21; and Heb 10:22. In support of the apostolic practice of water baptism he cites Acts

2:38–41; 8:35–38; 10:44–48; 11:13–18; 16:14–15,32–33; 19:1–7. He gives the following additional examples in *On Infant Baptism,* Acts 8:1–4; 9:1–19; 22:1–16. It should be noted that Mark 16:16 is the crucial text in this debate for Hubmaier as it is the clearer text that explains Matt 28:18–20 more fully.

Hubmaier also has compiled a series of texts that deal with children and original sin. Here the Old Testament dominates his choice and frequency of use. He proves that children are subject to the influence of original sin by citing Job 3:3; Ps 51:5; Jer 20:14. He supports this by references to Eph 2:3; 1 Cor 15:22, to show that children are by nature after the fall children of wrath, not of God. He does however propose that children before the age of reason, for which he does not give a specific date, do not know good or evil and are therefore not guilty of their own sin until they do know good and evil. His proof text for this proposition is Deut 1:39. He also maintains that it is not possible to live a sinless life after baptism, citing 1 John 1:8–10, a position and reference he holds in common with Zwingli.

The spiritual rebirth, which Hubmaier considers absolutely necessary before baptism takes place, finds its scriptural support in John 1:1, 12–14; 3:3–7; 1 Pet 1:3. Here Hubmaier sees the work of the Holy Spirit and the preached Word inextricably linked, by his identification of Christ as the Living Word of God being now embodied in the Scriptures as they are read and heard.

7

Making a Patchwork of Scripture
(Writings at Nikolsburg from July 1526 to July 1527)

INTRODUCTION

AFTER HIS RELEASE IN April 1526, Hubmaier went to Constance where he met with others who had fled Waldshut prior to its capitulation to the Austrian forces in December 1525. A Constance council member, Herr von Allopfenn had written a note to him on behalf of the Waldshut refugees about the time of his first interview with Zwingli and the other Zurich preachers. In it, he expressed their concern for their pastor and encouraged him to remain "patient and confident that God would help him in his time."[1]

Though his visit to Constance was only short, Hubmaier did have at least one conversation with the evangelical pastors of that city. In Zwingli's report of the conversation, he alleges that Hubmaier claimed to have defeated him on the question of baptism.[2] It is probable that it was here at Constance that Hubmaier retrieved the draft copies of his writings against Zwingli and Oecolampad, as well as his list of references on baptism taken from the church fathers.

Torsten Bergsten asserts that Hubmaier arrived in Augsburg at the beginning of May 1526. There he met with the evangelical pastors of the

---

1. *PY*, 154.
2. Bergsten, *Balthasar Hubmaier: Anabaptist Theologian*, 309.

city, and held discussions with them. Urbanus Rhegius, the Reformer of that city, who had been a fellow student of Hubmaier's at Freiburg and Ingolstadt, was included among the group. Again, Hubmaier referred to his ill-treatment at Zurich. Peter Gynoräus, who was attending at the invitation of Hubmaier, objected to Hubamier's claim that he had been tortured. Gynoräus was in Augsburg, having been expelled from Basel, and was reporting to Zwingli on the debates concerning interpretations of the Lord's Supper that were taking place in Augsburg.[3] It was also in Augsburg that Hubmaier became involved in a "spiritualist conventicle." Ludwig Hätzer had led this group until he was expelled from the city in the fall of 1525. He had been succeeded as leader by Hans Denck, who had previously met Anabaptists in St Gallen but had not joined them. During his two-month stay in Augsburg, Hubmaier transformed this group into a "congregationalist church," perhaps baptizing Denck, who in turn baptized Hans Hut.[4] It is, however, certain that Hubmaier worked closely with Denck during his time in Augsburg, establishing a relationship that has a definite influence on Hubmaier's later work on the freedom of the will.[5]

Hubmaier was not forced to leave Augsburg, as were Hätzer before him, and Denck after him. Nevertheless, he did leave, and arrived in the town of Nikolsburg (present-day Mikulov) in Moravia some time prior to July 21, 1526. Bergsten suggests that one of the appeals of Nikolsburg was that it was not at that time under Hapsburg control. As such, it offered a place of safety for one who was considered both a heretic and an insurrectionist. Not even the free city of Augsburg could give him that protection.[6]

At the time of his arrival, Nikolsburg had already been influenced by the evangelical preachers Hans Spittelmaier and Oswald Glaidt. There had also been a recent dialogue between the evangelicals and Utraquists.

Jan Dubcansky had arranged the dialogue in an attempt to unify these two groups. Though these groups did agree on seven theses that demonstrate unity on such issues as preaching the Word of God, marriage of priests, the removal of all things outside the Scriptures, and understanding the Lord's Supper as a remembrance feast, they did not come

3. Ibid., 311.

4. There is some dispute whether Hubmaier baptized Denck in Augsburg. Bergsten maintains that Hubmaier "apparently" baptized Denck. Bergsten, *Balthasar Hubmaier: Anabaptist Theologian*, 354. Packull strenuously denies this to give added weight to his theory of the independent origins of South German-Austrian Anabaptism. Packull, "Denck's Alleged Baptism," 327–38.

5. Bergsten, *Balthasar Hubmaier: Anabaptist Theologian*, 354–55.

6. Ibid., 311.

together as one group.[7] The theological influence of Zwingli is evident in the understanding of the Lord's Supper.

A further group, the *unitas fratrum*, or Bohemian Brethren, did not accept the Zwinglian view of the Lord's Supper, preferring to support Martin Luther's understanding of the real presence in the Eucharist. This made productive dialogue between them and Hubmaier, and later with the Anabaptists, highly improbable. That Hubmaier sought to convince them of his understanding of the Lord's Supper is seen in his dedication of his work *Form of Christ's Supper* (1526) to a leading noble of the Bohemian Brethren, Burian Sobek von Kornice.[8] However, Jarold Knox Zeman does not agree with Bergsten's view of Hubmaier's detailed knowledge of the Bohemian Brethren or the Czech Reformation, stating that Hubmaier's relationship to them was characterized by "ignorance and indifference."[9]

Nikolsburg was then representative of the predominantly German-speaking parts of Moravia, showing the influences of both the Lutheran and Zwinglian reformations that were seeking integration with the ongoing expressions of the earlier Hussite Reformation. The political and religious independence of the Lords of Liechtenstein, Leonhard and his cousin Hans, provided the secure setting in which such a diversity of religious views could peacefully coexist.

Bergsten concludes that by the time of Hubmaier's arrival in Nikolsburg, the Reformation there had received a Zwinglian stamp through the work of Spittelmaier and Glaidt. It was on this foundation that Hubmaier built his second Anabaptist church.[10]

OLD AND NEW TEACHERS ON BELIEVERS' BAPTISM

(Preface and Second edition, after July 1526)[11]

Analysis

The preface to both editions of this work is essentially the same. Even the date, July 21, 1526, is retained in the second edition. The major differences

---

7. Ibid., 317–18.
8. *PY*, 407; *HS*, 364.
9. Zeman, *Anabaptists and Czech Brethren*, 311.
10. Bergsten, *Balthasar Hubmaier: Anabaptist Theologian*, 319.
11. *PY*, 246–49, 264–74; *HS*, 241–55.

are in spelling, the vast majority of changes being the lengthening of shortened endings (sixty-two occurrences); for example, "e" to "en" (thirty-five examples), and in capitalization (sixty-one examples). There are also three printing errors, one of which occurs in the margin and gives John 14 as John 1. These changes in appearance do not change the content of the preface.

Hubmaier dedicates the work to Martin Göschl, formerly suffragan bishop of Olmutz, but now evangelical preacher at Nikolsburg. Göschl had been expelled from Olmutz because of his evangelical views.[12] In this work, Hubmaier skillfully uses the existing debate over the practice of the Czech Utraquists and the German-influenced Bohemian Brethren to admit children to the Lord's Supper, in order to introduce his own teaching against infant baptism. He notes the practice of those who admit children to the Lord's Supper (the Utraquists) as an act done out of "ignorance," and that they have only one argument against the Germans who oppose them: that the Germans baptize their children.[13] To counter their position the Germans argue that the Lord's Supper requires self-examination, something that children cannot do, basing their opinion on 1 Cor 11:28. To this the Czechs reply that children cannot believe and confess faith prior to water baptism, something that is equally demanded from Scripture. Hubmaier has the Czech protagonists cite his now familiar sequence of texts as proof of the need of prior faith and confession to water baptism (Matt 28:19f; Mark 16:16; Acts 2:38,41; 8:12, 38; 10:47–48; 11:16; 16:15, 33; 18:8; 22:16; Heb 1:22; 1 Pet 3:21).[14]

He rehearses the objection of his Zwinglian-influenced opponents, the Bohemian Brethren, who argue for faith that precedes baptism as an infused faith or foreign faith. He includes the faith of the church in his list of foreign faiths that are attributed to the child. Hubmaier had first noted foreign faiths in his work *On Infant Baptism*. Again he rejects foreign faiths since such faith does not come from the individual on the basis of the preached Word of God. He cites as the proof text for his position Rom 10:17[15] and includes a new thought at this point. He cites Augustine's famous dictum *"Euangelio non crederem"* ("I would not believe the gospel etc.") only to refute it, saying, "For if I did not believe the gospel I would

---

12. Bergsten, *Balthasar Hubmaier: Anabaptist Theologian*, 319–20.
13. *PY*, 246; *HS*, 227.
14. *PY*, 247; *HS*, 228.
15. *PY*, 247; *HS*, 228.

never believe the church, since the church is built on the gospel and not the gospel on the church."[16]

To support this view he cites first Paul and then Christ in 1 Cor 3:11 and Matt 16:18 to argue that the foundation to which Paul refers is none other than the individual's confession of faith that Jesus is the Christ the Son of the living God. This is the confession Peter made and that Jesus identified as the rock on which he would build his church.[17] This view of the confession as the basis on which the church is built was also introduced in *On Infant Baptism*, though not with reference to 1 Cor 3:11. Hubmaier continues to insist on the individual's confession of faith as the foundation of the church by using 1 Cor 3 and linking it to John 1:1, 14. Here he identifies the preached Word of God with God himself, who became human in Christ.

Hubmaier also notes the objection of those who say that since Christ has not forbidden infant baptism it can be safely administered to children. To this he answers with a phrase, "whatever Christ has not commanded in those things which concern the honor of God and salvation is already forbidden."[18] This phrase is very similar to his proposition cited in *On Infant Baptism*.[19] He replaces the earlier more general reference to those things commanded in Scripture with the more specific reference to the commands of Christ. This is in keeping with the immediately preceding identification of the preached Word of God with Christ.

As in the section where this statement occurs in *On Infant Baptism*, Hubmaier defends his hermeneutical principle by referring to Matt 15:13 as his central proof text. In *On Infant Baptism*, he begins with the Matthew reference and supports it with dire warnings from Gal 1:8f.; 2 Pet 2:1; Rev 22:18, and the command to go, teach, and baptize of Matt 28:19f.; while in this preface letter he begins with the sequence of references Luke 11:23; John 14:6; Deut 5:32, then adds 2 Pet 2:1; Rev 3:9; Matt 15:13; Mark 16:15.[20] The first sequence of texts focuses on the commands of God that

16. *PY*, 247; *HS*, 228.
17. *PY*, 247–48; *HS*, 228.
18. *PY*, 248; *HS*, 229.
19. *PY*, 280; *HS*, 261.

20. Bergsten does not give a verse for Luke 11 (*HS*, 243), while Pipkin and Yoder suggest Luke 11:45–52, the series of woes Jesus pronounces against the scribes and Pharisees. However, Hubmaier uses Luke 11:23 in a similar context at the end of *Old and New Teachers*, where he both quotes and cites the text. This use would suggest that Hubmaier is using this text in the preface, a text that was used by Fabri at Zurich and then by Zwingli against Hubmaier in support of the counter argument that it is

are alone to be obeyed and not to be deviated from in the least. Then there are the warnings against those liars who distort the Word of God, followed by the foundational text of Matt 15:13 that is then illustrated by Mark 16:15. Hubmaier argues that this command to preach the gospel immediately excludes the preaching of all that is not the gospel.[21]

To assist his argument Hubmaier then cites a theological axiom: *"Locus enim arguendi ab autoritate negatiue in Theologia est vrgentissimus"* ["in theology it is most compelling to argue a proof from negative authority"]. He demonstrates this by citing Heb 1:5 and its Old Testament source Ps 2:7, "to which angel has God ever said, 'You are my Son, etc.'" He explains it as follows: "It is as if he wanted to say: 'Since we do not find that in Scripture, then he said it to no one except to his dear Son, etc.' So also, as soon as Christ said to his disciples, 'go forth, teach all people and baptize, etc.' Matt 28:19, it is already forbidden to baptize those who have not yet been instructed in the faith."[22] This is the first time that Hubmaier has supported his argument by using an argument from the negative.

Previously he has insisted that by the "common law of justice" the burden of proof falls to the affirming not the denying. Since Zwingli and Oecolampad affirm infant baptism, they have the burden of proof.[23] He cites this axiom at the conclusion of a section where he rehearses Zwingli's argument against Johann Fabri at the First Zurich Disputation, where Zwingli has denied Fabri's use of Luke 9:50, "whoever is not against you is for you," by referring Fabri to Matt 15:13. However, by his use of this argument from the negative, Hubmaier tacitly approves the view that it is possible to prove the truth of a proposition from the negative.

Hubmaier also reiterates his conviction that the truth takes precedence over the unity of the church. He does this by citing 1 Cor 1:19 on the title page, "there must be divisions among you in order that those who are true may be revealed among you." This reference makes explicit what was implicit in the text of the first edition of this work, that for Hubmaier the unity of the church is no longer paramount; rather it is the declaration of truth that takes precedence. The divisions occurring among evangelical

---

permitted to do what is not forbidden. The Revelation reference is reduced to a footnote by Pipkin and Yoder, while Bergsten suggests verse 9 as the text Hubmaier has in mind, using the word "liar" as the link between 2 Pet 2:1 and this verse.

21. *PY,* 249; *HS,* 229.
22. *PY,* 249; *HS,* 229.
23. *PY,* 184, 283; *HS,* 179, 263.

Making a Patchwork of Scripture

preachers are necessary for they demonstrate to the world at large who is proclaiming the truth of Scripture.

The text of the second edition is expanded by reference to a further twelve teachers from the church's past and nine council decisions and is completely restructured in part one. Hubmaier gives two chronological listings, the first for the church fathers and popes and the second for the council decisions, citing a date for each in the margin. This strict chronology is occasionally disrupted. A major misrepresentation occurs when he attributes to Pope Leo 1 the date 836, when his papacy was between 440 and 461. There are other discrepancies in the dates, which detract from his attempt to show that infant baptism was not supported from the very earliest days of the church. Aeilus Donatus, an early fourth-century rigorist bishop, is dated as 137; Theophylact, an eleventh-century figure, is given the date 189; and Pelagius, early fifth century, is not only incorrectly dated 380, but also is described as the disciple of Augustine.[24] In addition, his numbering of the popes does not coincide with the present numbering used by the Catholic Church.

Nevertheless, it is obviously Hubmaier's intention to demonstrate in this second edition that there is a continuous sequence of witness against the practice of infant baptism from the earliest time of the church.

In the first edition, the evidence that Hubmaier presents can be summarized under five headings: 1) those are baptized who have stopped sinning and demonstrated a change in their life; 2) repentance and faith are necessary before baptism; 3) baptism is a sign that signifies to the recipient the certainty of the resurrection; 4) faith is not enough for salvation, there must be baptism as well; and 5) there must be teaching in the faith prior to baptism.

In the second edition, four new headings are added: 1) baptism was only practiced twice a year; 2) those who have received baptism from heretics must be baptized again, or better for the first time; 3) those unsure of their baptism should be baptized; and 4) children who die without baptism are saved since they are without the guilt of original sin. Only ten of the twenty-one new references come under these new headings, four under each of numbers 1 and 2, and one each under headings 3 and 4. The remainder all provide additional support to the previous headings numbered 2 and 5.

---

24. *PY*, 268; *HS*, 246. There is no indication of the source that Hubmaier uses to establish his dating.

Hubmaier does reduce his quotation of Tertullian, excising his reference to baptism being for those who have already stopped sinning. However, he does not remove his reference to this same theme from his section on Origen. Nevertheless, this topic has been reduced in its significance, as it was the first statement in the main text of the first edition, but is reduced to fifth place in the second. Such a statement about ceasing to sin would leave Hubmaier open to Zwingli's attack that the Anabaptists considered they were sinless and able to live without sin after baptism.

Hubmaier's selection of decrees from various councils does show an increased emphasis on discipleship and discipline; that is, the need for those who are baptized to live a life that shows the fruits of faith so that they are not excluded from the community of the baptized. He cites a decree from the Sixth Council of Carthage, which demonstrates that an examination of those who sought to be baptized took place a long time before the event. The candidates' responses were to include a confession of faith and a statement of "how they should live after baptism and avoid the ban."[25] He also refers to the Seventh Council of Carthage to show that female catechumens were also to be questioned prior to baptism, with the same emphasis on how they should live afterwards.[26]

These references to discipleship and discipline perhaps indicate Hubmaier's growing concern at this early stage about these matters in the church at Nikolsburg. Later it will be seen that these two topics dominate his thinking.

The second section of this later edition, which has references to the new teachers and begins with Desiderius Ersasmus, remains unchanged.

Use of Scripture

Compared with the first edition of this work, only four new biblical references are included in the second edition. The first is to Acts 2:38, where Hubmaier cites Augustine's use of the text to show the need of repentance prior to baptism. The second reference is related to Ambrose of Milan, who argues that the baptism of apostates and heretics does not "heal." To prove this he cites Rom 14:23, that all action not based on faith is sin. As an apostate or heretic has no faith, their baptism is ineffective. Every

---

25. *PY*, 273; *HS*, 249. The decree also included a mandatory period of abstinence from wine and meat that Hubmaier previously noted in his *Dialogue* as not being applicable to cradle babies.

26. *PY*, 273; *HS*, 249.

Making a Patchwork of Scripture

true sacrament requires word and deed; it does not rely on the external act, but on the internal confession of faith. The third reference is simply the expansion of a previous quotation of Basil the Great. Hubmaier now provides the Old Testament reference Gen 7 on which 1 Pet 3:20 draws for the image of the ark as the only symbol of baptism in the Old Testament.

The final new biblical reference comes from Hubmaier's new quotation of Rabanus of Metz, whom he cites in support of his view that instruction in the faith should precede baptism. Rabanus cites John 9:6f to support his contention: "Therefore Christ first covered the eyes of the blind man with mud and spittle and sent him to the water Siloam. . . . It is the same way that the baptizand is instructed in faith beforehand and brought believing to baptism, so that he may know what grace he receives therein and to whom he afterward owes obedience."[27]

Summary

This second edition of *Old and New Teachers,* and the preface letter, do show a continuing development in Hubmaier's selection of biblical material to support his interpretation of Scripture concerning baptism, though he does not change his basic position as previously outlined at the Second Zurich Disputation.

A BRIEF APOLOGIA

(1526)[28]

Setting

It appears that not long after his arrival in Nikolsburg, Hubmaier discovered that his Catholic adversaries were accusing him of a variety of charges. The list of accusations that he faced was an expanded version of charges that he had faced earlier at Waldshut and Schaffhausen.[29] He states:

> Since I am everywhere decried and denounced as a proclaimer of new teachings, alleging that I desecrate the mother of God, reject the saints, destroy prayer, fasting, Sabbaths, confession,

---

27. *PY,* 271; *HS,* 249.
28. *PY,* 296–313; *HS,* 270–83.
29. *PY,* 45; *HS,* 82: "a seducer of the people, seditionary, a Lutheran, a heretic."

Balthasar Hubmaier and the Clarity of Scripture

> that I despise the holy fathers, councils, and human teachings, attach no value to monasteries and priestly vows, nor to singing and reading in church. I make a mockery of extreme unction, which is also called the last baptism, and set up a new rebaptism. I break down altars and deny the flesh and blood in the mass. I am a revolutionary and a seducer of the people; I preach that one should not obey the government; nor pay interest or tithes. I secretly fled Regensburg. In sum: I am the very worst Lutheran arch heretic that one could find.[30]

It has been suggested by Bergsten that Hubmaier was encouraged to respond to these charges by the princes of Liechtenstein to prove his innocence.[31] This view is supported by Hubmaier in the work itself when he writes that he has been "prevailed" upon to write a defense against the accusations by "good lords and friends."[32]

Analysis

This catalogue of doctrinal and political accusations provides Hubmaier with the structure for the first half of his *A Brief Apologia*. He carefully answers each of these charges in the order they appear in the above passage.

He rejects the charge of starting a new teaching, insisting that he only preaches Christ crucified. He goes on to counter the charge by declaring that even Jesus and Paul were both falsely accused of propagating new teachings.[33] It is therefore not the charge that matters but the evidence to substantiate it.

He holds to the perpetual virginity of Mary, calling her blessed because she believed. In support of this view he cites the sequence of texts Matt 1:20; Luke 1:42; John 19:27; 7:14; 9:6. These are standard texts cited by the Catholic Church to support the doctrine of the perpetual virginity of Mary.[34]

With regard to honoring the saints, Hubmaier says he does so. The saints are God's instruments in whom he worked many miracles.[35] How-

---

30. *PY*, 298; *HS*, 273.
31. Bergsten, *Balthasar Hubmaier: Anabaptist Theologian*, 336.
32. *PY*, 307; *HS*, 279.
33. *PY*, 299; *HS*, 273.
34. *PY*, 299; *HS*, 273.
35. *PY*, 299; *HS*, 273. The text Gal 1 that Hubmaier cites does not supply any support for the point he is making.

Making a Patchwork of Scripture

ever, Hubmaier denies that the saints are mediators, as there is only one mediator, intercessor, and helper in our distress, Christ Jesus.[36]

Hubmaier rejects the accusation that he has destroyed prayer, arguing that he teaches that people pray without ceasing as Christ taught his disciples. This does not stop him from stating his displeasure at mumbled prayers that are said with the lips while the heart is nowhere in it. He cites as the proof texts for his opinion Luke 18:1–7; 1 Thess 5:17, and the synoptic parallels of the Lord's Prayer, Matt 6:5ff; Luke 11:1ff.[37]

Fasting provides a fascinating example of redefining a word so that the accusation can be denied. Hubmaier redefines fasting as refraining from excess, and accepting with thanks all food and drink taken in moderation. This, however, is a clear denial of the Catholic view of fasting that calls for abstinence from particular foods during certain times; for example, the Lenten fast.[38] His supporting texts are those common to the other Reformers, Rom 13:13; 14:14; 1 Tim 1:3; 4:3; Col 2:16; 1 Cor 8:8; 10:23–31; Acts 10:9–16; 11:4–9; 15:20, 29; Luke 10:7; Mark 15:11. These texts demonstrate a number of themes. They show that food is not of itself bad, and that all food is acceptable if received with thankfulness. They also show that those who demand abstinence are false teachers. The words of Jesus from Matt 15:11 are the only specific words quoted from Scripture, evidencing Hubmaier's continued understanding of the priority of the words of Jesus as proof for any doctrine.

The issue of the Sabbath receives the same redefining treatment as fasting. The true Sabbath is "abstaining from sin on all days."[39] However, Hubmaier's proof texts all come from the Old Testament, specifically the parallel versions of the fourth commandment, Exod 20:8–11; Deut 5:12–15. He supports the fourth commandment texts with two texts from Isa 58:13; 66:23, which speak of people desisting from their own ways as honoring God's Sabbath, and the worship of God continually from Sab-

---

36. *PY*, 299; *HS*, 273. The list of supporting texts Hubmaier uses is typical of texts chosen by the evangelical reformers when they refuted intercession by the saints: Matt 11:25–27; 1 John 2:1; 1 Tim 2:5; John 14:14.

37. *PY*, 299; *HS*, 273.

38. *PY*, 299; *HS*, 273–74. Cf. Zwingli's support of the printer Froschauer and his assistants who ate sausage during the Lenten fast of 1522. Zwingli, though present, did not participate in the meal. He later publicly defended their actions, first in a sermon on March 23, 1522, and then in a pamphlet *Choice and Liberty Respecting Food* (April, 1522), which may have been based on Luther's *On the Freedom of the Christian* (1520). Potter, *Zwingli*, 74–75.

39. *PY*, 299; *HS*, 274.

bath to Sabbath, respectively. What is significant is that Hubmaier fails to use any New Testament texts to support his view of the Sabbath. His normal pattern is to cite the words of Jesus, then of Paul or one of the other apostles in support, and finally Old Testament texts where applicable. New Testament texts were available to him, such as Matt 12:1–8 where Jesus declares himself Lord of the Sabbath, and Rom 14:1–6, where Paul speaks of every day being alike. However, it is unclear why he does not cite New Testament support for his view of the Sabbath.

Confession has its place in the life of all people who, following the example of such people as David, the prodigal, and the publican, should confess their sins to God. Hubmaier provides the biblical references to these episodes, 2 Sam 12:13; Ps 51; Luke 15:21; 18:13. Uncompromisingly, he declares auricular confession "vain," citing Matt 15:8–9 to support this view. Pipkin and Yoder, who follow Bergsten's suggestion, identify verse 8 as the particular text Hubmaier had in mind; that is, Jesus's quotation of Isa 29:13, which links the vain worship Isaiah identifies with the vanity of auricular confession.[40] This identification of a word common to both Hubmaier's statements and the passage referred to is a characteristic of Hubmaier's use of Scripture. It is also particularly helpful in identifying individual verses when Hubmaier piles up his biblical supporting texts.

In his reply concerning the church fathers, councils, and human teaching, Hubmaier reaffirms his basic agreement with the other Reformers, that Scripture is the "touchstone" by which all other sources of authority are tested (1 John 4:1). Where the church fathers, councils, and human teaching agree with Scripture, he accepts them because they are following Scripture and not human teaching. However, where they disagree with Scripture he commands them to get behind him, as Christ did Peter (Matt 16:23). He implies that his emphasis on Scripture as the standard against which all opinions are measured is not a new standard for it was also used by Augustine, Jerome, and in papal law itself. Paul is also interpreted as supporting Hubmaier's view. He cites the now familiar warning of Gal 1:8 that anyone who teaches another gospel, even an angel from heaven, should be accursed; thus identifying the gospel with the Scriptures as the standard against which all teaching is measured. Finally, the words of Jesus quoting Isaiah are used again, that "one honors God in vain with human teachings" (Isa 29:13; Matt 15:9). Here the Holy Spirit, Scripture, the Word of God, and the gospel are identified to be essentially the same.

---

40. *PY*, 299–300; *HS*, 274.

Concerning vows of monks, priests, and nuns, Hubmaier declares that they are of no value. Rather, they have been introduced by Satan. He contends that to live according to the baptismal vow would be more than sufficient for Christians. Laying additional burdens on people through these other vows would be unnecessary. However, Hubmaier does not supply any biblical references to support his opinion on vows.

Singing and reading in the church are acceptable to him if they are practiced in the spirit and from the heart, and with understanding of the words for the edifying of the church. This positive view of singing and reading is supported by New Testament references from Paul; 1 Cor 14:26; Col 3:16; Eph 5:19. However, Hubmaier is aware of a negative view of singing and reading that uses Old Testament texts for its support; namely, Mal 2:8, Ezek 33:31f; Amos 5:23. Hubmaier appears to give the New Testament priority over the Old in this matter. Zwingli, on the other hand, absolutely rejects singing in the church in favor of silent worship.[41]

In Hubmaier's exposition on extreme unction, there is a continuing expansion of the allegorical interpretation of the parable of the Good Samaritan, which formed the basis of his soteriology in the *Summa* and *On Christian Baptism*.[42] In this instance, it is joined with Jas 5:14, the traditional text on which the Catholic Church based its doctrine of extreme unction. The link for Hubmaier is the claim that the Catholic Church makes that the oil of extreme unction ascribes "forgiveness of sins."[43] He rejects the Catholic view by describing extreme unction as idolatry, for the oil, a physical element, has been elevated to have power greater than God. However, Hubmaier continues to interpret Jas 5:14ff to mean that people receive forgiveness of sins through anointing with oil. He does this by linking the word oil to the oil of the Samaritan (Luke 10:34ff), and with his view that there are three baptisms. The third baptism is described as martyrdom or the death bed.[44] Hence, Hubmaier can interpret Jas 5:14 to

---

41. Garside suggests from his study of Zwingli's *Sixty-Seven Articles* that Zwingli not only rejected music in the liturgy because it was "ostentatious and hypocritical," but from more fundamental scriptural grounds. He asserts that Zwingli rejected music and singing because God had nowhere commanded it! Garside, *Zwingli and the Arts*, 44.

42. *PY*, 84, 144; *HS*, 111, 158–59.

43. *PY*, 300; *HS*, 274.

44. Hubmaier previously described three baptisms in the *Dialogue*, but without a detailed explanation of the third baptism. *PY*, 189; *HS*, 182. Significantly this third baptism has become more specific in *A Brief Apologia*. Whereas in the *Dialogue* it was subsequent suffering, in *A Brief Apologia* it is martyrdom and the deathbed.

mean that the persecution that true believers face (2 Tim 3:12) describes the situation of those who are ill who call the priests to anoint them with oil. The oil becomes the oil of the comforting gospel, which prepares the believer to be meek and ready to suffer. "Thus the illness is lightened for us, and we receive the forgiveness of sins."[45] By referring to Rom 8:17, he makes explicit what was assumed to lie behind his works written during his imprisonment in Zurich; namely, that those who would be sons of God and joint heirs with Christ must share in the suffering of Christ. Suffering is nothing to be terrified about, the Christian is simply to follow the example of Christ who suffered to enter into his glory.

Hubmaier also extends the allegorical interpretation of the parable by describing the two coins left with the innkeeper as the Old and New Testaments that Christ left with the pastors and preachers who attend the sick sinner with the Word of God. Although Hubmaier's usage of Scripture gives priority to the New Testament, he nonetheless continues to maintain the unity of Scripture and the value of both Testaments for doctrine and Christian living.

Hubmaier responds to the charge of rebaptism with the now familiar argument that the baptism he teaches is the true baptism, supporting it with his usual sequence of references as used in the *Dialogue* and *On Infant Baptism*. He mocks infant baptism as infantile, for in infant baptism a child "two hours old" is asked in Latin "whether it renounces the devil and expecting it to answer in German . . . as if it had learned two languages in its mother's womb."[46] He affirms he knows of only one rebaptism, that of the disciples of John the Baptist in Acts 19:1ff.

Hubmaier demonstrates his previously unstated rule that only words that occur in Scripture are to be considered in doctrinal matters when he states that he does not recognize the word "Mass" as occurring in Scripture, except in Dan 11:38.[47] There the Vulgate renders *eloah ma'umzzin* (an idol named "god of fortresses") as *maozim, Mass*. This idol is to be honored with gold, silver, and precious stones. Hubmaier implies that the priests' Mass is likewise a matter of money, just like the Frankfurt fair,

---

45. *PY,* 301; *HS,* 274.

46. *PY,* 302; *HS,* 275–76. This appears to be a modification of a similar thought he used against Zwingli in the *Dialogue,* though there the question is asked in German, showing that Hubmaier was aware of the new liturgy for infant baptism that Zwingli had introduced in 1525.

47. *PY,* 302; *HS,* 276. For him the lack of the specific word "Mass" is a prima facie case that the doctrine of the Mass is a false teaching.

Making a Patchwork of Scripture

which is all about buying and selling. Hubmaier links his discussion of the idol in Daniel to his justification for tearing down the altars of the Mass by juxtaposing Paul's statement in 1 Cor 10:21, "for the table of the Lord has no communion with the table of devils," and the historical illustration of Dagon and the ark of God, 2 Sam 5:2ff.[48] Again Hubmaier uses a particular word, in this case "idol," to link together texts to support his argument, although in this instance there is no justification whatsoever to do so.

Hubmaier counters the accusation of denying the blood and flesh of Christ in the Mass by firstly decrying the priests as Mass merchants who "auction" off Christ's "crimson blood under the guise of bread and wine." For the second time, Hubmaier insists that Christ is not in the bread and wine as he is seated at the right hand of the heavenly Father. This echoes his statement in *Twelve Articles,* where he alludes to Acts 7:55 as the biblical proof for this view, though in this instance he does not provide any biblical reference in support.[49] He goes on to parody the Mass, "They raise you in the air, they make three pieces out of you, they drown you in wine, and finally crunch you with their teeth for the sake of money."[50] He suggests that this attitude of the greedy priests parallels the gratitude a cuckoo shows to its host. In the margin of the work he calls this a cuckoo Eucharist.

Hubmaier does not deny the charge of being a revolutionary; instead, he rejoices that he has been branded with the same name as was Christ, Jeremiah, Elijah, and Paul. Using the story of Ahab and Elijah, Hubmaier asserts that it was the bad advisers, "the Baalish bishops, monks, and priests," who lead Ahab into error. With this reference perhaps Hubmaier was thinking of the Lords of Liechtenstein who he sought to win for the Reformation.

Yet despite his willingness to be described as a revolutionary, he goes on to insist that he has always taught obedience to government. He bases this obedience on the simple assertion that God has hung the sword at the side of government, an allusion to Rom 13:4. This insistence on the validity of governments' use of the sword caused Hubmaier some difficulty in Waldshut, where he states that people "interrupted me openly in church on this point, defaming me as a blood sucker who does nothing but defend the governmental sword."[51] He goes on to qualify his position

---

48. *PY,* 302; *HS,* 276.
49. *PY,* 27; *HS,* 217. Cf. *PY,* 303; *HS,* 276.
50. *PY,* 303; *HS,* 276.
51. *PY,* 304; *HS,* 277. Bergsten notes the attitude towards the sword displayed by

on government by warning government to use the sword only according to God's direction; that is, to punish the evil and protect the righteous. He argues that people have a duty to be obedient to government, even under heavy burdens, as long as these are not contrary to God. If the burdens are contrary to God, echoing Peter in Acts 5:29, he states that people are to obey God rather than men.

He applies the same rule to bishops, abbots, monks, nuns, and priests, but with particular reference to "tearing them [the people] away by force from the Word of God."[52] He goes on to speak of interest and tithes, citing Matt 5:40 to confirm that he has always supported the payment of interest and tithes. He cites Luke 6, probably verses 34–38, as his text that proves that "if there were genuine brotherly love among us, it would indeed teach us to give and take interest."[53] He implies that Waldshut suffered the violent attacks of the Hapsburgs in 1525 because of the town's refusal to pay interest and tithes.

However, he insists that the real reason the people of Waldshut suffered was because of their desire to stay true to the Word of God. As evidence of the truth of this statement Hubmaier recalls some of the events of Waldshut's negotiations with the Austrian government at Breysach in Breisgau. There Waldshut's representatives promised to do all for the "Princely Majesty" just as their forefathers had done, including obeisance and tribute. With a rhetorical flourish, Hubmaier adds: "And if there were one stone buried sixty feet under the earth at Waldshut that were not good Austrian, then they would scratch it out with their fingernails and throw it into the Rhine."[54] The only request they made was to retain the "pure and clear Word of God." This request the councilors of the Princely Majesty rejected at Constance. There followed harrying and persecution of Hubmaier at the hands of Veit Suter, the Austrian representative, and Tegen Fuchs of Zurich. He continued to be pursued and accused by his Catholic adversaries, despite being released unconvicted of sedition by either Schaffhausen or Zurich. He claims that his accusers wanted to hand

---

Gross and Teck. These two men were dismissed from Waldshut because they would not carry the sword, though they would willingly assist in preparing the defenses of the town and stand guard. However, they do not display the full rejection of the sword as expressed by Conrad Grebel and the Swiss Brethren. Bergsten, *Balthasar Hubmaier: Anabaptist Theologian*, 244–45.

52. *PY,* 304; *HS,* 277.
53. *PY,* 305; *HS,* 277.
54. *PY,* 306; *HS,* 278.

Making a Patchwork of Scripture

him over for punishment without him receiving a hearing, though he continued to appeal for a fair hearing.[55]

Hubmaier cites a number of people as witnesses to the fact that he did not secretly flee Regensburg and Ingolstadt, a slanderous and defaming statement his opponents publish against him.[56]

With this statement concerning Regensburg and Ingolstadt, Hubmaier completes his answers to the charges he listed at the beginning of the work. He now commences a series of admonitions to government. This section of the work bears close resemblance to his earlier *An Earnest Christian Appeal* (1524), which is not surprising as he was in a similar situation there.

He reiterates his position that he is no heretic as he is willing to be instructed by the Word of God if he has erred.[57] However, no one has been able to show him differently from the Word of God, though one, whom he does not name, but is obviously Zwingli, has tried to teach him something other by means of "capturing, imprisoning, torture, and the executioner" in the Heretics' Tower.[58] Hubmaier regrets his weakness in Zurich, probably a reference to his recantation, yet sees in the humiliation of that experience a demonstration of God's love.[59]

He affirms again that Scripture is to be the sole judge of his teaching (John 12:48), while the government has authority to judge concerning everything else (Rom 13:4). In his *An Earnest Christian Appeal*, Hubmaier followed up this statement with his view on unequal punishment.[60] In *A Brief Appeal*, he makes no mention of this, inserting in its place a new theory that one should flee from tyranny and persecution. Paul provides an example of this when he fled Damascus and Christ instructed his disciples to do so in Matt 10:23. He adds that this is to take place "without violation of the divine Word and without vexation of the believers. But when the hour of our dying is at hand, which God only knows, then no fleeing will help us."[61]

55. *PY*, 307; *HS*, 279.

56. *PY*, 307; *HS*, 279.

57. *PY*, 46, 308; *HS*, 83, 279. He had also used this phrase at the end of his contribution to the Second Zurich Disputation. *PY*, 29.

58. *PY*, 308; *HS*, 280.

59. *PY*, 308; *HS*, 280. He includes the phrase "the son whom you love, you chasten" as part of a series of biblical texts for which he does not provide references.

60. *PY*, 308, cf. 47; *HS*, 280, cf. 84.

61. *PY*, 309; *HS*, 280. A group of Anabaptists who were confined to the Heretics' Tower escaped on March 21, 1526. The interrogation of two who were recaptured

Hubmaier then launches into a series of warnings to government not to use the sword that God has entrusted to them against the innocent. To do so will bring back on their own heads the judgments they decree. He rejects the defense that the lesser magistrate must obey his lord, citing the common Reformation counter argument that "one has to obey God more than people."[62] To substantiate his warnings against unjust government he provides a lengthy quotation from Isa 1:10–23.[63] At this point he introduces his exposition of Deut 1:16–17, which he used in his *An Earnest Christian Appeal,* and he argues for a hearing for those who have been accused of being agitators and heretics.[64] He adds a number of allusions that firstly, affirms government as the servant of God (Rom 13:4) and secondly, warns that the servant who knows the will of the master and fails to do it will receive many blows (Luke 12:47). He also adds the illustration from the Old Testament that God personally came down to earth to check that the accusations made against Sodom and Gomorrah were true, suggesting that government as the servant of God should follow the example set for it by its Lord.[65]

Again Hubmaier refers difficult cases to Moses, which this time he specifically identifies as the Scriptures, not just the five books of Moses.[66] These cases are defined as being "too difficult for the worldly government and would concern the faith of the Christian church." Worldly government is thereby restricted from directing the church in matters of the faith. Here is another probable legacy from Hubmaier's experiences at the hands of Zwingli and the Zurich Council. Hubmaier makes explicit the demarcation between faith, which is under the authority of the Word of God, and everything that pertains to the physical realm, which is under the authority of government. Hubmaier adds an expanded version of his list of texts from his *An Earnest Christian Appeal* to support his view.[67] What he fails

---

shows that staying and dying in the tower rather than attempt escape had been agreed to by Grebel, Blaurock, Mantz, and Ockenfuss. However when an opportunity presented itself whereby they could escape without causing "vexation" of the believers they took their chance. Hubmaier may well have been aware of their earlier decision; he was almost certainly aware of their escape. Harder, *Sources of Swiss Anabaptism,* 450. Pike seems to have erroneously included Hubmaier in this escape. Pike, *Story of the Anabaptists,* 45.

62. *PY,* 310; *HS,* 281. A quotation of Acts 5:29.
63. *PY,* 311–11; *HS,* 281–82.
64. *PY,* 43–45; *HS,* 80–82.
65. *PY,* 312; *HS,* 282.
66. *PY,* 312, cf. 43–44; *HS,* 283, cf.82.
67. *PY,* 44–45; *HS,* 82. Ezek 44:23–24; Luke 16:29; John 5:39; 12:47–48 (cf. *PY,* 312;

Making a Patchwork of Scripture

to repeat in this work is his conviction that the congregation is competent to judge these matters under the guidance of the Scripture.[68]

He concludes with a final admonition to the government to cease persecuting the innocent, and instead to turn to "preachers who will open up to you clearly and brightly his holy, living, and eternal Word."[69] Hubmaier uses as a "parable" the story of Paul's conversion on the Damascus road as the basis for this final admonition.[70] It is significant that Hubmaier has replaced the competence of the congregation to interpret and judge in difficult matters of faith with preachers who will clearly explain the text of Scripture.

Use of Scripture

This *Brief Apologia* demonstrates Hubmaier's continuing application of his hermeneutical principles and Scripture usages as we have seen them developed in his earliest works. There is evident within the text a dependence on earlier printed and preached works, as Hubmaier himself indicates.[71] With the wider range of topics addressed in this work, the ratio of references to the Old and New Testament differs dramatically from that in his works on baptism. Here there are twenty-five references to the Old Testament compared to seventy-nine to the New Testament, bringing the total number of references, quotations and allusions to twenty-nine and one hundred four for the Old Testament and the New Testament respectively.

The section on government alone provides thirteen of the twenty-nine Old Testament texts, demonstrating that for Hubmaier there is equality between the two Testaments when dealing with this topic. The remainder of the Old Testament texts are scattered unevenly across the rest of the topics Hubmaier addresses in this work. There are two examples of Old Testament references being given as well as the New Testament reference where it is quoted: Matt 1:20f.; Isa 7:14 (the perpetual virginity of Mary), and Matt 15:9; Isa 29:13 (people honor God in vain with

HS, 283); Isa 8:20; Ezek 44:23–24; Deut 18:15; 28:1; John 5:39; 12:47–48; Luke 16:29.

68. *PY,* 45; *HS,* 82.

69. *PY,* 312; *HS,* 283.

70. The wording of Hubmaier's text suggests that he has used extracts from the three accounts of Paul's experience in Acts: chapters 9, 22, and 26. *PY,* 312; *HS,* 283.

71. *PY,* 304; *HS,* 277. "Before long I will also have my writings published and thus bring into the open what I then preached publicly." *PY,* 307; *HS,* 279. "This was never accepted by my accusers, who openly pressed that I be handed over to them without being called to court, unheard and unconvicted, as I have also shown in public print in 1524," no doubt a reference to his *An Earnest Christian Appeal.*

human teaching). There are numerous texts cited as historical examples, both positively, as in David's confession of his sin, Ps 51; 2 Sam 12:13, and negatively as a warning to governments about persecuting the innocent; for example, the blood of innocent Abel (Gen 4:10).

As was pointed out above Hubmaier exclusively used the Old Testament as a source of proof texts to support his view of the Sabbath. He also introduced the spurious exegesis of Dan 11:38 linked to 1 Sam 5:2ff as part of his attack on the Mass.

There is also evident a new consistency in the way Hubmaier prefaces Old Testament quotations. Jehosaphat, Isaiah, and Moses are all said to have spoken by the "Spirit of God."[72] Although this phrase has been used previously, it becomes more consistently the way that Hubmaier introduces Old Testament quotations that relate to the role of government. This reinforces the identification that Hubmaier makes between Spirit, Scripture, and gospel earlier in this work.

With regard to the New Testament references, once again references to Acts dominate: eighteen of a total seventy-nine references. This raw score is, however, deceptive as twelve of these references are all contained in a now familiar sequence of references that Hubmaier uses to demonstrate that believers' baptism was practiced by the apostles following its institution by Christ. Luke comes a close second with fifteen references, while Matthew continues to score well with twelve references. Mark and John are both low scoring on two and six respectively. Four texts are cited from Romans, each of which relates to a different topic. Only 1 Corinthians scores as high as Romans; all other New Testament books are represented by fewer references.[73]

The majority of his references are used as supporting texts for a viewpoint he is expressing, which is based on another text that is used as a proof text. For example, Hubmaier uses Matt 1:20f as a proof text of the perpetual virginity of Mary, and goes on to support that with a series of other New and Old Testament references.

As was pointed out above, Hubmaier continues his allegorical interpretation of the parable of the Good Samaritan from Luke 10. He also cites Jesus's words, "they have Moses and the prophets" (Luke 16:29; 12:48) as a parable which indicates that Scripture is the sole authority to which appeals are to be made in matters of faith.[74]

---

72. *PY*, 309, 310, 311; *HS*, 280, 281, 282.
73. *PY*, 299; *HS*, 273.
74. *PY*, 312; *HS*, 283.

The large number of allusions identified come from the Synoptic Gospels, Acts, and Romans. Of the twenty-five synoptic allusions Hubmaier uses, twelve are based on his hermeneutic of personal identification. Hubmaier either identifies himself as sharing in Christ's sufferings, or with John the Baptist as one not worthy to untie the sandal of Christ. These synoptic parallels could be consolidated to just four, if all the Synoptic Gospels were considered. The allusions to Acts provide either historical examples used to demonstrate an action to be followed, or warnings of the consequences disobedience to the known will of God will bring. The allusions to Romans all relate to the basic proof text Rom 13:4, which Hubmaier uses to assert that government is a servant of God and wields the sword on his authority.

Summary

A Brief Apologia demonstrates that Hubmaier maintains his hermeneutical principles unchanged, though there is the possibility that he is no longer as certain about the role of congregational hermeneutic. His citation of Scripture shows a more balanced use of Old and New Testaments as he finds proof texts and supporting references from both Testaments. This reflects the wider sample of doctrines addressed in this work. It also suggests that he does not apply to all doctrines his principle that New Testament ceremonies must be determined by New Testament texts in all matters that relate to the church. This is particularly evident in his view of government, an issue on which he differed with other Anabaptists earlier in Waldshut, and later in Nikolsburg. This suggests that Hubmaier does not hold to the total subordination of the Old Testament to the New, as was the case with the Swiss Brethren.

A SIMPLE INSTRUCTION

(July–August 1526)[75]

Setting

A Simple Instruction was written approximately at the same time as the *A Brief Apologia*, as indicated by phrases common to both. It acted as

---

75. *PY*, 314–38; *HS*, 284–304.

Hubmaier's contribution to the debate on the Lord's Supper that was current in Moravia on his arrival.[76] Bergsten suggests that Leonhard von Liechtenstein had been baptized by Hubmaier and that both Spittelmaier and Glaidt had been won to the Anabaptist cause by the time Hubmaier completed the foreword.[77] Hubmaier is certainly fulsome in his praise of Leonhard von Liechtenstein, as demonstrated by his extravagant exposition of the Lord of Liechtenstein's name. At one point Hubmaier writes, "I observe that God has so inflamed Your Grace in a Christian fashion and especially blessed you not only with the external name of light, but also internally in the soul."[78] In Hubmaier's soteriology, such internal light is only possible through the Spirit who brings about the new birth that must precede the true baptism. Though not confirming that Leonhard was baptized at that time, it does show that Hubmaier considered him to have the prerequisite inner enlightenment, and was thus a proper candidate for baptism. The two preachers of Nikolsburg, Spittelmaier and Glaidt, are singled out for particular praise for the way they had brought the gospel to Nikolsburg and its territory.[79]

Analysis

This is a strongly polemical work, primarily targeting the Catholic doctrine of the Mass, though Hubmaier does also distance himself from Andreas Karlstadt and Zwingli. In a first short section, he presents in summary form fifteen different views of the Mass held by the Catholic Church. In this way, he sought to deflect the criticism of his Catholic opponents who cite the disunity of opinion among the evangelical preachers.[80] An even shorter second section is then devoted to the views of "present-day teachers," specifically Karlstadt and Zwingli, though these two are not named.[81] This division of material into old and new teaching parallels Hubmaier's presentation of references to baptism in his *Old and New Teachers*.

Though Hubmaier distances himself from Zwingli, he nevertheless adopts a view of the Lord's Supper that is very similar to Zwingli. Hubmaier

---

76. *HS*, 284.
77. *HS*, 284.
78. *PY*, 317; *HS*, 288.
79. *PY*, 317; *HS*, 288.
80. *PY*, 320; *HS*, 291.
81. *PY*, 321–22; *HS*, 291–92.

develops his symbolic understanding of the Supper as expressed in his *Several Theses* (1524), though there are important changes in emphasis.

Of greater significance is Hubmaier's restatement of his rule for the correct interpretation of Scripture, in this instance specifically related to texts on the Lord's Supper.[82] He first promulgated it as a general rule in his *Theses Against Eck* (No. XII).[83] Later he stated and applied this rule in *On the Christian Baptism*, where he deals with texts relating to baptism.[84] There are also phrases used by Hubmaier in *On the Christian Baptism* and the *Summa* that do not appear again in his writings until this work; namely, references to the "rough coat" of John the Baptist and the "sweet little Lamb Christ."[85] These renewed uses of phrases and restatement of hermeneutical principles indicate that Hubmaier was using his previous writings on baptism as background to this work. In those works, he had formally broken with Zwingli over the issue of baptism, not just because he reached a different conclusion but also because of hermeneutics. Now, in the debate over the Lord's Supper, Hubmaier uses the same hermeneutical principles to oppose both the Catholic view of the Mass and the Zwinglian method of interpreting Scripture used to support a symbolic view of the Supper as a memorial meal.

By distancing himself from Zwingli, Hubmaier is expressing more than bitterness because of his treatment in Zurich; he is continuing his debate with Zwingli about methods for correctly interpreting Scripture that began with the debate on baptism and find expression here in the debate concerning the Lord's Supper.[86]

A Simple Instruction came out in two editions, showing, according to Pipkin and Yoder, that it "touched upon an important issue and that it met a need in the Moravian debates."[87] The second edition shows evidence of corrected printing faults, but there are no changes to the meaning of the text itself.[88]

This is Hubmaier's longest exposition on the doctrine of the Lord's Supper. He begins by presenting fifteen opinions on the subject from the history of the Catholic Church. They range from a bare memorialism,

---

82. *PY,* 322; *HS,* 292.
83. *PY,* 53–54; *HS,* 89.
84. *PY,* 104–5, 109, 114; *HS,* 126, 130, 133–34.
85. *PY,* 316, cf. 85 and 145; *HS,* 287, cf. 111 and 159.
86. Bergsten, *Balthasar Hubmaier: Anabaptist Theologian,* 330.
87. *PY,* 314.
88. *HS,* 286.

where the symbols of the bread and wine are only "a sign and memorial" (No. 1),[89] to the Thomist view of the actual bodily presence of Christ under the accidents of the bread and wine (No. 7).[90] He also spent some time demonstrating the different views concerning the moment that the body of Christ becomes present in the Mass, at the speaking of the individual words *hoc est corpus meum*, or at the aspiration of the chalice (Nos. 12, 13).[91] He also notes the differences concerning the nature of the body of Christ in the Mass, whether it was his human body as it hung on the cross, or his post-resurrection body (Nos. 14 and 15).[92] He also notes the debate that the miracle of the Mass engendered about whether God is obliged to act whenever the priest performs the Mass (Nos. 8, 9).[93]

Hubmaier does not undertake a detailed rebuttal of these views, for his purpose is only to demonstrate to the reader the disunity among Catholic commentators on this teaching.

Hubmaier then briefly outlines his disagreement with the views of three present-day teachers. He rejects Karlstadt's "trope or type" interpretation of the word *hoc*; that is, that *hoc* does not point to the bread but to the body of Christ himself.[94] Previously Hubmaier had written to Oecolampad expressing his approval of Karlstadt's writings in which Karlstadt expressed this opinion.[95]

He goes on to reject Zwingli's interpretation of *"est"* as *"significat,"* which Zwingli had "proved" by his exegesis of Luke 8:4–15, the parable of the sower, and Gen 41:2–3, 26–27, the seven cows of Pharoah's dream. He had already rejected this conclusion of Zwingli's in *On Infant Baptism*, though without comment,[96] and in the concluding section of the *Dialogue*, probably written after Hubmaier's arrival in Nikolsburg, with the significant comment: "The judgment of Zwingli about bread and wine is pleasing. The manner of his judging is not pleasing."[97] Hubmaier amplifies this statement in this work with the comment: "For if this is the practice then no one would be certain as to where *est* [is] stands in the Scripture for *sig-*

---

89. *PY*, 319; *HS*, 290.
90. *PY*, 319–20; *HS*, 290.
91. *PY*, 319–20; *HS*, 290.
92. *PY*, 320; *HS*, 290.
93. *PY*, 320; *HS*, 290.
94. *PY*, 321; *HS*, 291.
95. *PY*, 68.
96. *PY*, 288; *HS*, 265.
97. *PY*, 230–31; *HS*, 212.

nificat [signifies] or for itself. And in the end there would be so many fights over words as there are *ests* and *ises* in the Bible."[98] This echoes Hubmaier's previously stated caution about using parables to establish doctrine, and the need to read Scripture for its simple meaning. In contrast to this arrogant dealing with Scripture, Hubmaier urges his readers to "look up, up, up," though he does not make clear what this injunction involves.[99]

He adds a third group of evangelical teachers who maintain that the body of Christ is a figurative body, though the bread is bread and the wine is wine. He makes no comment on this view. Instead, he goes on to reiterate his rule for correctly interpreting Scripture: "Where several sayings of the Scriptures are dark or presented very briefly, from which disagreement may follow, one should resolve these with Scriptures which are clearer or brighter—though on the same matter—setting them next to the dark or shortened sayings as much as one can have them at hand. One should ignite them and let them burn like many wax candles bound together so that a bright and clear light of the Scriptures breaks forth."[100]

This rule is then applied to the words of institution as they are found in Matthew, Mark, Luke and 1 Corinthians. The shorter records of Matthew and Mark are considered to be the darker texts, which are illuminated by the longer texts of Luke and 1 Corinthians. The later references provide Hubmaier with his major emphasis of this work, that in the Lord's Supper, "The bread offered, broken, taken, and eaten is the body of Christ in remembrance. Thus also the cup taken, distributed, and drunk is the blood of Christ in remembrance."[101] The words "in remembrance, or, in my memory" become the key to this interpretation, and Hubmaier uses the maxim "the preceding words should be understood according to the following words" to ensure that they are given priority in the interpretation of the words of institution.[102] While insisting that the bread is only bread and did not suffer for sinners, his hermeneutic, which demands that the simple reading of a text is to be accepted, urges him to state that the bread is the body of Christ. He does this without having to follow

---

98. *PY,* 321–22; *HS,* 291.

99. *PY,* 322; *HS,* 292. Perhaps Hubmaier has in mind his appeal to Jacob's ladder as an interpretive method: "right minded, truthful, and pious pastors" will use to show their congregations the way to heaven. *PY,* 337; *HS,* 304.

100. *PY,* 322; *HS,* 292. He first stated this rule in his *Theses Against Eck* (No. 12); *PY,* 53–54; *HS,* 89, but continued to use it consistently in his later writings *On the Christian Baptism* and *Dialogue. PY,* 104–5, 182; *HS,* 126, 177.

101. *PY,* 324; *HS,* 293.

102. *PY,* 324; *HS,* 293.

Luther, who argues for the actual bodily presence of Christ, or reverting to the dominant Catholic position of his day. Instead, he maintains that the bread is the body of Christ in remembrance. Hubmaier thus attempts to distance himself from his earlier identification with Zwingli's view that the bread is only a symbol that reminds the recipient of the body of Christ. The distinction he attempts to draw between himself and Zwingli is, however, eventually insignificant.

He presents a number of counter arguments that his Catholic opponents used against him. The first concerns the doctrine of transubstantiation formulated by Thomas Aquinas. It is rejected as "Anaxagorean" philosophy having no place in theology. Hubmaier asserts that by Thomas's interpretation "the word and meaning of Christ is ripped apart and violated."[103] This echoes a charge Hubmaier laid at Zwingli's door for his exposition of Mark 10:14.[104] He also repeats against the Sophists and Scholastics an accusation made against Zwingli, that they make difficult the simple meaning of the text.

The second counter argument comes in the form of a syllogism: "Everything which Christ said is so. Now Christ said concerning the bread, 'This is my body,' therefore it must be so."[105] Hubmaier rejects this syllogism by presenting one of his own, using as his second statement, Luke 14:26, "whoever does not hate father and mother cannot be my disciple," concluding that people should hate their parents. This is obviously ridiculous, and he suggests that a clearer text of Scripture is needed to make sense of this syllogism. He uses Mark 10:29, which adds to the Luke text the following words, "for my sake and the sake of the gospel when they depart from it." This proves for him the necessity to consider the "whole speech" and not just a part, which he then applies again to the texts of the words of institution to prove that the words "in my memory" are the key to correctly understanding the text "this is my body."

Hubmaier further demonstrates how he applies his principle of considering the "words that follow," by citing Mark 14:25, "Truly I say to you that I will not henceforth drink from the fruit of the vine, until the day that I drink it anew in the kingdom of God." He takes this to mean until after the resurrection and this allows him to then consider the meeting of Christ with the two disciples at Emmaus, where Christ is made known to

---

103. *PY,* 325; *HS,* 294–95. Luther used the same term to describe the result of Erasmus's hermeneutic in *On the Bondage of the Will,* 223–24.

104. *PY,* 231; *HS,* 212.

105. *PY,* 326; *HS,* 295.

them, not through the exposition of Scripture but in the breaking of the bread. Having met with Christ in the Supper these two then immediately go and proclaim the Lord's death to the other disciples in Jerusalem.[106] This supports his view of the necessity of the proclamation of the gospel at every sharing in the Lord's Supper.

To further support this view that the following words must be considered if a true interpretation of Scripture is to be made, he presents a number of "parables" which demonstrate that a statement makes sense only when all the speech is taken into consideration. He concludes that a further rule obligates Christians to speak simply and not with "empty speaking or figures of rhetorical persuasion."[107] He takes this rule from Augustine's *On Christian Doctrine*, and is the first occasion that he speaks favorably of this church father. This insistence on speaking with simplicity dominated Hubmaier's work against Oecolampad.

Hubmaier's exegesis of the main texts concerning the Lord's Supper follows. As in his *On the Christian Baptism*, Hubmaier quotes the texts in full, and then provides some minimal exposition of each reference. On occasion, he focuses on the individual words, which enables him to reject some Catholic practices. For example, from Matt 26:26, he takes the word "they" to prove that one person cannot celebrate the Supper alone, or the word "thanks," which he identifies with "blessed," and goes on to reject the Catholic Church's translation "consecrate."[108] The word "take" provides evidence for him that it is wrong to think of the Mass as a sacrifice, while consideration of the word "eat" leads him to ridicule the central action of the Mass when the priest raises the host, divides it into three parts, and immerses it in the wine.[109]

More commonly, he cites a short phrase from a verse and expounds it. In these instances, Hubmaier rehearses his previously stated views of the Supper being a memorial of the death of Christ, supporting it with a reference to Heb 9:16f, and insisting that the cup is the blood of Christ only after his death at the ninth hour.[110] The phrase "from the fruit of the vine" is used to demonstrate that the wine remained wine after the words

---

106. *PY*, 328; *HS*, 296–97.

107. *PY*, 328; *HS*, 296. Luther uses a similar phrase from Augustine to object to Erasmus's interpretation of Scripture by the use of tropes and figures. *On the Bondage of the Will*, 220–23.

108. *PY*, 329; *HS*, 297.

109. *PY*, 330; *HS*, 298.

110. *PY*, 330; *HS*, 298.

of consecration, just as it was so before them, a conclusion he supports by referring to Paul's words in 1 Cor 11:26, "whoever now eats from this bread and drinks from this cup of the Lord unworthily is guilty of the body and blood of the Lord."[111]

Hubmaier also develops the theme of the earnest desire of those who are to share in the Lord's Supper, by referring to the desire Christ had to share the Last Supper with his disciples.[112]

He interprets a number of passages to show that Christ cannot be humanly present in the elements of bread and wine. The phrase "until he comes" must mean that Christ is not present as it is no memorial if the one being remembered is bodily present.[113] He also provides a list of references without exposition that "testify that Christ Jesus ascended into heaven, sits at the right hand of God his heavenly Father, and also will not come from there until the time of the last day when he will come to judge the living and the dead. Just there he sits according to his humanity."[114]

Hubmaier also exegetes Acts 7:48ff. to attack the costly monstrances used to keep the host in after the celebration of the Mass. These little houses of wood, stone, silver, and gold are parodied by Hubmaier through several puns on the word monstrance as monsters and monstrous.[115]

The development in Hubmaier's teaching on the Lord's Supper follows a similar pattern of his teaching on baptism. He has located more supporting texts for his teaching, and though these texts are not central to his position, they do add a new emphasis. In this case, it is the idea of the bodily presence of Christ at the right hand of God that is the new emphasis. What is also significant is the reduction of emphasis on the idea of the Lord's Supper being a declaration of the obligation that the participant has to give body, blood, property, etc. for his or her neighbors as Christ did for the believer. This had been a dominant emphasis in his earliest work *Several Theses*, where he states that the body and blood of Christ on the cross became the believer's body and blood, so that the believer's body and blood is to be the same for the neighbor.[116] This theme does occur in

---

111. *PY,* 330–31; *HS,* 298, 301.
112. *PY,* 333; *HS,* 301.
113. *PY,* 333; *HS,* 300.
114. *PY,* 336; *HS,* 303.
115. *PY,* 335 cf. *HS,* 302. "Derhalb es alles vnnützer kosten ist, das man bissher an solche kostliche Mönster vnnd Monstrantzen glegt hat. Aber es hayssen wol Mönster vnnd Monstranntzen, a Mönstro, von eim mör wunnder, das auss dem mör kumbt, wie Johannes schreibt in der Offenbarung."
116. *PY,* 76; *HS,* 104.

A Simple Instruction, though without the frequency of the earlier work. In this work, Hubmaier makes the distinction that through faith in the work of Christ the believer receives forgiveness of sins, while it is in love that the believer obligates himself or herself to the neighbor when eating and drinking the bread and cup and promises "to let his flesh and blood be broken and sacrificed" for the sake of the neighbor.[117]

A striking omission in this work is any reference to the use of the vernacular as necessary for presenting the Lord's Supper, though this had been specified in his earlier work.[118] It is possible that this matter was no longer an issue for Hubmaier and other Reformers since it was now as commonplace to undertake the service of the Lord's Supper in the vernacular as it was to distribute the sacrament in both kinds to all who participated.

In the foreword of this work, Hubmaier undertakes an excessive exposition of the name of the Lord of Liechtenstein, Leonhard von Liechtenstein. By focusing on the individual components of this name, Hubmaier carries out a series of word studies in which he attributes to Leonhard the qualities of Old and New Testament saints as well as Christ himself. Leonhard is a Samson and a David, a figure of strength, manhood, and toughness. The story of Samson and the lion provides Hubmaier with a figure which teaches "that the beginning of a Christian life always looks frightening to our flesh and blood. . . . However, when the Spirit of God comes, then it all becomes sweet like honey, mild like the little Lamb Christ, and quite easy as the Lord himself told us."[119]

The word *Licht* gives Hubmaier the opening to discuss Christ the light of the world, who illumines all who join him in faith, and through them to influence those around them as they share the gospel. Leonard is to be blessed for supporting this proclamation of the gospel through his preachers, Spittelmaier and Glaidt.[120]

The word *Stein* is a figure of the Word of God on which all life is built. Hubmaier acknowledges that the Word of God is not only preached in the towns and territories of Leonhard, but it is also being lived out. Hubmaier encourages Leonhard to defend the gospel, citing a number of

---

117. *PY*, 334; *HS*, 301.
118. *PY*, 75; *HS*, 102.
119. *PY*, 316; *HS*, 287.
120. *PY*, 317; *HS*, 288.

Old Testament and Apocryphal examples of those who were victorious against overwhelming odds.[121]

Hubmaier concludes the dedication letter by identifying Nikolsburg with Emmaus, suggesting that the gospel manifested itself first at Wittenberg with Luther, but since then has moved on so that now Christ is made known in the breaking of bread. From this new Emmaus the gospel will be taken to be preached to other disciples. The emphasis is now on the central role of the preachers of the gospel who will take the gospel out into the rest of the world. This focus on the role of the preacher becomes increasingly important in Hubmaier's understanding. To be clearly understood Scripture must firstly be preached in its clear pure form. In his concluding statements, Hubmaier once again urges the people to pray that God would grant them preachers who will correctly teach the Word of God: "Yes, all of us, since we are all so careless, lazy, and slothful, should pray to God that he henceforth grant us right-minded, truthful, and pious pastors who show us the true ladder of Jacob to the heavens, Gen 28:12, on which we are again in the power of God helped out of the mire of this human error and may climb into eternal life."[122]

Once again these thoughts partially reflect Hubmaier's *On Heretics*, where he asserts the equal responsibility of both preachers and congregation for the errors that have overtaken the church. However, it is not the congregation that is now urged to search the Scripture to find the truth, rather they are urged to pray that God will give them pastors who will correctly teach them.[123] This is linked to the positive role that Hubmaier implies the Lord of Liechtenstein has to play in propagating the preaching of the gospel in his town and territories.

Use of Scripture

A consideration of the raw statistics of biblical references in this work gives a false impression of Hubmaier's use of Scripture. This occurs because the references from the dedicatory letter indicate a different usage of Scripture than those in the body of the text. In the body of the text, Hubmaier's references continue to be dominated by the New Testament, with Old Testament references being confined to citing Old Testament references quoted in the New Testament, or those Old Testament texts that

121. *PY*, 318; *HS*, 288.
122. *PY*, 337; *HS*, 304.
123. *PY*, 337, cf. 61; *HS*, 303, cf. 97.

provide historical examples that are to be followed or avoided. The New Testament texts are primarily proof texts, citing the words of institution, and other supporting texts.

In the dedicatory letter, Hubmaier uses ten Old Testament and one Apocryphal reference, and ten New Testament references. All of these references are either historical figures, which are used as types, or references to light and stone, which Hubmaier interprets allegorically. This usage of Scripture is rare in Hubmaier, and the concentrated application of this method of interpretation sets this dedicatory epistle apart from Hubmaier's other dedicatory letters.

Summary

This work is significant for Hubmaier's hermeneutic as it demonstrates his uniform application of his principles on both the Lord's Supper and baptism. In both doctrines, Hubmaier argues for the darker text of Scripture to be interpreted by the clearer text, that all the texts of Scripture on one topic be gathered together so that a correct judgment can be made, and that the simple meaning of the text is to be understood. He also uses the same phrase concerning making a "patchwork" judgment of Scripture instead of a perfect judgment.[124]

Hubmaier also demonstrates that he applies these rules in the same manner to both doctrines. He gathers together all the texts he considers to be central to the debate, uses the fuller text to interpret the shorter texts, and makes a conscious effort to consider the texts in their contexts. In these instances, it is specifically the "following" words that act as the interpretive key for the passage, while in his texts on baptism, it is both the preceding and following words that are to be taken into consideration.

---

124. *PY,* 327, cf. 189; *HS,* 295, cf. 182.

Balthasar Hubmaier and the Clarity of Scripture

A CHRISTIAN CATECHISM

(December 10, 1526, to early 1527)[125]

Setting

Bergsten notes that there was a dramatic increase in the number of adherents to the Anabaptist message in Nikolsburg soon after Hubmaier's arrival, and that the catechism he produced was a response to the need to instruct these converts in Anabaptist doctrine.[126] Hubmaier writes in the foreword that he has composed his catechism at the express wish of Göschl, the leading preacher in Nikolsburg.[127] He comments that it is not enough to know that one must be taught before baptism but what one is to be taught.[128] It is the content of doctrine that occupies the primary concern of Hubmaier in this work, though his instruction also includes sections on how the baptized person should then live in accordance with the instruction of Christ.

It has been suggested that the rapid growth of the Anabaptist church in Nikolsburg brought with it not only a need for explanation of Anabaptist doctrines of baptism and the Lord's Supper, but the need to maintain discipline within the members of the church.[129] Hubmaier's *A Christian Catechism* brings the topic of discipline firmly into the foreground, declaring it to be an essential part of the process of salvation along with baptism, which represents the vow of faith, and the Lord's Supper, which represents the obligation to love and do good works.

Analysis

Hubmaier dates the foreword to this work December 10, 1526, and the title page bears the date 1526. However, on the concluding page the date is given as 1527. It appears that the work was completed in December 1526 and printed in 1527.[130] The foreword also provides us with evidence

---

125. *PY*, 339–65; *HS*, 305–26.

126. *HS*, 306. What is not made clear is whether these converts were the residents of Nikolsburg or refugees from other areas.

127. *PY*, 344; *HS*, 310.

128. *PY*, 341; *HS*, 307.

129. Bergsten, *Balthasar Hubmaier: Anabaptist Theologian*, 328.

130. *HS*, 305

that Göschl, to whom Hubmaier had previously dedicated *Old and New Teachers* on 21 July, 1526, had by December of that year become part of the Anabaptist movement in Nikolsburg, for Hubmaier now not only calls him gracious Lord, but also brother.[131] Hubmaier also comments that he has used the names of the Lords of Liechtenstein as the questioner and respondent because of "the special inclination and affection" both he and Göschl have for them.[132] Leonhard was certainly baptized by this time, though it is unclear if Hans had received water baptism as the outward sign of faith. Nevertheless, Hubmaier prays that God would "preserve them to their end in his shelter, in his protection, and in a genuine, unadulterated, and Christian faith against all the onslaughts of sin, world, devil, and hell."[133] With these words Hubmaier appears to number these two nobles among the faithful.

In the foreword, Hubmaier closely identifies himself with Göschl, noting that they were both previously held captive to many "errors, hypocrisies, and evil abominations"[134] which they also taught others, by which they created many priests and monks. Hubmaier wrote *A Christian Catechism* in an attempt to redress the harm such actions caused. It is therefore not simply for the instruction of the young who are to be baptized, it is also an attempt to help open the eyes of those still trapped in the "mire and mud puddles of human precepts, of partiality of persons, of ancient practices and old customs."[135] *A Christian Catechism* is therefore an expanded version of the *Summa*, in which Hubmaier acknowledged his responsibility in teaching error to the people of Regensburg, Ingolstadt, and Friedburg, and sought to correct it. Hubmaier also uses some of the material from *A Brief Apologia* when he writes on topics such as Mary, the saints, images, fasting, Sabbath, singing, and confession. He does not, however, deal with obedience to the government in *A Christian Catechism*

---

131. *PY*, 340–41, cf. 246; *HS*, 307, cf. 227.

132. *PY*, 344; *HS*, 310. This format of a questioner and respondent is typical of later catechisms of the period, but not prominent among Catholic catechisms. See Janz, *Three Reformation Catechisms* and Zeman, *Anabaptists and Czech Brethren*, Appendixes 5 & 6, 330ff.

133. *PY*, 344; *HS*, 310.

134. *PY*, 343; *HS*, 308.

135. *PY*, 341; *HS*, 307. "Ein Christennliche Leertafel, die ein yedlicher mensch, ee vnd er im Wasser getaufft wirdt, vor wissen solle." has been variously translated. While Catechism is the most obvious choice, it does obscure the dual aim of this work. As the title suggests it is primarily for the preparation of candidates for baptism. However, it does have the important secondary role of education for the members of the gathered church.

as he does at length in *A Brief Apologia,* indicating that his focus is primarily on the life of the believer and the church, not the wider community.

Unlike other catechisms of that period, Hubmaier does not use the *Twelve Articles* or Creed as his framework for this manual of instruction, though he incorporates them in the body of his text.[136] Instead, Hubmaier focuses on the two institutions that Christ has left the church, baptism and the Lord's Supper, devoting a section of the work to each.

Part one of the catechism deals with the inward pledge of faith that is made public in water baptism. He develops his outline from the *Summa* and he prefaces his discussion of repentance with a brief series of questions and answers on the nature of man, God, and sin. Man is described as a tripartite corporeal being of body, soul, and spirit, created in the image of God. God is described as all powerful, all wise, and all merciful. The power of God is seen in creation, his wisdom is seen in the ordering and governing of all creatures, his mercy is seen in the sending of Christ to save the world from sin and to attain to eternal life. Sin is defined as every movement or desire that is contrary to the will of God, which is recognized in the law, specifically the Ten Commandments.[137]

Having thus described the predicament of people who have fallen into sin, Hubmaier goes on to describe the path sinners must follow if they are to be saved. He begins with the responses of repentance and prayer. Repentance he describes as self-accusation before God, asking for forgiveness and never again committing the sin, but rather living from then on according to the Word of God. Prayer is lifting up the mind to God in spirit and truth, as Christ taught his disciples to pray.[138]

At this point, Hubmaier introduces a distinction only hinted at in earlier works, the distinction between the promises of God and the gospel.[139] The promises of God "comfort and preserve the confessing sinner, so that he does not despair in his sins, for a Messiah will come and atone for the sins, to release the debtors from prison and to lead them with him

---

136. Examples of catechisms which are structured on the Creed, The Lord's Prayer, and the Ten Commandments can be seen in Janz, *Three Reformation Catechisms*. This work contains a Catholic catechism entitled "A Fruitful Mirror," 31ff; Luther's "Small Catechism," 181ff; and Hubmaier's Catechism. The "Catechism of the Bohemian Brethren" can be located in Zeman, *Anabaptists and Czech Brethren*, 330ff.

137. *PY,* 345–46; *HS,* 311–12. This echoed his earlier comment that the sinner is to repent of deeds and omissions that are contrary to the commands of God. *PY,* 144; *HS,* 158.

138. *PY,* 346–47; *HS,* 312.

139. *PY,* 347; *HS,* 312.

into the promised fatherland."[140] He then uses the illustration of pointing a sick man to the physician who will surely make him well but has not yet done so. This modifies Hubmaier's now familiar use of the parable of the Good Samaritan to describe the process of salvation.[141] While the wine remains the symbol of the sting of the law that brings the sinner to recognize his sin and repent, the oil, which was the comforting and healing gospel, is now divided into the promise that comforts and the gospel which heals: "The gospel . . . completely calms the person, helps him to rest in his conscience and makes him completely well, for it shows that the Law is now fulfilled in Christ, who has paid the debt of sin for us and has already vanquished death, devil, and hell."[142] To illustrate the difference between promise and gospel Hubmaier uses the example of the patriarchs. The patriarchs had the promise to comfort and preserve them in hell until Christ in his spirit came and preached the gospel to them. "Only then did they really live in Christ" and were "freed of their pains."[143]

Faith must follow the message of the gospel; not a dead faith which is unfruitful and without works of love, but a living faith that produces both the fruit of the Spirit and good works. The Christian faith is summarized in the *Twelve Articles,* which Hubmaier expands in one important point. Instead of the standard statement "I believe and confess the remission of sins," he modifies it to state, "I believe that by the command of Christ it [the church] has authority to forgive sins," a view he held in the *Twelve Articles.*[144]

Following faith, the sinner should desire baptism. Hubmaier's discussion of baptism follows his threefold division as first described in his *Dialogue.* The inner illumination of faith that occurs through the Word of God, which he calls spirit baptism, must be followed by water baptism, the sign of incorporation into the fellowship of the church. The sign of water baptism is also accompanied by oral public confession of belief in the forgiveness of sins and a vow to live according to the Rule of Christ and to accept brotherly admonition if the baptized person should fail to

140. *PY,* 347; *HS,* 312.

141. *PY,* 347, cf. 144; *HS,* 312, cf. 158–59.

142. *PY,* 347; *HS,* 312.

143. *PY,* 347–48; *HS,* 312. As illustrations of the promises of God, he also uses God's promise to the woman that her seed would crush the head of the serpent, and to Abraham that through his seed all the nations would be blessed. He contrasts the promises with the gospel, citing Rom 4:25, "Christ died for the sake of our sins and arose for the sake of our justification." *PY,* 348; *HS,* 313.

144. *PY,* 349, cf. 239; *HS,* 313, cf. 219.

live as they should. It is this true baptismal vow that the church had lost "for a thousand years."[145] His discussion of true baptism is completed by a reference to baptism in blood, which is defined as the daily mortification of the flesh until death.[146]

Hubmaier includes a very brief rebuttal of infant baptism and the charge of rebaptism. He reiterates his position, now familiar from his debates with Zwingli; infant baptism is no baptism, for the child cannot know what faith, Christ, or baptism is, therefore making infant baptism a mockery of the true baptism Christ instituted. On the subject of rebaptism, Hubmaier again makes the point that the issue is not individual opinion, but what the Word of God commands. Here there are echoes of his debate with the followers of Zwingli to whom he refers in his work against Oecolampad, who only cite the opinion of Zwingli and not the Scriptures.[147] He makes it plain that since infant baptism is no baptism, the water baptism of believers that he carries out is not rebaptism but true baptism.

The discussion of baptism and the pledge of faith draw Hubmaier to explore the doctrine of the church. He does this by asserting that Theses 9 and 10 of the Creed, which deal with the church, the fellowship of the saints, and the forgiveness of sins, are to do with baptism, by which the church opens the door of salvation.

Hubmaier distinguishes between the universal church and the particular church that is gathered together under one shepherd or bishop to receive instruction from the Word of God and to carry out the two sacraments that Christ has instituted. The daughter church has the same power to forgive or to exclude as the mother church, though the daughter church may err, whereas the mother church cannot.[148] He argues that the church is built on the "oral confession of faith that Jesus is the Christ, the Son of the living God." He goes on: "This outward confession is what makes a church, and not faith alone; for the church that has the power to bind and loose is outward and corporeal, not theoretical, and faith is inward. And although faith alone makes righteous, it does not alone give salvation, for it must be accompanied by public confession."[149]

With this strongly worded statement Hubmaier makes clear his earlier implications that faith is not enough for salvation. Salvation requires

145. *PY*, 349; *HS*, 314.
146. *PY*, 350; *HS*, 314.
147. *PY*, 283, 286–87; *HS*, 263, 264.
148. *PY*, 351–52; *HS*, 315.
149. *PY*, 352; *HS*, 316.

both inward faith and public oral confession of that faith. He continues to base this view on Rom 10:10. However, he now links salvation to identification with the physically gathered church. There is no salvation outside the church, and baptism is the outward symbol of the key that Christ has given that opens the door to salvation. In one regard, Hubmaier is close to Zwingli, Luther, and the Catholic Church, all of whom insisted that those who are saved are the members of the church marked by baptism. The difference is that Hubmaier defines the church as those marked by baptism on confession of an existing inward faith. For Hubmaier, this church is the visible gathered church, while the others speak more cautiously of the universal church.

The theses that speak of the fellowship of the saints and the forgiveness of sin provide Hubmaier with the framework for his discussion of discipline within the church. It is by the baptismal pledge that the members of the church subject themselves to one another for correction and reproof when they sin. It is from the command of Christ that the church has received authority to bind or to loose; that is, to forgive repentant members who have sinned or to exclude them from the church and thus presumably also from heaven and salvation.[150] Hubmaier gives only two causes for imposing the ban, or excommunication from the church, "refusal to be reconciled to the brother or to desist from sin."[151] He pointedly states that excommunication is not for "petty offences," something he accuses the "papists" of practicing.[152] However, the sinner who "desists from his sin, avoids the ways and paths that might cause him to fall again, and reforms" is to be welcomed back into the church with joy, as the father received the prodigal and Paul instructed the church at Corinth to do. By the act of readmission the church "opens the door of heaven for him and lets him return to the communion of the Lord's Supper."[153]

A short summary concludes the first part of *A Christian Catechism*: "Where water baptism in accord with Christ's institution is not reestablished and practiced one does not know who is a brother or sister, there

---

150. *PY,* 353; *HS,* 316.

151. *PY,* 353; *HS,* 317.

152. *PY,* 354; *HS,* 317. Later the imposition of the ban for trivial reasons was to provide a major issue of debate between Pilgram Marpeck and the Swiss Brethren. Klassen and Klaassen, *Writings of Pilgram Marpeck,* 367.

153. *PY,* 354; *HS,* 317.

is no church, no brotherly discipline or reproof, no ban, no Supper, nor anything that resembles the Christian stance and nature."[154]

Part two begins with the question: "What is the Lord's Supper?" Hubmaier has Hans, one of the Lords of Liechtenstein, respond: "It is a public sign and testimonial of the love in which one brother obligates himself to another before the congregation that just as they now break and eat the bread with each other and share and drink the cup, likewise they wish now to sacrifice and shed their body and blood for one another; this they will do in the strength of our Lord Jesus Christ, whose suffering they are now commemorating in the Supper with the breaking of bread and the sharing of the wine, and proclaiming his death until he comes."[155]

This is essentially a restatement of his teaching as most recently given in *A Simple Instruction*. However, there is a significant reordering of the various parts of his teaching. As in his earliest writing on the Mass, Hubmaier has underscored the importance of the vow of love for the neighbor by bringing it to the forefront of this summary.[156] He further sharpens the focus of his teaching on the obligation of love that he sees as an integral part of the Lord's Supper by having Hans conclude, "Precisely this is the pledge of love in Christ's Supper that one Christian performs toward the other, in order that every brother may know what good deed to expect from the other."[157] Though the second part of *A Christian Catechism* is centered on the pledge of love in the Lord's Supper, it is really an exploration of the subject of good works. Humbaier understands the pledge of love to involve an obligation to good works. These works are in no way meritorious in his thinking as they were maintained to be by the Catholic Church.

Hubmaier briefly explains his memorial understanding of the Supper. The bread and wine are memorial symbols of the suffering and death of Christ for the forgiveness of sins. Christ is not in the bread and wine, which are only bread and wine, he is seated at the right hand of God as the Christian's sole mediator and intercessor. As the sixth article of the Creed states, Christ will remain there until the day of his return when he will judge the living and the dead.[158] The Mass is repudiated as the idol

---

154. *PY*, 354; *HS*, 317.

155. *PY*, 354; *HS*, 317.

156. The understanding of the sacrament as an "oath" was used both by Zwingli and Erasmus. It is possible that Zwingli was influenced by Erasmus in this usage.

157. *PY*, 354; *HS*, 317.

158. *PY*, 355; *HS*, 318.

and abomination mentioned in Dan 11:31, which is honored with gold, silver, and gems, just as the Mass is, as he had already stated it in his *A Brief Apologia*.[159]

Hubmaier then begins a series of responses that on the one hand rejects what the Catholic Church teaches are good works, while maintaining that the works, when rightly understood, are to be continued. For Hubmaier, the correct understanding of the various works requires the redefinition of the terms. He begins with confession, which is still to be practiced, but not as the papists do; that is, auricular confession. Rather it is the direct confession of the sinner to God that is taught. Though he does not provide the Scripture references, the examples to be followed are the same as in his *A Brief Apologia*; that is, the prodigal, David, and the tax collector in the temple.[160]

Fasting is represented as daily eating and drinking in moderation, always with thanks as God has ordained. Unlike his statement in *A Brief Apologia*, Hubmaier this time gives a reason for fasting, "so that I do not overfeed the old Adam and he become insolent and cast the ark of the divine commands into the mud together with the stubborn ox."[161] By this allusion to 2 Sam 6:6, Hubmaier stresses the need for the daily mortification of the flesh, the taming of the old Adam to the will of Christ. If the old Adam reasserts its will over the life of the believer then both the flesh and the soul will be returned to the mire of sin. This prefigures Hubmaier's description of the struggle that goes on in the believer between the flesh and spirit. He begins to explain this in this work, but develops it more fully in his two works on the freedom of the will. Hubmaier also includes at this point instructions for how the master of a household should give thanks before and after a meal, and how he should speak with his household about the Word of God during the meal. He also warns "all who while eating swear, rave and curse by the flesh, blood, pains, wounds, and suffering of Christ, take the name of God in vain, slander their neighbor's honor and good reputation and speak ill of him, eat and drink the flesh and blood of men."[162]

Fasting and eating provide another example of the communal nature of the true Christian's life. Not only is there concern shown to maintain the honor of God and Christ, but the obligation of neighborly love is again

159. *PY*, 355, cf. 302; *HS*, 318, cf. 276.
160. *PY*, 356, cf. 299–300; *HS*, 318, cf. 274.
161. *PY*, 356, cf. 299; *HS*, 318, cf. 273–74.
162. *PY*, 356; *HS*, 319.

emphasized, this time in relation to what one says about others even in the privacy of one's own household.

Sabbath observance is dealt with briefly as the celebration of the eternal Sabbath, by which Hubmaier means that people should keep themselves from sinning and allow God to work in them to do His will.

Mary is again honored as the mother of God, who is blessed because she believed the message the angel delivered. She is described as "a pure, chaste, and spotless Virgin before, during, and after the birth."[163]

Hubmaier reiterates that the saints should not be called on by people to aid them when in distress. However, this time he includes Mary in this section, and develops his argument from his *A Brief Apologia*. Taking the words of Mary at the marriage feast in Cana, "do what my Son tells you," Hubmaier argues that to run to the saints or to Mary for help in our distress dishonors Christ. By doing so we show that we do not believe that Christ is the most merciful and most gracious one in heaven, our only intercessor and mediator, as Scripture tells us he is. We also disobey Mary and thus dishonor her, for we have not heeded her command to do what her Son commands.[164] He takes this argument one step further, declaring that to appeal to the saints is blasphemy against God, for it would be to accuse both Christ and Mary of misrepresenting the ways of God to us.[165]

Images are rejected totally since they are forbidden by God. This topic was not covered in his *A Brief Apologia*. However, Hubmaier had spoken on this issue at the Second Zurich Disputation, and we see here a development of that argument through the references Hubmaier provides in support. Previously he had cited only Old Testament references as proof texts to demonstrate the prohibition of images and idols in the church. That sequence of Exod 20:4–6; Deut 5:6–10; 7:25 is now extended by one reference to Bar 6:6 and to Gal 4:8; 5:1; 1 Pet 4:3f; 1 John 5:21. He also refers to Paul at Athens, an instance he had previously alluded to and now provides with its reference, Acts 19:23ff.[166] The inclusion of New Testament references indicates how Hubmaier has moved to rely more on it than on the Old Testament as a source of proof texts for doctrine. Hubmaier does maintain his opinion that the removal of images must

---

163. *PY*, 357; *HS*, 319. Hubmaier has added "during" to his description given in his *A Brief Apologia*, thus excluding any possible objection to the perpetual virginity of Mary. Cf. *PY*, 299; *HS*, 273.

164. *PY*, 357; *HS*, 319.

165. *PY*, 358; *HS*, 319–20.

166. *PY*, 358, cf. 25–26; *HS*, 320.

be preceded by clear teaching on the matter from the Word of God. In his earlier statement, however, he appears to be more confident that the inherent power of the Word of God will bring about change in people so that they will agree to remove the images from the church. In *A Christian Catechism*, he rewords this opinion, perhaps in the light of the present situation of the church in Nikolsburg. He writes, "But one should above all uproot such idols and images out of human hearts with the Word of God, or the outward destruction of idols is futile."[167]

The issue of singing is dealt with even more summarily than it was in *A Brief Apologia*. Singing is permitted if the words are intelligible and the singer is thoughtfully engaged in the act, reflecting on the meaning of the words.[168]

Under the rubric of the highest honor to God, Hubmaier undertakes an excursion into describing the works that are acceptable to God. It is not the works done with good intentions, as shown in the examples of Peter refusing to have his feet washed and Uzzah reaching out to steady the ark. Intentions have nothing to do with it; only those works are acceptable that God has commanded. The Christian discerns which works God commands by hearing the Word of God preached, and it is therefore the highest honor to God to hear and believe his Word as it is preached in the church.[169] Such preaching is summarized in the proclamation of love, love of God, and love of neighbor. This, Hubmaier asserts, fulfills the law and the prophets.

The good works that God commands are not possible in human strength, in fact God is seen as responsible for both the command to do the good works and the ability of the individual to do them. As a proof text Hubmaier cites Paul from Phil 2:13 that it is God who "works in us to will and to do the good."[170] This consideration of good works then leads Hubmaier into a discussion of the freedom of the will.

Hubmaier follows on from the proposition that man is incapable of doing good with the question, "Since man cannot do anything good, why does God condemn him?" He responds that God condemns people not for doing, but for not doing what God has clearly commanded them to do. He illustrates this with the examples of the teacher who beats the student

---

167. *PY*, 358; *HS*, 320.
168. *PY*, 359 cf. 300; *HS*, 320–21 cf. 274. In his earlier statement Hubmaier added the idea that singing must be edifying for the whole church.
169. *PY*, 358; *HS*, 320.
170. *PY*, 359; *HS*, 321.

for not learning, perhaps a reflection on his own experience as both pupil and teacher, and that of the husband who strikes his wife for not doing something the husband has commanded to be done, but never inflicting a beating for doing nothing.[171] He presses the point by raising a passage of Scripture that appears to indicate that it is within the capability of people to do good, "if thou wilt enter into life, keep the Commandments" (Matt 19:17). This text becomes one of Hubmaier's key texts in the debate concerning free will.

He indicates that the passages that deal with free will must be understood to relate to one of three conditions of people: how people were when they were first created, how they were after the fall, and how they are after being reborn through the Word God sent. He also makes explicit his presupposition that there is "something in us of God's likeness" that despite the fall has not been completely removed. Rather it is a "live spark covered with cold ashes" which is fanned to flame when the Holy Spirit breathes on the sinner through the proclaimed and believed Word of God.[172] Hubmaier is insistent that the Scriptures that deal with the free and bound will can only be judged correctly when the distinctions in human nature before the fall, after the fall, and rebirth through the Holy Spirit, are carefully noted.

He provides an example of incorrect interpretation by citing part of Rom 7:18, where Paul declares, "I know that nothing good dwells within me." It is wrong to conclude that there is nothing good in humanity from this text, for the words that immediately follow also need to be considered if Paul is to be understood correctly. Paul explains his comment by adding the words "in my flesh." Hubmaier then introduces an explanation of the tripartite anthropology that he introduced at the very beginning of this work. It is only the flesh that is totally corrupted by the fall and is irredeemable. The soul is wounded but capable of health again, while the spirit is held captive, and awaits liberation. The liberation of the spirit comes through the rebirth that Jesus spoke of, which also restores health to the soul, and makes the flesh completely harmless to the Christian.[173]

Hubmaier goes on to suggest that the passages in Scripture that attribute free will to people are there to awaken us from sleep and to "give us heart to resolve to do good and to accomplish this with the hope of divine help."[174] The will to do good, however, only exists in us after we have been

---

171. *PY,* 359; *HS,* 321.
172. *PY,* 360; *HS,* 322.
173. *PY,* 361; *HS,* 322.
174. *PY,* 362; *HS,* 323.

Making a Patchwork of Scripture

born again though the proclaimed Word and the Holy Spirit. He explains how this rebirth takes place by describing how God draws people to himself, firstly, through an outward drawing; that is, the public proclamation of the gospel, and secondly, through the inward drawing; that is, how God "illuminates the person's soul inwardly, so that it understands the incontrovertible truth, convinced by the Spirit and the preached Word in such a way that one must in one's own conscience confess that this is the case and it cannot be otherwise."[175]

In this short section on free will, Hubmaier demonstrates the application of his rule concerning the importance of interpreting a text by the words that follow. He had previously used this approach in his exposition of the words of institution of the Lord's Supper, where for him the crucial words are "in remembrance of me."[176] He also brings to the fore his understanding of humanity created in the image of God. People are not totally corrupted by the fall, though they are damned in the flesh because of the sin of Adam. This presupposition was totally rejected by Zwingli and Luther. On this matter Hubmaier sided with Erasmus and the Swiss Brethren.[177]

Scriptures are again noted that seem to contradict the belief in salvation by grace alone. How is it that Scripture promises rewards for our works? Hubmaier does not develop an answer in any depth; he simply attributes this phrase to the "gracious kindness" of God, and warns against presumptuousness that would consider the promised rewards as payment.[178]

A final section of *A Christian Catechism* deals with the question of those who hear but do not understand or do not want to obey the message they hear. Those who hear the Word of God outwardly but not inwardly are encouraged to pray in faith and ask for wisdom from God, who will certainly give it to them. Those who hear but either do not comprehend, or comprehend but do not obey, will stand condemned by their own unbelief. Hubmaier contrasts this personal unbelief and condemnation with personal faith and salvation.[179]

---

175. *PY*, 362; *HS*, 324.

176. *PY*, 324; *HS*, 293–94.

177. Friedmann comments that Hubmaier's anthropology "exerted the profoundest influence on incipient Anabaptism." Friedmann, *Theology of Anabaptism*, 58.

178. *PY*, 361; *HS*, 323.

179. *PY*, 363; *HS*, 324.

That Hubmaier considers inner faith alone insufficient for salvation is shown by the discussion concerning good works that immediately follows on from this reflection on condemnation though unbelief. Once again, it is the passage from Matt 25:34-36 that provides Hubmaier with the list of good works that Christ commands his disciples to do, while leaving them undone will bring condemnation on the day of judgment. In this way, Hubmaier brings to the attention of the catechumen that a living faith is required if they are to experience eternal life; that is, the "eternal, sure, and joyful vision of God's face, prepared from the foundation of the world for all believers in Christ who have performed works of mercy toward their neighbor."[180]

Hubmaier teaches that the shortest path to eternal life is that of the cross. The disciple of Jesus must expect to be persecuted and to bear his own little cross, accepting it with patience and joy.[181] He contrasts the reality of suffering that the true disciple of Christ will experience with the Catholic Church's cult of relics and pilgrimages. He had personally experienced one of the most extreme demonstrations of the excesses of the pilgrimage movement that his generation was to see. As pilgrimage preacher at the Chapel of the Beautiful Mary in Regensburg, he became appalled by the excesses of the pilgrims there after March 1519.[182]

In this work, some new material is introduced, most significantly the discussion on free will and good works that will dominate Hubmaier's writings in May and June of 1527. He briefly outlines his position and declares himself to be of a similar opinion to Erasmus.

He also makes more explicit his understanding that salvation is more than just inner faith and public oral confession. Salvation involves remaining within the church. Entry to the church is by water baptism, the pledge of faith, while remaining in the church involves fulfilling the pledge of love to one's neighbors made at the Lord's Supper; that is, to undertake the good works that Christ demands of all Christians. The part that discipline

---

180. PY, 364; HS, 325. Hell, on the other hand, is the "deprivation of the contemplation of God's face." PY, 365; HS, 326.

181. PY, 364; HS, 325.

182. Bergsten, *Balthasar Hubmaier: Anabaptist Theologian*, 60–62. A woodcut depicting the excesses of the pilgrims at the Schöne Maria chapel in Regensburg provided Ricker and Saywell with the opportunity to comment on the pilgrimage movement as follows: "Shrines also attracted crowds of pilgrims and worshippers, fervent and sometimes hysterical. Devotion to the shrines of the Virgin Mary was particularly intense, as this early sixteenth-century woodcut of the reputedly miraculous Schöne Maria in Germany indicates." Ricker and Saywell, *Renaissance and Reformation*, 32.

Making a Patchwork of Scripture

plays in defining who is in the church and who is excluded begins to be more and more crucial in Hubmaier's theology. The emphasis on the necessity of suffering is also a growing one.

Use of Scripture

His Scripture usage is not as full in this work as in some others. Though he repeats his material from *A Brief Apologia* on a number of topics, he does not always include the biblical references as he had done in the earlier work. Nevertheless, he does give ninety-five citations, fourteen Old Testament and eighty-one New Testament. These numbers increase to twenty-one and one hundred seven respectively when quotations without references and allusions are included. He continues to use the Old Testament chiefly as a source of historical illustrations (nine examples), while he uses it as a propositional proof text in eight cases, chiefly with respect to defining the commands that God demands people fulfill, the prohibition of images and idols, and the innocence of children from their own guilt, as they know neither good nor evil. There are four examples where Hubmaier uses Old Testament texts as supporting texts, and two instances where he gives both the Old Testament reference and the reference to its New Testament occurrence. In both instances he cites the Old Testament first, which is different to his previous method. However, this difference is not a significant shift in Hubmaier's attitude to the authority of the Old Testament. One example is primarily a historical reference, 1 Kgs 19:18; Rom 11:4, where God declares that he has preserved for himself seven thousand people who have not served Baal, which Hubmaier interprets as referring to the universal church. The other is a reference to Dan 11:31; Matt 24:15, where Jesus's words are used as the clearer text to identify the Mass with the abomination in the temple that Daniel sees. In this instance, though the Old Testament reference precedes the New, it is the New Testament words of Jesus that have priority in the interpretive process.

He also includes a reference to the Apocryphal book Baruch, which is only one of a series of references that develop his argument concerning the prohibition of idols and images in the church. The Baruch reference is, however, only a supporting reference and does nothing more than widen the sources that condemn idols.

The New Testament references are in the main proof texts or texts supporting the proposition of a proof text. These two types of usage account for eighty-eight of the one hundred seven New Testament references, quotations and allusions. There are twelve instances of references used as historical examples, particularly concerning restoration of repentant sinners; the prodigal Son mentioned twice, the repentant Corinthian, and the tax collector. There are five examples where Hubmaier uses another text as a clearer text by which he then gives the correct interpretation of the darker text. These include most significantly the Rom 7:18 text that becomes for Hubmaier the key text by which he then interprets all other texts that seem to deny any free will to people.

Hubmaier also uses two texts as metaphors, both in the dedicatory letter. One is an allusion to Christ being in the boat helping his disciples fish for men, the other is used by Hubmaier to interpret the history of the church in the German-speaking lands. He asserts that the church in that area has never been pure as it came there already mixed with error from Ireland and England. He states that the bishops and the people both slept as the tares were sown among the wheat, making them equally responsible for the present errors in the church.[183] Hubmaier's use of the Scriptures in this work is unremarkable, and remains consistent with his previous usages.

Summary

Hermeneutically Hubmaier continues to apply the same rules he has previously. As noted above, he utilizes his rule of the context of a passage to ascertain its true meaning in his consideration of the topic of free will. He also renews his emphasis on doing only what God commands, a part of his hermeneutic that had not received as much attention since his publication of *On Christian Baptism*.

THE GROUND AND REASON

(Autumn 1526)[184]

Setting

This work provides a second example of Hubmaier's practice of reissuing a previous work in a modified form. He had done this with the *Summa*, including it as the last chapter of *On the Christian Baptism*; now he takes

---

183. *PY*, 343; *HS*, 309.
184. *PY*, 366–71; *HS*, 3227–36.

from that same work the ten reasons why those who believe but have not yet been baptized should do so, modifies them and adds three new reasons, and issues it under the title *The Ground and Reason*.[185]

Bergsten, agreeing with Carl Sachsse, proposes that this work is to be identified with a work Hubmaier calls *What Christian Water Baptism Is* that he mentions in his preface to the *Dialogue* as being ready for printing.[186]

Analysis

Hubmaier dedicated the work to von Pernstein, a leader of the Utraquists and Lutheran sympathizer, who was a member of one of Moravia's leading families. Bergsten suggests that Hubmaier dedicated the work to him in order to win von Pernstein to the Anabaptist cause.[187] That von Pernstein was sympathetic to the Anabaptists is demonstrated by the protection he later offered some Anabaptist refugees.[188]

As Pipkin and Yoder note, this is a missionary tract, written to help those who cannot make up their minds about baptism. Hubmaier likens these people to Absolom who hung "between heaven and earth."[189] This metaphor takes on polemical overtones, however, when it is recognized that for Hubmaier baptism is the symbol of the key of admission to the church and therefore to heaven. To refuse to be baptized when one already has faith is to condemn oneself to exclusion from heaven. Hubmaier develops this theme in his new thirteenth reason. There he argues that water baptism and the forgiveness of sins are linked. Though water baptism does not grant remission of sins—that occurs through the power of the keys that Christ has granted to the universal church—nevertheless it is through water baptism that a person enters into the universal church "outside of which there is no salvation."[190] He argues that as much as a person thinks communion with the Trinity is important; or communion with the heavenly host or the universal church is important; or the forgiveness of sins

---

185. Cf. *PY*, 121–27; *HS*, 140–45.

186. *HS*, 327. Bergsten rejects Loserth's suggestion that this work should be identified with *Order of the Christian Church*.

187. *HS*, 327

188. *PY*, 366.

189. *PY*, 367; *HS*, 328.

190. *PY*, 371; *HS*, 335.

is important; that person should consider water baptism to be equally important.

The polemical warning becomes explicit in the final paragraph of this work, when Hubmaier states that those who fall have only themselves to blame. He then cites Luke 12:47 as a warning to those who ignore the clear command of God to be baptized, "Follow or you will be beaten with many strokes," one of Hubmaier's favorite polemical verses.[191]

The ten reasons from *On Christian Baptism* are taken over almost verbatim, with only minor changes in the spelling of some words. The most common change is *sy* replacing *sye*, and *Geend* for *Gond* in Matt 28:18. The other major change is the transfer of Scripture references from the body of the text to the margin in nearly every instance.

He begins with the command of Christ from Matt 28:18ff. Firstly, he contends that it is a command and secondly, that this command is given in the name of the Trinity. It is therefore a serious command and demands serious obedience.[192]

His third reason deals with the word order of Mark 16:15ff, which he summarizes as (1) go, (2) preach, (3) he who believes, (4) and is baptized, (5) will be saved. Supporters of infant baptism argue that these words only apply to those who need to have the gospel preached to them before baptism, but that they does not apply to infants. Hubmaier's response is to insist that they show him the command in Scripture where it says, "Go and baptize the infants of the believers, and after six or eight years preach to them the gospel."[193]

Hubmaier does add one long paragraph to reason four, dealing with the evangelical preachers' use of 1 Cor 7:2 to support their argument that "each" man should have a wife. Hubmaier urges consistent use of the Scriptures, and insists that the "each" of Acts 2:38 should have the same force, "each one of you be baptized."[194]

Exegesis of Hebrews 10:22ff provides Hubmaier with his fifth reason. He argues that those who want to go to God through the blood of Christ with a clear conscience must experience the washing of the body with water in baptism. If people do not believe that this is the true meaning of

---

191. *PY,* 371; *HS,* 336.

192. *PY,* 121–22; *HS,* 140.

193. *PY,* 122; *HS,* 141.

194. *PY,* 368; *HS,* 330–31. Perhaps Hubmaier has Zwingli in mind with this reference, as Zwingli had used this verse with exactly this sense in July 1522. Zwingli, *Petition of Eleven Priests,* 34–36.

Making a Patchwork of Scripture

these words of Scripture he challenges them to tear them out. However, that cannot be as the Word of God remains unchanged for eternity.[195]

His sixth reason is drawn from the book of Acts, which provides historical examples of those who could have argued that faith alone saved them, or that they already had the Holy Spirit, nevertheless were constrained by the serious command of Christ to be baptized.[196] However, here in *The Ground and Reason,* the modified version of *On the Christian Baptism,* Hubmaier deletes the reference to the twelve disciples of John the Baptist at Ephesus. This deletion causes some confusion in the references now cited in the margin. Though he retains the allusions to the Samaritans and Philip, Simon the sorcerer and the treasurer of Candice, he does not provide the reference to Acts 8. The allusion to Lydia and the Philippian jailer are given the wrong reference, Acts 10 instead of Acts 16, while the people who were baptized at Corinth are mentioned but cited at Acts 22 instead of Acts 18. These appear to be the careless errors of a printer who is resetting type.[197]

Reason seven has a section deleted that compares baptism and the Lord's Supper. In his earlier work, Hubmaier had sought to demonstrate that baptism was instituted as a command, "Go forth, teach, and baptize," while the Lord's Supper was not, for Paul says, "As often and as much as you do this."[198] This comparison with the Supper does not add to the strength of his argument, and in fact distracts from it. In this reason, he again emphasizes that baptism is a command and institution of Christ, and to declare that Christ did not institute baptism is to place oneself under the curse that Jesus uttered in Matt 5:18, they "will be called the least in the kingdom of heaven."[199]

The historical example of Naaman and Elisha provides Hubmaier with the context of his eighth reason. Naaman despised the simple instruction to wash in the Jordan, yet his obedience saw him cured and made whole again. Christians should not despise the command of God to be baptized in water, even though it seems such a trivial thing. To reinforce this point Hubmaier alludes to 1 Cor 1:19; God makes the wisdom

---

195. *PY,* 124; *HS,* 142.

196. *PY,* 124; *HS,* 142–43. He adds in the margin the example of the thief on the cross for whom faith alone was sufficient to save him. *HS,* 331.

197. *HS,* 331.

198. *PY,* 125; *HS,* 143.

199. *PY,* 125; *HS,* 143.

of the world foolishness and what is exalted before people an abomination before God.[200]

The ninth reason continues the theme of reason eight. All the commands of God as they are revealed in his Word are to be obeyed no matter how foolish they appear. He modifies this passage only by adding the biblical references Gen 2 and 17 for the illustrations of Adam and Eve, who were commanded not to eat the fruit, and the command to circumcise on the eighth day.

The final reason from the previous work focused on the necessity of baptism to define the visible church. Without baptism Hubmaier argues "there is no church nor minister, neither brother nor sister, no brotherly admonition, excommunication, or reacceptance."[201] The outward confession of faith that accompanies baptism makes manifest the faith of the heart, which in Hubmaier's soteriology is absolutely necessary, for faith in the heart is not enough for salvation. Baptism is also the link to defining the true visible church where not only baptism and the Lord's Supper are observed, but also admonition, ban, and readmission. It is therefore necessary that people are baptized so that the true church may be recognized and that it may function according to the Rule of Christ.[202]

With the three new reasons that Hubmaier adds, it can be seen how he brings into consideration both the present circumstances in which he was situated, and evidence from his more recent research and publications.

The eleventh reason clearly shows Hubmaier aware of his situation in Moravia, for he includes a reference to the Picards and their practice "today" of rebaptizing all those who were baptized by heretics. He holds this to be the proper course of action, citing the resolution of Cyprian and the Fourth Council of Carthage (255 AD), as he had done in the second edition of *Old and New Teachers*. It was decided that those baptized by heretics were to be rebaptized, since heretics did not received the power of the keys. Only the true church had received and retained that power. Hubmaier goes on to make the point that the Roman Church is considered by almost all evangelical preachers to be heretical. Those who have received infant baptism from that church have received heretical baptism, and therefore should be rebaptized. People should not refuse true baptism because of this "silly infant baptism."[203] In this reason, Hubmaier is also

---

200. *PY,* 126; *HS,* 144.
201. *PY,* 127; *HS,* 145.
202. *PY,* 127; *HS,* 145.
203. *PY,* 369, cf. 266; *HS,* 145, cf. 244–45.

making it plain that all those who remain in the Catholic Church, or claim to be evangelical but do not accept the true baptism, are outside the true church.

The short section deleted from the sixth reason constitutes the new twelfth reason. In this section, Hubmaier summarizes his argument against Zwingli's interpretation of Acts 19:1ff, which refers to the twelve disciples of John the Baptist who Paul baptized. He argues that it was the "high and earnest mandate of Christ" that moved these men to be rebaptized, and that people who have received infant baptism are obliged to do likewise by the institution of baptism by Christ. On the one hand, there is not a single letter in Scripture that can be regarded as commanding infant baptism. On the other hand, people have this plain command of Christ before them to baptize believers. Hubmaier then cites from "the very Christian epistle of James the warning, 'Whoever keeps all the commandments but fails in one point, is guilty of all'" (Jas 2:10), as a spur to encourage people in their decision to be baptized.[204]

The last reason, which focuses on the link between baptism, the power of the keys, and the forgiveness of sins, was briefly described earlier.

These three new reasons indicate Hubmaier's new emphasis on the nature of the church and the power of the keys that the church has received. He urges his readers to receive baptism so that the true church may be gathered and made visible, that discipline may be undertaken and those who bring shame to the name of Christ may be excluded, while those who truly repent may be readmitted.

People should desire baptism as much as they desire communion with God, the Father, the Son, and the Holy Spirit, with the heavenly host and the church, for in Hubmaier's opinion baptism is the symbol that Christ instituted to make the church visible. He is also at pains to encourage, even threaten, people to ensure that they are in the true church, for outside the true church, as defined by those who receive baptism, there is no salvation.

Use of Scripture

There are seven Old Testament references in this work, six of which are historical examples taken from Genesis, Deuteronomy, 1 Samuel, 2 Samuel and 2 Kings. Only one is used as a proof text (Deut 27:26), where Hubmaier modifies this curse of those who do not uphold the words of the

204. *PY,* 370; *HS,* 335.

law to more closely resemble the words of Jesus in Matt 5:18. He states that those who cannot say "Amen" with him; that is, they cannot agree with him that those who have faith and water and one willing to baptize them are obliged to be baptized, are still under the curse of the law.

There are twenty-nine New Testament quotations and allusions with references, with a further eleven stand-alone references. There are a further four quotations without references, and seven allusions without references, giving a total of fifty-one New Testament references, quotations, and allusions. Sixteen of these are from the book of Acts, nine being historical examples of the practice of baptism by the apostles; six refer to Acts 2:37–38 as a proof text of the institution of baptism, though it is Peter who is speaking and not Christ; the final reference being to Acts 19:1ff, a proof text for rebaptism. In citing texts from Acts, Hubmaier does not change his usage to his earlier works, particularly *On the Christian Baptism* and *Dialogue*.

References from Matthew fall in two main groups. The words of Christ that institute baptism Matt 28:18ff (four), which have parallel references in Mark 16:15f (four occurrences); and the words of Christ that grant the power of the keys to the church, Matt 18:15ff (five), which he supports with a reference to Matt 7:15 that issues a warning against the false prophets. He uses two texts from Matthew in his section on the baptism of John the Baptist, Matt 3:3, 12. The two remaining texts from Matthew both reflect Hubmaier's concern to prove that the words of Christ have eternal authority and must stand unchanged, Matt 5:18; 24:35.

All except one of the references to John are additional to those in *On the Christian Baptism*. Three refer to the power of the keys that Jesus granted to the church, reflecting Hubmaier's new interest in this subject, and three relate to the baptism of John the Baptist, all of which reflect Hubmaier's dispute with Zwingli over this issue. The other reference is to the foot washing incident, which Hubmaier uses as a New Testament illustration of the need for Christians to obey even what appear to be trivial commands from God.

The remaining New Testament references come from 1 Corinthians (three), only the reference to 1 Cor 7:2 being new; one from Hebrews (10:22f); one from James (2:10) and two references to the same text from 1 Pet 3:21.

Summary

Despite adding three new reasons for people to be baptized, Hubmaier does not change his basic hermeneutical approach. The emphasis remains on the authority of the words of Christ's institution of baptism as described in Matthew and Mark. The book of Acts continues to supply the historical illustrations of the practice of baptism by the apostles, with the words of Peter in Acts 2:38 being considered to have equal weight to those of Christ. In the paragraph Hubmaier adds to reason four, he demonstrates a rule not frequently used by him. He cites the verse from 1 Cor 7:2 to show that the word "each" should have a consistent meaning across Scripture. He has done a similar thing when arguing with Zwingli about faith having one meaning across Scripture and not a variety of meanings that theologians can pick and choose from as best suits their needs.[205] Hubmaier refers to this practice as a gloss of the same nature as the scholastic theologians who he rejected for their arbitrary handling of the Scriptures.

In his usage of Scripture and selection of material, the only change that is significant is the introduction of material from John 20:22ff as his primary proof text for the power of the keys that Christ gave the church. Otherwise, the pattern of choosing New Testament passages as proof texts and Old Testament texts as historical illustrations remains unchanged, as does his method of interpreting this material.

ON FRATERNAL ADMONITION

(Autumn 1526)[206]

Setting

This work is another of the works that Hubmaier appears to have written in the Autumn of 1526 that were ready for the printer by December of that year, but had to wait until early in 1527 to be printed. Bergsten identifies this work with one Hubmaier calls *An Order of the Christian Church*, which is mentioned in the preface to the *Dialogue*[207]. Bergsten also considers as "very improbable" Sachsse's proposal that Hubmaier had

---

205. PY, 192; HS, 185. The dispute is over the nature of faith exhibited by Simon Magnus, Acts 8:9ff.

206. PY, 372–85; HS, 337–46.

207. HS, 337.

completed the work before his arrival in Nikolsburg.[208] In his opinion, it is more likely that the work was written after Hubmaier's arrival in Nikolsburg in response to the need to teach on church discipline due to the rapid growth of the Anabaptist church there.[209] It is not dedicated to anyone, nor does it include a foreword, and is therefore much more difficult to date with any certainty.

The theme of this work had occurred in Hubmaier's earliest works, *Theses Against Eck*, *Summa* and *On the Christian Baptism*.[210] In these previous works, the theme is not developed extensively, though it is considered by Hubmaier to be important in the life of the church. In *A Christian Catechism*, the role of brotherly admonition and the ban become more crucial not only to the life of the church but also to its definition.[211] In this work, written about the same time as *A Christian Catechism*, fraternal admonition and the ban combine to become a third mandatory practice for the church, accompanying baptism and the Lord's Supper, all instituted by Christ and all essential for the church if it is to be the true bride of Christ. He makes this point abundantly clear in the sub-title of this work: *Where this [fraternal admonition] is lacking, there is certainly also no church, even if Water Baptism and the Supper of Christ are practiced.*[212]

It is, however, not simply a work of detached exposition on the subject. Certainly Hubmaier is responding to the lack of evident change in the lives of the people in his church, a change he believed to be a necessary manifestation of faith. Of equal concern to him was the theological half-truth that people were using to support their new "evangelical" lifestyles. Hubmaier accuses them of rejecting the Catholic Church's restrictions about taking a wife, fasting, praying, and sacrificing only to indulge in sexual misconduct, gluttony, drunkenness, and all manner of evil acts.[213] He alleges that they do so behind the "facade of the gospel." They assert that it is not possible for them to do any good work as all things, whether good or evil, have been ordained according to the providence of God.[214]

---

208. *HS*, 337–38.

209. *HS*, 337.

210. The link between the baptismal pledge and brotherly admonition was also stressed by Grebel and the other Zurich radicals, though they did not make the claim, as Hubmaier does, that without the practice of brotherly admonition there is no true church. Harder, *Sources of Swiss Anabaptism*, 288.

211. *PY*, 352–53; *HS*, 316.

212. *PY*, 373; *HS*, 338. This is the extended title.

213. *PY*, 375–76; *HS*, 340.

214. *PY*, 376; *HS*, 340.

Making a Patchwork of Scripture

It is then a polemical work aimed at a wider audience than the congregation of the Nikolsburg church. Hubmaier has all evangelical Christians squarely in his sights; that is, those who follow the teaching of Luther on the bondage of the will.

Analysis

The work begins with Hubmaier's understanding of the process of coming to faith and being incorporated into the church. He does not expand the early part of this process; that is, hearing the Word, accepting it, believing it, committing oneself publicly to God in water baptism, and pledging oneself to live a new life according to the command of Christ in the power of the Trinity.[215]

The new life is declared to be an ongoing struggle against sin, constantly denying its rule over the members of the body. People are called to submit the members of their bodies to God in obedience as instruments of righteousness. This is understood as the daily mortification of the flesh, or the baptism of blood of which he wrote in the *A Christian Catechism*.[216]

By the act of baptism people allow themselves to be marked, counted, and incorporated into the "holy universal Christian church" outside of which there is no salvation, as the illustration of the ark of Noah vividly demonstrates.[217]

Hubmaier's introduction of the theme of the universal church leads him to discuss the relationship between the universal church; that is, the mother church, and the particular church (in the margin he calls it the *ecclesia particularis*). The point of his discussion is that the daughter church, like the mother church and Christ the bridegroom, does the will of God so that God's will is done on earth.[218] He does not discuss the power of the church under the rubric of the keys as he had done in *A Christian Catechism*.

Using a medical analogy Hubmaier describes how at times radical surgery is required so that a corrupt part of the body does not destroy the whole. He asserts that all people are by nature children of wrath, and that Christians must progress and persevere in their new faith and not fall back

---

215. *PY*, 373; *HS*, 338.
216. *PY*, 373; *HS*, 338–39.
217. *PY*, 374; *HS*, 339.
218. *PY*, 374; *HS*, 339.

into sin. This, he argues, is accomplished by fraternal admonition.[219] It is implied by these statements that Hubmaier does not believe that the evil nature of people is totally removed when they believe and are baptized, but rather that the old Adam continues to fight against the new Christian nature for the whole of a Christian's life, a point he had made quite plain in *A Christian Catechism*.

To this point there is nothing new in Hubmaier's exposition of this theme. However, he now makes the dramatic claim that even if the gospel is heard, by which he means understood and believed, it is of no use. Similarly, water baptism and the Lord's Supper are in vain if fraternal admonition and the ban are not practiced along with them. Although he has stated the connection of admonition to baptism and the ban to the Supper in *A Christian Catechism*, he adds for the first time the above claim about the gospel, baptism, and the Lord's Supper being in vain without church discipline. To support his proposition he remarks, "this we have clearly seen and manifestly experienced in many places within a few years."[220] It is therefore not simply theological speculation that has brought Hubmaier to argue for church discipline as a mark of the true church; it is the everyday experience of the lack of impact of the evangelical gospel on the lives of those who "believe" that has urged him to take this stance.

He goes on to argue against the theological "half-truths" which people have used to justify their lack of changed behavior, and if Hubmaier's hyperbole were to be believed, their worsened behavior. He states that these evangelical Christians defend themselves by repeating the propositions: (1) "we believe, faith saves us" and (2) "we can do nothing good of ourselves."[221] Hubmaier allows that both of these statements are true, yet declares them to be a cloak under which people hide their wicked deeds.

To challenge these people with the Scripture, "Forsake evil and do good" only draws the rejoinder, "we can do nothing good, everything comes to pass according to the providence of God and necessarily."[222] This devious argument Hubmaier calls embroidering the Scriptures, a phrase reminiscent of his charge of those who make a "patchwork" of the Word of God.

By the restoration of admonition Hubmaier claims that these deceits will be exposed for what they are, and the "old Adam" will be confronted

219. *PY*, 374; *HS*, 339.
220. *PY*, 375; *HS*, 339.
221. *PY*, 375; *HS*, 339.
222. *PY*, 376; *HS*, 340.

with the truth and have to accept discipline now, or face it at the last judgment.[223] Hubmaier adds the significant comment that whether the one admonished accepts or rejects admonition, "we will have preserved our honor and conscience."[224] This indicates that for Hubmaier the baptismal vow and the pledge of love in the Lord's Supper place the church under an obligation to discipline an erring member for the sake of its own relationship with God. Later he makes it clear that failure to admonish an erring member will make the church a participant in the sin and equally guilty before God.[225]

Hubmaier proposes two categories of sins, public and private. Public sin is to be reproved publicly, so that others are not seduced to behave in the same way. He cites as an example the issue of interest charged on loans. Since the popes allowed a five percent rate of interest, people everywhere have made a "respectable business"[226] out of lending, and this against the clear Word of Christ in Luke 6:30. Hubmaier cites Paul from 1 Tim 5:20 as his proof text about reproving public sin, and supports it with a variety of New Testament examples: Christ who reprimanded Peter, Peter who rebuked Simon, and Paul who challenged Peter over his inconsistent behavior at Antioch (Matt 16:23; Acts 8:20; Gal 2:14).

In regard to public sins, there is no reference to the procedure for admonition that Christ outlined in Matt 18:15ff. Public sins are to be swiftly and decisively rebuked. Private sins, on the other hand, are to be dealt with by scrupulously following the procedure laid down in Matt 18:15ff. First go privately to the erring member, and confront the person with their fault. They hear you if they confess their sin, become obedient to the discipline of the church, repent of their sin, and vow to avoid it from that time on. If they hear you then you have "profited more than all the merchants of Venice," for you have restored the sinner to the church.[227] If the sinning member rejects your admonition, then take two or three witnesses, and command the person to accept fraternal admonition. They may invoke the Rule of Christ to do to others as you would have them do to you, by saying it is not right to publicly expose my private sin, as he would not want me to do so to him. In that case, the admonisher is to remind the recalcitrant one that a private meeting has already occurred but the warn-

223. *PY*, 376–77; *HS*, 341.
224. *PY*, 377; *HS*, 341.
225. *PY*, 379; *HS*, 342.
226. *PY*, 378, *HS*, 341.
227. *PY*, 379; *HS*, 425.

ing was not heeded. If the person continues to reject the admonition of the two or three witnesses, take the matter to the whole church.[228] Private sins include disputes between members who will not be reconciled. They are to be dealt with following the same procedure.[229]

Hubmaier insists that the command of Christ to admonish a sinning brother or sister comes in two sections. The first is the obligation to confront the sinning member. By doing so the individual who became aware of the private sin is not counted a participant in the sin. The second is the obligation of the sinner to accept admonition meekly and honorably.

Hubmaier notes another possible objection to carrying out fraternal admonition. He notes that Christ has given two kinds of commandments, one for admonition in Matt 18:15ff, and the other seemingly against it, Matt 7:4ff; Luke 6:42, where Christ commands that the one who would judge; that is, take the speck from his brother's eye, should first take the plank out of his own eye.

The response Hubmaier makes to this apparent contradiction is more pragmatic than theological. He simply asserts that the first command does not nullify the second, and that it is better to fulfill one than to neglect both.[230] He acknowledges that to fail to admonish another person because of the awareness of one's own sin would lead to the utter collapse of admonition.[231]

The second part of the work specifies the procedure for dealing with a nonrepentant sinner in the gathered church meeting. It repeats much of what has already been said, but with some differences in emphasis. Hubmaier begins this section with a warning about people being accountable to God for every vain word that they speak (Matt 12:36). He links this to the baptismal pledge that every member of the church has made. It is by this pledge, Hubmaier argues, that a person commits himself or herself to accept admonition. To ignore this and reject admonition is to place oneself before God for judgment and condemnation on the last day.[232]

---

228. *PY*, 379; *HS*, 342.

229. *PY*, 382; *HS*, 344–45. Zwingli challenges the *Schleitheim Articles* interpretation of this passage, suggesting that the Swiss Brethren have not followed it properly. Instead of three warnings followed by a public banning before the church, the Swiss Brethren incorporate the third warning in the act of calling the sinner before the church. Zwingli, *Refutation of the Tricks*, 181.

230. *PY*, 381; *HS*, 343.

231. *PY*, 381; *HS*, 344.

232. *PY*, 381; *HS*, 344.

Making a Patchwork of Scripture

There is also a short passage which proclaims triumphantly that when fraternal admonition is practiced "God will stand powerfully and wonderfully by his Word in such a way that the Christian brethren and the fellowship will be able to reconcile and conciliate such great causes and disunities, as could have not been judged in many years at great cost and with great damage."[233] Here Hubmaier once again espouses the view that the Word of God, where it is rightly followed, is powerful enough to accomplish what God promises.

Hubmaier also reiterates his view that it is not the signs that matter but what they signify. He had put this view forward in his earliest work *Several Theses*; now he argues in the same manner concerning fraternal admonition. The signs were instituted by Christ,

> to gather a church, to commit oneself publicly to live according to the Word of Christ in faith and brotherly love, and because of sin to subject oneself to fraternal admonition and Christian ban, and to do all with a sacramental oath before the Christian church and all her members, assembled partly in body and completely in spirit, testifying publicly in the power of God, Father and Holy Spirit, or in the power of the Lord Jesus Christ (which is all the same power), and yielding oneself to be in hand-pledged fidelity.[234]

He concludes that without baptism being properly carried out, it is not possible to undertake fraternal admonition in a good spirit: "For no one knows either who is in the church and who is outside. No one has authority over another, we are scattered to the winds like sheep without a shepherd."[235]

Use of Scripture

As an analysis of Hubmaier's Scripture usage makes clear, he continues to give most weight to the New Testament, principally to the words of Jesus, and then to the words of the apostles. There are forty-eight New Testament references in this work, twenty-two of which come from Matthew, two from Mark, four from Luke and two from John. There are a total of eleven references to Pauline epistles: 1 Corinthians being cited five times;

---

233. *PY*, 382; *HS*, 345.

234. *PY*, 384; *HS*, 346. Hand-pledged fidelity (*hanndtglober trew*). The image is of a solemn vow confirmed by shaking hands.

235. *PY*, 385; *HS*, 346.

Romans twice; and Galatians, Ephesians, 1 and 2 Timothy once each. Acts is cited four times, 1 and 2 Peter once each and Revelation once. On only eight occasions does Hubmaier refer to the Old Testament. One of the two references to Genesis is a general reference to the story of Noah and the ark, which supports his use of 1 Pet 3:21. The other is a metaphorical use of the "fig leaf fan" behind which Adam and Eve hid their nakedness. He relates this metaphor to those who hide their wrongdoing behind the phrase "faith alone saves us and not our works."[236] He refers to the Ten Commandments (Exod 20 and Deut 5) as passages from Scripture where God has laid down the precedents to be followed in exhortation and admonition. The other passages are the Sermon on the Mount (Matt 5, 6, 7) and Rom 12. Two Samuel 12:7 provides the only Old Testament example in the whole work. It relates the incident of the private sin of David with Bathsheba being confronted by Nathan the prophet. One of the two references to the Psalms (14:3) is a supporting proof text for his proposition that people are by nature children of wrath. Hubmaier cites Eph 2:3 as the primary proof text that describes people as by nature children of wrath.

Hubmaier uses the other reference to Psalms (50:18) to support Isa 1:23. He combines these texts to illustrate how failure to admonish the sinner is taken by God as participation in the sin and guilt of the sinner.[237]

Summary

Hubmaier raises a number of new issues in this work. Firstly, there is the necessity of practicing fraternal admonition and the ban if the church is to be a true church. Secondly, there is the thought expressed that the obligation to practice fraternal admonition is contained in the baptismal pledge. Thirdly, failure to practice fraternal admonition means the church is considered a participant in the sin and associated guilt. Finally, the baptismal pledge contains an agreement and obligation to meekly receive and submit to admonition.

Hermeneutically, Hubmaier again raises the issue of those who use "half-truths" to distort the message of the Scripture, just as the devil did when he tempted Christ (Matt 4:1–11). He reiterates that it is the clear Word of Christ that must be heard, and demonstrates this by citing Luke 6:30ff to reject the practice of charging interest. However, he fails to address a problem he raises in his debate with the evangelical Christians. They

236. *PY,* 376; *HS,* 340.
237. *PY,* 381; *HS,* 344.

state, "we believe, faith saves us" and "we can do nothing of ourselves."[238] Hubmaier acknowledges that these statements are true, yet declares them to be "half-truths," without providing any further explanation. Similarly, Hubmaier deals with the problem raised between the command to admonish and the command to refrain from judging in a pragmatic way. He can see the need for discipline in the church, therefore he gives priority to that need, interpreting the command not to judge as secondary. It is better to fulfill one command than do neither. This is clearly contradictory to his earlier hermeneutic that the commands of Christ are to be obeyed. The two appear to be in opposition, and his resolution contradicts his previously stated method of interpretation.

A FORM FOR WATER BAPTISM

(Autumn 1526)[239]

Setting

This work describes the final form of Hubmaier's baptismal liturgy, as it was practiced in the church at Nikolsburg and "elsewhere."[240] It is a short work that not only describes the procedure for baptizing, but also deals with three errors that still plague the church. Hubmaier maintains that two of the errors were held by the Catholic Church and are still held by the evangelicals, while the other error is held by the evangelicals alone. It can be seen then from these matters that Hubmaier was once again seeking to address evangelicals in Moravia who did not agree with his view of baptism, as well as provide instruction to the church in Nikolsburg.

Bergsten sees in Hubmaier's dedication of this work to Dubcansky an attempt by him to gain Dubcansky's support and thus to influence the development of the course of the Reformation in Moravia. It is conceivable that such an effect could occur as Dubcansky had already sought to direct the Reformation in Moravia by convening a dialogue between the Hussites and evangelicals there. Hubmaier stated, "We also ask the right hereby to give account of the same [baptism practice] publicly with the Word of

---

238. *PY,* 375; *HS,* 339.
239. *PY,* 386–92; *HS,* 347–52.
240. *PY,* 387; *HS,* 348.

God."²⁴¹ Jarold Knox Zeman rejects Bergsten's interpretation of the dedicatory letters to Czech nobles, arguing that Hubmaier had little knowledge of the various sections of the Hussite church, and that his personal contact with them was limited to one person, Jan Zeising, who had been expelled from the Czech Brethren. Further, Hubmaier did not avail himself of the opportunities to improve his knowledge of these churches, remaining basically oriented toward the Swiss and German Reformation.²⁴² Zeman comments further that there can be no doubt that the dedicatory letters to *The Ground and Reason, Form for Water Baptism,* and *Form for Christ's Supper,* all of which are dedicated to Czech nobles on the "left wing" of the Utraquist church, were the direct result of Zeising's visit to Nikolsburg. Zeising is shown to have had personal contacts with von Pernstein and Dubcansky, and he was to personally deliver Hubmaier's *Form for Christ's Supper* to Sobek.²⁴³ Yet this lack of personal contact and knowledge of the groups Hubmaier contacted through the dedicatory letters does not obviate the point that Hubmaier was seeking to win them to his view of baptism, the Lord's Supper, and church discipline.

It is also possible that Hubmaier was seeking political allies who could provide support or a safe haven if he was forced to flee Nikolsburg. It was at this time that the debate concerning the election of a new King of Bohemia occurred. Hubmaier's religious enemy, Archduke Ferdinand of Austria, was the leading contender for the position, a fact of which Hubmaier would have been well aware, and one that no doubt engendered in him a degree of fear. He comments in his dedicatory letter to Dubcansky, "woe to all those who would wash their rapacious hands in our innocent blood."²⁴⁴ He also uses a term *erbiettung* (Pipkin and Yoder translate it as "Christian challenge") in the margin that he had not used since his *An Earnest Christian Appeal* when he faced the threat of extradition into the hands of the Austrian authorities.²⁴⁵ Ferdinand was elected King of Bohemia on October 23, 1526, and one month later inherited the office of Margrave of Moravia.²⁴⁶ By July 1527, Hubmaier and his wife had been

241. *PY,* 387; *HS,* 349; Bergsten, *Balthasar Hubmaier: Anabaptist Theologian,* 339.

242. Zeman, *Anabaptists and Czech Brethren,* 175.

243. Ibid., 167.

244. *PY,* 387; *HS,* 349.

245. *PY,* 387; *HS,* 349. cf. *PY,* 40; *HS,* 78. The use of this term by Hubmaier would indicate that he felt himself to be in a similar situation to his position in Schaffhausen (September 1524). He used it then in his argument to seek political support in view of Austrian opposition.

246. Zeman, *Anabaptists and Czech Brethren,* 66; Bergsten, *Balthasar Hubmaier:*

Making a Patchwork of Scripture

delivered into Austrian hands, and both suffered martyrdom in Vienna in March 1528.[247] Bergsten dates the writing of this work in the fall of 1526 prior to Christmas, while Zeman dates it at the end of 1526.[248] It may have been that Hubmaier was also seeking the political support of the evangelical leaders of Moravia in preparation for renewed persecution at the hands of the Austrian authorities, as well as trying to further the Anabaptist cause.

Analysis

The work itself consists of two parts; firstly, the order of the baptismal service, including the words that the priest, candidate, and congregation are to say; and secondly, three errors that the church has fallen into regarding baptism. The order of the baptismal service begins with the candidate approaching the bishop of the church for baptism. The bishop then privately questions the candidate to ascertain if he or she has been sufficiently instructed in matters of the law, gospel, faith, and doctrines that concern the Christian life.[249]

If the bishop is satisfied that the person is sufficiently instructed in these matters, he takes the candidate before the gathered congregation and all pray that God "might graciously impart to this person the grace and power of his Holy Spirit and complete in him what has begun through his Holy Spirit and divine Word."[250] Here we see again an aspect of Hubmaier's soteriology, the joint working of the Holy Spirit and the Word in bringing salvation, with the implication that the process is not yet complete.

A prayer then follows for the whole congregation, which Hubmaier describes as people of many tongues assembled into a unity of faith so that they may have the fire of love kindled in them.[251]

Following these introductory prayers, the candidate, here called Jan, is questioned as to the faith that he holds and the baptismal pledge he will make.[252] The initial questions are simply the statements of the Creed

---

Anabaptist Theologian, 317.

247. Bergsten, *Balthasar Hubmaier: Anabaptist Theologian*, 337–39.

248. *HS*, 347; Cf. Zeman, *Anabaptists and Czech Brethren*, 165.

249. *PY*, 388. This emphasis on the necessity of this knowledge prior to baptism was previously observed in Hubmaier's *A Christian Catechism*.

250. *PY*, 388; *HS*, 349. A possible allusion to Phil 1:6.

251. *PY*, 388; *HS*, 349.

252. *PY*, 388–389; *HS*, 349–50. Hubmaier had used the names of those to whom he

rephrased as questions. These closely parallel Hubmaier's use of the Creed in his *A Christian Catechism*. He continues to emphasize that the church has the power of the keys; that is, the authority to forgive sins. He makes it plain that the church, by accepting the confession of faith and the pledge of the candidate given prior to baptism, and allowing the candidate to receive baptism, thereby assures the candidate of the forgiveness of sin.

The baptismal pledge explicitly includes a statement of willingness on the part of the candidate to obediently accept fraternal admonition. Previously, Hubmaier has argued that fraternal admonition is theoretically a part of the baptismal pledge. Now, he makes the theory explicit in the practice of the baptismal liturgy.[253]

After being baptized in the name of the Father, Son, and Holy Spirit for the forgiveness of sins, the bishop again prays for the candidate that his faith might increase and that he will persevere in the strength that God gives and be found in the Christian faith at the end.

The ceremony concludes with the bishop laying his hands on the head of the candidate and announcing that he or she is now counted among the Christian community and has the authority to participate in the use of the keys, in the Lord's Supper, and in prayer.[254]

In Hubmaier's liturgy there are echoes of the Catholic Church's sacraments of both baptism and priesthood. In both baptismal ceremonies the candidate is asked if they will renounce the devil and all his works. In the sacrament of ordination to the priesthood, the priest is declared to have the authority of the keys granted to him by the bishop on behalf of the pope. Priests are thus enabled to pronounce forgiveness of sins as a part of the sacrament of penance.[255] Windhorst has noted that Hubmaier retained the traditional schema of penance as the foundation for his baptismal theology. *Satisfactio* is seen to involve the entire Christian life, and is demonstrated in the works that occur as a necessary succession to that new life.[256] However, in this work the assurance of the forgiveness of sins

---

had dedicated his *A Christian Catechism*, Leonhard and Hans, for the questioner and respondent. He follows the same pattern here in *Form for Water Baptism*.

253. PY, 389; HS, 350.

254. PY, 389; HS, 350.

255. Zwingli had withdrawn the question of renouncing the devil from his Zurich baptismal liturgy, as he had also excluded any practice of exorcism. Zwingli, *Of Baptism*, 334f. Hubmaier had earlier ridiculed the exorcism of infants in *On the Christian Baptism*, suggesting that the devil could take the priest to court for falsely accusing him of being in the child. PY, 138; HS, 154.

256. Windhorst, "Anfänge und Aspekte," 153.

Making a Patchwork of Scripture

is not simply reliant upon the continued demonstration of good works. There is a movement back towards the function of the priests declaring forgiveness of sins. This reemphasis on the role of the priest speaking for the church is significant in Hubmaier's hermeneutical development.

The first error Hubmaier describes is calling infant baptism a baptism when it is clear that children do not know "what God, Christ, baptism, faith, or vow is."[257] He then cites the beast of seven heads and ten horns that sought to destroy the woman and her child (Rev 12), by this time a standard reference to the Catholic Church and papacy. Though it is not entirely clear why he uses this allusion at this point, it can be assumed that Hubmaier considered the woman as representative of the Anabaptists and the beast as the Roman Church, the major threat to the Anabaptists in Nikolsburg.

The second error is exclusively related to the evangelical churches. They have reinstituted the Lord's Supper in "both kinds," yet they have not obeyed the Scripture. Hubmaier maintains that there is a specified order to the occurrence of events laid down in Scripture. Previously he had used the same hermeneutical method to define the order by which one came to be baptized.[258] Now he used Acts 2:42 as the proof text that describes the sequence to be followed if the Lord's Supper is to be correctly reinstituted. The order is preaching, faith, confession, water baptism, and the breaking of bread. Since, in Hubmaier's eyes, evangelical preachers have rejected true baptism, their modification of the Lord's Supper is in vain.

He then adds a small paragraph on the problem of forbearance. He alleges that the evangelical preachers delay obeying the truth because of the weak in faith. He suggests that they justify their delay by showing that they are still with their congregations now, and preaching the gospel, whereas to have proceeded hastily would have meant their removal, and by implication hinder the proclamation of the gospel. To this Hubmaier responds with a vigorous assertion of the power of the Word of God to achieve what God sends it forth to accomplish, and a stinging rebuke for the lack of faith the evangelical preachers' attitude displays.[259] Hubmaier proposes his own rule on forbearance. He distinguishes between human

---

257. *PY*, 390; *HS*, 350.

258. *PY*, 390. Cf. 106, 129; *HS,*351. Cf. 127–28, 146.

259. *PY*, 390; *HS*, 351. It was the issue of forbearance that propelled Grebel and his circle into open opposition to Zwingli, as is demonstrated in the letter to Müntzer: "Pay no attention to the apostasy or to the unchristian forbearance, which the very learned foremost evangelical preachers established as an actual idol and planted throughout the world." Harder, *Sources of Swiss Anabaptism*, 288.

practices, such as eating or not eating meat, holidays, and so on, and true doctrine and Christian deeds. In the case of the former, it is possible to wait for a time, until the weak in faith have been instructed. In the latter case, the preacher must proclaim the truth in faith, and trust to the efficacy of the Word of God.[260]

He goes on to state: "For it is much better that a person should fall than that the Word should fall, for by the Word it will be very easy for him, as with Jacob's ladder, to be helped up again."[261] The intent of the statement is clear enough, that the Word of God provides a means for correction and rehabilitation of the fallen sinner. However, the reference to Jacob's ladder is not clear.[262]

The third error is that people have called the water of baptism a "sacrament," as they have done with the bread and wine of the Lord's Supper. This is wrong, for as Hubmaier reminds his readers, in Latin a sacrament is a commitment by oath. He argues that the baptismal vow and the pledge of love given at the Lord's Supper are the true sacraments.[263]

Use of Scripture

There is little in this work that is new in Hubmaier's teaching on baptism. What is significant is his vigorous restatement of the power and efficacy of the preached Word of God. As in his earliest statements on this subject, Hubmaier appeals primarily to the Old Testament for his proof texts; namely, Isa 40:8; 55:11; Jer 23:29. He adds Gen 1, presumably to draw attention to the creative power of the Word of God, and Jer 6, which may link to Jer 23:29, using the connecting image of the Word of God as a powerful fire that refines. He also cites Heb 4:12 and an obscure reference to Rom 1, perhaps focusing on Christ (the Word) declared to be the Son of God with power. The only other Old Testament reference is the allusion to Jacob's ladder, which was mentioned above.

---

260. *PY*, 391; *HS*, 351

261. *PY*, 391; *HS*, 351

262. Erasmus in his *Enchiridion*, had earlier made reference to Jacob's ladder as part of his hermeneutical method. As Jacob's ladder acted as a pathway between the earth and heaven, so seeking the spiritual meaning of the text would move the reader from the dead letter to the living Spirit. Torrance, "The Hermeneutics of Erasmus," 60.

263. *PY*, 391; *HS*, 352. Zwingli also describes a sacrament as an oath in *Sixty-Seven Articles* (1523), cited in Stephens, *Theology of Huldrych Zwingli*, 180.

Making a Patchwork of Scripture

The New Testament references are not dominated by long lists of historical accounts of the practice of baptism by the apostles. Acts is referred to only twice, Acts 2:38; 2:42. Matthew's record of the commission of the disciples in Matt 28:19 receives only one mention, while the usual accompanying reference to Mark 16:15f does not appear at all. There are two references to John's gospel. The first, John 6:53ff, demonstrates that Christ taught the truth at all times and left the result to God. In this instance, his hard teaching about eating his flesh caused offence and people left him. The other refers to Christ's healing of the blind man whom he sent to wash in the pool at Siloam. This is used as a prayer that Christ would in the same way open the eyes of his readers.

Both of Hubmaier's references to 1 Peter relate to Christ preaching to those in prison. These references have been taken over directly from the corresponding part of Hubmaier's *A Christian Catechism*.

The raw number of references, six and fourteen, for Old and New Testaments respectively, give a much higher ratio than is normal in Hubmaier's writings on baptism. However, the sample size is small and five of the six Old Testament references occur together and are related to the one theme of the power and efficacy of the Scripture. So even this work fits the general pattern of Old and New Testament citations for Hubmaier's writings on baptism.

Summary

Though Hubmaier's use of Scripture does not alter significantly in this work, there is a significant shift in his attitude towards the leader of the congregation, the priest or bishop. This is reflected in Hubmaier's description of the use of the power of the keys, which has been entrusted to the church for the forgiveness of sins. Though it is the church that is recognized as using the power of the keys, it is the priest who de facto uses the power, for it is the priest who conducts the interviews with those who seek baptism, and it is on his recommendation that a candidate comes to be baptized. In effect, the church rubber stamps what the priest recommends. This movement away from the congregational hermeneutic Hubmaier previously espoused is not explicit at this point. However, the sign of later movement is clearly signaled here.

A FORM FOR CHRIST'S SUPPER

(Autumn 1526)[264]

Setting

With this work Hubmaier completes his trilogy of liturgical texts written for the Anabaptist church at Nikolsburg. As Pipkin and Yoder comment, "These three texts and the preceding catechism constitute a rounded picture of Anabaptist church life."[265] It is also the third work that Hubmaier has dedicated to the theme of the Lord's Supper. Bergsten notes that it follows closely the Zwinglian liturgy, where the people are seated and receive ordinary bread and wine.[266]

In a postscript, Hubmaier dedicates this work to Sobek of Kornice, a middle level noble from a Bohemian family, whose influence extended into Moravia and Silesia. Sobek had studied at Wittenberg, and on his return to Prague became a bookseller and translated some of Luther's works. He may have provided the impetus for the invitation to Thomas Müntzer to come to Prague in 1521. In 1523, he was imprisoned for his support of the Lutheran cause in Prague. Upon his release, he moved to Moravia and joined the Bohemian Brethren in 1525. He also wrote a history of that group, the *Chronicle of the Bohemian Brethren 1482–1532*.[267]

Bergsten suggests that Hubmaier wrote this work and dedicated it to Sobek not only to explain the liturgy of the Lord's Supper as practiced in Nikolsburg, but also to win an influential convert to the Anabaptist movement.[268] In his dedication, Hubmaier states that he published the work so that others could not charge that the Anabaptists "fear the light," or that they have no reasons for practicing the Supper as they do.[269] It should also be noted that this work does not have the same polemical tone as his *A Simple Instruction* or *Form for Water Baptism*.

---

264. *PY*, 393–408; *HS*, 20:355–65
265. *PY*, 393.
266. *HS*, 353.
267. *HS*, 353.
268. *HS*, 354.
269. *PY*, 408; *HS*, 364–65.

Analysis

Hubmaier outlines in ten steps the Anabaptist church's practice of the Lord's Supper. To begin, they are to gather together at a set time and place so that the preaching of the gospel should not suffer. When they come together the people are to be modestly dressed, not contentious nor engaged in light talk.[270]

There follows a time of confession as preparation for the third step, the exposition of a suitable passage of Scripture. The fourth step emphasizes the communal hermeneutic of the Anabaptist church, as provision is made for a time of questions and explanations, where those who receive some message from God are permitted to share it with all present.[271] Due to a literal interpretation of 1 Cor 14:34f, women are excluded from this, and are instructed to ask their questions at home.[272]

The fifth step involves self-examination prior to participating in eating and drinking the bread and wine. This is a lengthy section which provides important information on Hubmaier's understanding of "fellowship" or participation in Christ (1 Cor 10:16).[273] He insists on a spiritual eating and drinking before partaking of the physical elements, otherwise the outward eating is a "killing letter."[274] Eating and drinking the bread and wine visibly confirms before the congregation the preexisting fervent hunger and thirst for Christ that Hubmaier defines as spiritual eating and drinking. He goes on to define the pledge of love that the participant confirms before the church in eating and drinking, as the true "sacrament," the giving of one's hand on the commitment that one is willing to offer one's body and blood for the fellow believers.[275]

This fellowship in the Spirit must exist before sharing the elements of the Supper, just as faith must precede baptism. Echoing his second new reason for being baptized, which he published in *The Ground and Reason*, Hubmaier this time applies it to the Lord's Supper. As much as a person cares about the flesh and blood; the suffering and death of Christ;

---

270. *PY*, 394; *HS*, 355.

271. Though Zwingli's "prophecy" school also allowed for discussion and questions, the preachers who exposited the Scriptures expected their interpretation to be accepted and not challenged by those unlearned in the biblical languages. Stephens, *Theology of Huldrych Zwingli*, 39–40, and Snyder, "Word and Power," 275.

272. *PY*, 396; *HS*, 356.

273. *PY*, 398; *HS* 358.

274. *PY*, 397; *HS*, 356.

275. *PY*, 398; *HS*, 358.

forgiveness of sins; brotherly love; communion with the Father, the Son, and the Holy Spirit; the heavenly host; the universal church, outside which there is no salvation—just so much should a person care about the bread and wine of the Supper.[276] However, this time Hubmaier reverses the idea to argue that where people do not desire baptism or the Lord's Supper there is no belief in Christ and no practice of Christian love.[277]

He concludes the fifth step by stating, "If now one had no other word or Scripture, but only the correct understanding of water baptism and the Supper of Christ, one would have God and all his creatures, faith and love, the law, and all the prophets."[278] In this sentence, Hubmaier makes it plain that fraternal admonition and the ban flow out of baptism and the Lord's Supper, since for him the first defines faith, while the second defines love; love of God and love of neighbor.

The sixth step speaks of the impossibility of loving our neighbor with the same self-sacrificing love as Christ has loved us. He argues that it is not enough for Christians to recognize sin or the distinction between good and evil by contemplating the law, God demands that they do what he commands. Although this is impossible for the flesh, it is possible for the newborn Christian who is completely free (except for the flesh) to will to do the good and to do it by the power God grants.[279] He acknowledges that the Christian still struggles against the old Adam, yet the sins that are committed are not damning if they are confessed, regretted, and rejected for the future.[280] The innate weaknesses of Christians are not damning because "in Christ we have all attained perfection and in him are already blessed."[281] This discussion of the will of the flesh and the will of the regenerate Christian receives greater attention in Hubmaier's two works on the freedom of the will.

There follows a prayer, requesting God to cause growth in faith among the faithful and to kindle love for one another. This seventh step is prolonged by a period of silence during which the congregation are encouraged to meditate on the sufferings of Christ. They then reverently and with hearts fervently desiring grace, corporately repeat the Lord's Prayer.[282]

276. *PY*, 399, cf. 370–71; *HS*, 359, cf. 335.
277. *PY*, 399; *HS*, 359.
278. *PY*, 399; *HS*, 359.
279. *PY*, 400; *HS*, 359–60.
280. *PY*, 401; *HS*, 360.
281. *PY*, 402; *HS*, 361.
282. *PY*, 402; *HS*, 361.

Making a Patchwork of Scripture

Those whose conscience is now untroubled before God following this exercise in self-examination and meditation on the sufferings of Christ and the meaning of loving one's neighbor, are then invited to make the pledge of love. First the congregation is asked if they will love God above all else. This requires the subjection of the carnal will to the divine will. This subjection is brought about by God working in the Christian through the divine Word.[283] To this an individual response is required.

A question is then asked concerning love of one's neighbor. This love of one's neighbor is expanded from Hubmaier's usual reference to Matt 25:34f, the works of brotherly love, by specifying obedience to parents and to all authorities (Eph 6:1–2; Col 3:20; Rom 13:1; 1 Pet 2:13f). It is Hubmaier's insistence that the Christian still owes obedience to the civil authorities that is the focus for the dispute in the Anabaptist church in Nikolsburg, and leads him to publish his views in *On the Sword*. This reference to obedience to all authorities in the pledge of love indicates that at this stage Hubmaier was continuing to teaching this view on government, a view he had also espoused in Waldshut.

The third question in the pledge of love deals with the desire of those taking the pledge to practice fraternal admonition, living according to the Rule of Christ so that no offence or harm is given to one's neighbor, and to practice the ban.[284]

When those present have individually voiced their desire to live by the pledge of love, the leader of the service begins the ninth step of the service, the distribution of the bread and the wine.

Here the words of institution from 1 Cor 11:23ff provide the words for the priest. The bread and the cup are offered into the hands of those participating, the participants apparently standing for this part of the service, for at the conclusion of the eating and drinking of the elements Hubmaier writes that the people should now be seated.[285]

The final step is an exhortation from the priest to first remind the congregation that by eating and drinking as they have just done, they have become "one loaf and one body," with Christ as their head. They must now become properly conformed to Christ, speaking and acting accordingly, giving no cause for those outside the church to blaspheme Christ and the church because of their behavior. To reinforce the seriousness of the situation Hubmaier invokes the woes of Matt 18:16 against those who

---

283. *PY,* 403; *HS,* 361.
284. *PY,* 403; *HS,* 362.
285. *PY,* 405; *HS,* 363.

bring shame to the name of Christ: "Woe, woe to him who gives offence! It would be better for him that a millstone should be hung around his neck and he should be cast into the depth of the sea."[286]

This warning leads Hubmaier to a final word on fraternal admonition and the application of the ban. Again he notes the distinction between the three warnings for private sins and the immediate public confrontation that follows public sins.[287] He exhorts them to live lives worthy of God, always being conscious of their baptismal commitment and their pledge of love, to which they have voluntarily committed themselves. They should watch and pray lest they fall into temptation, for they do not know the hour of their Lord's return, and he will demand of them an accounting (Matt 24:42; 25:13; Luke 16:2).[288]

It can be seen from this analysis that this work is not primarily concerned with describing the theological content of Hubmaier's teaching on the Lord's Supper. He indicates that he has done that elsewhere, presumably referring to his *A Simple Instruction*.[289] In step three Hubmaier gives a précis of a sermon on Luke 24:31ff as an example of how the priest should proclaim Christ from the Scriptures. He takes the words of the two disciples on the road to Emmaus and places them into the mouths of the congregation. At first they make a confession of faith, that Christ was "a man, a prophet, mighty in works and teaching before God and all people, how the highest bishops among the priests and princes gave him over to condemnation to death and how they crucified him, and how he has redeemed Israel; that is, all believers."[290] The initial "hope" of these two disciples is now declared to have become a reality. Christ has redeemed Israel.

The priest now takes up the words of Christ, rebuking those who are foolish and slow to believe all the things that Moses and the prophets have spoken. The priest speaks so as to "kindle and make fervent and warm the hearts of those at the table, that they may be afire in fervent meditation of his bitter suffering and death in contemplation, love, and thanksgiving."[291] The end result of such teaching is that the congregation again echoes the words of the two disciples, urging Christ to stay with them. Hubmaier

---

286. *PY*, 405; *HS*, 363.
287. *PY*, 406; *HS*, 363.
288. *PY*, 406; *HS*, 364.
289. *PY*, 403; *HS*, 361. A note in the margin.
290. *PY*, 394–95; *HS*, 356.
291. *PY*, 395; *HS*, 356.

does not here go on to draw out the inference that as Christ was made known to these two disciples in the breaking of bread, so he will be revealed afresh as the congregation participates in the elements, as he had earlier in the dedication of *A Simple Instruction*.[292] This is not exegesis but exhortation using the words of Scripture, or a paraphrase to stir up the emotional response of the hearers. The other passages that Hubmaier recommends to those who lead this service and are responsible for the exposition of Scripture, focus on the ideas of fellowship (1 Cor 10, 11) and on the words of Jesus in John 13–14, 15, 16–17, with which he encouraged his first disciples prior to the Passover celebration. The verses in John concern the need for a person's life to manifest the fruits of repentance (Matt 3; Luke 3) and the fear of God. This last subject uses the text of Sir 2 as its focus. The final verses of that chapter resonate with Hubmaier's theme of obedience to the commands of God and the preparation of a humble heart by those who fear the Lord. Obviously Hubmaier does not follow Zwingli in his rejection of the Apocrypha as a valid source for doctrine.

There is also a significant statement made by Hubmaier in his letter to Sobek. Having paraphrased article six of the Creed, that Christ has ascended and is seated at the right hand of the Father, from whence he will come to judge the living and the dead, he goes on to say: "Precisely that is our foundation, according to which we must deduce and exposit all of the Scriptures having to do with eating and drinking. Thus Christ cannot be eaten or drunk by us otherwise than spiritually and in faith."[293] When compared to his earlier works, this is a move in a new direction. Previously, the weight of Hubmaier's argument had rested on the assertion that the words "in remembrance of me" were the key to understanding the Lord's Supper as a memorial feast. He had gone so far as to describe his method of exegeting these verses as a general rule for the interpretation of Scripture; that is, that the words that follow in a text provide clarification of the preceding words.[294] He moves away from this grammatical argument to an assertion that the Creed provides him with the fundamental position from which all interpretation of texts related to the Supper must begin. This movement towards the universally accepted Creed as his basis for his theology of the Lord's Supper has occurred within a few short months of the completion of his *A Simple Instruction*.

---

292. *PY*, 318; *HS*, 289.
293. *PY*, 407; *HS*, 364.
294. *PY*, 324, 331; *HS*, 361, 299.

Balthasar Hubmaier and the Clarity of Scripture

Use of Scripture

There are two fascinating uses of allegorical interpretation of texts in this work. In both instances, Hubmaier refers to Old Testament texts. He cites Deut 6:8, "bind the commandments on your hands," and interprets it to mean fulfilling the commandments of God.[295] In the second instance, he uses the image of the Christian riding on a donkey and gaining mastery over it to describe the struggle of the Christian against the evil desires of the old Adam in him.[296] This image of the rider on an animal representing the will of God in man subduing and controlling the continuing evil in the Christian is common in the Reformation. However, Hubmaier takes the image one step further when he cites Exod 34:20 as a supporting text for this teaching. In this verse the firstborn donkey is to be redeemed with a lamb; if it is not redeemed its neck is to be broken. All firstborn sons are also to be redeemed by a lamb. Hubmaier takes this verse and urges that when the Christian reins in the will of the flesh it will break its neck. The flesh cannot be redeemed in this life even by the death of Christ the lamb of God.

Hubmaier makes few references to the Old Testament, consistent with his previous usage in works on the Lord's Supper. There are fifteen Old Testament references and the reference to Sirach that has been noted and commented on above. Hubmaier turns most in this work to the Psalms, using them as proof texts for the need for oral confession of faith (Ps 116:10), and not only to the command to do good to one's neighbor but also the possibility to do good (Ps 37:21, 26–27). Psalm 110:1 is cited along with Christ's use of it in Matt 22:44. The final reference is to Ps 32:1, "blessed are those whose sins are forgiven." (NIV) For Hubmaier this is a christological use of the Psalm since it is in Christ that the forgiveness of sins occurs. Hubmaier demonstrates this connection of the christological use of the Psalm by citing Paul's use of it in Rom 4:8.

In Hubmaier's New Testament references, his citations focus on the Synoptics: Matthew (twenty-seven), Mark (six), and Luke (twenty-one). John's gospel is cited fourteen times, two of these referring to the list of John 13–17, which Hubmaier nominates as suitable chapters from which to instruct the congregation concerning how to live an appropriate Christian life. As is to be expected in a work on the Lord's Supper, 1 Cor 10 and

---

295. *PY,* 400; *HS,* 360.

296. *PY,* 401; *HS,* 360. This image of the donkey being ridden features in the later debate on free will and is a major point of disagreement between Luther and Erasmus, as will be seen in the discussion on the topic of free will.

Making a Patchwork of Scripture

11 are often cited; sixteen of the total twenty-four citations of 1 Corinthians. Four instances of 1 Cor 14 provide Hubmaier with his evidence for establishing orderly procedures in the church. The other instances of Hubmaier's use of 1 Corinthians deals with church discipline of public offences (1 Cor 5:1f); warning against being a stumbling block to others (1 Cor 8:9); being one body in Christ (1 Cor 12:12); and disciplining the body to make it subject to God's will (1 Cor 9:27).

There is a marked increase in the use of Romans in this work: seventeen instances. Related to the theme of love of God and loving one's brother by living the Christian life, Hubmaier cites Rom 8:32 three times, as well as Rom 9:3; 12:9–21; 14:3. He is also concerned to emphasize the security the Christian has in Christ despite the ongoing struggle with sin. To support this teaching he cites Rom 8:1 twice, and Rom 4:5; 5:12. He is also involved in the debate on free will in this work, and cites in this regard Rom 2:7, 7:15ff, 7:18, 8:11, 10:5–8. The two remaining references to Romans deal with obedience to authorities (Rom 13:1ff) and an allusion to the need for any confession of faith to be made with heart and mouth (Rom 10:9–10). This increase in citations from Romans reflects Hubmaier's increasing concern with the debate on free will.

The remaining references and allusions are scattered across a wide range of Pauline epistles, with the remainder from 1 John (three), and 1 Peter (two).

Summary

Hermeneutically, this work shows Hubmaier moving from a grammatically based argument for a memorial interpretation of the Lord's Supper to one based on the Creed. It also provides an insight into Hubmaier's use of Scripture in a preaching context, where the emphasis is on stirring the emotions of his hearers by focusing them on the sufferings of Christ. This he achieves through the device of attributing to his hearers the words of the disciples as recorded in Scripture, while the preacher becomes the voice of Christ. Otherwise, Hubmaier continues to utilize Scripture in the way that he has done in the previous works.

ON THE CHRISTIAN BAN

(December 1526)[297]

Setting

With this work Hubmaier concludes his treatises on church order. He had earlier contended that there is no true church where baptism, the Lord's Supper, fraternal admonition, and the ban are not practiced according to the Word of God. In his three previous works, he has provided both a rationale for his liturgical forms, as well as suggesting the actual words to be used during the performance of these ceremonies. In this work, he completes this process by describing his teaching on the ban and a form of words that are to be used by the whole church when a member is banned. As Bergsten has noted, Hubmaier continues the train of thought that was begun in *On Fraternal Admonition*, but from the new starting point that the one to be dealt with is an unrepentant sinner.[298]

In a polemical section of the work, Hubmaier launches a stinging attack on the Catholic Church for its misuse of the ban. His major theme is that the ban has been used by the Catholic Church to coerce money from people, or to terrify secular power into submitting to the rule of the church, and not to protect the church from the shame that is brought on it by the evil behavior of sinning members.[299] Instead of these "holy belly fathers" imposing the ban, they themselves should be banned, for according to Hubmaier they are the notorious sinners mentioned by Paul.[300]

Hubmaier does not dedicate this work to anyone. In it, he refers to his earlier works on the Lord's Supper and baptism. An allusion to the star and the manger at Bethlehem led Johann Loserth to suggest a final

---

297. *PY*, 409–25; *HS*, 366–79.

298. *HS*, 366.

299. *PY*, 422; *HS*, 376. "Even for five shillings of hazel nuts, you would have to be struck immediately by the power of the invisible air-sword of their ban. . . . He did not properly give the small goose tithe or the offering penny. He called the abbot's concubine a harlot. Briefly: what has to do with the purses, the cakes, the money chests and the cellars of the religious, there the false ban, claiming to look like the wholesome ban of Christ, counter to the clear teaching of Christ and Paul, has become doorman, judge, hangman, and executioner." *PY*, 422–23; *HS*, 376.

300. *PY*, 423; *HS*, 376. Hubmaier uses *bauch* (belly) for *beicht* (confession), thus focusing his accusation on the priest confessors.

redaction of the work at about Christmas 1526. Bergsten and Pipkin and Yoder accept this view.[301]

Analysis

The structure of the work is set out by Hubmaier in the introduction. Rhetorically, he asks what is "necessary, useful and most helpful" to know about the ban? He suggests one needs to know, "what the Christian ban is, whence the church has this power, how to ban, and in what way one should deal with one who is banned."[302] He dedicates one section of the work to each of these questions, adding a final section describing "how to deal with the returning sinner."[303]

The ban is defined as "a public separation and exclusion of a person from the fellowship of the Christian church because of an offensive sin, from which this person will not refrain."[304] It must be applied in accordance with the command of Christ, being decided by the gathered church and publicly proclaimed.

Three reasons are given which describe why the ban is imposed. Firstly, so that the Word of God and the church is not "shamed, calumnied and despised"; secondly, so that novices and those weak in the faith are not caused to stumble or be corrupted by an evil example; and finally, so that the sinner might become aware of the misery their refusal to accept admonition is causing them, and thus be led to repent and renounce their sinful practices.[305] In section three on the imposition of the ban, Hubmaier replaces the second reason with a stronger warning based on 2 John 10. Here he warns that continuing fellowship with a known sinner brings those in contact with him or her under the same judgment, for they participate in their sin.[306]

Section two sees Hubmaier develop his view that Christ has granted to the church the power of the keys; the first key to forgive people's sins, the second to retain them if they are unrepentant. Whereas he had previously described the granting of the power of the keys to the church on the basis of the confession of Peter (Matt 16:16) and the authority that Christ

---

301. *PY*, 366; *HS*, 409.
302. *PY*, 410; *HS*, 367.
303. *PY*, 423ff; *HS*, 367.
304. *PY*, 410; *HS*, 367.
305. *PY*, 411; *HS*, 368.
306. *PY*, 417; *HS*, 372.

passed it on to the church (Matt 28:19ff; John 20:22f), now his argument is dominated by his understanding of order and hierarchy of authority. In the beginning, the Father alone had authority to forgive sins or to condemn. With the incarnation of the Son of God as Jesus of Nazareth, that authority was passed to him. The Son retained that authority only as long as he was bodily on the earth. After the resurrection, the Son transferred that authority to his spouse, the church, who continues doing the will of the Son and the Father, as long as the Son is not bodily present on the earth. When the Son returns, the church will meet him in the air and return the keys to him, for the authority of the church is restricted to the earth. Once the Son has completed the judgment of the living and the dead, he in turn will hand back the keys to the Father.[307]

Hubmaier notes the difference between the singular and plural "you" in Matt 16:18–19, interpreting the singular as referring to the unity of faith that the church has in the confession that Jesus is the Christ the Son of the living God, while the plural refers to the gathering of the church in that unity of confession to exercise the power of the keys, both for admitting and excluding.[308] That the church possesses this power of the keys after the resurrection of Christ, Hubmaier claims can be shown "more clearly than the sun" when the texts of John 20:22f; 1:32; Acts 2:1ff are considered.[309]

Two conclusions are drawn from the teaching that Christ is now bodily at the right hand of the Father. Firstly, Hubmaier, in common with Zwingli and his followers, maintains that Christ is not bodily present in the elements of the Lord's Supper, a position strongly advocated in *Form of Christ's Supper*. Secondly, and uniquely, he argues that if Christ were present bodily in the Supper, that would remove the power of the keys from the church.[310] Hubmaier continues that those who know how to speak correctly of the use of the Christian keys will also know the truth about baptism and the Lord's Supper.[311]

In the third section, Hubmaier outlines the procedure for the public proclamation of the ban. The one to be banned is reminded of the pledges and vows voluntarily taken at baptism and by previous participation in the Lord's Supper. A further reminder is given that the baptismal pledge included an agreement to accept fraternal admonition. However, this

307. *PY*, 415; *HS*, 370–71.
308. *PY*, 412; *HS*, 369.
309. *PY*, 413; *HS*, 369.
310. *PY*, 413; *HS*, 369.
311. *PY*, 413; *HS*, 369.

admonition has been rejected, despite the warnings given at first in private and then before witnesses and finally before the church.[312] After a short reiteration that the daughter church has the same power and authority as the mother church, there is a concluding declaration in which the unrepentant sinner is given over to "the devil for the destruction of the flesh so that the spirit might be saved on the day of the Lord Jesus" (1 Cor 5:1ff).[313]

The fourth section describes how those remaining in the church should behave toward any who are banned. In short, they are to have no "fellowship, not in eating, drinking, greeting nor having dealings with him in any other way" with them, for to do so would be to participate in their sin and face the same judgment.[314] This does not mean that all contact is to be eschewed, as works of necessity are still to be practiced. Only works of friendship are to be rejected. This puts the Jew and the pagan in a better position than the one who has been part of the church and is now excluded, for to the Jew and pagan the Christian is obliged to do both the works of necessity and to demonstrate friendship.[315] In words reminiscent of *On Heretics*, Hubmaier describes how the banned one is not to be struck, driven away, or killed. He also comments that the use of the ban within the church does not remove the sword from civil authorities.[316] Hubmaier declares that the church has a responsibility to judge only those within it not outside it.[317] Thus, he differentiates two different spheres in which judgments are made, and two distinct swords.

He also takes the opportunity in this section to reiterate his view that where baptism has not been restored according to the institution of Christ, then it is impossible to know who are brothers and sisters in the church, and it therefore becomes impossible to practice admonition or the ban.[318]

The final section deals with receiving back into the church someone who has been banned. The church is bound to joyously receive back any person who, having recognized their error and renounced their sin,

---

312. *PY*, 416–17; *HS*, 371–72. Earlier Hubmaier uses the term perjury to describe the breaking of the pledges made at baptism and the Lord's Supper.

313. *PY*, 417; *HS*, 372.

314. *PY*, 417–18; *HS*, 372–73.

315. *PY*, 419; *HS*, 374.

316. *PY*, 418, cf. *PY*, 60–64; *HS*, 373, cf. *HS*, 96–99, Articles 3, 4, 5, 14, 20–24 and 29. In *On Heretics* Hubmaier makes the distinction between the heretic who should be free of physical coercion, and evildoers, whom the civil authorities use the sword against to punish them for the protection of the good in society.

317. *PY*, 420; *HS*, 374.

318. *PY*, 420; *HS*, 374.

determining never to practice it again, repents and prays for God's grace, and returns to the church. This can happen many times, not just seven times, but seventy times seven, for whenever a sinner truly repents and returns to the church, and demonstrates the genuineness of their remorse by their changed life, the church, according to the command of Christ, must open her doors to that person.[319] To support this view Hubmaier links the saying of Jesus in Luke 17:4 with the seventy weeks of years mentioned in Dan 9:24, "This is to give us to understand that as often as a sinner genuinely finds remorse and sorrow for his sin, it is forgiven him through the suffering of Christ."[320] This use of the Old Testament should be noted, since Hubmaier has not previously used the Old Testament as a source that describes the sufferings of Christ.

The test of genuine repentance is a changed life that avoids everything that could attract the sinner back into error. If that change is not evident, then it is assumed that the repentance and remorse expressed by the penitent are not genuine.

Hubmaier acknowledges the difficulty of establishing the practice of fraternal admonition and the ban within the territories of "the mighty, great, and powerful Lords, cities and countrysides."[321] Perhaps there is in this thought a note of personal frustration. Although Hubmaier had dedicated his other liturgical works to powerful Lords of Moravia, his teaching and practice of baptism, the Lord's Supper, fraternal admonition, and the ban remained confined to Nikolsburg and its environs. Almost as an act of final rejection of both the Catholic Church and the other evangelical Reformers, Hubmaier declares that it is better to be with the despised manger of Bethlehem and the humble followers of Christ than to be in their majestic churches among the "high and spiritual princes and bishops Herod, Pilate, Annas, Caiaphas . . . and the painted wall Ananias."[322]

Once again Hubmaier returns to the theme of respecting persons more than the Word of God. By following after personalities, people are led into error. They should "look only at the bright clear stars of the Word of God which itself will show them the way to find a true church near Christ."[323]

319. *PY*, 424; *HS*, 377.
320. *PY*, 424; *HS*, 377.
321. *PY*, 424; *HS*, 377.
322. *PY*, 425; *HS*, 378.
323. *PY*, 425; *HS*, 378.

These final paragraphs of this work reveal Hubmaier still proclaiming the clarity of the Word of God and the ability of that Word to make itself understood to the humble and the simple of the world.

The presupposition that undergirds this work is once again the teaching of the bodily presence of the risen Christ at the right hand of the Father in heaven. As in the work on the Lord's Supper, this teaching provides the basis for arguing that Christ is not physically present in the elements of the Supper. In this work, it finds another application in regard to the authority that the church has to bind and to loose from sin. Where Christ is bodily present he alone has the power and authority to forgive or to bind sins. As Christ is no longer bodily present the church as his spouse is given the authority of Christ and exercises that authority, but only on earth, and only until Christ comes again.

There is also another example of Hubmaier's preoccupation with the order that God has placed in creation. We have seen him emphasize the order of the texts concerning baptism and also the Lord's Supper. Now he emphasizes the order there is between Father, Son, and the church. The authority to forgive sins passes from the Father via the Son to the church and back to the Son and finally the Father. Hubmaier does not state it but he implies that there is a sequence of discrete periods of time and only one of those named can exercise the authority to forgive sins in any one period. Thus, the Father exercises the authority to forgive sins from creation to the incarnation; the Son from the incarnation to the ascension; the church from the ascension to the second coming. Then the Son has the authority again from the judgment at his second coming to the time he hands all things back to the Father. Then the Father will be all in all. This division of time and authority finds significant expression in Hubmaier's later consideration of the salvation of the patriarchs. Whereas he had previously held that they languished in prison until Christ in the Spirit preached the gospel to them, later he will affirm that they were saved during the days of the Old Testament.

Use of Scripture

In this work, there is a reassessment of the place of the Old Testament in regard to the presence of Christ in history. This is indicated by the distinctive use Hubmaier makes of Dan 9:24, where he notes that the seventy weeks of years represent the suffering of Christ. Hubmaier has previously avoided identifying Christ in the Old Testament except in those references that Jesus himself or the apostles used in that way. Apart from this reference to Daniel, his use of the Old Testament remains consistent with previous works. There are three references to the Psalms and one to Exodus, giving a total of five Old Testament references.

His New Testament references, which total eighty-eight in this work, also remain consistent. The majority are taken from Matthew (twenty-five), thirteen of those referring to either the confession of Peter or the granting of the power of the keys to the church. The remaining twelve are generally supporting texts or historical references encouraging similar action or warning of dire consequences. Mark's gospel provides only two texts, each repeated twice. One refers to the authority to preach and baptize, the other to the place Christ has at the right hand of the Father. Luke provides Hubmaier with ten general references, and John with eleven, six of which relate to the power of the keys given in John 20:22ff. There are ten references to Acts, mostly historical examples. Twice Hubmaier uses Acts 1:9 in conjunction with Matt 16:16; John 20:22ff to argue for the authority of Jesus to bind or to loose from sin being given to the church after the ascension.

As expected, 1 Corinthians supplies Hubmaier with historical examples of the application of church discipline. One Corinthians 5:1ff accounts for six of the eight references made to 1 Corinthians in this work. Hubmaier also maintains in a marginal note that a public sin, such as what occurred in Corinth, must be dealt with immediately, and not according to the pattern of Matt 18:15f.[324]

The remaining references are of no particular importance to the discussion of Hubmaier's hermeneutic, as Hubmaier is simply supporting his arguments with various historical examples. For example, he suggests that those who have been banned be noted and their names sent to other fellowships so that they may be prepared beforehand should the banned one try to gain admittance. He uses the example of Paul naming various people as his proof for this view (2 Tim 1:15; 4:10, 14).[325] Hubmaier refers twice to 2 John 10 and alludes to it on one other occasion. This is his proof text by which he shows that continuing fellowship with one who is banned causes the individual or church that does so to participate in their sin and receive

---

324. *PY,* 418; *HS,* 373. Pipkin notes that Hubmaier was peculiar among Anabaptists in holding to this distinction between public and private sins that are to be dealt with in two distinct ways.

325. *PY,* 422; *HS,* 375.

Making a Patchwork of Scripture

the same judgment that awaits the unrepentant sinner. He makes the point more firmly in this work than he had done in *On Fraternal Admonition*.

Summary

There are, therefore, evident signals in this work and the other liturgical works that a change is occurring in Hubmaier's hermeneutic in this period, the autumn of 1526. Of particular significance is the new orientation Hubmaier is adopting towards identifying the sufferings of Christ in the Old Testament, and the division of history into three segments where only the authority of one person, Father, Son, or the bride of Christ is operative in the vital role of forgiving sins.

FREEDOM OF THE WILL I

(April 1, 1527)[326]

Setting

Hubmaier produced no further written works between the end of December 1526, when he completed his works dealing with the ordinances and discipline of the church, and April 1, 1527, the date on the foreword of his first book on free will. In that interval, the doctrine of free will came to be hotly debated in the Nikolsburg church, not so much as a theological issue but as a practical pastoral one. Hubmaier notes in the foreword to his first work that people have learned only two things from all the preaching of the gospel that has taken place, "We believe, faith saves us," and "We can do nothing good. God works in us the desire and the doing. We have no free will."[327] Hubmaier declares his pastoral concern when he decries that he has "heard of many people who have not prayed, fasted, nor given alms for a long time, for their priests say that their works are of no value before God."[328] Hubmaier's concern echoes that of Erasmus who writes in his work *De libero arbitrio* of the church fathers who have previously written on this subject, "Those who would avoid despair and complacency, but would inspire men to hope and Endeavour, attribute more to

---

326. *PY*, 426–48; *HS*, 379–97.
327. *PY*, 427; *HS*, 381. See also *PY*, 426 and *HS*, 379.
328. *PY*, 429; *HS*, 381.

free choice."[329] Denck makes the point that people use the doctrine of the bound will as a means of excusing themselves from the evil they commit while blaming everything on God, a point both Erasmus and Hubmaier also make.[330] In contrast, Luther takes up the debate with Erasmus from a theological perspective because he sees this doctrine as central to his whole theological position: "Indeed, as you should know, this is the cardinal issue between us, the point on which everything in this controversy turns. . . . So you see, that this problem is one half of the whole sum of things Christian, since on it both knowledge of oneself and the knowledge and glory of God quite vitally depend."[331] With Erasmus and Denck, Hubmaier affirmed a limited freedom of the will in humanity in contrast to Luther, Zwingli, and their followers, who totally deny any free will that can effect salvation in human beings.

Hubmaier's two writings on the freedom of the will have provided opportunity for scholars to investigate the influence of humanism and nominalism in early Anabaptism. Thor Hall, building on the pioneering work of Walther Koehler, and that of an earlier generation of Anabaptist researchers, such as Heinhold Fast and Harold. S. Bender, investigated the influence of Erasmus and humanism on Hubmaier and Denck by comparing their writings on free will. Having summarized the work of Denck and Hubmaier under twelve headings, Hall then notes the similarities that exist between them and Erasmus's view of free will.[332] Hall does not go so far as to claim that these similarities prove the influence of Erasmus in this matter, only that there is a "definite affinity between the views of the three men."[333] Bergsten acknowledges this work of Hall and introduces the work of Gerd Seewald, who demonstrated that Hubmaier's second work on free will has the same threefold division as Erasmus's *De libero arbitrio* and

---

329. *De libero arbitrio*, 51.

330. Denck, *Concerning the Law of God*, 125: "They would gladly do God's will but they excuse themselves and openly cast the blame on God, for they which, in short, not to be those people of whom the Lord said, He oft sought to gather them as a hen gathers her brood, but they would not." See *PY*, 429, *HS*, 381–82: "These are the half-truths under which we, as under the form of angels, protect all license of the flesh and blame all our sin and guilt on God " and *De libero arbitrio*, 96: "Why . . . grant anything to free choice? In order to have something to impute justly to the wicked who have voluntarily come short of the grace of God, in order that the calumny of cruelty and injustice may be excluded from God, that despair may be kept away from us, that complacency may be excluded also, and that we may be incited to Endeavour."

331. *De libero arbitrio*, 116–17.

332. Hall, "Possibilities of Erasmian Influence," 149.

333. Ibid., 164

numerous biblical texts in common.[334] Seewald also notes that Hubmaier probably made use of Luther's *On the Bondage of the Will* while writing his own contribution to the debate.[335] Bergsten also furthers Hall's work by demonstrating a verbal similarity that exists between Hubmaier's work and Denck's two works *Concerning the Law* and *Whether God is the Cause*. He also notes a similarity in their anthropology and in their distinction from Erasmus in as much as they "do not regard reason as the organ by which man accepts the activity of God within himself."[336] He concludes that Denck is the influence from whom Hubmaier drew these ideas.

Both David. C. Steinmetz and Walter L. Moore have analyzed these works of Hubmaier's and shown the continuity of thought that exists between Hubmaier's position and his earlier nominalist training, particularly the influence of the Old Franciscan doctrine of God and free will. While Steinmetz comments that Hubmaier "revived" these motifs in his debate on free will, Moore, who is in substantial agreement with Steinmetz's analysis, argues that Hubmaier never altered the position on free will that he had learned from his mentor and patron Johan Eck.[337] Moore reaches this conclusion by comparing Eck's *Chrysopassus* of 1524 and Hubmaier's two works on free will and his *A Christian Catechism*. Moore criticizes Steinmetz and Rollin Stely Armour for assuming that Hubmaier had once held to the same doctrine of grace as Luther or Zwingli. However, his limited selection of late texts from Hubmaier's works leaves him open to a similar objection. Moore has not presented an account of Hubmaier's understanding of grace from his early works to establish that Hubmaier never held a view of grace similar to Luther and Zwingli. The earlier analysis of Hubmaier's *Summa* and *On the Christian Baptism* do show Hubmaier adopting a view of grace and salvation that approximates to that of Luther and Zwingli.[338]

Steinmetz has also presented a comparison between the doctrine of Luther and Hubmaier on free will, noting that the crucial difference between them is in their anthropology. For Luther, the fall has affected the whole person; there is nothing good in humanity, everything is affected by concupiscence. Luther rejects any Platonic division of a person into

---

334. Bergsten, *Balthasar Hubmaier: Anabaptist Theologian*, 352.

335. Ibid., 353.

336. Ibid., 356.

337. Steinmetz, "Scholasticism and Radical Reform," 131; Moore, "Catholic Teacher," 74.

338. See the earlier analysis of *Summa* and *On the Christian Baptism* in chapter 5.

higher and lower faculties; that is, spirit and flesh. It was this division that allowed the nominalists to propose that something remained in human beings after the fall that was free to love God supremely.[339] Hubmaier, on the other hand, presents his trichotomous view of man, in which the spirit and the will of the spirit remain unblemished by the fall and concupiscence. Though the will of the spirit still desires the good, it requires the aid of external preaching and internal illumination by the Holy Spirit to bring the soul back to God. The flesh, however, remains totally corrupt both before and after restoration from the fall. This reliance on the external preaching of the Word is rejected by Gabriel Biel, though the Old Franciscan school affirms it, as does Eck.[340] The trichotomous anthropology of Hubmaier has generally been attributed to the influence of Erasmus. However, Gordon Rupp makes the telling point that this same anthropology "is found in Wessel Gansfort before him and in Cornelius Hoen among his disciples, and when we find it in Oecolampadius and Zwingli, we do not need to look to Erasmus as its author."[341] Indeed, Luther designates Origen as the creator of this "fable."[342] This trichotomous view of humanity should probably be regarded as part of the common knowledge of the age and not attributable to any particular person during the period of the Reformation. Nonetheless, Hubmaier's use of this anthropology is distinct and significant.

As interesting as the debate is concerning the various influences that impinged on Hubmaier in this area, of greater concern is the analysis of the hermeneutic of Hubmaier and the other major figures in this debate; that is Erasmus, Luther, and Denck. Rupp comments in his introduction to *De libero arbitrio* that the debate between Erasmus and Luther was not in itself a "very great debate. . . . At best, Erasmus prodded Luther into some splendid epigrams and into uttering hermeneutical principles of worth. At the worst, their debate slammed the door on any reconciliation

---

339. Steinmetz, "Luther and Hubmaier," 65–66. For a detailed description of Luther's anthropology compared with that of Thomas Aquinas see Janz, *Luther and Late Medieval Thomism*, 155–56. Janz argues that Aquinas in his *Summa* and Luther in his *Disputatio contra scholasticam theologian* shared a common Augustinian anthropology. The semi-Pelagian anthropology that Luther attacked was a blatant misrepresentation of Aquinas's position that Luther learnt from Karlstadt.

340. Steinmetz, "Luther and Hubmaier," 67. It would appear that Steinmetz has incorporated Moore's findings in this article, which is otherwise an expanded version of his "Scholasticism and Radical Reform."

341. Rupp and Watson, *Luther and Erasmus*, 5

342. *On the Bondage of the Will*, 317

between two great men, and embarrassed their common friends."³⁴³ It is in the area of hermeneutics that these works have not yet received due attention. Bergsten asserts that Hubmaier "borrowed from Erasmus the method of presenting this abundance of writing in favor of free will," but does not indicate if this included Erasmus's hermeneutical method as well.³⁴⁴ If Hubmaier had adopted Erasmus's hermeneutic as well as his division of the work as the format for presentation of his own argument, it would imply that Hubmaier radically changed his hermeneutical principles in response to this one issue. In the analysis of Hubmaier's two works on free will that follow, a careful comparison will be undertaken between Hubmaier's hermeneutic and the hermeneutics of Luther, Erasmus, and Denck. Only then will it be possible to indicate whether Hubmaier followed Erasmus or continued to develop his own position.

Analysis

In the preface to his first work on free will, Hubmaier indicates his pastoral concern about the lack of works of brotherly love that has grown out of a misrepresentation of the truth of Scripture. Some in his congregation claimed, "We can do nothing good. God works in us the desire and the doing. We have no free will." He challenged them that these were only half-truths, from which only half judgments can be drawn. He insists that for a whole judgment to be made the "counter Scriptures" must be laid beside them on the same scale, uniting them into a whole judgment.³⁴⁵ Hubmaier then adds that "whoever does not divide the Scripture in such a way eats of the unclean animals who do not part their hooves" (Lev 11:4).³⁴⁶ In order to uproot such tares, Hubmaier writes this first work on free will and promises a second work, which will "testify incontrovertibly and still more

---

343. Rupp and Watson, *Luther and Erasmus*, 1–2.

344. Bergsten, *Balthasar Hubmaier: Anabaptist Theologian*, 352.

345. *PY*, 428; *HS*, 381. This is one of the passages Bergsten notes as similar to Denck. "Whoever accepts [carnal] truth and overlooks spiritual truth, that is, who does not place [two] contradictions in Scripture on a balanced scale, still has whichever of the two he chooses, only a half-truth. A half-truth is worse than a lie because it will sell itself along with the truth." Denck, *Concerning the Law of God*. 143.

346. *PY*, 428; *HS*, 381. Luther uses the same image of the cloven hoof in *On the Bondage of the Will*, 157–58, also citing Lev 11. However, Luther is referring to choosing passages from the church fathers where they speak under the influence of the Spirit, and ignore what savors of the flesh, in short, choose what they say if it is against free choice and in support of grace.

powerfully with the Holy Scriptures to the freedom of the human being to do good and evil."[347] Only in his second work does Hubmaier demonstrate his method for resolving contrary texts.

The work is dedicated to Count George of Brandenburg-Ansbach, who was a follower of Luther. Bergsten notes that Count George was, until the time of the death of Ludwig of Hungary at the Battle of Mohacs in August 1526, the leader of the Lutheran party at the Hungarian court. It was Count George's position as a forceful representative of the Reformation in Silesia and Moravia that encouraged Hubmaier to dedicate this work to him.[348]

Hubmaier begins this work where he began his *A Christian Catechism*, with a definition of man as a corporeal and rational creature, created by God as body, spirit, and soul.[349] He elaborates what he means by humanity being created in the image of God by exegeting Gen 2:7. For the first time in his writings, Hubmaier uses Hebrew, Greek, and Latin to demonstrate that people were created with three essential substances. He cites the Hebrew *aphar* or *eretes*, which he says parallels the Greek *soma* and the Latin *corpus; neshamah*, which is translated as *pneuma* and *spiritus* respectively; and *nephesh*, which he gives as *psyche* and *anima*. In keeping with his earlier pronouncements that the German language is capable of providing understanding of Scripture, he also give the German for these three terms, "*Geist, Seel, Leib.*"[350] To support his contention that this tripartite view of man is thoroughly biblical, Hubmaier cites Paul's use of the terms in 1 Thess 5:23, as well as Heb 4:12, and the words of Mary in the Magnificat (Luke 1:46). In a more forced exposition of Matt 26:41, the words of Christ praying in the garden to have the cup removed from him, Hubmaier attributes the prayer to the saddened soul of Christ crying out according to the will of the flesh.[351]

According to Hubmaier, it follows that these three substances in people each have a will of their own. The will of the flesh does not want to suffer; the will of the soul is willing to suffer, but due to the influence of the flesh does not; and the will of the spirit has a strong desire to suffer. This reflects Hubmaier's interpretation of Matt 26:41. In Christ, who is the perfect representation of humanity, the spirit of Christ desired to

---

347. *PY*, 429; *HS*, 382.
348. *HS*, 379–80.
349. *PY*, 429, cf. 345; *HS*, 328, cf. 311.
350. *PY*, 429–30; *HS*, 382.
351. *PY*, 430; *HS*, 383.

suffer. However, the saddened soul of Christ, though willing to suffer, was hindered by the flesh, which did not want to suffer. Hubmaier supports this view by declaring that the three wills in man are spoken of in John 1:13; those who become children of God are born not of blood nor out of the will of the flesh nor out of the will of man (that is, the soul), but out of God.[352] For Hubmaier, this rebirth is essential if a person is to be saved eternally. He describes the rebirth as coming about through the water and the Spirit. The water he interprets to be the Word of God, "which is water to all who thirst for salvation, which Word is made alive in us through the Spirit of God, without which it is a killing letter."[353] The Word of God is the outward witness to the Spirit, the Holy Spirit is the inner witness, and conscience is the third witness that confirms that the testimony of the Word of God is true.[354]

Following this summary of his position, Hubmaier then proceeds to detail his understanding of humanity before the fall, after the fall, and after the restoration effected by God through the merits of Christ. He maintains that humanity before the fall was in all three substances and wills completely free to choose good or evil, life or death, heaven or hell. This is clearly stated in Eccl 15:14ff, the text Erasmus used to begin his discussion of this topic.[355] This view is later stated with reference to grace, "God created the human being so free that he was at first able without new grace to remain in his inborn innocence and righteousness unto eternal life."[356]

Through his disobedience, Adam lost this freedom for himself and for all his descendants. The result was evidenced three ways that align with flesh, soul, and spirit. Firstly, there is the irretrievable loss of the flesh, which is under God's curse to return to dust. Secondly, there is the wounding of the soul through its loss of the knowledge of good and evil so that it cannot refuse evil for it cannot distinguish good from evil, and must do the will of the flesh. Thirdly, there is the imprisoning of the spirit, which remains upright and guiltless, but unable to move the soul to do good. Hubmaier gives most attention to the place of the soul in God's order of salvation, for it is the soul that is reparable through the Word of God, while

352. *PY*, 431; *HS*, 383.
353. *PY*, 431; *HS*, 383–84.
354. *PY*, 431; *HS*, 384.
355. *PY*, 432–33; *HS*, 385. Cf. *De libero arbitrio*, 47.
356. *PY*, 443; *HS*, 393. This in contrast to Erasmus who states: "In man the will was so upright and free that, apart from new grace, he could continue in innocence, but apart from the help of new grace, he could not attain the happiness of eternal life which the Lord Jesus promised to his followers." *De libero arbitrio*, 48.

the body is only redeemable once it has returned to ashes and is raised a new body at the resurrection.[357] Hubmaier employs a similar figurative interpretation of the Genesis account of the fall to that of Erasmus. Eve is the flesh, while Adam is the soul, who for love of his flesh disobeys the command of God, bringing about the loss of all knowledge of good and evil.[358] For Hubmaier, in order to will good or evil requires first the knowledge of good or evil. That knowledge only becomes available again to humanity through the sent Word of God; that is, through the only begotten Son of God, Jesus Christ as revealed in Scripture.[359] This is in marked contrast to Erasmus's position, where he argued that through the law of nature the ancient philosophers, though they knew nothing of divine precepts, nevertheless gained a knowledge of God and what is good, and expressed that knowledge in leading virtuous lives.[360] Hubmaier is more in tune with Luther on this point, stating that Aristotle has "seduced" the scholastic theologians with his twofold division in humanity, the lower and higher natures, for he was unable to grasp "this breath of the living God with his natural and pagan understanding."[361]

The woundedness of the soul as a consequence of the fall is partially expressed as loss of the knowledge of good and evil, and thus the ability to will and to do good and evil. Yet there remains in the spirit of all people after the fall the "desire" to do good. Hubmaier describes this desire in terms of hunger and thirst, sustaining the metaphor of the Word of God as bread, water, drink, meat, and blood. God will not forsake such a "spirit-hungry" person, but will send an ambassador and letters, or if need be an angel, to instruct them in the Word of God.[362] However, even this power for willing what is good is attributed to God, for "it is not in us as if it were

---

357. *PY,* 435ff; *HS,* 386ff.

358. *PY,* 435; *HS,* 387. Cf. *De libero arbitrio,* 48. Erasmus argues that the will and reason of both Adam and Eve were corrupt, and that "this power of the soul with which we judge, and it matters not whether you call it nous, that is, mind or intellect, or logos, that is, reason, is obscured by sin, but not altogether extinguished."

359. *PY,* 439; *HS,* 390.

360. *De libero arbitrio,* 49. Erasmus goes on to acknowledge that this will that is able to do the good is useless for eternal life without the addition of grace by faith.

361. *PY,* 439; *HS,* 389. Cf. Luther's comment to Erasmus: "Moreover, you invented a fourfold grace to enable you to attribute some sort of faith and charity even to the philosophers; and with it a threefold law, of nature, works and faith, which is indeed a new fable, to enable you to assert that the precepts of the philosophers agree very markedly with the precepts of the gospel." *On the Bondage of the Will,* 176–77.

362. *PY,* 437; *HS,* 388 cf. *PY,* 363; *HS,* 324 where Hubmaier indicates that God will answer fervent prayer by sending a Peter from Joppa or an angel from heaven.

from us, for it is originally from God and his image, in which he created us originally." Nor can this breath of God in us be extinguished in people since God allows no one to be tempted beyond what they can bear (1 Cor 10:13).[363]

Ultimately, however, this "desire" in the spirit of people is extinguishable as punishment from God. Those who sin against the Holy Spirit will have the Holy Spirit taken from them, "without which Spirit our spirit is quite helpless." Those who sin against the Holy Spirit are described as those who deny free will in "the newborn human beings."[364] With his reference to 1 Cor 10:13 Hubmaier makes it clear that those who have the breath of God removed from them do so by their willful rejection of God and his Word.

It is in the third period, "Human Beings After the Restoration," that Hubmaier locates free will. The flesh remains totally corrupt, while the spirit now rejoices, and is ready and willing to do all good. The soul in its natural powers stands troubled between the flesh and the spirit. It has been awakened by the heavenly Father through the Word; made whole by the Son and enlightened by the Holy Spirit, so that it again knows what is good and evil; and has obtained again its lost freedom. The soul can now willingly be obedient to the spirit as it was in paradise. This is effected through the sent Word of God; that is, through the "only begotten Son, Jesus Christ."[365] The power of the Word of God to effect this change in human beings is supported by references to Ps 107:20; 119:25 as well as the words of Christ in John 8:31f. The emphasis is on the initiation of God in this process, "God speaks first and gives power through his Word." Later Hubmaier refers specifically to the regaining of knowledge of good and evil as the result of new grace and the drawing of the Father.[366] However, the cooperation of the individual is essential, as Hubmaier demonstrates by citing the popular saying, "God has created you without your help, but

---

363. *PY*, 437–38; *HS*, 389. In this section Hubmaier describes this part of human beings as the breath of God, in keeping with Gen 2:7, while in *A Christian Catechism* he uses the more mystical term "spark." *PY*, 360; *HS*, 322.

364. *PY*, 437; *HS*, 388.

365. *PY*, 439; *HS*, 390.

366. *PY*, 440. Cf. 444; *HS*, 390. Cf. 394. "Therefore this recognition and power of knowledge, willing and working must happen and be attained by a new grace and drawing of the heavenly Father, who now looks at humanity anew by the merit of Jesus Christ our Lord, blesses and draws him with his life-giving Word which speaks into the heart of a person." Denck, however, argues that God speaks to the heart of human beings "without any means." Denck, *Concerning the Law of God*, 119.

without your help he will not save you."³⁶⁷ Later he expresses the same thought but in terms of the grace of God, "If I now will, then I will be saved by the grace of God; if I do not will, then I will be damned, and that on the basis of my own obstinacy and willfulness."³⁶⁸ Hubmaier constantly stresses that God takes the initiative in the order of salvation, but that people are responsible to respond to God's offer of grace, and to fulfill the commands of God. In this way, he seeks to maintain that salvation is not due to human good works that merit God's grace, while at the same time insisting that sin and the loss of salvation is due to willful disobedience to the commands of God. Hubmaier begins with the presupposition that sin is not sin if it is not done willingly.³⁶⁹ In Hubmaier's understanding, for sin to be done willingly man must have a free will and a knowledge of good and evil.

The soul is now considered able to command the flesh to do the good; it tames the flesh and masters it so that "against its own inclination it must go into the fire with the spirit and the soul on account of the name of Christ." ³⁷⁰The soul is also free again to will evil and has a ready instrument in the flesh to perform it. Hubmaier warns that the soul should not procrastinate in its decision to follow the spirit, for if it hangs too long on this oak of human choice, it will be stabbed to death with three wounds, "consent, word, and deed."³⁷¹

Hubmaier is careful to explain that there remains imperfection in human beings, an imperfection due to the corruption of the flesh. However, the failures of the flesh are not injurious to the soul, for the divine commands are fulfilled in Christ. However, it is only in the ascended Christ that believers find their perfection, and not in their own bodies. He cites Augustine, "If the commandments of God are fulfilled . . . those other things not fulfilled by us are forgiven us."³⁷² Hubmaier uses the simile of the carpenter who uses a notched plane. The fault in the work lies not in

---

367. *PY*, 440; *HS*, 391.

368. *PY*, 442; *HS*, 392.

369. *PY*, 441; *HS*, 392. Erasmus holds to the same presupposition stating: "If the will had not been free, sin could not have been imputed, for sin would cease to be sin if it were not voluntary, save when error or the restriction of the will is itself the fruit of sin." *De libero arbitrio*, 50.

370. *PY*, 441; *HS*, 391.

371. *PY*, 440; *HS*, 391. This is a reference to the death of Absalom who had three spears thrust through his heart by Joab (2 Sam 18:14). Hubmaier here interprets these three spears to be three steps by which the soul again becomes the slave of the flesh.

372. *PY*, 441–42; *HS*, 392.

the carpenter but in the tool he uses. Nevertheless, the "divine Word is so powerful, authoritative and strong in the believers that the person (though not the godless one) can will and do everything that said Word commands him to want and to do."[373] This power of the Word causes the new birth in the Christian, without which it is impossible to enter the kingdom of God.

The image of Christ as the Samaritan and physician continues to feature in Hubmaier's portrayal of the order of salvation. However, he now identifies the wine and the oil used in the healing process as being applied to the inner and outer wounds that humanity has incurred due to Adam's disobedience. The inner wound is ignorance of good and evil, which is healed by the wine of the law. This is described as "new grace" by which all people are "taught anew what is truly good and evil before God."[374] The external wound of doing and acting, is healed by the oil of the gospel. By the gospel sin is made no longer damning "if we do not follow it wantonly." Therefore, in Christ the fall of Adam is made wholly innocuous for us and incapable of incurring God's condemnation. The centrality of Christ to this process is described by identifying how each of the three substances in Christ wins restored health and freedom for the three substances in all people.[375]

Hubmaier concludes this short introductory work with a polemical piece directed towards those who, by denying free will, shame and blaspheme God by implying that he is a tyrant who condemns people for something they cannot help but do. This denial of free will would overthrow the justifiable charge Christ brings against those who have not done what he commanded them (Matt 25:42). Similarly, Judas and Pilate could argue their innocence since they are not responsible for their sin, rather God is responsible since he created them and used them as unworthy vessels.[376] He goes on to protest against those who attribute their harlotry and

---

373. *PY,* 441, 444; *HS,* 391–92, 394. Luther uses a similar image of the notched carpenter's tool, *On the Bondage of the Will,* 233.

374. *PY,* 446; *HS,* 395. Earlier Hubmaier had described the effect of the law in three ways: to the flesh it brings recognition of sins, to the spirit it acts as an aid and witness against sin, to the soul it is a light "whereby it can see and learn the way of righteousness and flee sin and evil." *PY,* 442; *HS,* 393.

375. *PY,* 466; *HS,* 396. "For Christ with his Spirit has acquired for our spirit from the heavenly Father that the prison is not harmful to our spirit. And with his soul he has acquired for our soul that through his divine Word it is again taught and enlightened as to what good and evil is. Yes, also by his flesh he yearns for our flesh that after it has become ashes it may again be resurrected in honor and be immortal" (1 Cor 15:22).

376. *PY,* 447; *HS,* 396–97.

adultery to the necessity of God's will, and about the laziness and despair that the teaching of a bound will engenders. These people are waiting for a "special, unusual, and miraculous drawing of God . . . as if the sending of his holy Word were not enough to draw and summon them."[377]

Though Hubmaier notes in his foreword that the half-truths on which the doctrine of the bound will is based require that the contrary text be placed beside them so that a whole judgment can be made, he fails to do this at all in this preliminary statement on the topic. He leaves that part of the argument to his second book on free will. In this work, he is focused more on defining free will in relationship to his tripartite understanding of humanity.

Use of Scripture

In his use of Scripture, there is evidence to support the proposition that Hubmaier is increasingly relying on the Old Testament for material to argue for his point of view. Of the seventy-six Old Testament references he cites, thirty are from Genesis and twenty-three from the Psalms. Only Jeremiah (seven references); Isaiah (five references); Exodus, Deuteronomy, and Job (two references each) have more than one reference per book. The references from Genesis are almost entirely related to Hubmaier's discussion of the image of God in people and the three essential substances that comprise humanity. The references to the Psalms are of more interest with regard to Hubmaier's hermeneutic, for they show a definite shift in his understanding of Christ as the Word of God. Previously in his discussions on baptism, the physically present Christ speaks the words of forgiveness of sins that brings wholeness to the sinner. Now the sent Word of God is identified with the Word that God speaks in the Psalms. This Word is said to bring health (Ps 107:20; 119:11); to teach knowledge of good and evil or to bring enlightenment (Ps 119:7; 119:105); and bring life (Ps 119:107; 119:25). The power and effectiveness of the Word is also underlined by references to Isa 40:8; 55:11; Jer 6; 7; 23:29.

There is therefore a new identification of Christ with the Word of God that frees the effectiveness of Christ's work from the chronological constraint previously imposed. Prior to this work, restoration from the effects of the fall had to wait until Christ had come in the flesh. That this was Hubmaier's understanding is demonstrated by his conclusion that the patriarchs had to wait for their salvation until Christ had preached

---

377. *PY*, 447; *HS*, 397.

to them in the Spirit. It is also readily seen in his understanding that the church obtains the power of the keys to forgive sins only if Christ is no longer bodily present. Though Hubmaier has changed his appreciation of Christ as the Word of God, he does not specify whether the restoration from the fall has to wait until Christ has come in the flesh or whether the Word of God as spoken in the Old Testament effects the restoration of people after the fall, despite Christ having not yet suffered in the flesh. This is a significant development in Hubmaier's presuppositions and affects his hermeneutic, as it allows him to make much greater use of the Old Testament as a source of proof texts relating to salvation.

The New Testament references that Hubmaier cites also reflect a change in emphasis that is not entirely unexpected given the change in subject matter. Of the total of 117 references, Matthew's gospel and Romans share first place (twenty-five references each), while John's gospel follows closely with twenty-four references. Only Luke's gospel (thirteen) and 1 Corinthians (ten) have ten or more references. The other New Testament books used have five or fewer references. However, there is a change here as well. While Matthew has the greatest number of references, Hubmaier now uses this book principally as a source of illustrations to support various points. It is the book of Romans, particularly chapters 7, 8, 9 and 10 that provide the proof texts in his arguments for free will, along with John's gospel chapters 1 and 3. It is here that a link exists between Hubmaier's use of the logos theology of John's gospel and his identification of the Word of God in the Old Testament as Christ the sent Word of God.

Although there is evidence in this work of Hubmaier's awareness of Erasmus's *De libero arbitrio,* there is not enough to prove dependence. Hubmaier's citation of Scripture is independent of Erasmus in this work. Of the 169 separate references Hubmaier makes to Scripture, he shares with Erasmus only nine from the Old Testament, nine from the New Testament and 1 from the Apocrypha. If dependence were attributable on the basis of Scripture references in common, then Hubmaier would be dependent on Luther in this instance, for he shares with Luther ten Old Testament, twenty-four New Testament, and the same one Apocryphal text.

Summary

In this work, Hubmaier has made a dramatic change in one of his hermeneutical presuppositions; namely, his understanding of Christ as the sent

Word of God. Previously, Christ as the sent Word of God meant the physical incarnation of the Word of God in Jesus. Now, Hubmaier speaks of Christ as the sent Word of God in the Old Testament. In this use of Christ as the Word of God, Hubmaier means the *logos* that is independent of any physical constraints. This is not a view attributable to Erasmus.

FREEDOM OF THE WILL II

(May 20, 1527)[378]

Setting

With the publication of his second work on free will, Hubmaier completes the undertaking he had made in the preface of the first work. He dedicated this second work to Duke Friedrich II of Liegnitz, Brieg, and Wohlau in Silesia, who had been won to the Reformation by Caspar Schwenckfeld. When Frederick of Austria increased the persecution of Anabaptists and other evangelicals in 1528, many found refuge on the estates of Duke Friedrich, including Hubmaier's printer Simprecht Sorg and the preacher Glaidt.[379]

Bergsten refers to an unpublished work of Seewald, in which the latter compared Hubmaier's treatment of free will with that of Erasmus in *De libero arbitrio*. It is acknowledged that they both have a three-part division. In part one, both Hubmaier and Erasmus list and discuss texts of Scripture from the Old and New Testaments that support free will.[380] In part two, Erasmus discusses those passages that seem to oppose free will, while Hubmaier sets out his major theses to support free will. In part three, Erasmus draws together his conclusions for a moderating position, while Hubmaier discusses the arguments and texts opposed to free will.

378. *PY*, 449–91; *HS*, 398–431.

379. *HS*, 398.

380. *HS*, 399. Part three of Hubmaier's work is set out as a disputation, in which he identifies his friends in Nikolsburg who are in favor of the bondage of the will as the friends of Job. Hubmaier does not place his name before the answers he gives as he had done in his *Dialogue* and *On Infant Baptism*. "Now once again my good friends cry out (*Yetz schreyen abermals mein gutt freund*) . . . , Answer (*Antwurt*) . . ." *PY*, 482; *HS*, 424. Denck uses a similar structure in his works *Concerning the Law of God* and *Whether God is the Cause* : "You say (*Sprichst du*) . . . Response (*Antwort*) . . ." Denck, *Whether God is the Cause*, 26–27. Seewald's work was not available to compare these results of the usage of Scripture by Hubmaier and Erasmus.

In parts one and two, Hubmaier makes greater use of Erasmus, choosing the same texts and frequently in the same order. However, this similarity of chosen texts should not be overemphasized as evidence of theological dependence of Hubmaier on Erasmus.[381] Bergsten also notes positively Williams's comment that Hubmaier must have used Denck's *Whether God is the Cause*, something he goes on to demonstrate by showing literary similarities between Hubmaier and Denck on two topics; half-truths and sin that is recognized as punishment not being counted as sin.[382]

Analysis

In this second work on free will, Hubmaier sets out to demonstrate his method of determining a whole judgment by bringing together contrary texts that on their own give only a half judgment. In his dedicatory letter, he takes the example of Satan's temptation of Christ to show how Scripture can be misrepresented; a half-truth for a whole truth. It is the devil who whispers in one ear, while the Spirit of God speaks in the other. As soon as the Spirit speaks to any human being he may then immediately exercise free choice; that person is free to be obedient to God or to Satan.[383] Hubmaier had made this point clear in the title to this work, which states in part "that God by means of his sent Word gives power to all people to become his children and freely entrusts to them the choice to will and to do the good."[384]

His second major point in this prefatory letter relates to the saying of Christ, "If you will enter into life, keep the commandments" (Matt 19:17).[385] He comments that this verse "is more powerful in every single Christian heart as a testimony to the freedom of the human will than a big ship full of human glosses imported from foreign lands of carnal wisdom." His choice of this verse indicates his continued stress on the necessity of obedience to the stated commands of God as revealed in Scripture, principally in the words of Christ.

In part one, Hubmaier selects thirty Old Testament, New Testament, and Apocryphal texts, which he uses to describe humanity before the fall,

---

381. *HS*, 399.
382. *HS*, 399; Bergsten, *Balthasar Hubmaier: Anabaptist Theologian*, 355.
383. *PY*, 451; *HS*, 401.
384. *PY*, 450; *HS*, 400.
385. *PY*, 452; *HS*, 400.

Balthasar Hubmaier and the Clarity of Scripture

after the fall, and after restoration from the fall.[386] Humanity before the fall is described by reference to Eccl 15:14ff. Hubmaier interprets this as meaning that humanity before the fall was "so free and highly graced that he could remain in his created innocence and original righteousness without new grace, keeping the commandments of God and living eternally in rest, ecstasy, and joy."[387] He goes on to state that the human being did not embrace that freedom and became like an unreasoning animal, and henceforth became a "child of fire, of evil, and of death." It is therefore impossible for people either to know or to recognize good or evil, life or death, or to choose between them without a special new grace.[388] As explained in his previous work on free will, the fall does not affect the spirit in people, only the soul and the flesh. But God has come to our aid with a new and special grace through Christ. The effect of Christ's coming is now described in specific terms that demonstrate that everything the Christian possesses in this time of grace, the patriarchs and people of the "old marriage" also possessed through the promised Christ.[389] Here Hubmaier

386. Of the thirty references Hubmaier uses, twelve are from the Old Testament, seventeen from the New, and one from Ecclesiasticus. He begins with the reference to Eccl 15:14 as does Erasmus, and as does Luther in his response to Erasmus. There follow six Old Testament references in the order used by Erasmus, with the exception of Gen 6:3, which he has introduced here from Erasmus's part three. He shares six of these Old Testament references with Luther, the order of their appearance being altered by Luther discussing Deut 30:11ff earlier in his reply than in Erasmus's work; and Ps 51:5 as a reference to the impact of original sin, a topic not discussed by Erasmus in any detail. Of the seventeen New Testament references, Hubmaier shares nine with Erasmus. These show considerable variation in order of appearance compared to Erasmus. Philippians 2:13 and John 6:67 do not occur in Luther's treatment of the topic. Hubmaier has eight New Testament texts in common with Luther, seven of which are common to both Hubmaier and Erasmus. Only Eph 2:3 is used by Luther and Hubmaier but not found in Erasmus.

387. *PY*, 453; *HS*, 402. Luther rejects free will in man with regard to obeying the commands of God, even before the fall. He argues that man was free to choose only in relation to the lower creatures. As soon as God added his commandments and precepts man had no free choice but was under the direction of God. *On the Bondage of the Will*, 183.

388. *PY*, 454; *HS*, 403. Luther makes the same point in his discussion of Luke 23:34, "Father, forgive them; for they know not what they do." "For how can you will what you do not know? If you're not wise to it, you can't rise to it, surely." *On the Bondage of the Will*, 216.

389. *PY*, 454; *HS*, 403. Hubmaier supplies as references for this comment Gen 3:15; 22:18; 26:4; 28:14, all of which refer to the blessing of all nations through "the seed" promised by God. This concept of the seed becomes prominent in Hubmaier's hermeneutic, as he links this "seed" with the parable of the sower, where the seed is the Word of God, and identifies the Word of God with the eternal Christ.

Making a Patchwork of Scripture

makes explicit what was implicit in his changed Christology as shown in his first work on free will. There is no new covenant distinct from the old, "there is only one marriage and one church of the only bridegroom and Head, Christ Jesus."[390]

Human beings after the fall are described as having lost their freedom, become children of sin, wrath, and death, who without a special new grace of God can neither keep the commandments nor be saved. The Scriptures he chooses closely follow those of Erasmus, though he presents only a small selection of Erasmus's texts. He presents his Old Testament texts first, followed by New Testament texts, the latter all being from the works of Paul. To his choice of Erasmus's Old Testament texts, Hubmaier adds his familiar trio of texts on original sin, Job 3:3; Jer 20:14; Ps 51:5. His New Testament texts have no parallels in Erasmus. Hubmaier is concerned to emphasize the devastating effects of the fall on all humanity. Erasmus does not hold to the total corruption of humanity due to the fall, allowing some natural reason to remain, obscured, but not extinguished.[391] Luther on the other hand accused Erasmus of not understanding the full severity of the sin of Adam, which not only condemns all people, but has totally corrupted them.[392]

A selection of twenty texts follows showing the nature of human beings after restoration by Christ. People are said to receive again their freedom and a new grace "through the sent Word of God" to will and to do the good. This reception of new grace is described as a new birth effected through the power of the Word. However, this new birth does not affect the flesh, which continues to fight against the spirit. Yet the sin of the flesh does not condemn, for people awakened and born anew by the Word do not will nor walk according to the will of the flesh.[393]

---

390. *PY*, 454; *HS*, 403. This rejection of a division of the history of salvation at the point of the incarnation distinguishes Hubmaier from the Swiss Brethren. It also provides the basis from which Hubmaier can treat both Old and New Testaments equally without adopting the position of the Swiss Brethren, as expressed at the Bern Disputation in 1538, and many other Anabaptists; that is, the New Testament takes precedence over the Old. Davis, *Anabaptism and Asceticism*, 215–16.

391. *De libero arbitrio*, 48.

392. *On the Bondage of the Will*, 231. Luther also uses Ps 51:5 and Eph 2:3 in his discussion of the effects of the fall.

393. *PY*, 456–457; *HS*, 405. Erasmus speaks of grace abolishing sin so that it may be overcome, though grace does not uproot sin altogether. He also describes the action of grace in terms of the forgiveness of sins, whereas Hubmaier speaks of new birth. *De libero arbitrio*, 49. Erasmus's "probable opinion" concerning grace and free choice attributes most to grace and practically nothing to free choice, yet does not remove it

Hubmaier begins with Gen 4:5ff, a text Erasmus used to show Cain had rewards and punishment placed before him, and that the movement of the will to evil could be overcome.[394] Hubmaier ignores Erasmus's opinion about rewards and punishments, and simply maintains that the text shows Cain was able to master sin. He adds to Erasmus's view the comment that since Cain was born after the fall, the text applies equally well to all people born after the fall.[395] Luther attacked Erasmus's interpretation of this text in three ways. Firstly, Erasmus is inconsistent. Erasmus stated in his "probable opinion" that free choice cannot will the good, yet here maintains that free choice can overcome the motion of the mind to evil. Secondly, Luther argues that in Hebrew the future indicative is frequently used for the imperative, meaning that this passage shows what Cain ought to do, not what he can do. Thirdly, if the passage was indicative it would be a promise of God, and since God does not lie, the result would be that no person would sin, and then there would be no need of the law as precepts.[396] Later in this work, Hubmaier comments on this point of grammar, referring to the commandments in Exod 20 as had Luther, yet reaching different conclusions. Hubmaier states that the commandments are given in the indicative not the imperative, since God does not have to force the righteous to obey his commands, he simply has to show the way and the righteous joyfully follow without compulsion.[397]

---

completely. He denies that people can "will the good without peculiar grace . . . make a beginning . . . progress . . . (or) reach his goal without the principal and perpetual aid of divine grace." *De libero arbitrio*, 53. Hubmaier's emphasis on new birth reflects more of Luther's understanding as he states it in relation to John 1:12, "John is not speaking of any work of man, either great or small, but of the very renewal and transformation of the old man, who is a child of the devil, into the new man who is a child of God." *On the Bondage of the Will*, 217. The opportunity of this rebirth is the coming of Christ into the world through the gospel, which becomes effective through faith. However, this faith, willing, or believing, does not come from free choice.

394. *De libero arbitrio*, 54.

395. *PY*, 457; *HS*, 405.

396. *On the Bondage of the Will*, 189. He had made a similar point with regard to Eccl 15:14. In the phrase "if thou wilt" the verb is a subjunctive. Therefore, as the logicians say, a conditional asserts nothing indicatively. This point of grammar and the inconsistency between Erasmus's "probable opinion" and the assertion of free choice to fulfill the commandments of God without prior grace are Luther's major arguments against Erasmus's defense of free will. Erasmus is arguing against necessity as compulsion; Luther redefines necessity as "necessity of immutability," which he asserts does not involve compulsion. *On the Bondage of the Will*, 139.

397. *PY*, 466; *HS*, 412.

The second text Hubmaier cites, Deut 11:26ff, focuses on the ability of Israel to obey the commandments given them through Moses. It would be sacrilegious to say God used such "high words" just for fun and not with "earnest concern."[398]

Hubmaier deals with Deut 30:11 in similar fashion to his references on baptism in *On Christian Baptism,* as an extended quote with minimal comment. Hubmaier considers the Scripture to be so clear as to require no extensive interpretation. Hubmaier remarks: "See here, Christian reader, how bright and clear this Scripture shows us that God freely entrusted to the human being anew also after the Fall the choice of evil and good, blessing and curse, life and death. . . . [N]ot God, but we ourselves, out of free will, are responsible for our sins and eternal damnation."[399]

Erasmus focuses on key words in the text, "set before you," "choose," and "turn away," which he reasons would be "inappropriate" if there were no free will in human beings.[400] He also concludes from the words "in your heart," that God's commands are implanted in all people and that they are easy to do.[401]

Denck also makes use of this Scripture, insisting that the commands of God are in the Christian through the work of the Spirit, independently of the written word of Scripture.[402] Denck goes on to say, "Whoever esteems Scripture beyond its intention to inspire love of God makes of Scripture an idol and indoctrinates himself as those scribes who were unfit for the kingdom." This is a far cry from Hubmaier's position that the power of salvation is in the sent Word of God; that is, Jesus Christ, who is also identified as the preached Word of God. The Spirit of God illumines the soul of the human being, but not independently of the Scripture, as read or preached.[403]

---

398. *PY,* 458; *HS,* 405-6. Hubmaier uses a similar phrase when referring to the words of institution of baptism: "nowhere else in the Old and New Testaments can we find such high words put together in such an explicit and clear way. . . . [A] serious command demands serious obedience and fulfillment. . . . Christ did not use such precious words in vain as something which we might do or leave undone." *PY,* 122; *HS,* 140-141.

399. *PY,* 459; *HS,* 390.

400. *De libero arbitrio,* 55.

401. *De libero arbitrio,* 57.

402. Denck, *Concerning the Law of God,* 119. He links this view to Jer 31:34, a key verse for his understanding that God can make himself known to his people without the aid of any creaturely means.

403. *PY,* 439; *HS,* 390.

Luther contended that Erasmus proved too much for free will if his simile of the bound man, which he used to illustrate "choosing" and "turning," were to hold good. Luther claimed that it showed that free choice independent of grace does the good, not simply desires the good as Erasmus maintained.[404]

Hubmaier then lists four further Old Testament texts, all of which he argues reject the view that there is no free choice and that everything is done of necessity. With regard to the Isa 1:19 reference, Hubmaier paraphrases his opponents as saying, "God was mocking us when he commanded us to will something good."[405] Luther picked up this theme of the mocking God from Erasmus's treatment of Deut 30:15, 19, "Reason . . . thinks man is mocked by an impossible precept, whereas we say that he is warned and aroused by it to see his own impotence."[406] In his comments on Jer 18:8, 10 Hubmaier makes it plain that he is speaking of free choice that has been granted anew to human beings through the sent Word of God. He is therefore arguing for a freedom in people that relies on the new grace of God given in the power of the Word of God, yet cooperates with God to keep the commandments.

The New Testament texts supporting free will begin with Matt 19:17, followed by Luke 9:23 and John 14:15. They display Hubmaier's basic understanding that obedience to the commands of Christ and following

---

404. *On the Bondage of the Will*, 191. Erasmus uses the following illustration, "It would be as if one were to say to a man so bound that he could only raise his hand to the left: 'See, you have the best wine at your right hand you have poison at your left—choose which you will.'" *De libero arbitrio*, 55. Luther modifies the simile to show it is not ridiculous to say to someone totally bound, if he "maintains or ignorantly presumes that he can do what he pleases on either side of him," raise your hand on both sides, for this will show the falsity of his claim to posses freedom, or bring home to him his ignorance of his captivity and misery. *On the Bondage of the Will*, 192–93. In this work the use of similes and tropes to interpret Scripture is one major point of contention between Luther and Erasmus. Luther maintains "that neither an inference nor a trope is admissible in any passage of Scripture, unless it is forced on us by the evident nature of the context and the absurdity if the literal sense as conflicting with one or other of the articles of faith. Instead, we must everywhere stick to the simple, pure, and natural sense of the words that accords with the rules of grammar and the normal use of language as God has created man." *On the Bondage of the Will*, 221. In contrast Erasmus proposes as a key to interpretation the following: "I consider the best key toward the understanding of Holy Scripture is to consider what theme is examined in that passage; when that is determined, it will be useful to gather together what in parables and similitudes is relevant to our purpose." *De libero arbitrio*, 82–83.

405. *PY*, 460, *HS*, 407.

406. *PY*, 460; *HS*, 407. Cf. *On the Bondage of the Will*, 189 and *De libero arbitrio*, 54–55.

after Christ as his disciple are essential in the life of the believer. These are themes central to the Anabaptist understanding of Christianity. Matthew 23:37, which is first in Erasmus's list of New Testament texts, occupies fifth place in Hubmaier's. His treatment of this passage is taken over almost verbatim from Erasmus, as is his short comment on Rom 7:18f.[407] However, Luke 2:14, "Glory to God in the heights, peace on earth, and to humankind a good will," is an additional text to those used by Erasmus. Hubmaier reasons, "As glory is glory and peace is peace, so also is a good will a good will for humankind."[408] Philippians 2:13, which is for Luther a powerful verse against free will, is understood by Hubmaier in the same way as Erasmus, with the addition that Hubmaier understands both Luther's and Erasmus's interpretations to be "true if you regard the problem as a whole."[409] Here Hubmaier hints at his method of resolving half-truths and coming to whole judgments. He does not make his method explicit until part two of this work, reserving the demonstration of its application to part three.

Hubmaier introduces at this point two new texts that Erasmus does not use, both of which are aimed at overcoming the claim that all works even after grace happen by necessity. The first, 2 Cor 9:7, speaks of giving alms according to how a person has chosen previously to do, "not out of pity or necessity." This text from 2 Corinthians occurs again in Hubmaier's later interpretation of texts that appear to oppose free will. The second text is taken from Philemon, where Paul explains he desired Philemon's response to his request to be voluntary, not forced.[410]

The text John 1:11–12 provides Hubmaier with a further opportunity to reiterate his basic understanding of new birth: "God freely gives power and strength to all those to whom he sends his living Word, and gives them the free choice—if they desire it—in the power of the sent Word to become children of God. Whoever now is a child of God can will and do

---

407. Matt 23:37, *PY*, 461; *HS*, 408–9. Cf. *De libero arbitrio*, 59. Rom 7:18f, *PY*, 462; *HS*, 409. Cf. *On the Bondage of the Will*, 63.

408. *PY*, 462; *HS*, 409. "Glori seye Gott in der hohe, vnd fridt auff erden, vnd den menschen ain gutter will." Hubmaier notes in the margin, "A short and powerful Scripture." It is probably his own translation of the *Vulgate* "Gloria in altissimis Deo, et in terra pax hominibus bonae voluntatis." Luther translates this verse: "*Ehre sey Gott in der Hohe, und Friede auf Erden, und den Menschen ein Wohlgefallen!*" By his choice of ein Wohlgefallen, (a good pleasure) he removes any possibility of attributing a good will to man.

409. *PY*, 462; *HS*, 409.

410. *PY*, 463; *HS*, 409–10.

good, also not will and flee evil according to the will and pleasure of the Father."[411] Erasmus comments on this verse: "How can power to become children of God be given to those who are not yet children, if there is no liberty in our will?" Luther rejects this interpretation, stating that instead John means: "By the coming of Christ into the world through the gospel, whereby grace is offered and not work demanded, the opportunity is provided for all men . . . of becoming children of God if they are willing to believe. But the willing, this believing in his name, is not only something that free choice never knew or thought before, but still less something it can do by its own strength."[412] Luther later develops his understanding of the drawing of the Father by saying "that even the message of the gospel itself . . . is heard in vain unless the Father himself speaks, teaches, and draws inwardly." This inward drawing occurs through the outpouring of the Holy Spirit. Luther maintains there is an external drawing through the preached word, and an inner drawing through the illumination of the Spirit.[413] Erasmus had argued that the text did not speak of coercion or necessity, but rather as a sheep may be drawn to follow a green twig, so God knocks at our soul and we willingly embrace his grace.[414] Hubmaier does not adopt Erasmus's argument or simile. Instead he argues that free will exists "in those people drawn, illumined, and reborn by God, for to them the power is offered and given to become children of God in the power of his Word" (2 Pet 2, probably 1 Pet 1:23 and John 1:12). From his earlier work on free will, the illumination he speaks of parallels Luther's inner illumination of the Spirit. However, Hubmaier continues, "for although no one comes to Christ unless the Father draws him, it, nevertheless, does not follow . . . that all those come to Christ who have been drawn by the Father."[415] This conclusion would be anathema to Luther, as it limits the omnipotence of God.

The two remaining New Testament texts are treated summarily by Hubmaier. Hubmaier deals with John 6:67 as Erasmus had done. To ask, "Do you also want to go away?" implies it was in the power of the disciples

---

411. *PY*, 463; *HS*, 410.

412. *De libero arbitrio*, 60–61.

413. *On the Bondage of the Will*, 326–27.

414. *De libero arbitrio*, 80. This brings forth a retort from Luther about Erasmus's use of similes. He then adapts the image to fit the case of the godly, "who are already sheep and know God their shepherd; for they, living in the Spirit and moved by him, follow wherever God wills and whatever he holds out to them." *On the Bondage of the Will*, 327.

415. *PY*, 477; *HS*, 420.

Making a Patchwork of Scripture

to go away or remain.[416] The final text, John 8:31f, focuses on the integrity of Christ's promise that those who remain in Christ's word will know the truth and the truth will make them free. Christ then promises, if the Son makes you free, then you are truly free. To deny "true freedom in the believers denies Christ himself and the power of his Word through which we come to God."[417]

In this first part of this work, Hubmaier develops his earlier statements on humanity before and after the fall, and after restoration from the fall. The anthropology that dominated in his first work on free will continues inconspicuously to undergird this work. His main purpose in this first part of this work has been to describe the power of the Word of God to restore free choice in people. By using that freedom believers can cooperate with God to keep the commandments he has given through the teaching and life of Christ that they are called to obediently follow. He also makes explicit the effects his changed Christology implies. Hubmaier now understands the gospel to be effectively present as "promise" in the Old Testament and actual in the New. This is stated in terms of the "one marriage" which spans both Testaments. It also means that the words of Christ are no longer limited to the gospels, to Christ's use of particular Old Testament texts, or to acknowledged Messianic texts, as Hubmaier had earlier understood them to be. He therefore comes to hold a view of Scripture that is closer to Zwingli and Luther than to the Swiss Brethren.

Part two of this work is described by Hubmaier as "Several Very Useful Theses in This Matter, Set up in the Manner of a Disputation." There are three major themes in this part of the work. Considerable emphasis is given to describing the power of the Word of God to effect the restoration of free will in all people after the fall so they can obey the commands of God. The Word of God is variously identified as the comforting Word God spoke to Adam and Eve after the fall which clothed them to hide their nakedness, and as the powerful word Christ spoke which brought immediate and effective responses to his commands, "Stand up and walk. See. Hear. Stretch out your hand. Be cleansed."[418] This power, or grace of God, "which he bears to us and with which he embraces us," is offered through the preached Word. Power therefore lies within all people who have heard the preached Word to become children of God and to desire and complete

---

416. *PY,* 464; *HS,* 410. Cf. *De libero arbitrio,* 61.
417. *PY,* 464; *HS,* 410. The text is not cited by Erasmus nor is it discussed by Luther.
418. *PY,* 465; *HS,* 411.

the Father's will.[419] Using the parable of the sower Hubmaier claims that sonship is offered to all people impartially, "for the seed of the divine Word falls equally in four kinds of earth, it follows that we have equal power to accept the seed and bear fruit."[420] For Hubmaier, the power of the Word of God is not limited, as the example of the virgin birth of Christ testifies. That Peter hears and responds to the Word of God, while Herod does not, is due to the mercy of God, and is not a subject to be investigated or questioned. It belongs to the secret will of God.[421] Such is Hubmaier's understanding of the power and effect of the Word of God.

Using Erasmus's simile of the eye Hubmaier explains that a human being only has "the ability to see the light of faith through the Word of God, which he cannot see unless the light enters beforehand into his soul by heavenly illumination."[422] This inner and spiritual seeing is recognized as a grace of God. Where this grace exists, there is seeing, willing, and working.

Erasmus uses the illustration of the eye to support his argument that attributes entirely to grace the first impulse that stirs the soul, yet in performing the act allows something to human choice that has not withdrawn itself from the grace of God. Even in this act of cooperation grace is the principal cause. Free will is the secondary cause, and can do nothing without the principal cause.[423] Erasmus speaks of the sound eye that sees nothing in the dark and the blind eye that sees nothing in the light. As a sound eye can see nothing without the light, so free will can do nothing if grace withdraws from it. Nevertheless, when light; that is, grace, is infused in the eye, a person is still able to shut out the light so as not to see, or avert his eyes so that he no longer sees what he previously saw. For Erasmus, averting the eyes is a claim to "some merit."

---

419. *PY*, 468; *HS*, 413.

420. *PY*, 468. Luther vehemently rejects this conclusion. Though he agrees that the power of the Word of God is such that "the whole world of men would be converted by a single word of God once heard," it does not occur because of "the malice of Satan, who sits enthroned in our weakness, resisting the Word of God." *On the Bondage of the Will*, 167. Erasmus had argued that Scripture was obscure for the language of Scripture is adapted to the weakness of human understanding. It is the ambiguity of language that causes people not to understand the Word of God so that they are not converted. *De libero arbitrio*, 41.

421. *PY*, 469; *HS*, 414.

422. *PY*, 466; *HS*, 412.

423. *De libero arbitrio*, 90–91

Hubmaier's concern in using this illustration is to argue that by inner illumination, which comes through the Word of God, effected by the Holy Spirit, a human being can now see, will, and work in accordance with the will of God. This is not to claim some merit for believers as does Erasmus. The only merits Hubmaier ever speaks of are the merits of Christ by which salvation has been gained for sinners.

Luther does not refer to Erasmus's illustration of the eye, though he does provide a short explanation on grace and cooperation. Speaking of those whom God acts in by his Spirit, Luther maintains that God "actuates and moves them in a similar way" to those outside his kingdom. They follow and cooperate, "or rather, as Paul says, they are led." A person recreated by the Spirit of God "does nothing and attempts nothing toward remaining in this kingdom, but the Spirit alone does both of these things in us, recreating us without us and preserving us without our help in our recreated state."[424] Hubmaier and Denck (even more explicitly) argue that preservation in the kingdom of God depends on the cooperation of the believer through the action of free will to fulfill the commands of God.[425]

The second major theme relates to sin and evil. Does God work evil in people as well as good? If all things happen necessarily according to the will of God, then both good and evil are included in "all things." Therefore, God is responsible for evil. Hubmaier accepts that God is the cause of evil only in that he causes evil as punishment. Even this suggestion would be offensive to Erasmus's pious ears. Erasmus berates the defenders of necessity who argue that because God is God, all his works are supremely excellent. Therefore, what appears evil to us is, in the order of God, seen as a whole, as good.[426] Hubmaier's argument is closely related to Denck at this point, as Bergsten has shown.[427] Hubmaier maintains that all good is from God and is done in the power of the Word of God. Evil on the other hand, can be understood as coming from God only if it is recognized as

---

424. *On the Bondage of the Will*, 289.

425. *PY*, 471; *HS*, 415 cf. Denck, *Concerning the Law of God*, 139.

PY, 471; *HS*, 415. Erasmus states that it is better to say with Paul, "O the depth of the riches and wisdom and knowledge of God!" than "with wicked boldness to judge the divine counsels, which are beyond the investigation of man." *De libero arbitrio*, 93.

426. *De libero arbitrio*, 92. On the issue of God working evil in people he writes: "Moreover, those who deny free choice entirely, but say that all things happen by absolute necessity, aver that God works in all men not only good but evil works. Whence it would seem to follow that just as man can by no reason be said to be the author of good works, so he can in no way be said to be the author of evil works." This view "seems plainly to ascribe cruelty and injustice to God, a sentiment offensive to pious ears."

427. Bergsten, *Balthasar Hubmaier: Anabaptist Theologian*, 355.

punishment. The ability to resist the will of God occurs only where God offers the power to do so to people. Once people use this new free will it takes place "either for good or for punishment, which is also good to the one who recognizes its goodness."[428]

The third theme relates to the secret and the revealed will of God. It is not dealt with extensively at this point, yet it is crucial to Hubmaier's interpretation of Scripture. The secret will of God concerns all matters related to "God's omnipotence, omniscience, and eternal foreknowledge, predestination, providence, or reprobation." It is not permitted for people to search and inquire into these things, for to do so is to act like Adam and Eve, who sought to know more than they needed to become "like gods."[429] Instead, Christians are to listen to the "incarnated God," to pursue those things of which they are certain, principally those things to do with faith and love. "The true and simple will of God is that we hold his beloved Son Christ Jesus before our eyes and follow his life and teaching wherein lie all the law and the prophets."[430] This revealed will of God has two aspects: his will turned toward us, a will of love, and his will turned from us, a will of punishment.[431] Hubmaier later develops these views in part three. This distinction becomes crucial to Hubmaier's method for establishing a "whole judgment" when comparing contradictory texts.

He concludes part two with the assertion that theological disputes should be confined to the revealed will of God, which is made known in Scripture, and arguments about the omnipotence of God should be eschewed.[432]

In part three, Hubmaier deals with the counter arguments of those who support the view that everything, both good and evil, happens by

---

428. *PY*, 467; *HS*, 412–13. "Whoever recognizes that for him sin is a punishment, to him is sin not sin, but he will henceforth protect himself from the punishment, so that the punishment does not again become sin for him and condemning." Cf. Denck: "Whoever truly recognizes sin as a punishment, to him it is no longer sin and also harms him no more but is for him a wonderful means to perceive and love the ultimate good." Denck, *Whether God is the Cause*, 83.

429. *PY*, 467; *HS*, 413.

430. *PY*, 468; *HS*, 413. Later he uses a similar phrase, "we should always have before our eyes what God has commanded us," which he indicates is limited to the Scriptures. Election belongs to the secret will of God, therefore to "want to know outside of Scripture which people God wants to save or condemn is the worst serpent himself who counsels us so that we become gods, that is, naked and bare." *PY*, 470; *HS*, 414.

431. *PY*, 469; *HS*, 414. As Pipkin and Yoder note, this concern with the will of God is typical of late medieval nominalism.

432. *PY*, 468; *HS*, 413.

necessity. He notes that his opponents are his "dear friends" who come to him daily to dispute with him. He likens them to the "friends" of Job, calling them at various places by the names Eliphaz, Bildad, and Zophar. He presents sixteen "counter arguments" which have been used by them against free will. Each argument begins with a text of Scripture that seems to oppose free will. Hubmaier then categorizes the text as referring either to the hidden will of God, or to the revealed will of God as it is turned away from people; that is, as punishment. To rely only on such texts to establish a doctrinal position is to present only a half-truth. To make a whole judgment he brings other texts that he designates as the revealed will of God turned toward us; that is, to the love of God revealed in the cross of Christ. The hidden will of God denies any free will in humanity, for God is omnipotent and can will whatever he desires. The revealed will declares that God wants all people to be saved, while the revealed will turned away from us declares that those whose hearts are hardened and are consequently damned, are condemned by their own choice to follow evil and reject the good.

In the first set of disputed texts, Rom 9:18, the hidden will of God, is compared with John 3:16; 1 John 2:2; 1 Tim 2:6; John 1:9; and Mark 16:15 linked with John 1:12, the revealed and preached will of God. Hubmaier succinctly describes his hermeneutical method as follows: "Where one now confuses and mixes the two wills with one another there soon follows out of that a notable misunderstanding, error, and confusion of Scriptures. Therefore one should wisely divide the judgments in the Scriptures and ruminate truly on them in order to know which Scripture points to the secret will of God or to the preached."[433]

Hubmaier notes that the revealed will of God is described by the Scholastics as an "ordered" will, "since it occurs according to the preached word of the Holy Scriptures in which he revealed to us his will." He provides a number of examples that demonstrate the distinction between the hidden will and the revealed will of God. According to his secret will, God could damn Peter and save Judas without doing either injustice.

---

433. *PY,* 473; *HS,* 417. Erasmus makes a brief comment on the Scholastic distinction between the eternal will described as the necessity of consequence, and the revealed will as necessity of the consequent. He uses the example of Judas to explain that "it must necessarily follow that Judas should betray the Lord if God willed this to happen with his eternal will," but it does not follow "that Judas therefore betrayed necessarily, since this wicked business originated in a perverse will." *De libero arbitrio,* 68. Luther totally rejects this distinction between necessity of consequence and the consequent, describing the later as a "mere phantom" with which the Scholastics tried to console themselves. *On the Bondage of the Will,* 248.

But according to his revealed will God cannot send Jacob away without blessing him nor send the Cannanite woman away unheard nor withhold mercy from the weeping David (Gen 32:29; Matt 15:28; Ps 51). Hubmaier comments that the "divine prophecies" are so "powerful and forceful" in those who believe that "God is captured, bound, and overcome with his own Word by the believers."[434]

The second argument deals with the texts 1 Tim 2:4 and Rom 9:19. Hubmaier's friends combine these to argue that, since God wants all to be saved, it must happen. Again, the distinction between the hidden and the revealed wills is brought into play; 1 Tim 2:4 refers to the revealed will, while Rom 9:19 refers to the hidden will that it is unnecessary for people to explore. At this point, Hubmaier introduces his refinement of the revealed will, dividing it into the will of God turned toward us, by which God offers salvation to all, and the withdrawing will of God, by which he means that to those who "do not accept, hear, or follow after him, the same he turns himself away from and withdraws from and lets them remain as they themselves want to be."[435]

This distinction of the facing and withdrawing will of God is then applied to the example of the hardening of Pharaoh's heart, as discussed in Rom 9:17. God could have strangled Pharaoh from the moment he ordered the death of the male children of the Hebrews. Instead, God "keeps him in the mildness of his disposition as a tool of wrath," in order to show in Pharaoh his power as a warning to all other people.[436] Follow-

---

434. *PY,* 474; *HS,* 418. Luther maintains a similar position on the hidden and preached will of God. While discussing Erasmus's use of Ezek 18, he remarks: "Diatribe, however, deceives herself in her ignorance by not making any distinction between God preached and God hidden; that is between the word of God and God himself. God does many things that he does not disclose to us in his word; he also wills many things which he does not disclose himself as willing in his word. Thus he does not will the death of a sinner, according to his word; but he wills it according to that inscrutable will of his. It is our business, however, to pay attention to the word and leave the inscrutable will alone, for we must be guided by the word and not the inscrutable will." *On the Bondage of the Will,* 201.

435. *PY,* 475; *HS,* 418. Luther uses 1 Tim 2:4 and Rom 9:20, as does Hubmaier, to describe the revealed will of God and the correct response to the hidden will. *On the Bondage of the Will,* 202.

436. *PY,* 477; *HS,* 420. Erasmus explains these texts in a similar vein: "He (God) has mercy, therefore, on those who recognize the goodness of God and repent, but those are hardened who, by neglecting the goodness of God, persist in evil courses." He cites Origen and Jerome as authorities, quoting Jerome "God hardens when he does not at once punish the sinner, and has mercy as soon as he invites repentance by means of afflictions." *De libero arbitrio,* 65. Luther attacks Erasmus's exposition of

ing Erasmus, who follows Origen, Hubmaier notes that the text of Exod 9:16 reads, "for that reason I have awakened you," not "created you."[437] Luther strongly rejects this reading of the text, arguing that Pharaoh, like all people after the fall, was corrupted and born of ungodly seed. Therefore, God did create *(gemacht)* Pharaoh so that he might demonstrate his power in him.[438] Hubmaier argues that God awakened *(erweckt)* Pharaoh by using the plagues as an expression of his mercy, thus giving Pharaoh the opportunity to repent. By his revealed will God does not want to harden anyone, except those who resist their own conscience, as occurred in the case of Pharaoh.[439]

Then follows a discussion on the text "Jacob I loved, Esau I hated" (Mal 1:2f; Rom 9:13). Hubmaier provides a brief description of the themes Paul deals with in Rom 9–11, as the setting for the exposition of this text. Hubmaier proposes that in the references to Pharaoh and the potter and the clay, Paul is concerned with the theme of the omnipotence of God, while the reference to Jacob and Esau deals with divine foreknowledge. God's mercy toward the heathen is dealt with in chapter 11. Hubmaier considers only this last matter appropriate for investigation, as it is to do with the revealed will of God. The other three are all related to the hidden will of God.

---

these texts, rejecting that there is a trope here, rather that the literal meaning of the text "I will harden Pharaoh's heart" stands, and cannot be justifiably expressed as I will "give an occasion of hardening." Conscience will be left troubled by this method of interpretation, as Scripture would become unclear, obscure, and ambiguous if tropes and figures become the basis for interpreting Scripture. This would make Scripture fit with Anaxagoras's philosophy. *On the Bondage of the Will*, 223–24. Hubmaier makes a similar comment about Zwingli's use of tropes and figures as an interpretative method in relation to identifying the baptism of John with the baptism of Jesus. "One should not play tricks like that with the treasure of the divine Word, otherwise in the end, holy theology would become Anaxagorean philosophy." *PY*, 112; *HS*, 131.

437. *PY*, 477; *HS*, 420.

438. On the Bondage of the Will 231. Luther achieves this not from a literal rendering of the text, which he translates: "*Und zwar darum habe ich dich erwecket, dass main Kraft an dir erscheine, and mein Name verkundiget werde in allen Landen,*" but by arguing that God declared all things he made "very good" only before the fall; thereafter, all things were corrupted. The creative power of God continues to create, but now all people he creates are made from a corrupt seed, and cannot help but be corrupt. Using Erasmus's technique he provides a simile to describe his point; God continues to create human beings but after the fall, out of corrupt seed, so that as a wood-carver creates a rotten statue from rotten wood, so God creates corrupt people from corrupt seed.

439. *PY*, 478; *HS*, 420–21.

Nevertheless, Hubmaier argues, as does Erasmus, that Paul uses Rom 9:13 to suppress the arrogance of the Jews who believed they received the favor and grace of God from their blood relationship to Abraham.[440] He goes on to stress that those who argue for all things to happen by necessity, do so only to load their guilt on God. Instead of this, they should obey the commandments of God, as is plainly stated in Scripture, "If you would enter life, keep the commandments."[441] It was possible, Hubmaier claims, for Pharaoh, Judas, and Pilate to keep God's commands to them to do what appears evil without sinning. Abraham had received the command to kill Isaac, and could have done so, remaining innocent, if all he sought was to fulfill the command of God without any consideration for his own advantage. Pharaoh, Judas, and Pilate are condemned because they sought their own advantage and failed to submit their wills fully to God.

Hubmaier also gives brief consideration to the potter and the clay illustration in Rom 9:21. Unlike Erasmus, Hubmaier claims that we have been made vessels of honor through the Word of God that has been poured into us. It is therefore now our responsibility through the asserting of our will in cooperation with the grace of God to keep the vessel clean.[442] Erasmus deals with this text from the context of Jer 18, where the illustration of the potter and the clay is followed by an exhortation to penitence. It is the role of human beings to cooperate with God's grace by exercising free choice so that they merit eternal salvation.[443] Luther attempts to avoid some of Erasmus's argument by asserting that Paul does not take up this figure from the prophets, but from general usage. His usage of the figure is therefore not restricted to temporal afflictions as Erasmus maintains, but is specifically applied to the question of eternal salvation.[444] He also

---

440. *PY*, 479; *HS*, 412 cf. *De libero arbitrio*, 70. With regard to foreknowledge, Erasmus holds the position that God hates the unborn because he foreknows they will commit deeds worthy of hatred. This reflects his understanding of the necessity of the contingent. Erasmus also rejects the view that this text refers to anything other than temporal misfortune. Luther maintains that Paul cites the text to prove that it was not through any merit on the part of the two men that they attained what was prophesied about them. *On the Bondage of the Will*, 250. He also maintains that the phrase "Two people, born of you," indicates the text is relevant to the general question of salvation, and not simply to the temporal outcome of the older serving the younger. Luther achieves this by noting that the younger, Jacob, represents the future people of God; that is, all people God justifies through faith in Christ. *On the Bondage of the Will*, 251.

441. *PY*, 480, *HS*, 421.

442. *PY*, 481–82; *HS*, 424.

443. *De libero arbitrio*, 71–72.

444. *On the Bondage of the Will*, 255.

challenges the interpretation that Erasmus puts forward for 2 Tim 2:20, "if anyone purifies himself from these." Luther suggests it means that those who are vessels for honor keep themselves separate from the vessels of dishonor, not that they can purify themselves of their own filth, as the simile offered by Erasmus infers.[445] Luther also rejects the assertion that the fault must be the potter's and not the vessel's. The inference is that God acts unjustly if he willingly creates some vessels for honor and some for dishonor; that is, salvation and damnation. That, Luther says, is to do with the "majesty of God" and is not to be questioned by human reason.[446]

There follows in Hubmaier's work a series of eleven shorter arguments, dealing with texts that are not major texts in Erasmus, some not being considered by Erasmus at all. Hubmaier continues to resolve these arguments by applying his twofold division of Scripture. Those texts that argue for the abolition of free will are designated as either related to the secret will of God, or the will of God turned away from people. There continue to be echoes of Erasmus's arguments in these passages. At one point Hubmaier accuses his opponents of introducing strange glosses and produces as an example a gloss Erasmus attributed to Luther, "Stretch out your hand; that is, God stretches out the hand."[447] However, Hubmaier continues to stress the central role of the sent Word of God as described above, as for instance in John 15:5. In this text, "without me you can do nothing," he does not follow Erasmus's arguments relating to the use of such a phrase in common speech, or to taking the literal meaning of "do nothing" to include doing evil. If that were the case it would mean it is

---

445. Ibid., 256.

446. Ibid., 257–58.

447. *PY*, 483; *HS*, 425. Cf. *De libero arbitrio* 73. Erasmus claims those who suppress free choice gloss Eccl 15:14, "Stretch out your hand to whatever you will," to mean, "Grace will stretch out your hand to what it wills." He stings Luther into a spirited response with his retort that such a gloss of Scripture is a "forced and twisted interpretation." Erasmus argues that if those who oppose free choice insist on a literal interpretation of the passages dealing with the potter and the clay, or the craftsman and the tool, but deny the fathers' figurative interpretations, because they are only men, then is he not free to deny Luther's figurative gloss, since Luther too is only a man. Luther responds with his ruling about the inadmissibility of tropes and inferences unless forced by the context or absurdity of the literal sense as conflicting with the articles of faith. He then hotly denies ever having glossed Eccl 15:14 as Erasmus claims, stating that it can be interpreted according to the grammatical sense. He maintains that the text shows what is required of people, not what they are able to do. *On the Bondage of the Will*, 221–22.

impossible to sin without Christ participating in the sin.[448] Instead, Hubmaier interprets the verse from the wider context of the passage, "But if we remain in the vine, that is, in the knowledge of his divine Word, the same will teach us what we will, should do, and are able to do."[449] The verse is to be understood as relating to doing good and not about evil.

One text which Erasmus and Luther do not debate is Isa 45:7: "God makes the light and creates darkness. He makes peace and creates evil. I am the Lord who makes all things."[450] Hubmaier applies his distinction between evil as sin and evil as punishment. The evil Isaiah speaks of is the latter: "That evil God wills and does out of his justice. For where the justice of God does not act, there his goodness would be a cause of sins." To strengthen his case he notes that Christ speaks of evil in this way in Matt 6:34, "sufficient to the day is its evil." Yet his presupposition for denying that God is the creator of evil comes from a statement by Augustine, "Of what God is not the planter he is neither the maker nor effector." He maintains that it cannot be proved "from eternity" that God planted sin.[451]

In the debate over the text "God works all things in all things" (1 Cor 12:6), Hubmaier again differs from Erasmus in the way he handles the resolution of the text. Erasmus focuses on the problem of merit, rewards, and punishment, maintaining that if people do nothing it makes all the texts that speak of reward and punishment absurd. His resolution is to join together "the striving of our will with the assistance of divine grace."[452] Luther deals with the text from his understanding of the omnipotence of God. God continues to move men by his omnipotence, but they now being evil can only do evil, unless their evil nature first be cured. Therefore, the work God does through men can be said to be evil only in that God is the primary cause. However, God in himself is not evil, and is not responsible for the evil done. To further clarify his meaning, Luther uses his figure of

---

448. *De libero arbitrio*, 78.

449. *PY*, 486–87; *HS*, 427

450. *PY*, 488; *HS*, 428f.

451. *PY*, 488; *HS*, 429. This reflects his earlier position in his debate with Zwingli about baptism. There Hubmaier maintained on the strength of Matt 15:13 and Isa 29:10–12 that "every institution which God the heavenly Father has not implanted makes blind and should be uprooted." *PY*, 136; *HS*, 151–52. Hubmaier appears to have combined the idea of those things not planted by God will be uprooted, with Isaiah's warning, that God will blind those who present their own prophecies and visions as from God. There is therefore a polemical edge to Hubmaier's use of these references, for he implies that his opponent is presenting his opinion as the Word of God.

452. *De libero arbitrio*, 73–74.

Making a Patchwork of Scripture

the human will as a horse that God rides. If a horseman rides a lame horse then the way he rides must correspond to the nature of the animal. Only if the animal is cured will horse and rider compare well with others who ride sound horses. He also introduces the image of the carpenter cutting badly with a chipped and jagged axe to explain the same point.[453]

Hubmaier himself uses the image of a carpenter using a notched instrument, also arguing that the fault of the work lies in the instrument and not the carpenter.[454] His second method of dealing with this text is to note a distinction between Scripture speaking as God, and Scripture speaking at times as if everything is ascribed to human beings and God did nothing at all. When Scripture speaks as God, "the completion of all things" is attributed entirely to God. However, where Scripture speaks from the human perspective, everything is ascribed to the will of people and nothing to God. Even though Scripture ascribes everything to the work of human beings, they must always recognize that the work is all of God and that they are at best "useless servants."[455] He then states: "Whoever cannot accommodate himself to the two divisions of Scripture will often stumble. . . . For he will judge many half-truths to be full truths, which is the biggest error in dealing with Scripture."[456] To conclude his case he then lists fourteen counter Scriptures that he insists must be placed beside those texts that oppose free will so that a whole judgment may be made. Many have been previously used during the course of the preceding argument. Now they are simply quoted, assuming the reader can now correctly distinguish between those texts that deal with the hidden and revealed wills of God, and of the facing will of love and mercy, compared to the withdrawing will of punishment and hardening.[457]

---

453. *On the Bondage of the Will*, 232–33.

454 Here Hubmaier alludes to the figure of the defective instrument that he had specifically applied in *Freedom of the Will I*, PY, 441; HS, 391–92. Where Hubmaier applies this metaphor to the soul and flesh in human beings, Luther considers the imperfection to leave no part of man untouched.

455. PY, 489; HS, 429.

456. PY, 489; HS, 429.

457. PY, 491; HS, 431. Luther responds caustically to these distinctions. For him the acceptance of divine omnipotence and foreknowledge precludes any free will. Reason is offended and despairs at the idea that God condemns one to damnation solely on the basis of God's foreknowledge and omnipotence, with no injustice or lack of mercy on God's part. However, this is no more unreasonable than the opposite; that God elects some to salvation without regard to their works. Reason cannot grasp the things of faith. Luther insists that the despair that such an idea engenders shows human beings the total helplessness of their situation that is overcome only by the grace

Balthasar Hubmaier and the Clarity of Scripture

It can be seen then that Hubmaier closely follows Erasmus in the selection of texts used in the debate concerning free will, and that at times he cites Erasmus on some points almost verbatim. He also uses similes in the way Erasmus does, though nowhere near as many as Erasmus, while some of his similes he shares with Luther. He also shares with Luther a greater emphasis on the power of the Word of God to effect the transformation in all people by the outward preaching of the Word and the inner illumination of the Spirit. Erasmus, however, emphasizes more the role of reason that, unaided by Scripture and the Spirit, may do what is in itself to prepare for grace. Denck holds the position that the Spirit, unaided by the Scripture or any other material means, so enlightens the heart of the elect that they now know God, and no longer need Scripture, except as a witness against them in the eventuality that they sin in the future. For Hubmaier, Scripture is still necessary, as it is in Scripture that the commands of God are made plain to the world in the life and teaching of Jesus Christ. He has, however, now declared that the Word of Christ is equally in the Old Testament as in the New, therefore distancing himself from the Swiss Brethren who hold to the superiority of the New Testament over the Old.

Hubmaier is closer to Luther than to Erasmus or Denck in this matter of the power of the Word of God, preached and applied to the heart by the Spirit. However, Luther only holds this power to be theoretical, since the world and all in it, except the elect, are enslaved to Satan, who refuses to allow his slaves to hear the Word of God. Only the elect, whom God snatches from Satan, hear the Word of God as law, which brings them to despair and total reliance on the mercy and grace of God for their salvation. This, Luther maintains, is the only consolation that is possible for anyone. If salvation in any way depended on free choice and the works of man, it would not be certain and there would be no consolation.

Denck specifically rejects any proposal that the doctrine of election provides consolation for the elect.[458] Although Hubmaier does not spe-

---

of God. Because of the offence reason feels here, "there has been such sweating and toiling to excuse the goodness of God and accuse the will of man; and it is here the distinctions have been invented between the ordained and the absolute will of God, and between the necessity of consequence and the consequent, and so forth." *On the Bondage of the Will*, 244.

458. Denck, *Whether God is the Cause*, 107. "You say: We do not need foreknowledge, as you say, except for a consolation to all the elect that they may know that all their help and salvation lie in the hand of God and that no power is so mighty that it will or could wrest (it) from him. Response: This consolation you can give no one and also none can take from you, for, he who has committed himself to the chastisement of the Father [and who] has tasted partially the sweetness of the bitter cross, to him the

cifically attack the idea of foreknowledge and election providing consolation, he does use the same texts as Denck from Heb 6:4–6 and 10:26–31 together with 2 Pet 2:4 (a reference to the angels that are not spared God's judgment). Though he does not state his conclusion as forcefully as Denck, he nevertheless makes it clear that it is through continual obedience to the commands of Christ that believers demonstrate they remain in a state of forgiveness.[459] The major difference between Denck and Hubmaier is their understanding of the role of Scripture. Hubmaier sees God using the preached Word inseparably linked to the Holy Spirit to bring about regeneration and the renewal of the will to be obedient to His commandments. Denck, on the other hand, insists that those who have the truth receive it from God through the Holy Spirit without any material means, and that those who have the truth also have no further need of the written law and commandments, for they are now written on the heart of the believer. In this matter, Hubmaier is closer to Luther than to Denck or Erasmus.

Hubmaier is also closer to Luther in his understanding of Scripture being essentially clear and simple to understand. Luther speaks of an internal clarity that gives assurance to the individual believer and the ability to judge other peoples' dogmas according to the truth of the spirit within, though this judgment remains a personal thing. There is also an external clarity of the Scriptures that is tied to the preaching office and ministry of the Word, which allows the preacher of the Word to exhort and encourage Christians through the clear and certain exposition of the Word, and equally to judge the dogmas of all others according to the simple understanding of Scripture.[460] Luther does admit that there are some obscure texts in Scripture, but these are obscure only because of a lack of understanding of vocabulary or grammar. Even these obscure texts are not a mystery any more for all the mysteries of God that are necessary for the certainty of salvation have been revealed in Christ. Those obscure passages can therefore be brought into the light of Christ and their meaning sufficiently understood.[461]

Father reveals himself through the Spirit in defiance before all his enemies, but, not the less, [that he] fear God and despise no one. For whom God has received in faith he can and will reject again if he does not remain in faith, since he did not spare the angels because they were so secure that they thereby developed satisfaction in themselves and forget God."

459. *PY*, 471; *HS*, 415 cf. Denck, *Concerning the Law of God*, 139; Denck, *Whether God is the Cause*, 107, an allusion to the angels not being exempt from God's judgment.

460. *On the Bondage of the Will*, 159.

461. Ibid., 110–12.

Balthasar Hubmaier and the Clarity of Scripture

Hubmaier had previously alluded to the same quotation from Augustine that Luther used to refer to the need to speak simply and not with persuasive rhetorical images.[462] From his usage of Scripture and his comments about its clarity, Hubmaier continues to view Scripture as clear to understand. However, he has now introduced a number of distinctions that must be applied if the correct interpretation of Scripture is to be obtained. These distinctions Luther considers invalid, though he introduces his own: law and gospel or promise; the two kingdoms; and the assertion that all Scripture speaks antithetically, particularly where it speaks of Christ.[463]

Use of Scripture

Hubmaier's changed appreciation of the Old Testament is also clearly demonstrated in his references to Scripture. Of the 380 references, quotations and allusions identified in this work, one hundred fifteen refer to the Old Testament. The most frequently cited books are Genesis (thirty-three), Psalms (eighteen), Isaiah (eighteen), and Deuteronomy (ten). All the other Old Testament books have less than ten texts cited per book. The majority of the Genesis references are related to the three stages of man; prefall, postfall, and postrestoration. Hubmaier also includes his sequence of references to the promise of God to bless all people through the "seed," as was previously mentioned. In this way, he links up the prophecies of the Old Testament with their fulfillment in Christ, yet not as he had done previously with the incarnate Christ. He underlines the shift in his christological understanding by his references to the Psalms, where he understands any reference to the Word of God as a reference to the sent Word; that is, the preincarnate Christ. He also uses Luther's reference to Ps 107:20, as he had done in his first work on free will, to refer to the healing power of the Word of God. In this appreciation of the healing power of the Word of God present in the Psalms, Hubmaier is returning to an earlier position he maintained that may have been founded on Luther's exposition of the Psalms.[464] Hubmaier also shares with Luther references

---

462. Ibid., 170. Cf. *PY,* 277; *HS,* 259.

463. Ibid., 323, 327.

464. *PY,* 115; *HS,* 134. This reference, which is in *On the Christian Baptism,* demonstrates how the apostles preached Christ by referring to the promise of the sent Word in such Old Testament texts as Ps 107:20, and the fulfillment of the promise at the incarnation. Luther also used this Psalm but without the concept of progressive

Making a Patchwork of Scripture

to Ps 51:5 concerning David's declaration that he was born in sin. Both use this verse to discuss the serious consequences of the fall, a reference and thought lacking in Erasmus's discussion of free will.

With regard to the New Testament, Hubmaier makes 262 references, quotations and allusions. There has been a discernible shift in his choice of books as sources for his texts. Romans is the most frequently cited New Testament book (fifty-two), closely followed by John (fifty). Then follows Matthew (thirty-seven), Luke (twenty-two), and 1 Corinthians (eighteen). All other New Testament books are cited less than ten times. In the Romans citations, ten are from chapter 8 and fourteen from chapter 9, where the examples of Pharaoh, the potter and the clay, and Jacob and Esau are dealt with. These he shares in common with Luther and Erasmus, indicating that to some degree the ground for the debate was predetermined and the references to Scripture simply reflect that. References to Romans and John's gospel also dominate the scriptural citations of both Erasmus and Luther. Romans 7:18 is cited five times. For Hubmaier, as for Erasmus, this text of Paul's is used to demonstrate that Paul considered that there exists in human beings a desire to will the good. The difference between Hubmaier and Erasmus relates to how grace and enlightenment are given and received in people. For Hubmaier, it is the Word of God that is the primary means by which God through his Spirit enlightens and renews free will in people. For Erasmus, it is reason that is enlightened so that people can know and will the good. For him, enlightenment happens without a special role for Scripture.

John's gospel has replaced Matthew as the most frequently cited gospel. Hubmaier employs the first and third chapters of John as the sources from which to prove his understanding of regeneration, the new birth. Of the fifty-eight references to John, twenty-eight come from these chapters, and half of these relate to John 1:11–12, his central text to explain how through the sent Word God grants to all people the power of free will. He adds to this five references to 1 Tim 2:4 to prove that the revealed will of God is that all people should be saved. Matthew's gospel proves to be a

---

revelation from promise to fulfillment. For Luther the gospel is as effective in the Old Testament as in the New to "heal," for there is only one covenant. *On the Bondage of the Will*, 201. Progressive revelation makes it possible to distinguish between the promise of the gospel in the Old Testament and its fulfillment in the New. The Word does not "heal" in the Old Testament. Marpeck most forcefully presents the idea of progressive revelation of the gospel and relates it specifically to the salvation of the patriarchs. William Klassen, *Covenant and Community*, 136.

Balthasar Hubmaier and the Clarity of Scripture

source for historical examples and scriptural similes by which Hubmaier bolsters his arguments.

Comments have been made in the preceding text on Hubmaier's use of 2 Cor 9:6. For Hubmaier, this text clearly demonstrates free choice over necessity, since the cheerful giver whom God loves must have determined beforehand to give generously. Luther would not object to this understanding of free choice as it relates to the lower matters of everyday living and not to eternal salvation. It has also been noted how Hubmaier's use of Heb 6:4–6 and 10:26–31 parallels that of Denck.

This work is very heavily supplied with Scripture texts in the margins, some of which, according to Pipkin and Yoder, seem "marginally related at best."[465] While it is true that Hubmaier cites chapters of Scripture that do not readily appear related to his arguments, there are only three instances where it remains uncertain to which part of the chapter he is referring. As with all Hubmaier's previous citations of Scripture, there is a clear relationship between the words of the text and the order of the Scripture references as they appear in the margin. Hubmaier is not only trying to demonstrate by this extensive array of scriptural texts that his sole authority in matters of doctrine and Christian practice is Scripture, as Pipkin and Yoder suggest, he is also supporting his case with specific and relevant scriptural references.[466]

Hubmaier's use of the Apocrypha remains limited to Ecclesiasticus. Like Erasmus, Hubmaier uses this text as the starting point for the debate in this work. Otherwise Hubmaier provides only one other reference to the Apocrypha which also comes from Ecclesiasticus.

Hubmaier shares more Old Testament texts with Erasmus (nineteen) than with Luther (seventeen) or Denck (six). When New Testament texts are considered the position changes, and Hubmaier shares thirty-eight texts with Luther, twenty-six with Erasmus, and twenty-four with Denck. That Hubmaier has more texts in common with Luther than Erasmus in the New Testament reflects the closer affinity Hubmaier has with Luther on subjects such as the new birth and the power of the Word of God. Hubmaier's independence is seen in his exegesis of Gen 1–3, from which he establishes his anthropology. Hubmaier's main link with Denck is their use of Heb 6:4–6 and 10:26–31. Both use these texts to prove that salvation is dependent on continual obedience to the revealed will of God. The difference is that for Hubmaier the revealed will of God is confined to

---

465. *PY*, 450n5.
466. *PY*, 450n5.

Making a Patchwork of Scripture

Scripture, while for Denck it is written on the hearts of believers and is independent of Scripture.

Summary

The above analysis makes it clear that while Hubmaier followed Erasmus in the choice of his texts and in some of the similes he used in his arguments, there are significant hermeneutical differences that cannot be overlooked. Any suggestion therefore that Hubmaier simply followed Erasmus's hermeneutical method as well as his Scripture texts must be viewed with great caution. It has been shown that Hubmaier also has a number of hermeneutical features in common with Luther, particularly with reference to the role of the Word of God and the Spirit. However, as Steinmetz has indicated, it is the basic anthropological difference between Hubmaier and Luther that leads them to opposing positions in the debate of free will.[467] It also needs to be noted that Hubmaier and Luther differ fundamentally with reference to ecclesiology. For Luther, the true church is hidden. For Hubmaier, the church is both hidden as the universal church, and visible as it finds expression in the gathered community of believers. This community is defined by its practice of baptism, including the vow of faith; its celebration of the Lord's Supper with the pledge of love; and its practice of fraternal admonition and the ban. It is this visible church that must be kept pure, so that the Lord is not shamed before unbelievers by the conduct of its recognized members. Any antinomian tendency, a theology which Hubmaier faced in some members of the Nikolsburg church through their interpretation of Luther's doctrine of the bound will, must be challenged, for the believer is not only justified in Christ through faith, but must show that faith in acts of brotherly love. Only in this way does the believer fulfill the commandments of Christ.

In common with Denck, there is in Hubmaier the understanding that to be Christ's true disciple includes suffering with Christ, as the believer carries the cross of Christ. What he does not share with Denck, is the latter's insistence on the elect not only having God in them, but through "resignation" *(gelassenheit)*, the total surrender of the will, their being in God.[468]

---

467. Steinmetz, "Luther and Hubmaier," 59. Hubmaier's anthropology does not have a prominent place in this work. It is given a full explanation in his first work of free will. Nevertheless, his position underpins the whole of this second work and occasionally becomes specific.

468. Denck, *Whether God is the Cause*, 93.

From this discussion of Hubmaier's theology of free will and his hermeneutic in relation to that topic, it can be seen that he slavishly follows neither Erasmus nor the Swiss Brethren nor Denck. He agrees with them on the conclusion that human beings after receiving grace can will and do good in cooperation with God's continuing grace. In this conclusion, he opposes Luther and Zwingli. However, his presuppositions about the nature of Scripture and the role of the Spirit bringing enlightenment in association with the Scripture is much closer to Luther than to Erasmus or Denck. In addition, his new position concerning the "one marriage" in the Old and New Testaments, and his understanding of Christ acting to save in the Old Testament, leads him to move dramatically away from the Swiss Brethrens' presupposition that the New Testament is superior to the Old. It contains the words of Christ that surpass the words of Moses as the master of the house is greater than the servant.

Despite all the texts held in common with Erasmus and Luther, Hubmaier remains his own man, seeking to uphold a middle course between Luther and Erasmus. While adopting a position similar to Luther on the power of the Word of God and the work of the Spirit through the Word, he nevertheless holds to a limited free will that cooperates with the grace of God to fulfill the commands of Christ. His ecclesiology further makes his position distinct from those of Luther and Erasmus, neither of whom accepted the idea of a gathered confessing church that sought to fulfill the Word of Christ in their life of discipleship as evidence of the new birth that had occurred in them. Their good works of brotherly love, the outworking of their pledge to love one another at the Lord's Table, acted as confirmation of their faith, which they had declared in baptism. Without that correspondence between faith and works, Hubmaier implied that people could not be assured of their salvation.

ON THE SWORD

(June 24, 1527)[469]

Setting

Within the Anabaptist movement the relationship of the church to governing authorities provoked considerable debate and brought forth a number

---

469. *PY,* 29: 492–523; *HS,* 24: 432–57.

of writings that sought to define that relationship. One such writing was produced in Schleitheim on February 24, 1527, when representatives of the Swiss Brethren agreed on the seven theses of the Brotherly Union.[470] The same issue was also hotly debated in the Anabaptist church of Nikolsburg, and resulted in Hubmaier completing this work on June 24, 1527, some four months after the Schleitheim meeting.

The events leading up to Hubmaier addressing this topic are complicated by a related dispute between Hubmaier and Hut. Hut appears to have arrived in Nikolsburg from Passau sometime after April 21, 1527, and became embroiled in the debate then occurring over this issue.[471] However, there were more issues involved in this public argument than just the question of the use of the sword. Eventually a disputation between Hubmaier and Hut took place, which led to Hut being threatened with imprisonment.[472] Bergsten suggests that Hubmaier wrote *On the Sword* in response to the disputation with Hut over the latter's eschatology and his negative opinion about government.[473] He rejects Sachsse's opinion that Hubmaier was aware of the *Schleitheim Articles* and wrote in response to them.[474] However, this work does not reflect the full extent of the topics discussed at the disputation nor does Hubmaier mention Hut by name in this work, as he does in his final statement produced in Vienna for Fabri.

Werner O. Packull has presented a reconstruction of the topics of the disputation. He begins with the eleven statements Hut recalled at his trial in Augsburg.[475] He adds to these the four statements not mentioned

---

470. Yoder, "Schleitheim Brotherly Union," 27–54.
471. Herbert Klassen, "Life and Teaching of Hans Hut," 182.
472. Bergsten, *Balthasar Hubmaier: Anabaptist Theologian*, 361–62.
473. HS, 432–33.
474. HS, 432.
475. Packull, *Mysticism*, 102.
(1) that Christ was not God's Son.
(2) that Christ was merely a prophet.
(3) that Mary had more than one husband.
(4) that the angels had become men with Christ.
(5) that when a man is possessed by a good angel he can only do good, and when possessed by a bad angel only evil.
(6) that Hut and his followers put stock in visions and dreams.
(7) that Hut had set a definite date for the pending judgment.
(8) that with Scripture one received the truth and also falsehood.
(9) that Christians would judge the world.
(10) that no prince or power in this world has accepted or recognized the truth.
(11) that power should be taken from the government and given to the Christians.

by Hut but mentioned in *Die Nikolsburger Artikel*, that Fabri claimed to be Hubmaier's.[476] Packull adds further topics concerning the Lord's Supper, baptism, and eschatology, the evidence for these being adduced from statements on the disputation by Hubmaier, Hut, and Hans Nadler, a follower of Hut. Allowing for overlapping of topics from the various lists Packull indicates that a list of sixteen of the fifty-two theses Hubmaier produced for the disputation can be reconstructed.[477] He also notes that in *The Chronicle of the Hutterian Brethren*, the Nikolsburg Disputation was confused with a later debate concerning community of goods that took place between Jacob Widemann and Spittelmaier. This confusion left the impression that Hubmaier was mainly concerned with Hut's position on nonresistance.[478] He concludes that *On the Sword* represents a continuation of Hubmaier's "running battle with the Swiss Brethren rather than with Hut's followers."[479] This conclusion is supported by the preceding analysis of Hubmaier's writings on baptism, where he distances himself from the position of the Zurich Anabaptists on a number of points that Zwingli sought to attribute to him as well, particularly their view of the magistracy.

The work is dedicated to another representative of a leading Moravian noble family who was a known Lutheran sympathizer, "Lord Arkleb of Boskovic and Erna Hora at Vranoy, First Secretary of the treasury of the Margraviate of Moravia."[480] Hubmaier expresses his intention in the title

---

476. Packull, *Mysticism*, 99–100.

(1) The Gospel should not be preached in churches but only secretly and clandestinely in houses.

(2) Christ was conceived in original sin.

(3) The Virgin Mary is not the mother of God but only the mother of Christ.

(4) Christ was not God but a prophet to whom the speech of God or Word of God was commanded.

(5) Christ did not make satisfaction for the sins of the entire world.

(6) Among Christians there should be neither force nor authority.

(7) The day of judgment is to be expected within two years.

(8) The angels were conceived with Christ and accepted the flesh with Him.

477. Packull, *Mysticism*, 100. Packull does not date the disputation as definitely as Bergsten, who follows Seebass's date of May 12 and 13. Bergsten, *Balthasar Hubmaier: Anabaptist Theologian*, 363.

478. Packull, *Mysticism*, 104. Packull notes that Stayer "definitely destroyed" the myth that Hut was a representative of the "nonresistance" position. See Stayer, *Anabaptists and the Sword*, 162–65.

479. Packull, *Mysticism*, 104.

480. *PY*, 494; *HS*, 434. Bergsten notes the coincidence that Lord Arkleb died in Vienna on the same day as Hubmaier, March 10, 1528. *HS*, 433.

and dedicatory letter to this work that he will examine the Scriptures that "many brethren" cite to prove that a Christian is not to sit in authority nor to wield the sword. He also makes clear that the opinion he puts forward here has always been his opinion: he has written about it and taught it as well as having preached on it in Waldshut.[481] Pipkin and Yoder note that Hubmaier's position on civil authority is close to that of Luther and Zwingli, a point well demonstrated by comparing Zwingli's reply to the *Schleitheim Articles* and Hubmaier's responses to those texts of the *Schleitheim Articles* he cites in this work.[482]

Analysis

Following his now familiar method of presenting Scripture texts with a short analysis and comment, Hubmaier here selects fifteen passages of Scriptures that his "brethren" use to argue against government and a Christian's involvement in government. He begins with John 18:36, "My kingdom is not of this world." His "brethren" use this to argue that Christians should not carry the sword because the kingdom of Christians is not of this world, just as Christ's kingdom is not of this world. He counters this reasoning in two ways; firstly, the text says how things should be, not how they are; secondly, that Christ alone can say this, for he alone is without sin. As sin clings to Christians all their lives, so they remain of the kingdom of the world, something they themselves confess when they pray, "thy kingdom come."[483]

Though the *Schleitheim Articles* do not use this text, the idea of the total separation of the Christian from the world is presented as Thesis IV: "Now there is nothing else in the world and all creation than good and evil, believing and unbelieving, darkness and light, the world and those who are [come] out of the world, God's temple and idols, Christ and Belial, and none will have part with the other."[484] Here the Swiss Brethren reject any participation of the Christian in the world on the understanding

---

481. *PY*, 495; *HS*, 435. Hubmaier's earlier teaching on the magistracy finds its clearest expression in *On Heretics* and in his *An Earnest Christian Appeal*.

482. *PY*, 493.

483. *PY*, 496; *HS*, 436. Zwingli comments on the *Schleitheim Articles* view that since a judge is fleshly he cannot be of the kingdom of God and that all people, while remaining in the body, remain apart from the kingdom of God. Yet the judge who acts righteously, with equity and justice does so from God, for such attitudes do not come from the flesh. Zwingli, *Refutation of the Tricks*, 204–5.

484. Yoder , "Schleitheim" 38.

that the Christian is one with Christ; he is the head and Christians are his members. The members are to be of the same mind as Christ; if they were not they would be a kingdom divided against itself and would fall.[485]

Hubmaier develops his argument against this position in two ways. When discussing the seventh selected text, Matt 18:15ff, which his opponents use to prove that government among Christians makes the ban worthless, he argues that the divine command that established authority to protect the good and punish evil continues to be valid today. God established authority in response to sin entering the world when he gave Adam outward and temporal authority over Eve (Gen 3:16). That authority was passed on to "special and God-fearing people" and by the command of God became established in kingship through Samuel. Temporal authority was established by God because of sin, and as long as sin continues, temporal and outward authority shall also continue.[486] Government must, therefore, be accepted with thanks as a gift from God. The ban is also commanded by God, but it is for the admitting of the holy to communion and the exclusion of the unworthy. It functions within the church according to the mandate that Christ gave in the power of the keys.[487] The ban is to be used against secret sins, where the sword should not be used. Citing Christ's encounter with the adulterous woman (John 8:10ff), Hubmaier comments that Christ demonstrates that his office is different from that of the judge; he has come to forgive sins, not to pass judgment. That Christ does not condemn the woman results from the lack of judgment according to the law. If she had been condemned according to the law of Moses, Christ would not have interfered with the judgment. Since no one has judged her, Christ exercises his office and forgives her.[488] The *Schleitheim Articles* also use this Scripture to demonstrate the difference between mercy and judgment; Christians are to follow Christ's example of mercy

---

485. Yoder, "Schleitheim" Article VI, 41.

486. *PY*, 505; *HS*, 442–43.

487. *PY*, 504; *HS*, 442. Hubmaier presents a short summary of his teaching on the ban and the power of the keys that does not differ from his previous teaching on the subject as published in his *A Catechism* and *On the Ban*.

488. *PY*, 506; *HS*, 444. Zwingli discusses this passage focusing on the distinction that must be drawn between Christ in his divinity, omnipotence, and providence, and Christ during his mission. While on earth, Christ never took the role of a judge. However, now that he has ascended and sits at the right hand of the Father, he again acts as a judge. Therefore, it is possible to be a Christian judge. Zwingli, *Refutation of the Tricks*, 199–200.

rather than the law of the Father.[489] The Swiss Brethren drew a distinction between mercy that only applies to the church as the kingdom of Christ, and the law that applies to the world. The harsh judgment of the law therefore cannot apply to the church, only brotherly admonition and the ban acting as expressions of mercy. For Hubmaier, the distinction is between the office of Christ to show mercy and the office of authorities to defend the good and punish the evil. These are not mutually exclusive since sin continues in Christians just as in the world, and must also be punished.

The second response Hubmaier makes to the dualism of the Swiss Brethren occurs in his discussion of the fifteenth selection of Scripture. Here he gives a summary of his opponent's position, "Christ is our Head and we his members." Since Christ is the head of the body, and he did not strive but went patiently to death, so the members must do the same.[490] Firstly, he notes a distinction between the divine and the Christian. According to this Christians are by nature children of wrath, not of God. Therefore, Christ is not their head by nature. Christians become members of Christ in soul and spirit through faith in the forgiveness of sins and not in the flesh that remains guilty before God and opposed to his will. Secondly, though Christians are children of God through faith, they do not all have the same office; some are preachers, some protectors, some peasants, some do other things. All the good works they do flow from faith. Government, according to its office, undertakes the work of protecting orphans, widows, and the righteous. This is the command of God.[491] Hubmaier's argument rests on the distinction that exists between Christ and Christians by nature, and between individual Christians by virtue of the office they are commanded by God to fulfill.[492] The Swiss Brethren see no such distinctions, particularly between the head and the members who are one through faith.

The third and fourth passages that Hubmaier treats are used by his "brothers" to argue that Christians should not use fire, water, sword, nor gallows (Luke 9:54–56), neither should they be judges nor sit on councils nor carry the sword (Luke 12:13f). Hubmaier links together passages

489. Yoder, "Schleitheim" Article VI, 40.

490. *PY,* 518; *HS,* 453–54.

491. *PY,* 519; *HS,* 454.

492. Zwingli attacks the Swiss Brethren's use of the term "outside the perfection of Christ." He maintains that the term "perfection" applies only to Christ, and that as long as a Christian remains in the body he is outside the perfection of Christ. He concludes, "wherever the members of Christ do not arrive at the measure of the perfection of the head there is need for the sword." Zwingli, *Refutation of the Tricks, 197.*

five and six (Matt 5:40; 1 Cor 6:7f), as both relate to the topic of Christians appearing before a court. These concerns closely reflect those of the Swiss Brethren who compiled the *Schleitheim Articles*. They formulated their thesis on the sword by discussing the following series of questions: "whether a Christian may or should use the sword against the wicked for the protection and defense of the good, or for the sake of love?"; "whether a Christian shall pass sentence in disputes and strife about worldly matters, such as the unbelievers have with one another?"; and "whether the Christian should be a magistrate if he is chosen thereto?"[493]

Hubmaier responds by noting the distinction that exists between the office of Christ and that of temporal authority. It was not Christ's office to bring judgment in fire or water, but to bring salvation to those who believe. He rejects this attempt to have him make a temporal judgment (Luke 12:14), but his rejection of the role of judge did not mean a total rejection of all temporal judgment. This Hubmaier infers by paraphrasing the words of Christ: "It is as if he wanted to say, 'Surely you can find other judges. I am not here to interfere in the office and mandate of others. On the contrary, the office and orderly mandate has been given by God to the government to protect and guard the godly and punish and kill the evil ones.'"[494] He then discusses Luke 12:13f as a separate text, but uses the same distinction between the office of Christ and of government. His point in this second exposition of Luke 12:13f is that only those people are to be judges who are called and elected to be such. To support his case he cites the examples of Abraham, Moses, and Phineas, who were elected to the task of judge and used the sword to execute God's judgment.[495]

The thirteenth passage, Luke 22:25f, is taken by the "brethren" to mean that there should be no government among Christians on the understanding of Christ's words that they are not to rule like worldly kings. Here Hubmaier notes that Jesus spoke to the disciples as preachers of the Word of God. The role of the preacher of the Word of God prohibits him becoming enmeshed in the affairs of the world, as the pope and bishops

---

493. Yoder, *Legacy of Michael Sattler*, 39–40.

494. *PY*, 500; *HS*, 438. Zwingli makes a similar comment on this verse, saying that Christ "openly teaches that there was some judge to whom they could refer the case, but Christ was not he, so he made no decision." Zwingli, *Refutation of the Tricks*, 200.

495. *PY*, 501; *HS*, 440; Exod 2:12; Gen 14:14ff; Num 25:7f. These examples do not provide useful support for his argument. Moses took it on himself to intervene in the argument between the Egyptian and the Israelite, killing the Egyptian as a result. Similarly, Phineas killed the idolatrous Israelite at Baal Peor on his own initiative, not by the specific command of God or Moses.

have erroneously done. Christians should flee from the heavy responsibility of civil office, but where called on to fulfill it, they are not to dominate, but be servants. He arrives at these conclusions by considering the wider context of the passage, and making a whole judgment. He concludes that God has not forbidden government but shown the distinction between the office of preacher and civil authority.[496]

The fifth and sixth passages are cited by the "brethren" as proof that "a Christian may not be a judge." Hubmaier admits that among Christians it is a sin for them to seek the courts to settle disputes over temporal goods. However, from the wider context of 1 Cor 6; that is, verses 1–6, he maintains that a dispute before a Christian judge stops those who are quarrelling from adding sin on sin. He suggests that Paul seeks to shame the Corinthians for taking their disputes to unbelieving judges and urges them instead to appoint judges from among themselves to settle such matters. From this he infers that the sword is also permitted to the Christian: "If then, a Christian, by the power of the divine Word, may and should be a judge with the mouth, he may also be a protector with the hand of the one who wins justice and may punish the unjust. For of what use would the law, court, and judge be if one were not allowed to carry out and enforce the punishment on the evildoers?"[497] Citing 2 Chr 19:15–17, he comments, "This Scripture is given to us as well as to those of old because it concerns brotherly love."

---

496. Zwingli also interprets Luke 22:25f from its wider context and arrives at the same conclusion as Hubmaier. Zwingli understands Christ to be speaking to his disciples, who are preachers of the Word (citing John 20:21 as his supporting text). The office of the magistrate is therefore to be avoided by them as a snare. Yet the office of magistrate is not thereby forbidden to all Christians. Peter and Paul wrote to many Christians who held such high positions, and did not discourage them from their work. This proves for Zwingli that the office is not forbidden to Christians. Like Hubmaier, he goes on to maintain that people should not put themselves forward for such positions. Zwingli, *Refutation of the Tricks*, 202–3.

497. *PY*, 503; *HS*, 441. Zwingli also links together these sayings of Paul and Christ. While Paul admonishes Christians to bear injury rather than to litigate, it does not follow that a Christian may use the courts or be a judge. Similarly, while Christ warned his disciples against entering into lawsuits "because of the danger, since it often occurred in fact that he who hoped to return from the court a winner was thrown into prison till he could pay the whole debt," this warning does not mean Christians cannot use the courts. Zwingli, *Refutation of the Tricks*, 200–201. Both Hubmaier and Zwingli make use of a wider context of the verses to obtain their conclusions. Hubmaier is more literal in his exposition as he maintains that it is sin for Christians to go to court at all.

Balthasar Hubmaier and the Clarity of Scripture

The distinction between the office of Christ and government finds another expression when Hubmaier deals with passages nine and ten, (Eph 6:14f; 2 Cor 10:4f). The sword referred to in these passages is the spiritual sword, the Word of God that Christ used to combat Satan when tempted in the wilderness, the very sword Christ said he had come to bring.[498] In part, Hubmaier agrees with the claim that his opponents make that the weapons of the Christian are "not made from iron or long wood, but the gospel. . . . the faith . . . the Word of God."[499] However, he accuses them of error because they do not recognize that there are two swords spoken of in Scripture, the spiritual sword spoken of in these texts, and the physical sword Paul speaks of in Rom 13. The two swords belong to different aspects of the body. The physical sword relates to the flesh, while the spiritual sword relates to the soul. The physical sword may also be called a spiritual sword when it is used according to the will of God.[500] It is the attitude of the government that determines whether the physical sword is used according to the will of God. Any government that seeks its own power, pomp, and circumstance wields the physical sword contrary to the will of God. The will of God can be clearly determined from Scripture, and so government can be judged as to whether it wields the physical sword in accordance with the will of God.

The use of distinctions between different categories of texts as a method for maintaining the truth of both texts had previously been used by Hubmaier in his writings on free will. The method again becomes prominent in his resolution of the text Matt 5:21, "you shall not kill." He asks, "How can killing and not killing go together?" for the people of the Old Testament had commands both to kill and not to kill. His reply begins with a sequence of sixty-eight references to Scripture covering different

---

498. *PY,* 509; *HS,* 446. Matt 4:1–11; 10:34.

499. *PY,* 508; *HS,* 445–46. The *Schleitheim Articles* use a similar image: "The weapons of their battle and warfare are carnal and only against the flesh, but the weapons of Christians are spiritual, against the fortification of the devil. The worldly are armed with steel and iron, but Christians are armed with the armour of God, with truth, righteousness, peace, faith, salvation, and the Word of God." Yoder, *Legacy of Michael Sattler,* 40–41. Zwingli does not deal with this text exegetically but polemically, contrasting the weapons with which magistrates are armed and those he says the Anabaptists wield. "So earthly magistrates, they say, are armed with brass and iron; Catabaptist with hypocrisy and evil speaking, lies, injury, discord, faithlessness, disaster and the word of the devil—to give them altogether the gifts that are theirs in place of what they claim for themselves." Zwingli, *Refutation of the Tricks,* 205–6.

500. *PY,* 510; *HS,* 447. He cites Isa 1:17; Jer 21:12, 22:3 as the clear will of God for government actions. *PY,* 499, 512; *HS,* 438, 449.

topics, all apparently contradictory texts.[501] Almost quoting from *Freedom of the Will I*, he writes, "Therefore one should divide the hooves of the Scriptures, Lev 11:3, and chew them well before one swallows them, that is, believe or one will eat death therein and through half-truths and half-judgments deviate far, far from the whole truth and seriously go astray."[502]

To demonstrate his method, he chooses the words of institution for the Lord's Supper, reiterating his earlier view that the whole truth is obtained only when the following words, "do this in memory of me," are taken into consideration. He then applies the same method to the text from Matt 5:21, suggesting that the type of killing of which Christ speaks is killing that "happens out of anger, mockery, or despising." Just government does not kill in this way, but by the command of God. Those whom the government calls to assist carrying out the command of God are not murderers, but servants of God.[503] He concludes: "That those who do not want to kill the evildoer but let them live, are acting and sinning against the commandment, 'You should not kill.' For whoever does not protect the righteous kills him and is guilty of his death as much as the one who does not feed the hungry."[504]

Hubmaier also deals with this theme when discussing Matt 5:43f, a text that relates to loving one's enemies. By a syllogism he proves that Christian government has no enemies, for it hates and envies no one, and enemies are only those whom one hates and envies.[505] So when the government uses the sword to punish it does so out of brotherly love according to the command and mandate of God. That obeying the command of God and killing are not mutually exclusive, Hubmaier proves by alluding to God's command to Abraham to kill Isaac, a point he also made in *Free-*

---

501. *PY*, 512; *HS*, 449. Some of these contradictory texts were dealt with in his writings on *Freedom of the Will II*.

502. *PY*, 514; *HS*, 450.

503. *PY*, 515; *HS*, 450. He does note that not all people who are called the servants of God necessarily do the will of God. He cites the case of the devil and Nebuchadnezzar who are so called, noting that the difference is in the attitude with which the servant applies punishment. The true servant of God acts out of compassion, while the devil and Nebuchadnezzar seek only their own benefit and the disadvantage of the people. *PY*, 500; *HS*, 439.

504. *PY*, 516; *HS*, 451.

505. *PY*, 511; *HS*, 448. He makes the same point in reference to the fourteenth passage, Rom 12:19f, "do not avenge yourselves," referring the reader to his comments on passages 10 and 11. It is impossible for the Christian government to seek vengeance as vengeance comes from wrath, and that is not the source of the Christian government's motivation.

dom of the Will II.[506] Obedience to the command with the right attitude should be the primary concern of the Christian; that is, selflessly seeking only the will of God.

The question of the commands of God is also raised in the second passage presented for discussion, Matt 26:52–54. Christ commands Peter to put his sword away and this is considered proof by Hubmaier's opponents that Christ commands Christians to have nothing to do with the physical sword. Hubmaier responds by asserting that Christ is only saying that the sword is not to be wielded by those who are not duly authorized.[507] Secondly, he maintains that Christ only meant for Peter to sheath the sword, not throw it away, for the following words, "whoever takes up the sword shall perish by the sword," indicates that Christ confirms that those who use the sword for violence and their own ends should be punished by the sword.[508] Thirdly, he notes that Peter erroneously drew his sword trying to prevent the will of God from occurring. For Christ the hour had come, and Peter was wrong to try and prevent the will of God being fulfilled. From this Hubmaier understands that Christians should keep on protecting the innocent until sure that the hour of their death has come. The authorities therefore are obliged, "for the sake of the salvation of their souls to protect and guard all innocent and peaceful people."[509] However, the authorities "will have to wait a long time" before they ever hear God command them to cease protecting the innocent.

The final passage Hubmaier presents for consideration is his text that proves government authority to be from God, Rom 13:1ff. His argument rests on the understanding that God has established temporal authority by his command and that "obedience consists in all that which is not against God." Government that seeks to do the will of God by protecting the good and punishing the evil is not against God, and Christians are obliged to obey and assist in the task of government when called on by such a government.[510] The text, "the authority does not bear the sword in vain," is

---

506. *PY,* 511, cf. 480–81; *HS,* 448, cf. 423.

507. *PY,* 497, *HS,* 436.

508. *PY,* 498, *HS,* 437.

509. *PY,* 499, *HS,* 438.

510. *PY,* 520; *HS,* 455. Hubmaier used the same mode of argument when he wrote some of his most scathing condemnations of Zwingli for being inconsistent. Zwingli had not allowed Fabri to argue the admissibility of evidence on the grounds that it was "not against God," then Hubmaier used the same approach as part of his argument against Zwingli's defense of infant baptism. However, Hubmaier no doubt felt he was consistent, as he cites a plain positive command of God which for him established

the most frequently cited in this work, and is Hubmaier's foundational text that establishes the use of the sword by government wherever there is flagrant sin and evildoers.

Hubmaier goes on to warn that it is the responsibility of the people to test the spirit of the government to prove if it is acting according to the will of God. Should a government be "childish or foolish" and "not competent" to rule, then its citizens may escape it legitimately and accept another, though this is possible only if it is done "lawfully and peacefully . . . without great damage and rebellion." If the government cannot be replaced in this way, it must be endured by God as punishment for sin.[511]

Hubmaier thus affirms that the sword has a place among Christians. A Christian may be a magistrate if called upon by the governing authorities to occupy that position. Christians also owe allegiance to their government and should pay taxes and contribute to its defense as requested. He maintains that a Christian government is better than a non-Christian one, and that the more pious a magistrate the better for the community. In all these conclusions, he agrees with Zwingli, and at times arrives at them using the same interpretations. He differs from Zwingli most noticeably on the question of rejecting an unbelieving government.

Hubmaier's vehement rejection of the conclusions of his opponents as "trash," which they present under the "appearance of spirituality and the pretence of humility," are not quite as strong as Zwingli's condemnations

---

temporal authority.

511. *PY*, 520–21; *HS*, 455. Zwingli adds an enigmatic warning to magistrates: "Here meanwhile, magistrates and judges, be ye mindful of your duties, for not otherwise is horror of you conceived than because those who render right to everyone are so rare among you, especially in this time when all abounds in violence and cruelty." Zwingli, *Refutation of the Tricks*, 205. As can be seen from this comment of Zwingli, he does not go as far as Hubmaier, who allows greater individual questioning of government. This is perhaps surprising in Hubmaier, if he was seeking to win the assurance of the local Moravian nobles by demonstrating his commitment to Christian magistracy. However, the political context of Moravia makes this understandable. The Catholic Hapsburg rulers were beginning to pressure the Moravian nobles to eradicate Lutherans and other heretics and sectarians from their lands. This policy could also be turned against themselves as Utraquists and Bohemian Brethren. Therefore, Hubmaier was providing in these words a way for the common people to reject a non-Christian government, though not by force of arms. In this emphasis upon the right of the common people to reject non-Christian governments, Hubmaier differs from Luther. For Luther resistance by a lesser magistrate against a superior authority occupied his thought considerably after 1528, culminating with the formation of the Schmalkaldic League in February 1531.

of the Catabaptists, yet damaging enough as they are expressed by one who is a leader in their own group.[512]

Use of Scripture

Hubmaier's use of Scripture in this work continues to reflect his growing reliance on the Old Testament. Of the total 197 references, quotes and allusions, fifty-seven relate to the Old Testament. Genesis is referred to most frequently of the Old Testament books with eight references. Three of the eight refer to the establishment of authority in the world due to the sin which affected all people through the fall. This is part of Hubmaier's main argument for the continuation of authority within the world and among Christians. God, by his declaration that Adam would have authority over Eve, established the principle of order and government for the world, which became focused in temporal authority when Samuel appointed a king for Israel, 1 Sam 8:5. Hubmaier adds to this his anthropological understanding of humanity in which the flesh in the Christian remains flesh and the instrument of sin. In this way, the Christian remains in the world where sin still requires authority to deal with it.

Hubmaier continues to focus on obedience to the commands of God.[513] Three other references from Genesis refer to God's command to Abraham to kill Isaac. Since what God commands is good, it must be possible to fulfill the command without sinning.[514] From this text he proves that it is possible to use the sword without sinning.

He also uses a series of texts, Isa 1:17; Jer 21:12; 22:3, (each twice) along with Ps 62:11; Mic 6:8; Nah 3:1ff; Zeph 3:1f; Zech 7:9f and all of Habakkuk, to define the role of godly government: to free the oppressed from persecution, protect widows and orphans, and to act justly and show mercy.[515] This provides a measure against which to test temporal authority to see if it is doing the will of God, and if it is not then it may be removed peacefully or escaped from.

---

512. *PY*, 521; *HS*, 456. With condemnation like this it is no wonder that Hut fled, and that Glaidt, who had first housed Hubmaier on his arrival in Nikolsburg and who took Hut's part in the Nikolsburg disputation, also fled and worked alongside Hut in his ministry in Vienna in June 1527. Herbert Klassen, "Life and Teaching of Hans Hut," 183.

513. Walter Klaassen identifies obedience to the commands of God as one of Hubmaier's basic hermeneutical principles. Klaassen, "Speaking in Simplicity," 146.

514. *PY*, 511, 499, 514; *HS*, 448, 438, 450.

515. *PY*, 499, 522; *HS*, 438, 456.

Making a Patchwork of Scripture

The majority of the remainder of the Old Testament references are historical examples of kings acting as good or bad magistrates, though some references occur in the list of contradictory texts.

The majority of the New Testament texts (forty-two) are from Matthew's gospel. This reflects the preference of Hubmaier's opponents for quoting from Matthew, particularly chapter 5. Luke and John are the next most frequently cited gospels (twelve each), followed Mark's gospel (three).[516] In his exposition of these and other New Testament passages, Hubmaier's constant complaint against his opponents is that they do not take notice of the wider context of the passage quoted. He states this with reference to Luke 22:25f, "Therefore dear brothers, do not make patchwork of the Scripture, but place the preceding and the following words together into a whole judgment, so that you then obtain a perfect understanding of the Scriptures."[517]

After Matthew's gospel, the next most frequently cited book is Paul's Epistle to the Romans (twenty-eight). Eighteen of these references come from Rom 13 and 8 of these refer to verse 4. This is Hubmaier's key New Testament proof text that verifies that government as established in the Old Testament, continues in the New Testament and to the present day. Yet surprisingly, it is not the standard text of Rom 13:1ff that provides the foundation for Hubmaier's retention of government. Rather, it is his sequence of arguments based on Gen 3–4; that is, his references to the origins of sin and the establishment of authority in the world as a consequence. This order of authority finds further legitimization when Samuel establishes kingship in Israel by the command of God.

Summary

As was noted above with respect to the twelfth passage Hubmaier discusses in this work, recognizing distinctions between different categories of Scripture is essential if a whole judgment is to be made, and half-truths avoided. This method of interpretation involves certain presuppositions

---

516. Three of the five references from Matthew that Hubmaier attributes to his opponents come from Matt 5, four from Luke and one from John. They do not cite Mark at all.

517. *PY,* 517; *HS,* 453. With reference to Ephesians 6:14f he urges, "I beseech you, for the sake of divine love, that you start to read eleven lines above the verse to the Ephesians which you introduce." *PY,* 509; *HS,* 446. Walter Klaassen states that viewing a passage in the context of the preceding and following verses is another of Hubmaier's hermeneutical principles. Klaassen, "Speaking in Simplicity," 147.

Balthasar Hubmaier and the Clarity of Scripture

about the categories into which the Scriptures are placed. For example, Hubmaier and Zwingli both distinguish between Christ in his omnipotence as a judge, and the incarnate Christ who rejects the office of judge for the role of Savior. Previously, Hubmaier has noted the distinctions between the ordained and absolute will of God, between evil as punishment and evil as sin resulting from the unredeemable flesh that remains in human beings. Each text of Scripture is held to be true, but the whole truth is only discerned when the proper distinctions are observed so that a text is not applied to the wrong issue. This is the major development in Hubmaier's hermeneutic that has occurred in his writings on free will and the sword.

Previously in his writings on baptism, the principle that Scripture interprets Scripture meant that for texts concerning the same theme, the clearer text interpreted the darker text, the clearer text being understood in its plain clear literal sense.[518] Hubmaier's hermeneutical method is therefore quite distinct from that of the Swiss Brethren in this respect, and from Denck and Hut, who resolve contradictory texts by subsuming the physical within the spiritual.[519] Packull comments that although Hubmaier uses the resolution of contradictory texts as part of his argument to overcome the literalism of his opponents' interpretation of Scripture, a feature of Swiss Brethren hermeneutic, he has not adopted the more mystical principles of Hut and Denck.[520]

Hubmaier has in common with other Reformers of his day an understanding of the limited superiority of the New Testament over the Old. He demonstrates this in his discussion of Luke 6:27ff and Matt 5:38ff. In

---

518. Walter Klaassen, "Speaking in Simplicity," 146. This is very close to Luther's understanding of the external clarity of Scripture, as was seen in the comparisons between Hubmaier and Luther on free will.

519. Denck explains the resolution of contradictory texts as follows: "Concerning the Spirit's teaching, Scripture gives clear testimony, however, in a fashion that appears contradictory in many places to those for whom it has not been sealed by the Spirit of God . . . Two opposing texts must both be true. But one is locked up within the other as the lesser in the greater, as time within eternity, place within infinity." Denck, *He Who Loves the Truth*, 165. Of the forty contradictory couplets Denck cites, only seven appear in Hubmaier's list of texts (Nos. 1, 12, 14, 16, 18, 22, 29). The same theme is expressed by Hubmaier and Denck in one other couplet, though they use different passages for the first text: Hubmaier 1 Tim 2:4 and Mark 16:16; Denck No. 27, Rom 11:32 and Mark 16:16.

520. Packull, *Mysticism*, 104. Packull goes on to conclude from this that Hubmaier's *On the Sword* was written not against Hut but against "Anabaptists of Swiss Brethren derivation."

these passages, Jesus speaks of the Old Testament practice of taking an eye for an eye and turning the other cheek. Hubmaier comments: "In this matter there is now a higher stage in the New Testament than in the Old: the slandered and injured do not sue, but still the government punishes. In the Old Testament the injured one sued and the judge punishes."[521] This is a qualified superiority of the New Testament over the Old, which makes the individual believer responsible for fulfilling the commands of Christ, while the commands of God given in the Old Testament for the suppression of evil through ordained authority continue to be practiced by government.

With the publication of this work, Hubmaier confirmed that he held to a form of Anabaptism that was distinct from that of the Swiss Brethren, with whom he had earlier been in contact in Zurich, and from the South German Anabaptism of Denck and Hut. Though Hubmaier had contact with Denck in Augsburg on his way to Nikolsburg, and later with Hut in Nikolsburg itself, their influence on his hermeneutic is limited. The differences between Hubmaier and other Anabaptists are most noticeable not only in the subject matter of his disputation with Hut, but also in the manner in which Hubmaier carried out that disputation. Hubmaier used a combination of verbal bullying and denying his opponents an opportunity to participate fully in the debate. Hubmaier was dictating to Hut and his followers, not engaging in seeking to clarify doctrine through the process of congregational hermeneutic. In this attitude, he betrays himself and moves back toward the hermeneutical presuppositions of Zwingli and the other magisterial Reformers who gave authority to the preachers as the interpreters of the Word of God, using the magistrate as the power to enforce obedience to their interpretation.

That Hubmaier's action was not acceptable to the church at Nikolsburg is demonstrated by the fact that Hubmaier was forced to account for his actions before the whole church on the following day.[522]

---

521. *PY,* 508; *HS,* 445.

522. Bergsten, *Balthasar Hubmaier: Anabaptist Theologian,* 361, citing the *Chronicle of the Hutterian Brethren,* 48.

Balthasar Hubmaier and the Clarity of Scripture

SUMMARY OF WRITINGS AT NIKOLSBURG FROM JULY 1526 TO JULY 1527

These works were all written by Hubmaier after his arrival in Nikolsburg. They demonstrate continuing doctrinal development and refinement of his views, as well as changes in his hermeneutical approach.

Doctrinally, Hubmaier develops his understanding of the church, defining it to be represented as both the universal church of all the saints, and the local expression of the church as the gathered community of those who have been admitted to that community on confession of faith. That vow of faith is demonstrated through baptism by water, and sustained in that community by the vow of love that it makes when sharing in the Lord's Supper. The church has been given the power of the keys by Christ until his bodily return, whereupon the church returns the power to loose and to bind to Christ. This power to forgive sins or to bind the sinner finds expression in the concepts of fraternal admonition and the ban. Without the practice of these disciplines within the church, the church is not a true church. In this way, Hubmaier adds the idea of church discipline to those of baptism and the Lord's Supper as the third mark of the church. He also focuses on the structure of the church and writes three liturgical works that outline not only the doctrine of baptism, the Lord's Supper, and fraternal admonition, but also how these acts are to be carried out as part of the services of the church when gathered together for worship.

Two debates within the Nikolsburg church drew from Hubmaier statements on other significant doctrines that were contentious during the Reformation: freedom of the will and the relationship between the church and government.

With his work on free will, Hubmaier makes explicit his anthropology, which had only been glimpsed in earlier statements in *On the Christian Baptism*. He now plainly advocates a view of human beings as tripartite; that is, in all people there are three essential substances, body, soul, and spirit. Each of these substances has its own will, and each of the parts is variously affected by the fall and the restoration from the fall. This anthropology is linked with the introduction of an understanding of a distinction in the will of God. God's will can be viewed as both ordained and absolute. Hubmaier owes his understanding of the will of God in this way to his scholastic background, in particular to the influences of the Old Franciscan tradition via the teaching of Eck. Combining these two ideas allows Hubmaier to maintain on the one hand a limited freedom of the will in the imprisoned yet unharmed spirit that continues in human

Making a Patchwork of Scripture

beings after the fall, while on the other hand holding to the total corruption of the flesh, the instrument of an evil will. The soul stands between the two, following the flesh until it receives grace through the preached Word of God and the illumination of the Spirit, by which it is healed and empowered to join with the spirit in human beings and forces the flesh to obey the will of God, doing what God commands.

The second dispute saw Hubmaier develop more fully what he had previously only said in passing. He insists that government is ordained by God and is to be obeyed, and that it is permitted for a Christian to be a magistrate and to carry and use the sword without sinning.

Hermeneutically, there are a number of significant developments and changes in his presuppositions that occur in these writings, as well as the continuation of many of his methods.

He continues to use his basic principles that the commands of God are to be obeyed. However, he makes a distinction between the commands of God and the commands of Christ that was not previously apparent. God established authority on the earth because of sin. Since sin continues on the earth after the restoration from the fall, authority also continues, even among Christians, because they too continue to be subject to sin. Therefore, Christians must obey the command of God that establishes authority and be subject to temporal authority. However, within the church, the command of Christ is of higher priority. Christians are called on not to follow the Old Testament pattern of seeking recompense by litigation, but rather to bear with persecution and slander. The suppression of evil for the sake of the righteous is the office of the government, and Christians when called on by government should obediently fulfill the roles of magistrate and executioner with no fear of sinning.

Hubmaier comes to use as a significant method of interpretation of Scripture the idea of distinctions between various categories into which the different texts of Scripture can be placed. All texts that speak of the physical sword and punishment relate to the office of the God ordained authorities; those texts that speak of the spiritual sword relate to the church and the office of Christ and the apostles, to forgive sins. He uses distinctions in the same way in his work on freedom of the will. In his works on free will, resolving apparently contradictory texts of Scripture involves recognizing the distinction between the ordained and absolute will of God, and applying the distinction to the various texts of Scripture. Here he makes explicit his underlying assumption that all Scripture speaks the truth, and that the contradictions are only apparent. The theme of resisting half-truths and making whole judgments, which has grown over the course of the period of these works, comes to dominate his hermeneutical method in the last three works discussed above. It is a method by which Hubmaier not only resolves contradictory texts but also seeks to combat an excessive literalism of some Anabaptists within the Nikolsburg church. In this matter, he has distanced himself further from the Swiss Brethren's hermeneutical approach as demonstrated by Conrad Grebel and the *Schleitheim Articles*.

Hubmaier also demonstrates a growing dependence on the Old Testament as a source of texts from which to argue theological matters. The Old Testament is no longer primarily a source book of historical examples that are to be followed or avoided. In particular, the books of Genesis, Psalms, and Isaiah become important in Hubmaier's theology and hermeneutic. From Genesis, Hubmaier draws texts from chapters 1, 2, and 3 to establish his tripartite anthropology and his understanding of the establishment of authority to suppress the effects of sin. He also relies on God's command to Abraham to kill Isaac as proof that it is possible to obey the command of God and do what appears evil without sinning.

The Psalms become a source of texts that demonstrate that the Word of God, which he identifies as Christ the sent Word of God, has equal authority and power in the Old and New Testament. This reflects Hubmaier's new understanding of Christ as the *logos* who speaks with one effective voice, bringing salvation across both Old and New Testaments. This point is clearly demonstrated by Hubmaier's changed attitude to the patriarchs. In his *A Christian Catechism*, he maintained that the patriarchs must wait for Christ to come and preach the Word to them so that they may be saved and not merely comforted by the promise of the coming Christ. In *Freedom of the Will II*, he declares that the patriarchs have in the promise of the coming Christ all that the Christians have in the incarnate Christ. He argues for this understanding of the effective work of redemption on the presupposition that there is only "one marriage" in Old and New Testaments. If there is only one bride, there can only be one church, and those in the church must be those Christ has saved.

Isaiah also becomes more prominent in Hubmaier's usage, providing proof texts for the virgin birth and for the will of God concerning how governments should act.

The New Testament continues to provide the majority of Hubmaier's citations, though the prominence given to Matthew's gospel and Acts is replaced by John's gospel and Romans. In part, this is due to the change in subject matter. As Hubmaier moves on to themes other than baptism, his references to Acts diminish to negligible numbers. In passages where he describes the process of salvation, he continues to refer to his allegorical interpretation of the parable of the Good Samaritan. However, the dominant references relating to salvation are now drawn from John chapters 1 and 3. There are now few references to Matt 28:18ff and Mark 16:15f, which previously had provided Hubmaier with the foundation of his order of salvation.

The interaction of the preached Word and the inner illumination of the Spirit continues to be a prominent theme in these works, though as noted above, the definition of the Word of God is now broadened beyond the words of Jesus in the New Testament. In this way, the idea of following the teaching and example of Christ, which Hubmaier still insists on in these works, is expanded to allow Christians to follow the examples of all who have the Spirit of God in both Old and New Testaments. Thus, he overcomes the limitations that following the example of Christ would impose on Christians; for example, carrying and using the sword and being magistrates. The Swiss Brethren insisted on following the example of Christ in a narrower sense, limiting their actions to the practices of Christ and the apostles in the New Testament. The result of this presupposition for the Swiss Brethren was the rejection of all participation in the world. Hubmaier, on the other hand, not only allows the godly example of Old and New Testament saints to be followed, he applies his hermeneutic of distinctions so that the office of Christ to forgive sins is distinguished from the office of the magistrate to punish evil for the sake of order and protection of the good. This distinction allows Hubmaier to identify the church as the body that exercises the power of the keys, or the spiritual sword, while the individual member of the church, who continues to exist in both the world and the church due to the tripartite nature of human beings, can accept the role of magistrate and wield the physical sword without sinning.

8

Judge Me According to the Word of God
(Writings at Kreuzenstein Castle from January to March 1528)

APOLOGIA

(January 1528)[1]

Setting

SOMETIME BETWEEN JUNE 24 and July 22, 1527, Hubmaier and his wife Elsbeth were arrested and imprisoned by the Austrian authorities. On the latter date, King Ferdinand I of Austria ordered Freiburg to gather evidence for Hubmaier's trial, and that the evidence should then be forwarded to the government at Ensisheim. A similar directive went to the government in Innsbruck.[2] It remains unclear whether Hubmaier and his wife were arrested in Nikolsburg or whether, having accompanied the Lords von Liechtenstein to Vienna, they were arrested there.[3] Ferdinand's

---

1. *PY*, 30: 524–62; *HS*, 25: 485–91.
2. Bergsten, *Balthasar Hubmaier: Anabaptist Theologian*, 377.
3. Ibid., 377–78. Bergsten notes the discrepancy in the *Chronicle of the Hutterian Brethren*, which reported the events. See Hutterian Brethren, *Chronicle of the Hutterian Brethren*, 46–47.

letters make it clear that the major charge against Hubmaier was insurrection, relating to his time in Waldshut, though heresy was also a consideration. Ferdinand later demonstrated his religious zeal against heretics in the number and severity of decrees against heretics in his domains.[4]

Hubmaier was removed from Vienna to the Kreuzenstein Castle ruins where he remained until March 1528. He describes himself as "a prisoner in heavy bonds and have been for a long time in severe sickness, cold and wretchedness, without books, and in my head and memory am quite weak and clumsy," a description that closely parallels his experience under arrest in Zurich.[5] For at least some of that time he was separated from his wife, a separation he felt keenly.[6]

Towards the end of 1527, Hubmaier requested permission from Ferdinand for discussions with Johann Fabri. This request was granted. As a result Fabri, in the company of Marcus Beckh of Leopoldsdorf, the procurator or provincial administrator, and Ambrosius Salzer, Rector of the University of Vienna, held discussions with Hubmaier that lasted several days.[7] The result of the discussions is the present work, which Hubmaier dated January 3, 1528.[8]

In twenty-seven theses, Hubmaier presents his confession of faith dealing with the issues raised during the discussions with Fabri and his colleagues. Fabri provides his account of these events in his *Ursache*. Pipkin

---

4. See Zeman, *Anabaptists and Czech Brethren*, 194–200 for some of Ferdinand's decrees against heretics and Anabaptists and a description of the persecution of Anabaptists at his hands from August 20, 1527 through to September 1528.

5. PY, 526; HS, 461 cf. PY, 243; HS, 223; PY, 172–73; HS, 169–70.

6. PY, 545; HS, 477.

7. PY, 525; HS, 460. Hubmaier thanks Ferdinand for granting the interview with the three men mentioned.

8. Only a handwritten manuscript of the work survives. Bergsten presents the findings of a comparison between the handwriting of this work and "authentic" handwriting of Hubmaier, concluding that it is a "contemporary copy." HS, 459–60. Pipkin and Yoder state more strongly that the manuscript "is not from Hubmaier's hand." PY, 525. However, Estep in his translation of Bergsten's biography of Hubmaier, maintains that it is "preserved for us in his handwriting." Bergsten, *Balthasar Hubmaier: Anabaptist Theologian*, 378. Packull suggests that Hubmaier wrote a preliminary confession that was in the hands of Ferdinand by July 29, 1527. This informed the King of the activity of Hut and his followers in the area of Vienna. Packull, *Mysticism*, 141. Bergsten states that Hubmaier wrote a supplementary confession on the topics of baptism and the Lord's Supper in February 1528 that was sent to the King, though the present document was held back by the Lower Austrian government because it was an unsatisfactory "half-opinion." Bergsten, *Balthasar Hubmaier: Anabaptist Theologian*, 379. Of the three confessions that this reconstruction requires, only the *Apologia* has survived.

and Yoder note approvingly Carl Sachsse's comment that everything Hubmaier says in this work echoes his earlier writings.[9] Certainly, Torsten Bergsten is correct to show that Hubmaier tried to present his theology in the best possible light to his Catholic examiners, distancing himself from both the evangelical Reformers and Anabaptists such as Hans Hut.[10] While it is true that Hubmaier has differentiated his teaching from that of the Reformers, it should also be noted that in his earlier writings he shares a number of key principles with the Reformers. These include the focus on the preached Word of God, and the gospel that brings ontological change in human beings through the inner working of the Holy Spirit in cooperation with the Word of God. In the *Apologia* Hubmaier frequently refers to these more Catholic topics as presented in his *A Christian Catechism* and *Twelve Articles*, as proof that he has maintained his Catholic-sounding position throughout.[11] However, Fabri and his colleagues were unconvinced of Hubmaier's recantation. Although Hubmaier dressed his *Apologia* in words that in the main could bear a number of interpretations, he has little to say on the key issues of baptism and the Lord's Supper. What he does say on these two topics is not a recantation but an offer to "postpone these two articles" until a council has called and dealt with them. If that is not satisfactory Hubmaier states his willingness to be examined by Ferdinand, his council, and universities, "to give answer with the holy Scriptures on all the articles" ascribed to him.[12] Though trying to maintain his position that it is Scripture that judges doctrine and not human beings, Hubmaier nevertheless significantly compromises his principles at this point, for he

---

9. *PY*, 525.

10. *HS* 458–59. Bergsten identifies which theses of Hubmaier's are most distant from the teachings of the Reformers. In Theses 1 and 2 Hubmaier corrects the Reformation teaching of *sola fide*; Theses 5–7 are directed against teaching on predestination and in support of free will; and Thesis 18 presents a positive statement on celibacy, which is his most positive Catholic statement and most removed from the teaching of the Reformers. Against the teaching of Hut are Thesis 14, "On the Last Day"; Theses 25–26, "On Baptism" and "The Lord's Supper"; and Thesis 27, "On Government."

11. *PY*, 358ff, 362; *HS*, 320–21, 323–24; *PY*, 236; *HS*, 216.

12. *PY*, 557–58; *HS*, 487–88. In his *Theses Against Eck*, No. IX, Hubmaier wrote, "Search in Scripture, not in papal law, not in councils, not fathers, not schools; for it is the discourse which Christ spoke which shall judge all things. He is the truth, the plantation, and the vine." *PY*, 53; *HS*, 88. Later in *A Brief Apologia*, he wrote: "I test the holy fathers, councils, and human teachings by the touchstone of Holy Scripture. If they measure up with it, then I am believing the Scripture. If they do not conform to it, I command them to get behind me, as Christ did to Peter when he was not minded according to the will of God." *PY*, 300; *HS*, 274.

has maintained that his teaching on baptism and the Lord's Supper are in accordance with Scripture and need no further examination by people.

On February 26, 1528, Ferdinand wrote to the Lower Austrian government angrily demanding that it expedite the case against Hubmaier. In a reply to Ferdinand, the government sought to excuse itself for the delay by indicating that Hubmaier had not supplied a recantation as he had promised to Fabri and the other examiners, but only a "half-opinion."[13]

Hubmaier was returned to Vienna, where he was examined under torture, and wrote a testimony *(urgicht)* which according to Fabri was "read publicly in the presence of many thousands."[14] The content of this testimony indicates that the charges of insurrection and sedition arising from the events in Waldshut in 1524–25 and Hubmaier's involvement with the peasants' army at that time were the main focus of the Austrian government. The question of baptism and the Lord's Supper are mentioned only briefly, with a cursory reference being made to Hubmaier's recantation of believers' baptism at Zurich.[15]

While the trial focused on Hubmaier's involvement with the peasants' army, the Austrian authorities were also aware of his religious convictions. Hubmaier's failure to recant his opinion on baptism and the Lord's Supper provided sufficient grounds for the Austrian authorities to condemn him as a heretic. Hubmaier died the prescribed heretic's death, burning at the stake. He died on March 10, 1528. His wife, Elsbeth, was drowned in the Danube three days later. In this way came to an end the pilgrimage of an independent thinker, who took aspects from medieval Catholicism, the evangelical Reformers, and the Radical Reformers, and combined them into a form that reflected his own unique experience of that time. As Bergsten has shown, Hubmaier left a legacy of literature to the Anabaptist community that continued to influence their theology, particularly in the areas of baptism, the Lord's Supper, free will, and church discipline. He also notes that Hubmaier's opinion on community of goods, the sword, and government did not have a continuing positive influence among Anabaptists.[16] However, Hubmaier's opinions on these latter doctrines have continued to produce a negative effect among present-day Mennonites and Hutterites.

---

13. Bergsten, *Balthasar Hubmaier: Anabaptist Theologian*, 379.
14. *PY*, 563.
15. *PY*, 565.
16. Bergsten, *Balthasar Hubmaier: Anabaptist Theologian*, 385.

Balthasar Hubmaier and the Clarity of Scripture

Analysis

The majority of the theses Hubmaier presents are dealt with summarily. His usual method is to present a series of Scripture quotations combined with short expository comments, prefaced by a short thesis and followed by a slightly longer concluding remark. In seventeen of the twenty-seven theses, Hubmaier refers to specific works where he deals with the thesis under discussion. In three other theses, No. 1 ("On Mere Faith"), No. 3 ("On Christian Liberty"), and No. 18 ("On Virginity and Widowhood"), he makes the more general allusion to having commented on the thesis in his "booklets." In seven theses: No. 4 ("On the Fear of God"), No. 5 ("On Conscience"), No. 13 ("On Purgatory"), No. 14 ("On the Last Day"), No. 15 ("On Prayer"), No. 19 ("On Fasting"), and No. 20 ("On the Sabbath"), he makes even more generalized references to having preached, stated, or admonished people concerning the thesis in question. In some instances, he makes no reference to having previously dealt with the thesis at all. This evidence is particularly relevant with respect to theses 13, 18, and 19, for Hubmaier had previously dealt with these theses in such a way that his statements in this work show a radical change of opinion. Hubmaier also deals with three other of the theses under specific headings or in specific ways in his previous writings.[17]

Thesis 1, "On Mere Faith," and Thesis 2, "On Good Works," are closely related. Concerning faith, Hubmaier states, "Mere faith alone is not sufficient for salvation." To support this view he cites Rom 10:10, "For man believes with his heart and so is justified, and confesses with his lips and so is saved." His interpretation of this verse, however, identifies oral confession with exercising faith in good works, bypassing the link between oral confession of faith and water baptism that has been an essential aspect

---

17. Thesis 13, "On Purgatory," cf. *Eighteen Theses* No. 14, *PY,* 34; *HS,* 74; *On the Christian Baptism, PY,* 83; *HS,* 110; *Dialogue, PY,* 185; *HS,* 179.
Thesis 14, "On the Last Day," cf. *A Christian Catechism, PY,* 364; *HS,* 325.
Thesis 15, "On Prayer," cf. *A Christian Catechism, PY,* 347, 363; *HS,* 312, 324.
Thesis 18, "On Virginity and Widowhood," cf. *Eighteen Theses* Nos. 15 and 16, *PY* 34; *HS* 74.
Thesis 19, "On Fasting," cf. *A Christian Catechism, PY,* 356; *HS,* 318.
Thesis 20, "On the Sabbath, cf. *A Christian Catechism, PY,* 357; *HS,* 319.
His comments on purgatory and celibacy in his earlier works are more polemical toward the Catholic Church than his comments on the other theses, which indicates a greater change on Hubmaier's part to allow for a favorable interpretation by Fabri and the others. The other theses referred to here are dealt with by Hubmaier in such a way as to expand on his opinion as it was previously stated. This will become evident in the discussion on the individual theses that follows.

of his teaching on baptism.[18] He introduces a new supporting text, 1 John 3:18f, which admonishes the reader to love not in words but in deeds and truth. Hubmaier thus emphasizes the necessity of good works accompanying faith, a point he made in his *A Christian Catechism* under the distinction between dead and living faith.[19]

The general theme of antinomianism that he refers to in his earlier works is reiterated here. People, he claims, want to be "truly evangelical" but do not undertake any works of brotherly love. This he continues to deplore as he had done in his "booklets."[20]

In Thesis 2 he stresses the place of good works, citing references from Scripture he has previously given in his works *Form for Christ's Supper* and *Freedom of the Will II*.[21] The Scripture references are obviously considered clear in themselves since Hubmaier simply cites the texts without adding any exposition. His final comment reflects his position as expressed in *Freedom of the Will II*, "Those who say they can do nothing good deceive themselves and there is no true faith in them."[22]

His thesis "On Christian Liberty," (Thesis 3), continues on the theme of faith and the necessity of good works. Faith without good works "adulterates Christian liberty into carnal license."[23] He cites Gal 5:13f and 1 Pet

---

18. *PY*, 526; *HS*, 462. Cf. *Eighteen Theses*, Nos 1–4, *PY*, 32; 72. The *Eighteen Theses* comes from Hubmaier's pen before his adoption of adult baptism. In it, there is no mention of the necessity of oral confession of faith. Instead, faith must be manifest in "gratitude toward God" and "works of brotherly love." While in his *Theses Against Eck* No. 1–4, *PY*, 51; *HS*, 88, faith and oral confession of faith are linked with specific reference to Rom 10:10, there is no link between oral confession and the baptismal pledge. In his *Dialogue*, *PY*, 193; *HS*, 185, Hubmaier links faith, oral confession, and the works of faith in the general context of baptism. In a summary at the end of his *Twelve Articles*, Hubmaier alludes to Rom 10:10, stating, "This is my faith, which I confess with heart and mouth and have testified to publicly before the church in water baptism." *PY*, 240; *HS*, 220. In his discussion of the church in *A Christian Catechism*, Hubmaier states that the church is built on the oral confession that Jesus is the Christ. He continues, "This outward confession is what makes a church, and not faith alone." *PY*, 352; *HS*, 315–16. Earlier, he describes the baptismal pledge as this oral confession before the congregation. *A Christian Catechism*, *PY*, 350; *HS*, 314.

19. *PY*, 348; *HS*, 313.

20. *PY*, 375f; *HS*, 339–40. *PY*, 427–29; *HS*, 381. He also produces a scathing anti-clerical polemic on the same point in *On the Christian Ban*, *PY*, 422f; *HS*, 376.

21. *PY*, 401–2; *HS*, 360; *PY*, 490; *HS*, 430. He adds to his list of references given in *Freedom of the Will II* the Markan parallel 3:25 to Luke 8:21 and the new Scripture 1 Cor 3:8.

22. *PY*, 528; *HS*, 463.

23. *PY*, 528; *HS*, 463.

2:16 as warnings about using Christian freedom as carnal license. He links this thought with the distinction between the carnal Christian and the Spirit-led Christian, citing Rom 8:6, 13; Gal 5:24f; Gen 6:3, references he acknowledges he had previously used in his *A Christian Catechism*, with the exception of Gen 6:3.[24] He introduces for the first time in relation to this topic the method of interpretation that he has developed in his last three writings. He places John 8:36 beside Luke 9:23 and its parallel reference Mark 10:38. Christ has made you free it is true; nevertheless it is freedom to be "servants of the cross." Similarly, in response to the objection of the "carnal Christians" who argue on the basis of 1 Tim 1:9 that there is no law for the just, Hubmaier presents his view that the law is to be kept by Christians since Jesus said in Matt 5:17ff that he had not come to abolish the law, nor was the law to be relaxed in the least point. To this he adds the word from James that transgression in one point of the law makes the offender guilty of them all (Jas 2:10).[25]

Thesis 4, "On the Fear of God," is essentially a new theme in Hubmaier's teaching, though he states that he has preached on it "so earnestly that many people hated me for it and said I was trying to make monks and nuns of them."[26] He suggests that the fear of God involves people always remembering that God is merciful and faithful to those "who keep before their eyes his covenant and his law" (Ps 25:10). Again this theme is a warning to those who would presume on the mercy of God and make their freedom in Christ into carnal license.

Although Hubmaier has not previously made a specific thesis of conscience in his teaching, its role is of great importance to him. This can be seen in his earlier writings and in his determination to stand by the essential truths of his teaching on baptism and the Lord's Supper. In this thesis, Hubmaier teaches that the Word of God reveals God's will through the commandments of God. Obedience to the commandments results in people having a good conscience before God, while disobedience brings

24. *PY*, 529; *HS*, 463–64 cf. for Gal 5 *PY*, 348; *HS*, 313; or Rom 8 *PY*, 360; *HS*, 322.

25. *PY*, 529–30; *HS*, 464.

26. *PY*, 531; *HS*, 465. He makes his first use of Deut 10:12; Josh 24:27; Mal 1:6; Luke 1:50; Ps 25:10; Luke 12:5 in this thesis, while using the illustration of Abraham's willingness to kill Isaac as an example of one who feared the Lord. Previously this illustration from Gen 22 has been used to demonstrate that it is possible to obey God's commands, even to do what appears evil, without sin. *PY*, 480–81; *HS*, 423. He also uses the example of God sending someone to instruct Cornelius, a God-fearing man, in the Christian faith. This usage of Cornelius for such a purpose is consistent with previous uses. *PY*, 363; *HS*, 324; *PY*, 437; *HS*, 388.

about self-accusation and loss of uprightness of heart.[27] Where someone has been made aware of sin through conscience according to the plumb line of Scripture, they must with Peter "weep bitterly, repent and show remorse, grief and repentance for the sin" and thus reconcile themselves "again to God and achieve peace through a good conscience."[28] Hubmaier equates conscience with faith by citing Rom 14:23. Where the text states, "Everything that does not come from faith is sin," Hubmaier interpolates "conscience" into the verse stating "for what is not of faith is contrary to conscience and what is against the conscience is against God and is sin."[29]

Conscience also played a role in Hubmaier's own conviction and death. Twice in Hubmaier's *Vienna Testimony*, which Fabri reports was read publicly in Vienna, Hubmaier is said to have confessed to actions that were against God and his conscience.[30] Whether Hubmaier had said this is open to debate, since it was a tactic of all those involved in the disputations of that day to charge opponents with acting contrary to their conscience.[31] Nevertheless, in this work Hubmaier does make specific reference to being compelled by his conscience to maintain his opinion on baptism and the Lord's Supper.[32] It should also be noted that Hubmaier reflects his personal experience in his teaching. Though he does not use the term "conscience"

---

27. *PY*, 531; *HS*, 465.

28. *PY*, 532; *HS*, 466. This teaching strongly echoes Hubmaier's previous teaching on conscience, particularly in *Freedom of the Will I*, where he uses the same illustration of conscience as the gnawing worm, *PY*, 431; *HS*, 384. In *A Christian Catechism*, Hubmaier is at pains to demonstrate that conscience is the spark of God that remains in all people after the fall. It has been covered in ashes, but not quenched completely. If one blows on the spark it will once again burn. The breath which blows on this spark is the Holy Spirit, which Christ breathed on his disciples on Easter Day (John 20:22), and the church continues to breathe on the soul through the proclamation of the Word of God. Thus the wounded soul is re-awakened. *PY*, 360; *HS*, 322. In his earlier work *On the Christian Baptism*, Hubmaier had emphasized more the link between the preached Word of God that convinces the hearer of the truth of the Gospel and the confession of faith. Faith is in turn connected to baptism, as baptism is the outward expression of existing inward faith. Baptism also indicates that there already exists a good conscience toward God. This good conscience is based on the assurance the Holy Spirit brings that the gospel is true. Hubmaier makes this point through the exposition of 1 Pet 3:20f. *PY*, 106, 117, 134; *HS*, 127, 136, 149–50.

29. *PY*, 531; *HS*, 465.

30. *PY*, 564

31. Hubmaier had charged Zwingli with doing this. *PY*, 231; *HS*, 212. Zwingli in turn had charged the Swiss Brethren with the same fault, describing it as hypocrisy. Zwingli, *Refutation of the Tricks*, 167ff.

32. *PY*, 556; *HS*, 486.

in the final paragraph of his *Twelve Articles*, nevertheless the cry to remain in the faith, which he confessed at baptism, is that of one who had recently under torture been forced to recant his beliefs against his conscience.[33]

Hubmaier refers his readers to his second work on free will in which he attacked the "harmful error" that all things happen by necessity. Though citing the same Scriptures as in his two works on free will, Hubmaier does give priority to 2 Cor 9:7 in this discussion. For him, this text proves unequivocally that Christians can perform good works that are not of necessity. However, in this instance he moves away from the context of the passage; that is, giving alms, and applies it to angels and human beings, who God created reasonable beings. They are to "praise, honor and magnify" God "without compulsion and unforced."[34] His teaching on this point is in harmony with his previous works. In conjunction with this attack on necessity he again stresses that good works must flow from renewed free will; that is, the works of praying, fasting, and giving alms, as he had done in *Free Will I*.[35]

He follows on his discussion of "necessity" with a discussion of free will (Thesis 7). He alludes to Martin Luther's comment that free will is an empty and useless title, a statement Desiderius Erasmus attacked in his work *De libero arbitrio*. Erasmus accused those who made such statement of calling God a tyrant and blaming God for the unrighteousness of sin.[36] Matthew 25:42ff becomes the proof of his charge against those who deny free will, for Christ would not be able to legitimately accuse the sinners that they did not feed him, or visit him as he had commanded them to do unless they were free to do so. In this section on "free will," Hubmaier adds nothing new to his previous detailed statement in his two booklets on the subject, booklets he refers his readers to for a fuller explanation of his position.

Like his thesis on conscience, the eighth thesis on "Remorse, Sorrow and Repentance" sees Hubmaier bring together some texts of Scripture that he has previously used with reference to this theme, with the addition of a number of other texts used for the first time.[37] He refers to his booklets

---

33. *PY*, 240; *HS*, 220.

34. *PY*, 532; *HS*, 466. Cf. *PY*, 463, 475; *HS*, 409, 418; and *PY*, 444; *HS*, 394.

35. *PY*, 534, cf. 428–29; *HS*, 468, cf. 381.

36. *PY*, 534; *HS*, 467 cf. Erasmus, *De libero arbitrio*, 54 and Luther, *On the Bondage of the Will*, 177ff.

37. *PY*, 536–37; *HS*, 469–70. Jer 18:8, 10; 2 Sam 12:13; Ps 51:17. The new texts are from the New Testament, Luke 19:8 (Zacchaeus); Luke 7:37 (the prostitute who anointed Christ's feet). Cf. *PY*, 378–79, 412, 425, 460; *HS*, 342, 369, 378, 407.

On Fraternal Admonition and the *On the Christian Ban* for his previous teaching on the subject, particularly with regard to the point that compensation for sins should be made "according to the nature of the sins."[38] What he does not indicate is that his earlier view of repentance, or more accurately the lack of true repentance as made clear in *On the Christian Ban*, is in the context of a harsh anticlerical polemic directed against Catholics. If his Catholic examiners had read the passages he had pointed them to, his writings would not have endeared him to them.[39] Using the example of the woman who anointed Christ's feet, Hubmaier claims that this is a true act of repentance. Whereas previously she had submitted herself to sin, now she submits her members to "servitude to Christ." He had previously described repentance as "accusing oneself of sin before God, asking him for forgiveness, and thenceforth never again committing it; that is the highest form of repentance."[40]

Theses 9 and 10 deal with the subject of "the Virgin Mary." Hubmaier had previously dealt with this thesis in his earlier booklets *Twelve Theses*, *A Brief Apologia*, and *A Christian Catechism*. Hubmaier introduces a typological interpretation of Gen 3 and 4 to prove the virginity of Mary. The Genesis passages make clear that Eve, though betrothed to Adam, was a virgin when God foretold that her seed would crush the serpent's head. For the typology to be consistent, Mary, who was betrothed to Joseph, fulfilled the promise of God to Eve when she bore the Christ child. Hubmaier concludes that Mary must have been a virgin also.

He also makes comment on Jewish interpretation of Isa 7:14 that legitimately translates "virgin" as "young woman." He rejects this view, saying it changes nothing with regard to the perpetual virginity of Mary on two grounds: firstly, Eve was referred to as "woman" throughout the Genesis narrative, but this did not mean that she was not a virgin; secondly, that if a young wife bears a child, this is not a sign but the ordinary course of nature, which contradicts Isaiah's statement that the event of the birth is to be a sign to Israel.[41] Hubmaier had indeed previously vigorously maintained the view that Mary was a virgin before, during, and after the birth of Christ.[42] Similarly, he maintains his orthodoxy concerning

---

38. *PY*, 537, cf. 380, 419; *HS*, 470, cf. 343, 374.
39. *PY*, 422, *HS*, 376.
40. *PY*, 537, cf. 346–47; *HS*, 470, 312.
41. *PY*, 537, *HS*, 471.
42. *PY*, 357; *HS*, 319 cf. *PY*, 236; *HS*, 216, "the pure and eternally chaste virgin;" *PY*, 299; *HS*, 273: "I confess the pure Virgin Mary to be a chaste maiden before and after

Mary, in that he affirms her to be *theotokos* and not merely *Christotokos*, as the Nestorians erroneously maintained. Two texts combine to prove this proposition, Luke 1:43, where Elizabeth describes Mary as "the mother of my Lord," and John 19:25, where Mary is identified as the mother of Jesus. Hubmaier reasons: "If Mary is the mother of Jesus and the Lord Jesus is true God, it must follow that Mary was the mother of the true God. This logic cannot be refuted by any Christian."[43] He does carefully distinguish between Christ's divinity and humanity. Mary is only his mother according to his humanity, and not his divinity.

It would appear that behind the discussion of these two theses lies the *Nikolsburg Theses*. The third of the *Nikolsburg Theses* states: "The Virgin Mary is not the mother of God but only the mother of Christ."[44] That this is probable is supported by later references Hubmaier makes to his dispute with Hut concerning the last day, baptism, the Lord's Supper, and government. Yet Hubmaier does not identify Hut as teaching *Christotokos* theology, which would have further distanced himself from his Nikolsburg opponent.

Hubmaier affirms again his belief "that Jesus is Christ, the only begotten Son of the living God, true God and Man, conceived of the Holy Spirit, born of Mary, the eternally chaste Virgin," adding that he believes that Christ fulfills the promises and prophecies of God. This confession is the same as Peter's (Matt 16:17f), on which the church is built.[45] Hubmaier builds his case for the deity of Jesus, stating that the Old Testament clearly indicates that a man would be conceived on earth without the seed of man and be born of a virgin, and that this man would be truly God. Hubmaier identified this man as Jesus Christ.

As he indicates, this statement is in agreement with his view of Jesus as previously recorded in the *Twelve Theses*.[46] In that earlier work Hubmaier does not supply an extensive list of Scripture references to support his view. While he does provide an extensive list in this thesis of the *Apologia*, many of the texts are not identifiable. Hubmaier appears to simply be piling up texts as if to prove his faithfulness to Scripture, but instead

---

the birth."

43. *PY*, 538, *HS*, 471–72.

44. See Packull, *Mysticism*, 99. Packull accepts the authenticity of the *Die Nikolsburger Artikel* as representative of Hut's position. He therefore rejects the earlier generally agreed position expressed by Williams that the theses were forged. Williams, *Radical Reformation*, 1992, 342n70.

45. *PY*, 539; *HS*, 472.

46. *PY*, 235–36; *HS*, 216–17.

is devaluing Scripture. Heinrich Bullinger accused the Swiss Brethren of indulging in this practice.[47] As with the thesis on Mary, this thesis on the deity of Christ was included in the *Nikolsburg Theses*.[48]

The thesis "On Original Sin" attacks Zwingli's position. Though this is not stated explicitly, it would be obvious to any reader who checked that Hubmaier is referring to *On Infant Baptism*. There he specifies Zwingli as the originator of the teaching that original sin is a weakness and not damning.[49] In this present thesis he states simply, "Original sin is not only a weakness, but is a damnable sin of those who are not in Christ and who walk according to the flesh, it is also the matrix and root of all sins."[50] It appears to be Hubmaier's view that Scripture speaks clearly on this matter for he cites texts of Scripture without further comment. With the exception of Romans 7:18–20 and 5:12 Hubmaier had used the other six texts he cites here in his booklet against the evangelical preachers at Basel.[51]

In his discussion concerning purgatory (Thesis 13), Hubmaier makes use of Paul's comments in 1 Corinthians 3:10–15 to indicate that there is the heavenly kingdom for those who have built on Christ with gold, silver, and precious stones, and "hell is a purgatory for those who have built on Christ with wood, hay, and stubble." For those outside of Christ there is only everlasting fire. He states that besides heaven and hell he knows of no "special purgatory" in Scripture. He also cites Christ's comments in Matt 5:25 with reference to agreeing with your accuser or face being put in prison until the last penny has been paid. Though not stated explicitly, Hubmaier reverts to a medieval interpretation of this text that identifies "prison" with purgatory. He also cites Christ's words from Matt 12:32, along with its synoptic parallels, in which is made a distinction between two kinds of sins; those against the Son of Man that will be forgiven, and those against the Holy Spirit that "will not be forgiven neither in this age nor in the age to come."[52] He concludes, "It follows on the authority of the Word of Christ and of Paul that there is forgiveness of sins in the other world, or these three texts cannot be completely understood."

47. Fast and Yoder, "How to Deal with Anabaptists," 90.
48. Packull, *Mysticism*, 100. It is Thesis 4 on the list.
49. *PY*, 284–85; *HS*, 263.
50. *PY*, 540; *HS*, 473.
51. He also deletes Jer 20:14, a text he has always previously cited in conjunction with Ps 51:5; Job 3:3. Hubmaier continues to make use of these two later texts in this case. Cf. *PY*, 152, 204, 218, 284, 431, 434, 455; *HS*, 149, 193, 203, 263, 384, 386, 404.
52. *PY*, 541; *HS*, 474. Zwingli had previously explicitly rejected the identification of prison with purgatory. Zwingli, *Sixty-Seven Articles*, 336–38.

Previously, Hubmaier had not been so evasive in his statements concerning purgatory: "Whoever would look for purgatory, on which those whose God is their belly have been building for years, is looking for Moses' grave, which he shall never find."[53] In *On the Christian Baptism*, he had also spoken of teaching "useless things" about a wide range of doctrines, including purgatory, concerning which the "red whore of Babylon" deceived him.[54] In his debate with Zwingli over baptism, Hubmaier reminds Zwingli of his statement at the Second Zurich Disputation that "the Scriptures know no purgatory, only hell and heaven." Hubmaier was in total agreement with Zwingli's denunciations of purgatory at that meeting, as well as with his method of biblical interpretation, to which Hubmaier drew Zwingli's attention by introducing this statement in his debate with Zwingli.[55]

It is therefore evident that Hubmaier is not only being deliberately evasive by describing part of hell as a purgatory where it is possible to receive forgiveness of sins, he also introduces the notion that "there is forgiveness of sins in the other world," an opinion that is contradictory to his teaching on the power of the keys. Previously, he has taught that forgiveness of sins belongs to Christ, who transferred the power to the church at his ascension. The church uses that power of the keys to admit and exclude people not only from its membership on earth but also in heaven. He maintains that only when a person is part of the church can they be assured of salvation, for there is no salvation outside the church.[56] In this thesis on purgatory, Hubmaier makes a large concession to his doctrine of the church and to soteriology. His teaching on the doctrine of the church is further compromised in later theses in the *Apologia*.

In his discussion on the last day (Thesis 14), Hubmaier does not direct his readers to a specific work where he previously dealt with the

---

53. *PY*, 34; *HS*, 74. *Eighteen Theses*, No. 14.

54. *PY*, 83; *HS*, 110. Cf. Hubmaier's similar confession of promoting "many errors, hypocrisies, and evil abominations" by which he had a part in creating many priests and monks, although he asserts this happened through ignorance. Although he does not list the errors specifically in this instance, it would have been impossible for him to have examined people for the priesthood without having taught the doctrine of purgatory, a foundation of the whole penitential system of the medieval Catholic Church. *PY*, 342; *HS*, 308.

55. *PY*, 185; *HS*, 179.

56. *PY*, 239; *HS*, 219. The teaching on remission of sins through the power of the keys becomes a central theme Hubmaier developed in his Nikolsburg writings.

theme, though he does deal with it specifically in his *A Christian Catechism*.[57] There Hubmaier refers to 1 Thess 4:16ff; John 5:29 as the Scriptural basis for his teaching on the day of judgment. In the *Apologia* he discusses Matt 24; Luke 21; Mark 13. Hubmaier employs his method of a clearer text interpreting a darker text. In this case Mark 13:32f clarifies Matt 24:36, for "Mark records Christ's words even more clearly." Hubmaier also cites from 1 Thess 5:1ff. The point he is making in the *Apologia* is that the exact time of the judgment day is not known to anyone except the Father alone, whereas in his earlier treatment he was making the point that the day of judgment would see the resurrection of all people, those who have done good to eternal life, and those who have done evil to "the resurrection of the judgment."

The change of emphasis has been brought about because Hubmaier wants to focus his readers' minds on the difference there is between himself and Hut. Hubmaier maintains that Hut has misled the "simple folk" with the idea of a "definite time for the last day, namely now at this very next Pentecost."[58] Hubmaier attributes Hut's error to faulty mathematics. The identification of Dan 12:7 and Rev 13:5 saw Hut calculate that there were three-and-one-half "ordinary years" until the last day. Hubmaier challenges this conclusion, stating that they are "Danielic years" or "sun years" and the final figure, allowing for leap years, is 1,277 ordinary years.[59] The crucial point is not that Hubmaier and Hut determined a specific period of time from the prophecies of Daniel and Revelation, but that Hut nominated a specific date at which the last day would occur. Hubmaier states that he "unambiguously told him openly and earnestly and rebuked him for exciting and misleading the simple populace without basis in the truth."[60]

---

57. *PY*, 541f, cf. 264; *HS*, 110, cf. 325.

58. *PY*, 542; *HS*, 475. *Die Nikolsburger Artikel*, No. 7 reads, "The day of judgment is to be expected within two years." Zeman has shown that Ferdinand's repression of the Anabaptists was in part inspired by the "chiliastic expectations of the end of the world at Pentecost 1528" (31 May). He gathered evidence of this expected overthrow of the government from the records of trials of Anabaptists in Ferdinand's domains. Zeman, *Anabaptists and Czech Brethren*, 194ff.

59. Packull notes how the debate over eschatology between Hubmaier and Hut was carried on by Hut's follower Leonhart Schiemer, who rejected the idea of taking "days for years" and the arithmetic that arrived at 1,277 years, arguing that the result should be 1,290 years. Joachimists used two figures in their reckoning, 1,260 and 1,290 years. Packull, *Mysticism*, 110.

60. *PY*, 543; *HS*, 475.

Balthasar Hubmaier and the Clarity of Scripture

Hubmaier concludes with his own warning of the imminence of the day of judgment, citing Jas 5:9, "Behold the Judge is already standing at the door." Hubmaier has consistently held the view that the last day is imminent. In his preface to the *Dialogue* with Zwingli he warns, "for the last times are here" of which Christ spoke in Matt 24.[61] Yet nowhere in his writings does he nominate a specific day or date; instead he uses the concept of the day of judgment as a warning that people ought to do that which God has clearly commanded them to do.

In the fifteenth thesis, "On Prayer," Hubmaier specifically identifies prayer as the way a person must first make some amends to God's injured righteousness due to our wickedness before God will forgive our sin. He summarizes his position thus: "As truly as God is just he will forgive no man his sins unless he has first prayed."[62] He then provides a long series of Scripture references that begin with the teaching of Christ on prayer, Matt 7:7; John 16; Matt 6, with the parallel text Luke 11, and the parable of the judge and the widow, Luke 18. He then presents a list of examples that show "how beneficial" prayer is (Gen 20:17; Exod 32:31f; Num 11:4f; 16:22f; 1 Kgs 8:22f; 17:1; Dan 9; Matt 26:36ff; Luke 1:13; John 4:46f; Jas 1:5f; 5:13f). Another series of texts follow that demonstrate appropriate attitudes to prayer; for example praying on our knees or with upraised hands; beating our breasts and falling on our faces; praying with weeping hearts and eyes and with a loud voice (Acts 7:59f; 2:36; 21:5; 1 Tim 2:8; Luke 18:13; Matt 26:39; 1 Sam 1:11ff; Luke 11; Matt 27:46ff and Luke 23:46). These texts provided Hubmaier with a pattern for public prayer, which by his own testimony, he followed, "I have led in praying the Mea Culpa or the Lord's Prayer or a psalm with a very loud voice and kneeling." That he interpreted such texts literally is also demonstrated in his use of Acts 3:1, 10:3 as the basis for reintroducing prayer at the ninth hour. It was at that time that the people went to pray at the temple and was also the time that God answered Cornelius's prayer.

In this thesis on prayer, Hubmaier makes his only reference to a source other than Scripture from which he draws material to support his teaching. He cites Pliny's letter to the Emperor Trajan as evidence that the Christians rose before dawn to pray, evidence corroborated by Eusebius

---

61. *PY,* 176; *HS,* 172. Hubmaier takes the reference to the sun and moon losing their shine, and stars falling from heaven, and applies it to Zwingli and other preachers who have become objects on which people depend instead of God. For Hubmaier "respecting persons" above the Word of God is an error he sees occurring in Zurich and other places where people look more to men for direction than to God himself.

62. *PY,* 544; *HS,* 476.

in his *History of the Church*. Perhaps these two authors were less controversial to cite than Augustine, Jerome, or Origen, though why he should choose to use these extra-biblical authorities at all when he does not do so in any other part of this text is surprising.

Though Hubmaier does not indicate that he has addressed this topic of prayer previously, he has done so briefly in his *A Christian Catechism*, and in a way more closely related to this statement in Thesis 15 than in his first book on free will. In the latter work, prayer is not related to making amends for God's injured righteousness, rather it is the cry of the soul to which God responds by sending a Philip or Peter to proclaim the Word of God. Through this comes recognition of sins, the truth of the gospel, and the inner illumination of the Holy Spirit in the new birth.[63] Thus in this thesis, as in his thesis on purgatory, Hubmaier makes a significant shift in his soteriology, a shift back to an Occamist position that God will not deny his grace to those who do that which is in them.

The sixteenth thesis deals with confession. Hubmaier distinguishes three kinds of confession; (1) confession to God, (2) confession to another person we have offended as Christ taught in Matt 5:23f, (3) confession to the church for the remission of sins. It is this final kind of confession that

---

63. *PY*, 437; *HS*, 388. Hubmaier's opponents cite Jer 10:23 as proof that neither the way nor the path is in the power of the human being. In *Freedom of the Will II* Hubmaier comments: "The prophet speaks here of those things which concern the salvation of the soul in which the human being, outside of the divine Word and leading, is completely helpless and wholly ignorant.... If now God sends his Word, them the human being is able to know, desire, and walk the way of the divine footsteps, as the counter scriptures show clearly." *PY*, 484–85; *HS*, 426. Steinmetz has argued that Hubmaier follows the Occamist principle, "to those who do what is in them God does not deny his grace." He notes that this principle operates at two levels; (1) reason and revelation, and (2) grace and free will. For those who have never heard the gospel there are two resources in them which operate to aid their return to God, the unfallen will of the spirit, or conscience, and revelation of God in nature. The invitation to salvation comes through the external proclamation of the Word of God. Where that proclamation is not understood, prayer operates as an action that is possible for all people prior to grace. Steinmetz, "Luther and Hubmaier," 68–69. What Steinmetz has not included in his analysis of Hubmaier's teaching on free will is Hubamier's view that reason and conscience are inoperative in people prior to God sending his Word. *PY*, 439; *HS*, 390. As with Luther, Hubmaier uses Ps 107:20 as a text to support his view that healing comes only through the sent Word of God. In this second work on free will, Word is identified as Christ, the *logos*, whose power has illuminated all people of the Old and New Testaments. *PY*, 454; *HS*, 403. Heathens may be aware of God through conscience and revelation in nature, but they cannot be saved until the gospel is preached to them. For Hubmaier, people cannot fulfill the Occamist principle and "do what is in them," even pray, as a preparation for grace, either in the area of reason and revelation, or grace and free will.

occupies Hubmaier's discussion. He presents his view of the power of the keys as the foundation on which this remission of sins is based, a view he has taught in his booklets *On the Sword* and *On the Christian Ban*.[64] There is however one very significant difference between Hubmaier's previous teaching and his position in the *Apologia*. In *On the Christian Ban*, Hubmaier focuses on the change from the singular you *(dir)* to the plural you *(Ir)* stating that the plural "signifies the unity of the church."[65] The power of the keys to admit and to exclude is therefore used by the whole church as a gathered community. In the *Apologia* Hubmaier qualifies his previous statement, saying the "church then has the authority by Christ's command to forgive and remit the same sins through its priest and dispensers of the Word of God, as Christ promised such authority to the church."[66] Confession is seen as the approach of the penitent to receive the remission of sins, yet the dispensation of that remission is now located in a selected group within the church. This closely resembles the Catholic Church's view of confession and is another significant move away from Hubmaier's previous understanding of the church and soteriology.

The following thesis on the church (Thesis 17) sees Hubmaier develop this statement on the role of the priest or congregational leader in the church. Again speaking of the power of the keys he states that the authority, which Christ has given to the particular or daughter church, is now given over to its "chosen, established, and ordained minister and priest." "Now," he continues, "whoever hears and is obedient to the priest is also obedient to the particular church as the daughter; whoever is obedient to the daughter is obedient to the mother; whoever is obedient to the mother is obedient to her bridegroom and husband Christ Jesus; whoever is obedient to Christ Jesus is obedient to his heavenly Father, who is the source of all authority."[67] He refers to his works *On the Christian Ban, On Fraternal Admonition* and *A Christian Catechism*, where he has taught the distinction between the mother and the daughter church that differ, not in their authority, but only in that the daughter church may err. However, he nowhere in those works teaches obedience to the priest as being equivalent to obedience to Christ and to the Father.[68]

---

64. PY, 545–46; HS, 477. Cf. *On the Sword*, PY, 504–5; HS, 442; *On the Christian Ban*, PY, 411–13.

65. HS, 368.

66. PY, 412; HS, 368 cf. PY, 545; HS, 477.

67. PY, 547; HS, 478.

68. Pipkin and Yoder note Hubmaier's use of the term "priest" in this passage,

A further concession to his Catholic examiners is seen in the eighteenth thesis, "Of Virginity and Widowhood." He states the proposition on which he bases his new opinion as follows: "That human state is higher which is nearer to its original source." Virginity is thus higher than marriage, which is in turn higher than widowhood, although all of them are pleasing to God and honorable. To prove his case he cites the "clear testimony of Scripture," beginning with Matt 19:12 where Christ teaches concerning eunuchs. He comments on this verse that it shows "that those who keep their virginity do well, for virginity is much better and more beneficial to the kingdom of God than marriage and widowhood."[69]

He follows up this medieval exposition of the text from Matt 19 with Paul's teaching on celibacy from 1 Cor 7. He does not exegete at all these words of Paul. Rather, only a summary comment is given to the effect that the words teach the superiority of virginity over marriage. He claims that John teaches the same truth in Rev 14:4: "These are they who have never been defiled with women, for they are virgin. They follow the Lamb wherever he goes." Concerning widowhood, Hubmaier cites Paul's instructions to Timothy on the subject (1 Tim 5:3ff). It is inferred that a simple literal interpretation of the text is to be accepted, as Hubmaier adds no exposition of the passage. He refers his examiners to his booklets where he has frequently complained against those who desire to be good evangelicals, but mean by that carnal liberty. What he does not do is to refer them to his earliest writing where he proposes the theses, "To forbid marriage to priests and then to tolerate their carnal immorality is to free Barabbas and to kill Christ; To promise chastity in human strength is nothing other than to promise to fly over the seas without wings."[70] Thus, Hubmaier compromises another position which he held previously, and which he acted on when he married Elsbeth Hugline in Waldshut on January 13, 1525, before becoming an Anabaptist preacher.[71]

---

conceding that it "may be partially an adjustment to his Catholic judges." Though Hubmaier has used the term "priest" previously, nevertheless he has moved significantly away from the congregational view he had previously espoused back to a more hierarchical view. Though this is not a sacerdotal view, it does mirror the magisterial churches of Zwingli and Luther, where the authority of the priest over the congregation is established by magisterial authority.

69. *PY*, 548; *HS*, 479. Zwingli cites the same passage, arguing that celibacy is a gift of God given to a few people and not to all. It is therefore not a binding law for all priests, but only for those who can "receive it." Zwingli, *Petition of Eleven Priests*, 30–32.

70. *PY*, 34; *HS*, 74. *Eighteen Theses*, Nos. 15 and 16.

71. Bergsten, *Balthasar Hubmaier: Anabaptist Theologian*, 205–6.

Theses 19, "On Fasting," and 20, "On the Sabbath," had previously been briefly dealt with in this order by Hubmaier in his *A Christian Catechism* and *A Brief Apologia*.[72] In *A Brief Apologia*, fasting is defined as eating and drinking in moderation with thanksgiving, this statement being modified in *A Christian Catechism* with the addition of an allusion to 2 Sam 6:6. Moderation in food and drink is encouraged so that the "old Adam" is not overfed and becomes insolent, casting "the divine commands into the mud together with the stubborn oxen."[73]

The Scriptures Hubmaier cites in this thesis share only two texts with his previous statements, the 2 Samuel reference and a general reference to Acts 10, poorly chosen since Peter was not fasting when he received the vision of the clean and unclean animals but was waiting for food to be prepared (Acts 10:10). The Scripture references he cites in this thesis are all historical examples of prayer and fasting. It is this link to prayer that is the focus of his discussion. He states, "And if I were to give advice in these dangerous times, I would advise, and also do it myself, that one should fast often and hold general assemblies in prayer, that God may graciously turn his anger and wrath away from us and aid us to come again to peace in soul and body."[74] Using images of Gog and Maggog from Ezek 38–39 and Rev 20, he warns of impending doom from a foreign people, no doubt a reference to the Turkish threat, ever present in his day.[75]

Though maintaining that voluntary fasting and self-denial on all days are of value, in keeping with his previous views, he nevertheless asserts that choosing a "particular day" helps a person "be better fitted to pray." He then adds the significant statement, "Likewise, a king may also do so with his people and particular church"; that is, the king has authority to set aside particular days on which all his subjects must fast.[76] In the theses on confession, the church, and virginity Hubmaier has made concessions that compromised the congregational basis of his ecclesiology. In this thesis, he compromises his view of the church's independence from temporal authority in all matters to do with the salvation of people. This indicates

---

72. *PY*, 356–57; *HS*, 318 cf. *PY*, 299; *HS*, 273–74.

73. Hubmaier provides the 2 Sam 6 reference in this thesis on fasting. *PY*, 550; *HS*, 481.

74. *PY*, 550; *HS*, 481.

75. Interestingly Hubmaier provides a series of references (Wis 3; Isa 54:1; 2:19f; Hos 10:8) that could all have been included in one reference to Luke 23:29–30. In fact, Hubmaier uses the words from Luke 23: 29–30 but does not supply the reference.

76. *PY*, 549; *HS*, 481.

a move away from congregationalism toward the magisterial form of the church.

The move from the general position that all days are alike for the Christian to that of a particular day is significant, as is again demonstrated in the twentieth thesis "On the Sabbath." Hubmaier proposed the first view in his *A Brief Apologia* and *A Christian Catechism,* but now adopts the latter view. "Although to a Christian every day is a Sabbath Day, in that he should rest from sinning, Sunday is especially mentioned in Scripture as being the Lord's Day."[77] That God established the Sabbath is obvious from Scripture when simply understood for the texts are clear (Gen 1, 2; Exod 2:8–11, and the parallel reading in Deut 5:14). The change from Sabbath to Sunday is accounted for by reference to Josh 10:12–13. The sun and moon stood still for Joshua for twenty-four hours until the enemies of Israel were defeated. In Jesus this type is fulfilled. When Christ, our Joshua, had overcome his enemies and ascended into heaven, the Sabbath was moved forward twenty-four hours. Typology has been an increasingly familiar method of interpretation in Hubmaier's hermeneutic during the later stages of his writings from Nikolsburg, and continues to appear in this final writing.

Concerning the works of the Sabbath, Hubmaier cites the example of Christ and Paul, "to rest in God, to preach his Word, to read, hear, prayer, consider the hour to be reconciled to God and to perform deeds of mercy towards one's neighbor."[78] While accepting some holidays, such as Christmas, Easter and Pentecost, Hubmaier reiterates his thesis "that feast days are not to be multiplied," a position he defended twenty years before at Freiburg during his student days.

Concerning food (Thesis 21), Hubmaier cites Rom 14:20 as a cautionary note. While all food may be eaten in moderation and with thankfulness, a Christian should not eat anything that would cause another to stumble. While Hubmaier does not make this qualification in his *A Christian Catechism,* he does state it plainly in his *Form for Water Baptism.*

Concerning forbearance he states this rule:

> In those things which have to do with human practices, such as eating meat or not eating meat, holding or not holding holidays etc., one may well forbear and do or admit something for the sake of the weak, but only for a time until our neighbor is better instructed in the Word of God, and so that Christian freedom

---

77. *PY,* 551, cf. 299, 357; *HS,* 482, cf. 274, 319.
78. *PY,* 552; *HS,* 483.

> should not be made into a new human law. But in true doctrine and in Christian deeds, one must freely proclaim and do what God has commanded us and not otherwise, and trust again to the Word of God for its efficacy.[79]

It could be understood from this rule that Hubmaier, while appearing to make concessions to his Catholic examiners, is at least in his own mind only forbearing until they be taught differently from the Word of God. This is the case in respect to his articles on food, fasting, and the Sabbath, yet the case is different with respect to "true doctrine." In Theses 25 and 26 on baptism and the Lord's Supper, which are central to Hubmaier's position as an Anabaptist, he proposes a "postponement" until the next Christian council is assembled and can deal with the two theses in question. If Ferdinand is not willing to wait until then, they are to be examined by the King, his council, and universities.[80] Hubmaier has withdrawn from his stated belief in the power and efficacy of the Word of God, which he encouraged other timid preachers to believe in, and to preach the truth without any other consideration than being obedient to the revealed commands of God.[81]

In this thesis on food, Hubmaier again slips in his polemic against those who consider themselves "truly evangelical," those who "seek their gospel alone in eating meat and taking wives," citing his opinion against such people from his booklet *On the Christian Ban*.[82]

The power of the Word of God is introduced in Hubmaier's discussion of the Ten Commandments. As he has argued consistently in his works from the Second Zurich Disputation through to his booklet *On the Sword*, obedience to the commands of God is necessary if people are to be saved. In his books on free will, he made the point that once the command of God is heard, then ability to do what is commanded is given. He reiterates that position in this thesis.[83] He maintains that it is possible to

---

79. *PY*, 391; *HS*, 351.

80. *PY*, 557–58; *HS*, 487–88.

81. Immediately prior to Hubmaier adopting an Anabaptist theology and practice, he had written in his *An Earnest Christian Appeal* that he regretted having not preached the whole truth as he had known it for some two years previously, in order to spare the weak in faith. *PY*, 46; *HS*, 83. A few months later, he wrote to Oecolampad declaring that the time was right to declare the whole truth publicly. *PY*, 69.

82. *On the Christian Ban* contains a polemical piece against Catholic Church authorities. *PY*, 422f; *HS*, 376. He refers to "evangelicals" in *On Fraternal Admonition*, *PY*, 375f; *HS*, 340, and *Freedom of the Will I*, *PY*, 427–29; *HS*, 381.

83. *PY*, 555; *HS*, 485.

do all that God commands through the power of the Word of God. By way of comparison, the words of human beings do not have strength in them to accomplish what they command, as for example in the contest between Moses and the magicians of Pharaoh, Exod 8. He also presents Christ's words to the man beside the pool at Bethesda, John 5:8. The man received strength and the power to stand on the authority of Christ's words, "Rise, take up your bed and walk." As he believed and desired, so it happened.[84] Though the thesis refers to the Ten Commandments, Hubmaier has a much broader view of the commandments of God. Previously he had identified the commands and teaching of Christ with the commandments of God. In this thesis that identification is absent, and a more specific Old Testament view of the commandments is presented.

His treatment of "the ban" (Thesis 23) is dealt with briefly, as Hubmaier directs those who would seek to know more of his teaching to his specific work *On the Christian Ban*. He presents without comment a series of Scripture texts, Matt 18:15–18; 1 Cor 5; 2 Cor 2; 1 Tim 1:20; 2 Thess 3:6; Titus 3:10; 2 John 10, all of which he uses in *On the Christian Ban*.[85] The ban has been instituted by Christ, and Hubmaier claims that Christ speaks through these Scriptures. He summarizes his opinion of the ban in the statement, "without the key of the ban the church cannot remain upright."[86] Hubmaier's opinion of the ban had increased over the period of his time in Nikolsburg. In his *Twelve Articles* the focus was on baptism and the Lord's Supper, but by the time he wrote *On Fraternal Admonition* the practice of admonition and the ban are as essential to the church as baptism and the Lord's Supper.[87]

Thesis 24, "On the Intercession of the Saints," is very short. Yet in the brevity of this thesis Hubmaier again manages to adapt his previous statements on the role of the saints as intercessors so that it is more acceptable to his Catholic questioners. Previously, Hubmaier had stressed the sole role of Christ as mediator and intercessor. Now, he uses the concept of the unity of those who are in heaven with Christ to suggest that as Christ intercedes for those on earth, the saints who are members of his body and

---

84. *PY*, 554; *HS*, 484. Hubmaier had used this reference to John 5:8 in *Freedom of the Will II* (*PY*, 465; *HS*, 411), but he has not "always and everywhere" used this text as he claims in his Kreuzenstein *Apologia* (*PY*, 554; *HS*, 484). He also introduces some new texts to support his argument, Deut 27:26; Prov 7:1–3; 1 John 2:4; 2 Kgs 22:13.

85. *PY*, 555; *HS*, 485–86 cf. *PY*, 420–23; *HS*, 374–76.

86. *PY*, 556; *HS*, 486.

87. *Twelve Articles*, *PY*, 239; *HS*, 219. Cf. *On Fraternal Admonition*, *PY*, 384f; *HS*, 346.

at one with his will intercede along with him.[88] Hubmaier does maintain his previously stated position that people should not call on the saints for help and salvation, adding Rom 8:34 to references cited in his *A Christian Catechism* (Matt 11; 1 Tim 2:5; 1 John 2:1).[89]

In Theses 25 and 26 Hubmaier discusses baptism and the Lord's Supper together. He begins by raising the difference that existed over these two doctrines between himself and Hut. What he does not make clear is the content of the difference. Werner O. Packull has noted the influence of Hut on several of Hubmaier's followers, particularly in the light of the debate between the two men. Packull indicates that the disagreement over the Lord's Supper centered on Hut's "cross mysticism" interpretation of the Supper. For Hut, and later his follower Hans Schlaffer, the Lord's Supper is understood as "commemorating and celebrating the members" oneness with their head in suffering."[90]

Hubmaier, on the other hand, insists that the Lord's Supper is a public confession of the pledge of love the members of the body of Christ make to one another, demonstrated primarily in works of brotherly love as well as in sharing in the sufferings of Christ for the sake of one's neighbor and the gospel. Hubmaier also maintains that Christians will suffer, since they are required to take up the cross of Christ and follow in the path he walked.[91]

With regard to baptism, Hut linked baptism with his eschatological views. Baptism was the seal that marked out the 144,000 mentioned in Rev 7:1ff.[92] It is highly probable that Hubmaier objected to the eschatological connections that Hut made between baptism and the Lord's Supper, and the pending day of judgment that would see Christians rise up against the government.[93] These considerations led Hubmaier to declare that the teachings of the two men were "as far apart as heaven and hell, east and west, Christ and Belial."[94]

Hubmaier prefaces his short statements on baptism and the Lord's Supper with the remark, "I am convinced and powerfully compelled in my conscience that I will stand by what I have written in my books on

---

88. *PY*, 556, cf. 357, 299; *HS*, 486 cf. 319 273.
89. He deletes his *A Christian Catechism* references to John 2:5, 10:9; 14:6.
90. Packull, *Mysticism*, 114.
91. *PY*, 560, *HS*, 489-90.
92. Packull, *Mysticism*, 81.
93. *PY*, 560, *HS*, 490.
94. *PY*, 557, *HS*, 487.

these two points."[95] In these comments he introduces no modification of his earlier position on these two topics. The concession he does make has been noted earlier, a concession to forebear preaching on these matters until a church council has decided and pronounced on them. He does try and qualify this concession by insisting that any decision must be made according to the Scriptures.

The final Thesis, "On Government," sees Hubmaier present his view of temporal authority in keeping with his statements on the issue as presented in *On the Sword*. He begins with the thesis that people are to be obedient to government "in everything that is not contrary to God." He later clarifies his meaning by noting that people owe obedience to temporal authorities with all temporal things, but that the soul belongs to God.[96] He cites the familiar texts that refer to government, Rom 13:1ff; 1 Pet 2:13-17, Titus 3:1; 1 Tim 2:1f. However, on this occasion he does not begin with his references to Genesis as he did in *On the Sword*, thus avoiding the more complex justification of authority by referring to the continuation of sin in the believer and the establishment of divine order in the world.

As in the preceding theses on baptism and the Lord's Supper, Hubmaier distances himself from Hut, who he claims has by his teaching on those themes provoked "conspiracy and sedition."[97] This was the very charge that the Austrians were leveling at Hubmaier, for in their view he had provoked rebellion in Waldshut by preaching his doctrine on baptism and the Lord's Supper.

Hubmaier concludes his *Apologia* with an appeal to Ferdinand for mercy and pardon, declaring that he would from then on conduct himself "in such a way that your Royal Highness will be pleased, and will direct the people with great earnestness and high zeal to worship, to the fear of God and obedience, in whatever place I am appointed to."[98] It is doubtful that Hubmaier really thought it possible that Ferdinand would pardon him and appoint him to a parish in his domains.

---

95. *PY*, 556, *HS*, 486-87.
96. *PY*, 558-59, *HS*, 488-89.
97. *PY*, 560, *HS*, 490.
98. *PY*, 561, *HS*, 490.

SUMMARY OF WRITINGS FROM JANUARY TO MARCH 1528

Hubmaier thus presented his final confession of faith, a confession that saw him make concessions to his Catholic inquisitors, but only in those areas he considered "human practices." Theologically he did not make concessions on the three fundamental doctrines of baptism, the Lord's Supper, and the ban, though pragmatically he agreed to defer preaching on these topics until after a decision had been made by either a church council or the universities.[99]

Of greater significance are his concessions in ecclesiology, specifically the removal of the power of the keys; that is, the forgiveness of sins, from the gathered church to an elite group of priests and preachers of the Word of God.

Hermeneutically, the trend towards older medieval methods of interpretation and presuppositions continues, as does the use of typology. There is also a continuation of the importance of the Old Testament as a primary source of references independent of the sayings of Christ. Genesis again dominates the count, nineteen of the eighty-four Old Testament references, followed by Isaiah (twelve), Deuteronomy and Psalms (eight each), and Jeremiah (six). With the discussion of eschatology taking a prominent place Daniel is well represented with five references. Hubmaier uses the Apocrypha five times in this work and the familiar reference to Eccl 15:14 is used to support free will. The other references provide examples of prayer and the need to pray (The Prayer of Azariah, which occurs in the Apocryphal version of Dan 3, The Prayer of Manasseh, and a general reference to the Wisdom of Solomon), or to the need to fear God (Eccl 2:1, 16), or to the declaration that the barren are blessed on the last day (Wis 3:13), a text discussed above.

With regard to the New Testament, Hubmaier reverts to using Matthew most often, fifty-two of the 231 New Testament references, quotations

---

99. Williams rejects the view that Hubmaier's concessions were mere expediency. Rather, it "was in keeping with his conviction that the universally operative Holy Spirit, which, according to his trichotomous scheme, moved freely in each redeemed person, would operate most effectively in a universal council where the divisiveness and partiality of fleshly wills could be offset by the dynamic presence of the Spirit of God to impart clarity and strength to their collectivity of the spirit-wills and psychic preferences." Williams, *The Radical Reformation*, 1992, 338. What Williams does not note is Hubmaier's following concession in which he will allow himself to be examined by Ferdinand, his council, or universities. This would make Williams's contention about a universal council difficult to sustain.

and allusions. Luke follows with thirty-one references, closely followed by John (twenty-six) and Romans (twenty-three). Only Acts (fifteen), Mark (thirteen) and 1 Corinthians (ten) have ten or more references.

Long sequences of texts are a noticeable feature of this work, as with his work *On the Sword*. There is also an increase in the citation of synoptic parallel references, and a decrease in the number of Old Testament texts being cited along with their New Testament occurrence. This is particularly noticeable when this work is compared with Hubmaier's pre-Nikolsburg works on baptism.

This final work from Hubmaier's pen does indicate a continuing movement away from the hermeneutic of the Swiss Brethren and the South German mysticism of Hut, back towards a more medieval hermeneutic that saw the literal sense of a text as only one of four valid interpretations that could be discovered in every text of Scripture. This trend is observable in Hubmaier's Nikolsburg writings, and is accelerated by his imprisonment and the desire to present his *Apologia* in ways that were the least likely to offend and most likely to receive a favorable reading.

That Hubmaier failed to receive mercy and pardon from the Catholic Austrian authorities is evidenced by his death. However, he did maintain a good conscience toward God concerning baptism and the Lord's Supper by maintaining his views on these crucial issues, urging the Emperor to "judge according to the Word of God."[100] In light of his refusal to budge on these items, the *Chronicle of the Hutterian Brethren* identify him as "Brother" Balthasar Hubmaier, and include him among their list of Anabaptist martyrs.[101]

---

100. *PY*, 558; *HS*, 488.

101. Hutterian Brethren, *Chronicle of the Hutterian Brethren*, 49.

9

Hubmaier's Hermeneutic: "Truth is Unkillable"

HAVING COMPLETED THE ANALYSIS of Hubmaier's works, it remains to draw together the various themes of his hermeneutic that have been identified. They will be used as headings in the following discussion.

A description of the development of Hubmaier's hermeneutic over the course of his career as an Anabaptist Reformer follows. Where pertinent, comparisons are drawn between Hubmaier on the one hand and the Swiss Brethren, Erasmus, Zwingli, and Luther on the other.

To conclude this work, an assessment of Hubmaier's hermeneutic with specific reference to the theme of the clarity of Scripture is undertaken. It is argued that in this regard Hubmaier more closely followed the Magisterial Reformers, such as Zwingli and Luther, than either the Swiss Brethren, Hans Denck, Hans Hut, or Erasmus.

SCRIPTURE

In common with the evangelical Reformers, Hubmaier holds to the formal principle of *sola scriptura*. Primarily, Scripture is considered to be the only authority by which matters of faith and practice in the church are to be judged. Other possible sources of authority, such as the church fathers, councils, decretals, and the tradition of the church, are to be accepted as authoritative only in so far as they can be demonstrated to agree with Scripture. Hubmaier maintains this opinion of the authority of Scripture consistently throughout his writings, varying it only in his final writing, the *Vienna Testimony*. Even in this final writing the concession he makes in agreeing to postpone his teaching on baptism and the Lord's Supper until the matter has been discussed by a General Council, or has been examined by representatives of Ferdinand of Austria, is qualified by the formal principle that the examination take place only according to Scripture.[1] Even in his extreme need to modify his position so that it would be favorably viewed by the Catholic Austrian authorities, Hubmaier continues to challenge them on this fundamental premise on which the work of all the Reformers was built.

Compared with Zwingli and Luther, Hubmaier has a broader view of the canon of Scripture. Whereas Zwingli and Luther both specify those books of Scripture they accept as canonical, specifically rejecting the Apocrypha, Hubmaier nowhere in his writings attempts this. In his earliest statements as a supporter of Zwingli he simply states that the Scriptures, both the Old and New Testaments, are canonized and sanctified by God.[2] At no time in the course of his later writings does he give cause to think that he has changed his view. His actual use of texts indicates that he considered the Apocrypha equally useful for determining doctrine and practices in the church. This attitude to the Apocrypha is made more discernible in his final work, the *Vienna Testimony*, though it is evident in other works across the whole period of his writings. In this attitude toward the Apocrypha, Hubmaier more closely mirrors the attitude of Erasmus, the Swiss Brethren, and the South German Anabaptists. Hubmaier's pattern of citing from Scripture generally follows that of Erasmus, giving priority to Matthew over John, though this trend is reversed in his writings on free will. Luther gives priority to the Pauline epistles and the gospel of John.

The relationship of the Old Testament to the New became a crucial matter of dispute between Zwingli and his successor Heinrich Bullinger on the one hand, and the Swiss Brethren on the other. For Zwingli and Bullinger Scripture is "flat"; the event of the incarnation does not dramatically alter the way the Old Testament is interpreted. For them, the principle of the one covenant dominates, allowing them to identify circumcision from the Old Testament with water baptism in the New. For the Swiss Brethren the incarnation is a vital turning point in world history and for the interpretation of the Old Testament in particular. The incarnate Christ, Jesus,

---

1. *PY* 558; *HS* 487.
2. *PY* 23.

comes to fulfill the law and establish a new covenant between himself and the church. The words and life of Jesus become determinative for doctrine and practice. Where there appears to be conflict between the two Testaments, such as in killing, taking oaths, and so on, the words of Jesus in the New Testament have priority over the Old Testament prophets.

In his earlier writings about baptism and the Lord's Supper, Hubmaier demonstrates his affinity with the views of the Swiss Brethren. He gives priority to the words of Christ by focusing on Christ's words of institution for both baptism and the Lord's Supper. He also adopts the principle that Christ's methodology of citing Old Testament texts gives those texts continuing validity, a method he insists must also be adopted by those who now read the Scriptures. His priority of the New Testament over the Old reaches its fullest expression in his writing against the preachers at Basel. There he insists that, since baptism is a New Testament ceremony, only a clear word from the New Testament is to be permitted in the discussion of that doctrine.[3]

However, this priority of the New Testament does not continue in Hubmaier's discussion of free will or the sword. By way of contrast, Hubmaier's understanding of the unity of Scripture, which he maintains is always present, comes to dominate and is effectively demonstrated by considering his use of Scripture texts. In his works on free will and the sword, the ratio between the Old and New Testament texts cited is reduced when compared with those of his earlier writings. In particular, Genesis becomes a prominent source of texts to establish his tripartite anthropology and the need for temporal authority in response to the entrance of sin into the world.

The unity of the Testaments is further demonstrated in Hubmaier's response to the challenge of those in the Nikolsburg church who reject his claim that it is within the Christian's power to do the works that God has commanded. He reemphasized the unity of the Scriptures by speaking of it in terms of the one marriage that spans both Testaments. This view of the one covenant is based on an altered emphasis in his Christology—he moves away from stressing the incarnation to recognizing the effective work of Christ in the promise of salvation in the Old Testament. The promise is not merely made by the Father in anticipation of the incarnation; the promise already contains the reality of forgiveness for those who believe the Word of God, for the Word of God is always powerful and

---

3. *PY* 288; *HS* 265.

effective to accomplish what it declares. That Word of God is Christ, the *logos*.

Thus, in regard to the unity of the Testaments Hubmaier initially demonstrated a similarity to the two evangelical Reformers, Luther and Zwingli, and to some degree to Erasmus. He then moved closer to the Swiss Brethren up to the end of 1526, when he began to move away from them again so that the distinction between the Testaments is no longer as great for Hubmaier as for the Swiss Brethren.

CLARITY OF SCRIPTURE

The clarity of Scripture is a crucial element in the hermeneutical debate of the Reformation. Scripture is considered clear and its true meaning easily understood, even by those who are not theologically educated. Although Hubmaier does not specifically discuss the clarity of Scripture, he nevertheless maintains a position closer to that of Zwingli and Luther compared to Erasmus. Particularly in his earlier writings, Hubmaier is constantly declaring that the Word of God is clear, pure, and simple. He is referring to the literal sense of Scripture that is made known to the reader and hearer of the Word of God through the Holy Spirit. This understanding of the Holy Spirit working with the proclaimed Word of God is close to Luther's understanding of the interrelation of the Word of God and the Holy Spirit. Zwingli places more stress on the independence of the Spirit from the external and material word, a position to which Denck and Hut approximate. Erasmus holds to the work of the Spirit being only partial; the Spirit does not wholly enlighten nor does the Spirit enlighten all in the same way.

Initially, Hubmaier demonstrates a great reserve toward any interpretation based on figures, metaphors, similes, parables, and allegories, particularly in his debate with Zwingli over baptism. Zwingli is therefore closer to Erasmus at this point than is Hubmaier, for Zwingli follows more closely Erasmus's advice concerning the careful study of the figures of speech as a tool for interpreting obscure texts. For Hubmaier, the baptismal texts are not obscure and therefore there is no need to resort to artificial interpretations based on synecdoche, similes, and figures.

However, for Hubmaier, like all the Reformers, there are obscure or dark passages of the Scriptures. One such group of texts relates to the hidden will of God. Interpretation of these texts requires a different form of exegesis from his previous method. Whereas previously the principle that the clearer text illuminates the darker text meant that a clearer or fuller text provided a grammatically based explanation of the darker text, now two seemingly contradictory texts are brought together and the apparent paradox is resolved by designating the texts to different categories. Both texts are held to be true, since all Scripture is inspired by the one Spirit. The resolution is arrived at by recognizing that some texts apply to the omnipotence of God and his absolute will, while others apply to the ordained will of God. Scripture is still described in terms of its clarity and the onus is on the interpreter correctly dividing Scripture, so that error is avoided.

For Luther the thesis of the clarity of Scripture can never be compromised. Since the Holy Spirit brings illumination and the mysteries of God are now fully revealed in Christ, the only possible obscurity in Scripture is due to human ignorance of grammar and vocabulary. Even that is no hindrance to understanding the full revelation of God, for passages that are dark can be interpreted by placing them beside those parts of Scripture where the same theme is dealt with and the interpretation is certain. It is not Scripture that is obscure, as Erasmus maintains, rather God has continued to keep himself in his omnipotence veiled from us. However, all that God reveals to us in Scripture is clear.

For Erasmus, the clarity of Scripture is only partial, and is only certain in the revelation of what the message of the gospel is. By that, Erasmus means that all people may know what God expects of them in the way they are to live. For Erasmus, God has made the gospel abundantly clear in the incarnation. In Christ, God is revealed as limiting his omnipotence and acting only out of goodness and love. Through the life and teaching of Christ, God demonstrates all that is to be done by the Christian. This incarnate Christ is to be encountered in reading Scripture. However, there are issues relating to those doctrines—such as omnipotence, predestination, and foreknowledge—that still remain dark and obscure, despite God having spoken of them in Scripture. The illumination of the Spirit is not sufficient to ensure certainty. Neither can human wisdom combined with spiritual wisdom attain certainty in these matters, as the mixed opinions of the church fathers on these matters demonstrate. Therefore, it is best not to make assertions, but in moderation to allow a difference of opinion as long as it does not contradict the teaching of the church.

Neither Luther nor Zwingli is willing to tolerate Erasmus's opinion. For Zwingli, the Spirit's illumination is complete and lasting in those who believe. By their possession of the Spirit they are assured that they have believed correctly, for the truth is plain and there can be no error for those with the Spirit. Those who do not agree with Zwingli thereby demonstrate that they do not have the Spirit and are therefore excluded from salvation. Luther speaks of the internal and external clarity of the Word of God: the internal clarity is produced by the illumination of the Spirit that gives believers the assurance that they have believed correctly; the external clarity is tied to the office of the preacher of the Word of God. The preacher is not only assured of the certainty of his own faith but is able to test the orthodoxy of all other teaching and to present the truth of the gospel to others. Certainty and truth dominate the views of Luther and Zwingli, as compared to Erasmus's more circumspect desire for moderation so as to avoid schism and violence.

Hubmaier is closer to Zwingli and Luther in this regard, since for him the truth is of paramount importance, *"Die wahrheit ist untödlich."* He demonstrates this in his debate with the preachers at Basel, where he insists that truth, not faith and love, must determine interpretation of the Scriptures.

Initially, Hubmaier emphasized the role of the congregation in determining the correct interpretation of Scripture. There is a role for those who are educated in theology, but it is not to dictate the correct understanding of Scripture. Similarly, there is a place for the study of the biblical languages in helping to interpret the darker passages of Scripture. Nevertheless, the fundamental innovation of Hubmaier's early hermeneutic that cannot be overlooked is the aspect of congregational participation in the determination of the correct understanding of Scripture. That Hubmaier maintained his position on this point into his first six months in Nikolsburg is demonstrated by his *Form for Christ's Supper,* where there is time specifically set aside for the congregation publicly to enquire and seek the correct understanding of Scripture after the preacher has expounded the text of the day.[4] However, there is also in these writings a growing emphasis on the role of the preacher as the central figure in the life of the congregation and in the interpretation of Scripture.

This attitude to the dominant role of the preacher became practically evident in Hubmaier's handling of the disputation with Hut. It was not the congregation that determined the correct understanding of Scripture. Instead, Hubmaier with his supporters dictated their views to Hut and his supporters, insisting that they adopt Hubmaier's opinion. On this occasion, the Lords of Liechtenstein provided the disciplinary force, imprisoning Hut overnight, rather than the church being involved in the

---

4. *PY* 395; *HS* 356.

proceedings as it should have been if Hubmaier had followed his own formula for discipline within the church. One consequence of the treatment of Hut during and after the debate was Hubmaier's appearance before the gathered church where he gave an account for his actions.[5] Later, in his *Vienna Testimony*, Hubmaier formally declared that the role of discipline resided in those who were priests and preachers of the Word.

In this respect, Hubmaier came to approximate toward a more magisterial understanding of the interpretation of the Scriptures; that is, correct interpretation resides in those who are appointed to the task of preaching. This had been Zwingli's response to the challenge of the Anabaptists in Zurich. Not only had he restricted the interpretation of the Scriptures to those who were duly appointed by the City Council to the office of preacher, but also those who held that office were to be instructed in the biblical languages. Without the biblical languages Zwingli insisted that people could not correctly understand Scripture. He also, through the City Council, had the private reading and exposition of Scripture suspended, and instituted his prophecy school, where the leading preachers of Zurich expounded the text of Scripture in the three biblical languages, followed by a German summary. Luther followed a similar course of action in Wittenberg. Preachers were to be authorized by the University of Wittenberg before they could preach the Word of God. Melchior Hoffman is an example of one who went to a great deal of trouble to obtain such a letter of authorization that then allowed him to preach in Silesia.[6]

The clarity of the Scriptures also involved the issue of translations into the vernacular. Erasmus had urged such translations to be made, convinced that the most uneducated people could encounter the living Christ in the Scripture and be changed as a result. Both Zwingli and Luther undertook translations of the Bible into the vernacular of their respective regions, and both encouraged the reading of Scripture. However, unlike Erasmus, the reading of Scripture was to provide confirmation of the truth proclaimed through the preached Word of God. It was the preached Word of God, free from the letter of the text, that the Holy Spirit used to bring inner illumination to people. Though the preached Word is based on the written word and cannot be independent of it, Hubmaier and Denck do not place the same emphasis on the Spirit working through the written word. Hubmaier follows Zwingli and Luther in identifying the action of the Spirit most closely with the proclaimed Word of God. Denck on the

---

5. Bergsten, *Balthasar Hubmaier: Anabaptist Theologian*, 361.
6. Deppermann, *Melchior Hoffman*, 60.

other hand goes so far as to separate the illumination of the Spirit from the written word, though the written word is to be retained as a witness against those who have once been illuminated by the Spirit and later deny the obedience they owe to Christ.

Methodologically Hubmaier, like Zwingli, Luther, the Swiss Brethren, and the South German Anabaptists, is indebted to Erasmus. Scripture is understood to interpret Scripture. The clear text interprets the darker text; texts on a particular theme are to be gathered together to illuminate the darker text on the same theme; the words that proceed and follow must be considered, as must the wider context of a text. The basic grammatical and historical methodology that Erasmus outlined in his *Paraclesis* is to be observed in Hubmaier as it is in Luther and Zwingli. There is also in Hubmaier a stronger association with Erasmus because of his shared tripartite anthropology. This leads to a greater use of figurative interpretation in his later writings from Nikolsburg, though Hubmaier has always retained some allegorical and tropological interpretation. As was noted above, Hubmaier does not totally follow Erasmus's method for resolving the debate on free will. He does not begin with the premise that there are obscure passages of Scripture that cannot be interpreted; rather he maintains that all the passages of Scripture declare the truth, and interpretation involves correctly dividing the Scriptures into passages that relate to distinct themes. Though Erasmus also used the division of Scripture into different categories, he does not believe that the final truth on matters relating to God's "hidden will" can be known. Truth is not certain, only what God has shown us in Christ is; that is, matters of love and faith. Hubmaier insists that truth does matter, and has priority over faith and love when these two principles are invoked to interpret Scripture against its clear sense in order to maintain the outward unity of the church and civil peace.

THE COMMANDS OF GOD AND FORBEARANCE

Fundamental to Hubmaier's hermeneutic is his proposition that the Christian is to be obedient to the commands of God. What God commands to be done is considered good, because God himself is good. It is implicitly understood that the Christian can fulfill what God commands through the enabling work of the Spirit. This view becomes explicit in the debate over free will. Hubmaier is not concerned, as is Erasmus, to argue that people do good works so that God is obligated to extend to them his grace. Rather, Hubmaier insists on the prior action of God in both prevenient grace and a special new grace made available through the proclaimed Word of God. People cooperate with God, and are held responsible for using or not using the enabling power of God to fulfill the commands to do good that God has given in Scripture.

Hubmaier also focuses on the negative of this thesis, declaring that all those things that God has not commanded are forbidden to the Christian. In this he agrees with Zwingli's use of the same proposition at the First Zurich Disputation, where it was used to attack the Roman Catholic view of purgatory. In this Hubmaier differs from Luther, and the later Zwingli, both of whom support the view that what is not forbidden in Scripture is allowable. This latter proposition became a focal point in the debate between Hubmaier and Zwingli over infant baptism. Hubmaier argued that there is no clear word commanding baptism of infants, while there is a clear command to baptize believers, therefore baptizing infants was forbidden. Zwingli insisted that there was no word forbidding baptism of infants and it was therefore permissible. Hubmaier accused Zwingli of inconsistency on this point. Zwingli replied that water baptism had nothing to do with salvation, as this was a spiritual matter and dependent on faith alone. Water baptism was therefore in Zwingli's estimation *adiaphora*. It was an external material sign that did not affect salvation and could therefore be decided according to the rule of faith and love. In practice that meant that the unity and peace of the community of Zurich were best served by continuing the practice of infant baptism.

For Hubmaier, baptism with water had been instituted by Christ himself with serious words of command and these could not be ignored. It was therefore not a matter of indifference, but affected the honor of God. Hubmaier also insisted that internal faith alone was not enough for salvation. According to Rom 10:10 it must be accompanied by an oral public declaration of that faith. Faith may justify, but only when linked to oral confession of that faith does salvation follow.

Hubmaier did add a qualification to this thesis concerning the commands of God: those things that are not commanded are forbidden in matters of the honor of God and the salvation of souls. This qualification had been drawn from him by Zwingli during their debate, as Zwingli had shown that without the qualification the rule could be applied with absurd consequences. What Hubmaier does not do is to define just what matters he considers are incorporated in this qualification. Later, in *A Form for Water Baptism*, he proposes a rule on forbearance that does describe those things that may be considered matters of indifference, at least until people have been better instructed in the Word of God. He writes: "In those things which have to do with human practices, such as eating meat or not eating meat, holding or not holding holidays, etc., one may well forbear and do or admit something for the sake of the weak, but only for a time until our neighbor is better instructed in the Word of God, and so that Christian freedom should not be made into a new human law."[7] However, he holds that in matters of true doctrine and Christian deeds these must be proclaimed, trusting in the efficacy of the Word of God to accomplish its purpose. It is better for people to fall from the Word of God than for the Word of God to fall; better that the "Word of truth" be proclaimed and those offended by it fall away than to compromise the truth.

Earlier, in his *Letter to Oecolampad* (January 16, 1525), Hubmaier had described his own practice of continuing to baptize infants because of the weakness of faith of the parents, while continuing to proclaim the truth of the Word of God on the matter.[8] In his *Vienna Testimony*, Hubmaier acts on the first part of his rule, allowing the continuing practice of fasting and special holidays, though with the added provision that the civil authority has the right to direct the church in these matters. Hubmaier cautiously suggests a moratorium on these matters and the crucial issues of the Lord's Supper and baptism until the church at a General Council has made a final declaration on all these things.[9]

However, in his earlier work *On the Christian Baptism*, Hubmaier argues strongly against forbearance, declaring that to preach only the gospel automatically excluded forbearance concerning "human teachings, laws, dreams, and legends."[10] To demonstrate his meaning he lists examples of those things that would be allowable if the rule of allowing what is not expressly forbidden were to be followed: baptizing animals; circumcising girls; holding vigils for the dead; calling wooden idols the saints; taking infants to the Lord's Supper; blessing palm branches, herbs, salt, butterfat, and water; and selling the Mass as a sacrifice. These issues are not considered matters of indifference, for he adds, "Realize what a nice double popery we would set up again if it were acceptable to juggle outside the Word of God in those matters which concern God and the souls."[11] Only Scripture is to direct the preaching and life of the Christian.

7. *PY* 391; *HS* 351.
8. *PY* 72.
9. *PY* 549–53, 557–58; *HS* 480–83, 487–88.
10. *PY* 136; *HS* 151–52.
11. *PY* 136; *HS* 152.

Those who follow the rule of Luther and Zwingli add to Scripture and are therefore under the curse God prescribed for such destroyers of his Word.

Hubmaier thus demonstrated in his attitude to forbearance a pattern of development that is mirrored in other aspects of his theology. He begins his Reformation work in close harmony with Zwingli's approach, and at times Luther's and Erasmus's as well. During his time as an Anabaptist writer in Waldshut he moves closer to the more urgent demand for reform, ignoring the argument of forbearance for those weak in faith, and demanding the proclamation of the gospel as it is found in the words of Scripture alone. After some time in Nikolsburg, Hubmaier encounters challenges to his teaching from two directions. Firstly, there are those who urge a new legalism that has grown out of their literal interpretation of Scripture and the priority of the Words of Christ. Forbearance is overridden; a new law of conformity is expected of those who are within the church. To this new legalism, Hubmaier responds by reintroducing the idea of forbearance in those things that are human teachings. He then extends the determination of these human teachings to the civil authorities in a final compromise in his last writing. Secondly, there are the antinomians. Hubmaier charges them with no longer practicing brotherly love on the basis of an erroneous understanding of the doctrine of free will.

CHRISTOLOGY

It is also in the writings from his time in Nikolsburg that we see Hubmaier dramatically alter his Christology, which in turn affects his hermeneutic. This is particularly clear in his discussions of the Creed relating to the *descensus*. In his Nikolsburg works written before 1527, Hubmaier maintains that Christ's redemptive work remains incomplete for the patriarchs until after the incarnation and death of Christ. The patriarchs only had the comforting promise of the gospel until Christ in the Spirit brought them the good news of the gospel and effected forgiveness of sins. However, with his writings on free will this position changes so that the patriarchs already have in the promise what the church has in the gospel. The effective work of Christ is thus extrapolated into the past, breaking the sequential pattern Hubmaier has previously maintained regarding the work of Christ and salvation.

Previously, Hubmaier had described the process of salvation in a modified economic Trinitarian manner. According to this model the Father begins the process with the promise of the seed in Gen 3, which is repeated to Abraham, Isaac, Jacob, and David. The second stage when the Son has authority begins when the promise is fulfilled in the incarnation. There Christ offers forgiveness of sins to those who believe him and obediently follow his commands. The third period begins at the ascension when the authority to forgive sins is passed to the church, which represents Christ during his bodily absence. However, it is the Holy Spirit working through the Word of God, proclaimed and read, who brings about faith and salvation. This faith and obedience to the earnest command of Christ finds expression in water baptism and the Lord's Supper. Hubmaier thus separated the Spirit from the bodily presence of Christ on earth. This allowed him to maintain a theology of the Lord's Supper that did not require the bodily presence of Christ nor to have Christ present to accomplish the work of salvation. The inner work of rebirth is the work of the Spirit, while the declaration of the forgiveness of sins through the proclamation of the gospel is the work of the church that represents Christ during his bodily absence.[12]

However, when the redemptive work of Christ is viewed as being effective in the Old Testament, this economic Trinitarian view is no longer tenable. Instead, Hubmaier comes closer to the position of Luther and Zwingli, who see Christ effecting salvation in all the Scriptures through the work of the Spirit.

GOVERNMENT

With regard to the question of government, Hubmaier always held an independent view to that of the Swiss Brethren and the South German Anabaptists Denck and Hut. In his early writings, he does not specify in detail his reasons for supporting government as God ordained, nor why a Christian can be a magistrate. He undertakes this task specifically against those he calls Anabaptist brothers during his final months in Nikolsburg. The basis of his argument is the continuation of sin in the life of the believer. The healing of the wounded soul and the freeing of the spirit in people after the Holy Spirit has brought enlightenment does not solve the problem of sin completely, as the flesh remains always willing and capable of sin. To deal with this problem of sin God has ordained fraternal admonition and the ban in the church. The world remains under the dominion of Satan and the effect of sin. To deal with the evil that results from sin in the world God has ordained civil authority. The Christian who is called upon

12. Rempel, "Christology and the Lord's Supper," 74–75.

by duly authorized civil powers is in a better position to administer justice than those who are not believers. John D. Rempel notes that the dualism in Anabaptism is between the church and the world, and not between Spirit and matter as for the other evangelical Reformers. For the Anabaptists the church becomes the point of contact between Spirit and matter.[13]

It is precisely at this point that Hubmaier's understanding of the church differs from the Swiss Brethren. Whereas the Swiss Brethren can dismiss magistracy, oaths, and killing because these are outside the perfection of Christ that is the church visibly present on earth, Hubmaier denies that the church represents the perfection of Christ on earth. The individual believer knows that perfection is located in Christ and that Christ is not on earth. Christ in his perfection is seated at the right hand of the Father. While on earth the individual and the church both remain subject to error and outside the perfection of Christ that will come only with the return of Christ. Hubmaier also consistently maintains that the authority of the church to guarantee forgiveness of sins through the proclaimed gospel depends on the physical absence of Christ. It is not the work of the Spirit separating the church from the world that occupies Hubmaier, rather it is the ongoing impact of sin in both the believer and the world.

This focus on sin is more akin to the views of Luther and Zwingli. Unlike them, however, Hubmaier maintains that the preached Word of God is necessarily effective on those who hear it. Through the preached Word the Holy Spirit makes the letter of the law alive, enlightens the soul, bringing knowledge of sin and the total dependence on God. Those who hear the preached Word are thus enabled to recognize the truth of the gospel and the opportunity to respond to the offer of forgiveness. The hearers are responsible before God for the acceptance or rejection of the offer, but not the faith to believe, since faith is a work of God. Luther and Zwingli differ in their assessments of the power of the Word of God to necessarily effect salvation in the hearer. For Zwingli, this places too much stress on a material object, thus diminishing his view that salvation is entirely dependent on the Spirit free from all material substances. For Luther, to tie salvation to the proclaimed Word of God, even with the Spirit responsible for the process of salvation, is to limit God's omnipotence.

---

13. Ibid., 18.

ANTHROPOLOGY

Underlying Hubmaier's position on the magistracy is his tripartite anthropology that presupposes human beings are composed of three parts; body, soul, and spirit. Though this is a view of humanity that Erasmus does sometimes express, it is not his dominant view. Erasmus prefers the Platonic twofold distinction of body and spirit as this corresponds more closely with his preferred two senses in Scripture, letter, and spirit. Luther rejects any division of people into two or three natures, and deals with the person as a whole. There is therefore in Luther's anthropology no part of a person that is not totally affected by the fall, no undamaged image of God remaining in humanity that might "do that which is in it," thereby obliging God to extend his grace to it. Zwingli holds to a twofold division in man: the body; and the inward man, or soul, or spirit, all these terms being used interchangeably. It is the soul that acts as the focus of God's saving work in people. Though the soul is the point of contact with people, it does not possess the ability to respond to God.[14] Hubmaier is thus closer to Zwingli than to Luther as regards his anthropology and the action of God through the Spirit to effect salvation. However, they differ markedly on the role of the Scripture in that process of salvation. On that matter Hubmaier is closer to Luther.

CONSCIENCE

A further aspect crucial to Hubmaier's hermeneutic is the role of conscience. Initially, conscience is spoken of by Hubmaier in terms of faith. Through the proclaimed Word the Spirit brings knowledge of sin and of grace in Christ. It also makes known the fact that through Christ the law has been fulfilled and that the believer has a gracious Father in heaven who forgives sins. This guarantee of forgiveness of sins brings peace and rest to the conscience of the believer.[15] Hubmaier maintains that this knowledge of a good conscience toward God is nothing but faith.[16] Through the action of conscience, believers know when they have transgressed the commands of God. Conscience thus plays a key role in recognizing if faith has been maintained, and whether a person is still within the church, outside of which there is no salvation.

14. Stephens, *Theology of Zwingli*, 145–46.
15. *PY* 116; *HS* 135.
16. *PY* 134; *HS* 150.

In his writings on free will, Hubmaier moves to a position where he identifies conscience with the image of God in people. It is linked to the spirit of a person and not the soul, so that even though human beings retain a part of the divine image, they are not able to recognize what is good or bad until the Spirit of God enlightens them in association with the preached Word. Hubmaier maintains that the spirit of human beings remains imprisoned and unable to affect people as a consequence of the fall. Conscience is therefore not a source of knowledge of good and evil in human beings as it is for Erasmus. In this way Hubmaier, like Luther and Zwingli, can reject the wisdom of the ancient philosophers as a second source of authority to supplement the Bible. Only in the pages of Scripture is knowledge of good and evil found, and that knowledge is made known only through the work of the Spirit.

LANGUAGES AND INTERPRETIVE METHOD

Like all other evangelical interpreters of the Bible in that period, Hubmaier attacks the method of interpretation used by the scholastic theologians. He employs the same attack on Zwingli, accusing him of introducing foreign glosses and "serpent questions," just as the scholastic theologians do, thus making dark what is clear and simple in the Word of God. However, like all the others in this period, he is not so displeased with the Scholastics' method as to avoid using it when it might help his cause. He quite freely uses syllogisms against Zwingli, and readily adopts a non-literal interpretation of texts. He extends the allegorical interpretation of salvation as described in the parable of the Good Samaritan over five writings, beginning with the *Summa* (1525) and culminating in *On Free Will 1* (1527). He frequently makes use of parables to reinforce a point that he has made from the exposition of a text, and increasingly in the writings of 1527 resorts to figurative interpretation of certain texts. There is also a marked increase in his use of typology in his last writing, a form of interpretation that is not seen during his period as an Anabaptist author, but is present prior to his public commitment to that position.

He is also prone to invoking axioms of dialectic in his debate with Zwingli, such as the proposition that the burden of proof lies with the affirming.[17] Dialectic remains a useful tool for interpretation but, like Erasmus, he prefers the simple meaning of Scripture drawn from those passages that are clear. In passages that are obscure or dark, the biblical

---

17. PY 184; HS 179.

languages are useful for interpretation, but the interpreter must beware that by using the biblical languages and dialectic they do not obscure that which is generally clear and plain.

Hubmaier consistently appeals to German vernacular translations of the Bible as presenting the clear and plain meaning of the text. His early statements appealing to German translations "fifty or one hundred years old"[18] is contrasted with Zwingli's appeal to Hebrew, Greek, and Latin translations. He accused Zwingli of creating a "false New Testament"[19] with his new German translation. On the very rare occasions when he cites Greek and Hebrew he is careful to provide German translations.[20] Not only does he consistently appeal to German translations, he consistently preaches in German to Germans so they might understand the clear, plain meaning of the Word of God.

For Hubmaier, the essence of the gospel read and preached in the vernacular is clear and plainly understood by all people, since the Spirit accompanies the Word to bring enlightenment and give understanding. Scripture should therefore be proclaimed and read in the vernacular for the benefit of all people.

ASSESSMENT

Walter Klaassen's assessment of Hubmaier's hermeneutic, though brief, does provide a useful base from which to begin. He notes Hubmaier's adherence to the principle of *sola scriptura*, suggesting that Hubmaier was more radical than Luther and Zwingli in his rejection of the church fathers, the prestige of contemporary theologians, tradition, or social order, if the truth of Scripture was thereby compromised. Klaassen identifies the limited role Hubmaier grants to scholarship, particularly to interpretations that rely on the biblical language. Hubmaier is convinced that scholars use linguistic tricks to confuse and hide the simple meaning of the text. Manifest reason is not specifically identified as an interpretive principle, but it remains part of Hubmaier's method. For Hubmaier, common sense allows only one interpretation of the most significant passages of Scripture. For example, common sense demands that children cannot believe or are able to receive instruction, and are therefore not to be baptized since faith follows hearing and understanding the gospel. Klaassen notes

18. *PY*, 80.
19. *PY*, 182.
20. *PY*, 429–30.

Balthasar Hubmaier and the Clarity of Scripture

Hubmaier's insistence on the consistent use of interpretive principles, particularly the principle that the command includes the prohibition of its opposite. Similarly, what is not commanded is forbidden in matters central to the Christian faith. Klaassen emphasizes that the role of obedience that Hubmaier demanded is required of believers with regard to the commands of God. Klaassen also identifies the principles that Scripture interprets Scripture; the clearer passages interpret the darker; and the preceding and following words provide a context that must be considered if the text is to be understood correctly. He also notes that, for Hubmaier, interpreting Scripture involves a willingness to admit that one does not know the answers to some questions; for example, are children not in need of salvation as they have not sinned? Hubmaier answers that he does not know, while the Swiss Brethren adopt the position that children do not need salvation.[21] Klaassen based his analysis of Hubmaier's hermeneutic primarily on the latter's baptismal writings. It is not surprising then that Hubmaier's hermeneutic appear very close to those of the Swiss Brethren, given Hubmaier's understanding of baptism was accepted by the Swiss Brethren. However, Klaassen also makes the point that Hubmaier's view of the church and the relationship of two Testaments is not identical to that of the Swiss Brethren. In fact, as has been shown above, Hubmaier's view of the church and its relationship to the world provides one of the fundamental differences in his hermeneutic presuppositions that allowed Hubmaier to maintain his support for a Christian magistracy throughout his whole career.

In his analysis, Rempel suggests that Hubmaier's pneumatology is the key to understanding not only his anthropology, ecclesiology, Christology, and theology of the sacraments, but also his whole theology.[22] While this insight has value, it suffers from the same limitations as Klaassen's assessment of Hubmaier; that is, it is based on a limited selection of sources in Hubmaier's corpus. Hubmaier does argue for a sequential work of the Trinity to bring about salvation in his baptismal and Lord's Supper writings, with the work of the Spirit occupying the central role after the bodily ascension of Christ. However, this is not Hubmaier's final word on the matter. As was noted above, Hubmaier changes his Christology in his writing on free will, so that the sequential nature of God's saving acts no longer dominates. In these writings on free will, God saves equally effectively through Christ, the divine Word of promise in the Old Testament,

---

21. Klaassen, "Speaking in Simplicity," 139–47.
22. Rempel, "Christology and the Lord's Supper," 53.

as he does through Christ, the incarnate Word, and the proclaimed Word of the gospel. Hubmaier maintains that the proclaimed Word is made alive by the Spirit. The progressive revelation of God's salvation, on which the Swiss Brethren based their understanding of the superiority of the New Testament over the Old, is thus removed. This allows Hubmaier to give equal weight to the commands of God in the Old Testament, which establish order and authority for the control of evil, and to insist that such commands are still valid in the world and the church today. Rempel's assessment that Hubmaier viewed "the Incarnation as a unique moment of divine revelation, superseded by the coming of the Spirit" and that this view was at "the heart of Hubmaier's picture of creation," presents an incomplete assessment.

Klaassen is correct to say that Hubmaier did not apply his hermeneutic consistently, for as this work has demonstrated Hubmaier changes his presuppositions and his methods of interpretation during the course of his career as a reformer. He begins by adopting a position closer to Zwingli, then moves closer to the Swiss Brethren as he becomes more confident of the power of the Word of God to effect change in those who hear the preached word. This period of his hermeneutic is dominated by the theme of simplicity and truth. The truth of the Scripture cannot be compromised for the sake of the weak in faith; the speed of reform need not be slowed to accommodate their tardiness. In Waldshut, with the support of one-third of the town council and the citizens, he pushed through his Anabaptist reform of the church. Then came his flight from Waldshut to Nikolsburg via a traumatic time in Zurich.

In his early writings from Nikolsburg, the same tendency to view the words of Christ in the New Testament as superior to Old Testament dominates his assessment of Scripture. Scripture is the sole authority for both faith and the practice of the believer. Obedience to the commands of Christ and the interpretation of Scripture by Scripture, following Erasmus's method, reaches its high point in his writing against Oecolampad and the preachers at Basel.

However, with the challenge that arises from within the Nikolsburg church, first from the antinomians, and then from those who introduce a new legalism compared with the freedom that the Christian has in Christ, Hubmaier begins to adapt his theology and his hermeneutic. Hubmaier's response is to emphasize the role of the church in disciplining recalcitrant members. Fraternal admonition is recognized as an additional mark of the church, along with baptism and the Lord's Supper. It is the role of the church to ensure that the believer remains within the visible local church, outside of which there is no salvation. The Holy Spirit brings the believer into the church and enables the believer obediently to fulfill the commands of Christ to love the neighbor and carry out works of brotherly love. However, when the believer fails, it is the church that has the authority from the Father, and not the Holy Spirit, to guarantee forgiveness of sins and readmit the sinner on hearing a confession of repentance and seeing a change in life that eschews sin.

In this period there is also a new emphasis on a tripartite anthropology. This aspect of Hubmaier's theology allows him to emphasize his view that people are responsible for accepting or rejecting the grace God makes available to them, through the soul that has been awakened by the Holy Spirit using the proclaimed Word, and is again free to respond to the grace of God.

Hubmaier also introduces a refinement of the principle that the clear text interprets the dark text. Interpretation depends on the correct division of Scripture into different categories. Apparently contradictory texts of Scripture that constitute paradoxes of faith can be resolved, not by denying the truth of one or the other as; for example, when Luther denies free will, but by asserting that both texts are true. This position is tenable as long as the correct category is applied to each text. This idea of the division of Scripture into categories is dominant in his work *On the Sword*.

In this way Hubmaier moves away from both the antinomians and new legalists, and back towards a position that is akin to that of the Magisterial Reformers, giving greater say to those who are learned in the biblical languages, and to those who preach the Word of God. He also demonstrates this movement away from the literalism of the Swiss Brethren through his increased use of interpretation by the spiritual sense of figures, types, and allegories. There is also a movement towards adopting the position that those things that are not forbidden are allowed in human matters.

Through this investigation of Hubmaier's hermeneutic, a pattern has become observable which is comparable to the development of Zwingli in particular, but to some extent also to that of Luther. Hubmaier has begun his career as a reformer in close allegiance with Zwingli, both theologically and hermeneutically. He then moves closer to the Swiss Brethren in their hermeneutic concerning baptism in particular but also the Lord's Supper. However, when he is challenged by forces within his own church that jeopardize the continuity of his reform program in Nikolsburg, Hubmaier modifies his hermeneutic towards that of Zwingli, and away from a literalism that invokes the defense of the truth by the simple reading of Scripture. Hubmaier becomes willing to compromise truth for the sake of unity and peace based on the hermeneutic of faith and love.

Although Hubmaier attached his motto "Truth is unkillable" to nearly all his works, his hermeneutic shifted in the last six months in Nikolsburg to indicate that the hermeneutic of faith and love had begun to dominate. During his captivity in Zurich an appeal to faith and love had enabled him to change his position on baptism. Now in Nikolsburg it had reasserted itself to qualify his interpretation of the Scripture so that the fledgling church at Nikolsburg would receive the support of the Lords of Nikolsburg, without which it could not survive.

In this respect, Hubmaier is closer to the Magisterial Reformers, who underwent a similar development in their hermeneutic and theology. By invoking the clarity of Scripture, and providing translations in the vernacular, they encouraged lay people to read and understand the Scripture for themselves. However, when these same people arrived at conclusions that differed from their own, the Reformers modified their position on the clarity of Scripture, restricting interpretation of Scripture to the few who were educated in the biblical languages. In this way, they established a new popery of theologians as Hubmaier had predicted. After being challenged by Hut, Hubmaier appears also to have limited the correct understanding of Scripture to the elected preachers of the Word of a given congregation. In this respect, he also shows himself to have moved closer to the Magisterial Reformers toward the end of his time in Nikolsburg, while continuing to emphasize the congregation's responsibility to elect and judge the preacher.

Though Hubmaier remains an enigma in Anabaptist research, this investigation of his hermeneutic has allowed his place in the fluid matrix of the early Reformation to be more firmly fixed. He follows no one theologian totally, but draws from all the main Reformers, Erasmus, Luther, and Zwingli. Throughout his career as an Anabaptist he maintained his distinctive position on Christian magistrates that separated him from the Swiss Brethren; he also maintained a distinctive hermeneutic that tried to avoid literalistic and legalistic interpretations of Scripture. For the sake of the ongoing security of the Nikolsburg church, Hubmaier shifted his position on the presupposition that faith and love take priority over truth, by admitting a degree of forbearance for the weak in faith that he had rejected during the time when he was closest to the Swiss Brethren. Hubmaier's hermeneutical development reflects the degree of support he had from civil authorities and the degree to which he felt that the reform of the church that he had instituted was threatened, either from external forces such as the Austrian Catholics or from those who opposed his theology from within the church. When threatened, Hubmaier tended to emphasize the magisterial aspects of his hermeneutic; when secure, he emphasized a more literal interpretation of the Scriptures akin to the Swiss Brethren's position, but not identical to it.

The Nikolsburg church that Hubmaier tried to preserve did fragment after his death. William R. Estep suggests the cause was the lack of strong leadership among the "more constructive Anabaptist party."[23] While strong leadership is certainly one issue, a more fundamental issue was the shift in hermeneutic that Hubmaier had introduced.

As has been demonstrated, Hubmaier shifted his hermeneutic towards the view of the Magisterial Reformers in the crucial area of the clarity of Scripture. No longer did the correct understanding of Scripture emanate from the gathered community of the church. Rather, the interpretation of Scripture was vested in the leader of the congregation, the preacher of the Word of God. In this way, Hubmaier sought to overcome the disruption being caused by Hut and Jacob Wiedemann, and to avoid the potential for fragmentation based on strong personalities insisting on particular ideas as essential to the church.

Hubmaier did not survive long enough to establish his unique form of the church, with its combination of Anabaptist and magisterial features. If he had survived to establish his church he would have continued to struggle with the tension created by his ecclesiology. For him, that challenge inherent in individualizing faith and the consequent emphasis on the right of the individual to read and interpret Scripture may have eventually forced him to become like the magisterial churches of Luther and Zwingli, using the power of the magistrate to enforce doctrinal uniformity. Alternatively, he may have reverted to a congregational hermeneutic and faced the possibility of losing the protection of the Lords of Liechtenstein, and the continuing fragmentation of the church when strong personalities with differing interpretations of Scripture arose.

He may however, have decided to live with the tension and trust to the power of his own personality to overcome opposition and maintain the unity of the church. His followers in Nikolsburg attempted this latter option. However, those who attempted to lead the Nikolsburg

---

23. Estep, *The Anabaptist Story*, 68.

Anabaptist church following Hubmaier's lead did not have the personality to overcome the internal opposition within the church. Consequently the expression of the Anabaptist church that Hubmaier had created faded from Anabaptist history.

Bibliography

PRIMARY SOURCES

Denck, Hans. *Concerning the Law of God*. In *The Spiritual Legacy of Hans Denck: Interpretation and Translation of Key Texts*. Studies in Medieval and Reformation Thought XLVII. Edited and translated by Clarence Bauman, 118–59. Leiden: Brill, 1991.

———. *He Who Loves the Truth*. In *The Spiritual Legacy of Hans Denck: Interpretation and Translation of Key Texts*. Studies in Medieval and Reformation Thought XLVII. Edited and translated by Clarence Bauman, 160–77. Leiden: Brill, 1991.

———. *Whether God is the Cause of Evil*. In *The Spiritual Legacy of Hans Denck: Interpretation and Translation of Key Texts*. Studies in Medieval and Reformation Thought XLVII. Edited and translated by Clarence Bauman, 72–117. Leiden: Brill, 1991.

Die Nikolsburger Artikel. In *Bayern I. Quellen zur Geschichte der Weidertaufer*, Vol II. Edited by Karl Schornbaum, 65–66. Leipzig, 1934. Reprint. New York: Johnson, 1971.

Erasmus, Desiderius. *De libero arbitrio*. In *Luther and Erasmus: Free Will and Salvation*, edited and translated by E. G. Rupp, 35–100. Library of Christian Classics XVII. London: SCM, 1969.

Fabri, Johann. *Ursache warum der Wiedertäufer Patron und erster Anfänger Doktor Balthasar Hubmaier zu Wien auf den zehnten Marz 1528 verbrannt wurde*. Vienna, 1528.

Harder, Leland. "The Second Zurich Disputation." In *The Sources of Swiss Anabaptism: The Grebel Letters and Related Documents*. Classics of the Radical Reformation Vol. 4. Edited by Leland Harder, 234–51. Scottdale, PA: Herald, 1986.

———, editor. *The Sources of Swiss Anabaptism: The Grebel Letters and Related Documents*. Classics of the Radical Reformation Vol. 4. Scottdale, PA: Herald, 1986.

Hubmaier, Balthasar. *Apologia*. In *Balthasar Hubmaier: Theologian of Anabaptism* [hereafter *PY*]. Classics of the Radical Reformation Vol. 5. Edited and translated by H. Wayne Pipkin and John H. Yoder, 524–62. Scottdale, PA: Herald, 1989.

———. *A Brief Apologia*. In *PY*, 296–313.

Bibliography

———. *A Brief "Our Father."* In *PY*, 241–44.
———. *A Christian Catechism.* In *PY*, 339–65.
———. *Dialogue with Zwingli's Baptism Book.* In *PY*, 166–233.
———. *An Earnest Christian Appeal to Schaffhausen.* In *PY*, 40–48.
———. *Eighteen Theses Concerning the Christian Life.* In *PY*, 30–39.
———. *Eine ernstliche Christliche erbietung an einen ersamen Rath zu Schaffhusen, durch doctor Baldazar Hubmor von Fridgerg, Pfarren ze Walshut beschehen.* 1524. Original relocated in Stadtarchiv Schaffhausen. Lodged as AA 4, 42, & 73.
———. *A Form for Christ's Supper.* In *PY*, 393–408.
———. *A Form for Water Baptism.* In *PY*, 386–92.
———. *Freedom of the Will, I.* In *PY*, 426–48.
———. *Freedom of the Will, II.* In *PY*, 449–91.
———. *The Ground and Reason.* In *PY*, 366–71.
———. *Interrogation and Release.* In *PY*, 160–65.
———. *Letter to Oecolampad.* In *PY*, 67–72.
———. *Letter to the Zurich Council.* In *PY*, 90–92.
———. *Old and New Teachers on Believers' Baptism.* In *PY*, 245–74.
———. *On Fraternal Admonition.* In *PY*, 372–85.
———. *On Heretics and Those Who Burn Them.* In *PY*, 58–66.
———. *On Infant Baptism Against Oecolampad.* In *PY*, 275–95.
———. *On the Christian Ban.* In *PY*, 409–25.
———. *On the Christian Baptism of Believers.* In *PY*, 95–149.
———. *On the Sword.* In *PY*, 492–523.
———. *A Public Challenge to All Believers.* In *PY*, 78–80.
———. *Recantation at Zurich.* In *PY*, 150–59.
———. *Several Theses Concerning the Mass.* In *PY*, 73–77.
———. *A Simple Instruction.* In *PY*, 314–38.
———. *Statements at the Second Zurich Disputation.* In *PY*, 21–29.
———. *Summa of the Entire Christian Life.* In *PY*, 81–89.
———. *Theses Against Eck.* In *PY*, 49–57.
———. *Twelve Articles in Prayer Form.* In *PY*, 234–40.
———. *Vienna Testimony.* In *PY*, 563–65.
Hutterian Brethren, editor and translator. *The Chronicle of the Hutterian Brethren.* Vol. 1. New York: Plough, 1987.
Klassen, William, and Walter Klaassen. *The Writings of Pilgram Marpeck.* Classics of the Radical Reformation, Vol. 2. Scottdale, PA: Herald, 1978.
Luther, Martin. *On the Bondage of the Will.* In *Luther and Erasmus: Free Will and Salvation*, edited and translated by E. G. Rupp and A. N. Marlow, 101–334. Library of Christian Classics XVII. London: SCM, 1969.
———. *Concerning Rebaptism.* In *Luther's Works*, Vol. 40, edited and translated by Conrad Bergendorf, 229–62. 1958. Reprint. Philadelphia: Fortress, 1975.
———. *To the Christian Nobility of the German Nation Concerning the Reform of the Christian Estate.* In *Luther's Works*, Vol. 44, edited by J. Atkinson and translated by C. M. Jacobs, 115–217. 1966. Reprint. Philadelphia: Fortress, 1973.
———. *Treatise on Good Works.* In *Luther's Works*, Vol. 44, edited by J. Atkinson and translated by W. A. Lambert, 21–114. 1966. Reprint. Philadelphia: Fortress, 1973.
Oecolampad, Johann. *Ein Gesprach etlicher Pradikaten zu Basel gehalten mit etlichen Bekennern der Widertaufe.* Basel, 1525.

Bibliography

Pipkin, H., Wayne Walker, and John H. Yoder, editors and translators. *Balthasar Hubmaier: Theologian of Anabaptism*. Classics of the Radical Reformation, Vol. 5. Scottdale, PA: Herald, 1989.

Sattler, Michael. "The Schleitheim Brotherly Union (February 1527)." In *The Legacy of Michael Sattler*. Classics of the Radical Reformation Vol. 1. Edited and translated by John Howard Yoder, 27–43. Scottdale, PA: Herald, 1973.

Westin, Gunnar and Torsten Bergsten, editors. *Balthasar Hubmaier: Schriften* [hereafter HS] (Quellen und Forshungen zur Reformationsgeschichte Band XXIX. Quellen zur Geschichte der Taufer IX. Gütersloh: Gütersloher Verlagshaus Gerd Mohn, 1962).

Zwingli, Huldrych. *Antwort über Balthasar Hubmaeirs Taufbüchlein*. In *Huldreich Zwinglis sämtliche Werke*, Vol. IV. Corpus Reformatorum 91. Edited by E. Egli, G. Finsler, and W. Kohler, 585–647. Leipzig: Heinsius, 1927.

———. *Exposition of the Sixty-Seven Articles*. In *Huldrych Zwingli Writings*, Vol. 1. *The Defense of the Reformed Faith*. Pittsburgh Theological Monographs, New Series, 12. Edited and translated by Edward J. Furcha, 4–373. Pittsburgh, PA: Pickwick, 1984.

———. *Of Baptism*. In *Zwingli and Bullinger*. Library of Christian Classics XXIV. Edited by G. W. Bromiley, 119–75. London: SCM, 1953.

———. *Of the Education of Youth*. In *Zwingli and Bullinger*. Library of Christian Classics XXIV. Edited by G. W. Bromiley, 96–118. London: SCM, 1953.

———. *On the Clarity and the Certainty of the Word of God*. In *Zwingli and Bullinger*, edited by G. W. Bromiley, 49–95. Library of Christian Classics XXIV. London: SCM, 1953.

———. *The Petition of Eleven Priests to be Allowed to Marry, July, 1522*. In *Ulrich Zwingli 1484–1531: Selected Works*, edited by S. M. Jackson, 25–39. Philadelphia: University of Pennsylvania Press, 1972.

———. *The Preaching Office*. In *Huldrych Zwingli Writings*. Vol 2. *In Search of True Religion: Reformation, Pastoral and Eucharistic Writings*. Pittsburg Theological Monographs, New Series Vol. 12. Edited by H. Wayne Pipkin, 147–86. Pittsburg, PA: Pickwick, 1984.

———. *Refutation of the Tricks of the Catabaptists, 1527*. In *Ulrich Zwingli 1484–1531: Selected Works*, edited by S. M. Jackson, 123–258. Philadelphia: University of Pennsylvania Press, 1972.

———. *Von der Taufe, von der Weidertaufe, und der Kindertaufe*. In *Huldreich Zwinglis sämtliche Werke*. Vol IV. Corpus Reformatorum 91. Edited by E. Egli, G. Finsler, and W. Kohler, 206–337. Leipzig: Heinsius, 1927.

SECONDARY SOURCES

Aldridge, John William. *The Hermeneutics of Erasmus*. Basel Studies of Theology 2. Zurich: EVZ, 1966.

Armour, Rollin Stely. *Anabaptist Baptism: A Representative Study*. Scottdale, PA: Herald, 1966.

Bainton, Roland H. "The Bible in the Reformation." In *The Cambridge History of the Bible: The West from the Reformation to the Present Day*, Vol. II, edited by S. L. Greenslade, 1–37. Cambridge: Cambridge University Press, 1963.

Bibliography

———. *Here I Stand: A Life of Martin Luther*. Nashville: Abingdon, 1978.

———. "The Left Wing of the Reformation." In *Studies on the Reformation: Collected Papers in Church History*. Series 2, 119–29. Boston: Beacon, 1963.

Beachy, Alvin J. *The Concept of Grace in the Radical Reformation*. Nieuwkoop, Netherlands: de Graaf, 1977.

Bender, Harold S. "The Anabaptist Vision." In *The Recovery of the Anabaptist Vision*, edited by G. F. Hershberger, 29–56. Scottdale, PA: Herald, 1957.

———. *Conrad Grebel c.1498–1526: The Founder of the Swiss Brethren Sometimes Called Anabaptists*. Studies in Anabaptist and Mennonite History, Vol. 6. Scottdale, PA: Herald, 1950.

———. "The Pacifism of Sixteenth-Century Anabaptists." *Church History* 24 (1955) 119–51.

Bergsten, Torsten. *Balthasar Hubmaier: Anabaptist Theologian and Martyr*. Edited and translated by W. R. Estep. Valley Forge, PA: Judson, 1978.

———. *Balthasar Hubmaier: Seine Stellung zu Reformation und Täufertum (1525–1528)*. Kassel, Germany: Oncken, 1961.

Biesecker-Mast, Gerald. *Separation and the Sword in Anabaptist Persuasion: Radical Confessional Rhetoric from Scheitheim to Dordrecht*. Telford, PA: Cascadia, 2006.

Bornkamm, Heinrich. *Luther in Mid-Career 1521–1530*. Translated by E. T. Bachmann. London: Darton, Longman and Todd, 1983.

Brewer, Brian. "A Response to Grace: The Sacramental Theology of Balthasar Hubmaier." PhD diss., Drew University, 2003.

Bromiley, Geoffrey, editor. *Zwingli and Bullinger*. Library of Christian Classics XXIV. London: SCM, 1953.

Burger, Edward K. "Erasmus and the Anabaptists." PhD diss., University of California, Santa Barbara, 1977.

Busser, Fritz. "Zwingli the Exegete: A Contribution to the 450th Anniversary of the Death of Erasmus." In *Probing the Reformed Tradition: Historical Studies in Honor of Edward A. Dowey, Jr.*, edited by E. A. McKee and B. G. Armstrong, 175–96. Louisville, KY: Westminster/John Knox, 1989.

Caner, Emir. "Balthasar Hubmaier and His Theological Participation in the Reformation: Ecclesiology and Soteriology." *Faith and Mission* 21.1 (2003) 32–66.

———. "Truth is Unkillable: The Life and Writing of Balthasar Hubmaier." PhD diss., University of Texas at Arlington, 1999.

Christ, Christine. "Das Schriftverständnis von Zwingli und Erasmus im Jahre 1522." *Zwigliana* 16.2 (1983) 117–25.

Clasen, Claus-Peter. *Anabaptism: A Social History, 1525–1618*. Ithica, NY: Cornell University Press, 1972.

Cooper, Brian David Raymond. "Human Reason or Reasonable Humanity?: Balthasar Hubmaier, Pilgram Marpeck, and Menno Simons and the Catholic Natural Law Tradition." PhD diss., University of St. Michael's College, 2006.

Davies, Rupert E. *The Problem of Authority in the Continental Reformers: A Study in Luther, Zwingli and Calvin*. London: Epworth, 1946.

Davis, Kenneth R. *Anabaptism and Asceticism: A Study in Intellectual Origins*. Studies in Anabaptist and Mennonite History, Vol. 16. Scottdale, PA: Herald, 1974.

———. "Erasmus as Progenitor of Anabaptist Thought and Piety." *Mennonite Quarterly Review* 47 (1973) 163–78.

———. "Vision and Revision in Anabaptist Historiography: Perceptional Tensions in a Broadening Synthesis or Alien Idealization." *Mennonite Quarterly Review* 53 (1979) 200–208.

DeMolen, Richard L., editor. *Essays on the Works of Erasmus*. New Haven: Yale University Press, 1978.

———. "Introduction. Opera Omnia Desiderii Erasmii. Rungs on the Ladder to the Philosophia Christii." In *Essays on the Works of Erasmus*, 1–50. New Haven: Yale University Press, 1978.

Deppermann, Klaus. *Melchior Hoffman: Social Unrest and Apocalyptic Visions in the Age of Reformation*. Edited by B. Drewery. Translated by M. Wren. Edinburgh: T. & T. Clark, 1987.

Dipple, Geoffrey. "Response to Snyder's 'The Birth and Evolution of Swiss Anabaptism.'" *Mennonite Quarterly Review* 80 (2006) 657–60.

Dolan, John P. "Review of I. B. Horst, *Erasmus, the Anabaptists and the Problems of Religious Unity*." *Mennonite Quarterly Review* 43 (1969) 343.

Dorey, Thomas A., editor. *Erasmus*. Albuquerque: University of New Mexico Press, 1970.

Dyck, Cornelius J., and Dennis D. Martin, editors. *The Mennonite Encyclopaedia*, Vol. 5. Scottdale, PA: Herald 1990.

Ebeling, Gerhard. *Evangelischen Evangelienauslegung*. Munich: Lempp, 1942.

———. "The New Hermeneutic and the Young Luther." *Theology Today* 21 (1964) 34–46.

Endres, Ernst. "The View of Balthasar Hubmaier of the Church: A Church-Historical Perspective." DD diss., University of Pretoria, 2003.

Estep, William R. *The Anabaptist Story*. Grand Rapids: Eerdmanns, 1975.

———. "The Anabaptist View of Salvation." *South Western Journal of Theology* 20 (1978) 32–49.

Evans, Gillian R. *The Language and Logic of the Bible: The Early Middle Ages*. Cambridge: Cambridge University Press, 1984.

Fast, Heinold. "The Dependence of the First Anabaptists on Luther, Erasmus, and Zwingli." *Mennonite Quarterly Review* 30 (1956) 104–19.

Fast, Heinold, and John Howard Yoder. "How to Deal with Anabaptists: An Unpublished letter of Heinrich Bullinger." *Mennonite Quarterly Review* 33 (1959) 83–95.

Ferrario, Fulvio. "L'anabattismo delle origini e il problema ermeneutico." *Rassegna di Teologia* 4 (1988) 382–400.

———. *La "Sacra ancora" il principio scritturale nella Riforma zwingliana, 1522–1525*. Turin: Claudina, 1993.

Finger, Thomas. "Response to Snyder's 'The Birth and Evolution of Swiss Anabaptism.'" *Mennonite Quarterly Review* 80 (2006) 660–66.

Forstmann, H. Jackson. *Word and Spirit: Calvin's Doctrine of Biblical Authority*. Stanford: Stanford University Press, 1962.

Franzmann, Martin H. "Seven Theses on Reformation Hermeneutics." *Concordia Journal* 15 (1989) 337–50.

Friedmann, Robert. "Book Review." *Mennonite Quarterly Review* 36 (1962) 356–58.

———. *The Theology of Anabaptism: An Interpretation*. Scottdale, PA: Herald, 1973.

Friesen, Abraham. *Erasmus, the Anabaptists, and the Great Commission*. Grand Rapids: Eerdmans, 1998.

Bibliography

―――. *History and Renewal in the Anabaptist/Mennonite Tradition.* North Newton, KS: Bethel College, 1994.

Furcha, Edward J. "In Defense of the Spirit. Zwingli Authenticates His Reforms [in Sixteenth-Century Zurich]." In *Prophet, Pastor, Protestant: The Work of Huldrych Zwingli after Five Hundred Years,* edited by Edward J. Furcha and H. Wayne Pipkin, 43–58. Allison Park, PA: Pickwick, 1984.

Garside, Charles. *Zwingli and the Arts.* New Haven: Yale University Press, 1966.

George, Timothy. *The Theology of the Reformers.* London: Apollos, 1988.

―――. *Reading Scripture with the Reformers.* Downers Grove, IL: InterVarsity, 2011.

Gingerich, Ray. "Response to Snyder's 'The Birth and Evolution of Swiss Anabaptism.'" *Mennonite Quarterly Review* 80 (2006) 670–74.

Goertz, Hans-Jürgen. *The Anabaptists.* Translated by Trevor Johnson. New York: Routledge, 1996.

―――. "History and Theology: A Major Problem of Anabaptist Research Today." *Mennonite Quarterly Review* 53 (1979) 177–88.

―――, editor. *Umstrittenes Täufertum 1525-1975 Neue Forschungen.* Göttingen: Vandenhoek and Ruprecht, 1975.

Goldingay, John. "Luther and the Bible." *Scottish Journal of Theology* 35 (1982) 33–58.

Goncharenko, Simon Victor. "The Importance of Church Discipline within Balthasar Hubmaier's Theology." PhD diss., Southwestern Baptist Theological Seminary, 2011.

―――. *Wounds that Heal: The Importance of Church Discipline within Balthasar Hubmaier's Theology.* Eugene, OR: Pickwick, 2012.

Gonzalez, Antonia Lucic. "Balthasar Hubmaier and Early Christian Tradition." PhD diss., Fuller Theological Seminary, 2008.

Graffagnino, Jason J. "The Shaping of the Two Earliest Anabaptist Catechisms." PhD diss., Southwestern Baptist Theological Seminary, 2008.

Grant, Robert M. *A Short History of the Interpretation of the Bible.* London: A & C Black, 1965.

Hall, Thor. "Possibilities of Erasmian Influence on Denck and Hubmaier in Their Views on the Freedom of the Will." *Mennonite Quarterly Review* 35 (1961) 149–70.

Harwood, Adam. *The Spiritual Condition of Infants: A Biblical-Historical Survey and Systematic Proposal.* Eugene, OR: Wipf and Stock, 2011.

Hayden-Roy, Priscilla. "Hermeneutica Gloria vs. Hermeneutica Cruis: Sebastian Franck and Martin Luther on the Clarity of Scripture." *Archiv für Reformationsgeschichte* 81 (1990) 50–67.

Hershberger, Guy F., editor. *The Recovery of the Anabaptist Vision: A Sixtieth Anniversary Tribute to Harold S. Bender.* Scottdale, PA: Herald, 1957.

Holland, Robert C. "The Hermeneutics of Peter Riedeman (1506–1556) with Reference to 1 Corinthians 5:9–13 and 2 Corinthians 6:14–7:1." ThD diss., Basel, 1970.

Janz, Denis R. *Luther and Late Medieval Thomism: A Study in Theological Anthropology.* Waterloo, ON: Wilfrid Laurier University Press, 1983.

―――, editor. *Three Reformation Catechisms: Catholic, Anabaptist, Lutheran.* New York: Mellin, 1982.

Jones, Keith. *A Believing Church.* Didcot, UK: The Baptist Union of Great Britain, 1998.

Klaassen, Walter. *Anabaptism: Neither Catholic Nor Protestant.* Waterloo, ON: Conrad, 1973.

———. "The Bern Debate of 1538: Christ the Center of Scripture." *Mennonite Quarterly Review* 40 (1966) 148–56.

———. "Speaking in Simplicity: Balthasar Hubmaier." *Mennonite Quarterly Review* 40 (1966) 139–47.

———. "Word, Spirit, and Scripture in Early Anabaptist Thought." PhD diss., Oxford University, 1960.

Klager, Andrew P. "Balthasar Hubmaier's Use of the Church Fathers." *Mennonite Quarterly Review* 84 (2010) 5–65.

———. "'Truth Is Immortal': Balthasar Hubmaier (c. 1480–1528) and the Church Fathers." PhD diss., University of Glasgow, 2010.

Klassen, Herbert C. "The Life and Teaching of Hans Hut (Pt 1)." *Mennonite Quarterly Review* 33 (1959) 267–304.

Klassen, Ryan. "Wielding Two Swords: Ecclesiology and Social Ethics of Balthasar Hubmaier." MA thesis, Providence Theological Seminary, 2005.

Klassen, William. "Anabaptist Hermeneutics: The Letter and the Spirit." *Mennonite Quarterly Review* 40 (1966) 83–96.

———. *Covenant and Community: The Life, Writings and Hermeneutics of Pilgram Marpeck*. Grand Rapids: Eerdmans, 1968.

———. "The Hermeneutics of Pilgram Marpeck." ThD thesis, Princeton Theological Seminary, 1960.

———. "History and Theology: Some Reflections on the Present Status of Anabaptist Studies." *Mennonite Quarterly Review* 53 (1979) 197–200.

Kreider, Robert S. "Anabaptism and Humanism: An Inquiry into the Relationship of Humanism to the Evangelical Anabaptists." *Mennonite Quarterly Review* 26 (1952) 123–41.

Künzli, Edwin. "Antwort an Paul Marti von Edwin Künzli." *Zwigliana* 9.6 (1951) 375–77.

———. "Quellenproblem und Mystiche Schriftsinn in Zwinglis Genesis- und Exoduskommentar: Erster Teil." *Zwigliana* 9.4 (1950) 185–207.

———. "Quellenproblem und Mystiche Schriftsinn in Zwinglis Genesis- und Exoduskommentar: Zweiter Teil." *Zwigliana* 9.5 (1951) 253–307.

Lienhard, Marc, editor. *The Origins and Characteristics of Anabaptism/Les Debuts et les Caracteristiques de l'Anabaptisme*. The Hague: Nijhoff, 1977.

Littell, Franklin H. *The Origins of Sectarian Protestantism*. New York: Macmillan, 1964.

Lindberg, Carter. "Fides et Intellectus ex Auditu: A Response to Hans-Jürgen Goertz on 'History and Theology.'" *Mennonite Quarterly Review* 53 (1979) 189–92.

Loserth, Johann. *Doctor Balthasar Hubmaier und die Anfänge der Wiedertaufe in Mähren*. Brunn, Germany: Rohrer, 1893.

MacGregor, Kirk R. *A Central European Synthesis of Radical and Magisterial Reform: The Sacramental Theology of Balthasar Hubmaier*. Lanham, MY: University Press of America, 2006.

———. "The Sacramental Theology of Balthasar Hubmaier and Its Implications for Ecclesiology." PhD diss., Iowa State University, 2005.

Macoskey, Robert A. "The Contemporary Relevance of Balthasar Hubmaier's Concept of the Church." *Foundations* 6 (1963) 99–122.

———. "The Life and Thought of Balthasar Hubmaier, 1485–1528." PhD diss., University of Edinburgh, 1956.

Bibliography

Marti, Paul. "Mysticher Schriftsinn und wissenschaftliche Auslegung des alten Testaments." *Zwigliana*, 9.6 (1951) 365–74.

Mau, Wilhelm. *Balthasar Hubmaier* Abhandlungen zur mittleren und neueren Geschichte 40. Berlin: Rothschild, 1912.

McClendon, James William Jr., "Balthasar Hubmaier, Catholic Anabaptist." *Mennonite Quarterly Review* 65 (1991) 20–33.

———. *Systematic Theology: Ethics*. Nashville: Abingdon, 1986.

McDill, Michael W. "The Centrality of the Doctrine of Human Free Will in the Theology of Hubmaier." PhD diss., Southeastern Baptist Theological Seminary, 2001.

McGrath, Alister Edgar. *The Intellectual Origins of the European Reformation*. Oxford: Blackwell, 1987.

———. *Reformation Thought: An Introduction*. Oxford: Blackwell, 1988.

McMullen, William. "Church Discipline as a Necessary Function of the Visible Church in the Theology of Balthasar Hubmaier." MA thesis, Southeastern Baptist Theological Seminary, 2003.

Moore, Walter L. "Catholic Teacher and Anabaptist Pupil: The Relationship between John Eck and Balthasar Hubmaier." *Archiv für Reformationsgeschichte* 72 (1981) 68–97.

Munro, Marita R. "The Theology and Practice of the Lord's Supper in the Writings of Balthasar Hubmaier." M.Th thesis, Baptist Theological Seminary, Ruschlikon, Zurich, 1990.

Murray, Stuart. *Biblical Interpretation in the Anabaptist Tradition*. Kitchener, ON: Pandora, 2000.

Nam, Samuel Beyung-Doo. "A Comparative Study of the Baptismal Understanding of Augustine, Luther, Zwingli and Hubmaier." PhD diss., Southwestern Baptist Theological Seminary, 2002.

Newman, Albert Henry. *A History of Anti-Pedobaptism: From the Rise of Pedobaptism to AD 1609*. Philadelphia: American Baptist Publishing Society, 1897.

Oberman, Heiko Augustinus. *The Harvest of Medieval Theology: Gabriel Biel and Late Medieval Nominalism*. Durham, NC: Labyrinth, 1983.

Oyer, John S. "Goertz's 'History and Theology': A Response." *Mennonite Quarterly Review* 53 (1979) 192–97.

———. "Topics for Research in Anabaptism." *Mennonite Quarterly Review* 55 (1981) 381–83.

Packull, Werner O. "Denck's Alleged Baptism by Hubmaier: Its Significance for the Origins of South German-Austrian Anabaptism." *Mennonite Quarterly Review* 47 (1973) 327–38.

———. *Mysticism and the Early South German-Austrian Anabaptist Movement 1525–1531*. Studies in Anabaptist and Mennonite History Vol. 19. Scottdale, PA: Herald, 1976.

———. "A Response to 'History and Theology: A Major Problem in Anabaptist Research Today." *Mennonite Quarterly Review* 53 (1979) 208–11.

Parker, Thomas Henry Louis. *John Calvin*. Tring, UK: Lion, 1975.

Pater, Calvin Augustine. *Karlstadt as the Father of the Baptist Movements: The Emergence of Lay Protestantism*. Toronto: University of Toronto Press, 1984.

Payne, Ernest A. *The Anabaptists of the 16th Century and Their Influence in the Modern World*. London: Kingsgate, 1949.

Payne, John. "Towards the Hermeneutics of Erasmus." In *Scrinium Erasmianum*, Vol II, edited by J. Coppens, 13–49. Leiden: Brill, 1969.
Pike, E. C. *The Story of the Anabaptists*. Eras of Nonconformity II. London: Law, 1904.
Pipkin, H. Wayne Walker. "The Baptismal Theology of Balthasar Hubmaier." *Mennonite Quarterly Review* 65 (1991) 34–53.
———. *Essays in Anabaptist Theology*. Elkhart, IN: Institute of Mennonite Studies, 1994.
———. *Scholar, Pastor, Martyr: The Life and Ministry of Balthasar Hubmaier (ca. 1480–1528)*. Prague: International Baptist Theological Seminary, 2008.
Poettcker, H. "The Hermeneutics of Menno Simons: An Investigation of the Principles of Interpretation Which Menno Brought to His Study of the Scriptures." PhD diss., Princeton Theological Seminary, 1961.
Potter, George Richard. *Zwingli*. Cambridge: Cambridge University Press, 1976.
Preus, James S. *From Shadow to Promise: Old Testament Interpretation from Augustine to the Young Luther*. Cambridge: Harvard University Press, 1969.
———. "Old Testament Promissio and Luther's New Hermeneutic." *Harvard Theological Review* 60 (1967) 145–61.
Raeder, Siegfried. "The Exegetical and Hermeneutical Work of Martin Luther." In *Hebrew Bible/Old Testament: The History of Interpretation. Vol. 2. From Renaissance to the Enlightenment*, edited by Magne Saebo, 363—406. Göttingen: Vandenhoeck & Ruprecht, 2008.
Randall, Ian. *Communities of Conviction: Baptist Beginnings in Europe*. Scharzenfeld, Germany: Heufeld, 2009.
Reinke, D. R. "From Allegory to Metaphor: More Notes on Luther's Hermeneutical Shift." *Harvard Theological Review* 66 (1973) 386–96.
Rempel, John D. "Christology and the Lord's Supper in Anabaptism: A Study in the Theology of Balthasar Hubmaier, Pilgrim Marpeck, and Dirk Philips." ThD diss., University of St Michael's College (Canada), 1988.
———. *The Lord's Supper in Anabaptism: A Study in the Theology of Balthasar Hubmaier, Pilgram Marpeck, and Dirk Philips*. Scottdale, PA: Herald, 1993.
Ricker, J., and J. Saywell, editors. *Renaissance and Reformation: The Dawn of a New Age 1400–1550*. Toronto: Clarke, Irwin, and Co., 1973.
Roth, John D., and James M. Stayer, editors. *A Companion to Anabaptism and Spiritualism, 1521–1700*. Leiden: Brill, 2007.
Rothkegel, Martin. "Anabaptism in Moravia and Silesia." In *A Companion to Anabaptism and Spiritualism 1521–1700*, edited by John D. Roth and James M. Stayer, 163–215. Leiden: Brill, 2007.
Runia, K. "The Hermeneutics of the Reformers." *Calvin Theological Journal* 19 (1984) 121–52.
Rupp, E. Gordon, and Philip S. Watson, editors. *Luther and Erasmus*. Louisville, KY: Westminster/ John Knox, 1969.
Sachsse, Carl. *Dr Balthasar Hubmaier als Theologe*. Neue Studien zur Geschichte der Theologie und der Kirche 20. Berlin: Trowitzsch und Sohn, 1914.
Scott, Tomas. "Reformation and the Peasants' War in Waldshut and Environs: A Structural Analysis. Part I." *Archiv für Reformationsgeschichte* 69 (1978) 82–102.
———. "Reformation and the Peasants' War in Waldshut and Environs: A Structural Analysis. Part II." *Archiv für Reformationsgeschichte* 70 (1979) 140–69.

Bibliography

Seebass, Gottfried. "Müntzers Erbe. Werk, Leben und Theologie des Hans Hut." PhD diss., Heidelberg University, 1972.

Seewald, Gerd. "Balthasar Hubmaier and Civil Government." Typed manuscript, Ruschlikon Baptist Seminary, Ruschlikon-Zurich, 1953.

Shantz, D. H. "The Ecclesiological Focus of Dirk Philips' Hermeneutical Thought in 1559. A Contextual Study." *Mennonite Quarterly Review* 60 (1986) 115–27.

Sider, Ronald J. *Andreas Bodenstein von Karlstadt: The Development of His Thought 1517–1525*. Studies in Medieval and Reformation Thought 11. Leiden: Brill, 1974.

Snyder, C. Arnold. *Anabaptist History and Theology*. Rev. ed. Kitchener, ON: Pandora, 1997.

———. "Beyond Polygenesis: Recovering the Unity and Diversity of Anabaptist Theology." In *Essays in Anabaptist Theology*, edited by H. Wayne Pipkin, 1–33. Elkhart, IN: Institute of Mennonite Studies, 1994.

———. "The Birth and Evolution of Swiss Anabaptism, 1520–1530." *Mennonite Quarterly Review* 80 (2006) 501–645.

———. "The Influence of the Schleitheim Articles on the Anabaptist Movement: An Historical Evaluation." *Mennonite Quarterly Review* 63 (1989) 323–44.

———. "Modern Mennonite Reality and Anabaptist Spirituality: Balthasar Hubmaier's Catechism of 1526." *The Conrad Grebel Review* 9 (1991) 37–51.

———. "Word and Power in Reformation Zurich." *Archiv für Reformationsgeschichte* 81 (1990) 263–85.

Stayer, James M. *Anabaptists and the Sword*. Lawerence, KS: Coronado, 1972.

———. "Die Anfänge des schweizerischen Täufertums im reformierten Kongregationalismus." *Umstrittenes Täufertum 1525–1975 Neue Forschungen*, edited by Hans-Jürgen Goertz, 19–49. Güttingen: Vandenhoeck & Ruprecht, 1975.

———. "Introduction." In *A Companion to Anabaptism and Spiritualism 1521–1700*, edited by John D. Roth and James M. Stayer, xiii–xxiv. Leiden: Brill, 2007.

———. "Let A Hundred Flowers Bloom and Let A Hundred Schools of Thought Contend." *Mennonite Quarterly Review* 53 (1979) 211–18.

———. "A New Paradigm in Anabaptist-Mennonite Historiography?" *Mennonite Quarterly Review* 77 (2004) 297–307.

Stayer, James M., and Werner O. Packull, editors and translators. *The Anabaptists and Thomas Muntzer*. Toronto: Kendall/Hall, 1980.

Stayer, James M., Werner O. Packull, and Klaus Deppermann. "From Monogenesis to Polygenesis: The Historical Discussion of Anabaptist Origins." *Mennonite Quarterly Review* 49 (1975) 83–121.

Steinmetz, David C. "The Baptism of John and the Baptism of Jesus in Huldrych Zwingli, Balthasar Hubmaier and Late Medieval Theology." In *Continuity and Discontinuity in History: Essays Presented to George Huntston Williams on the Occasion of his 65th Birthday*, edited by F. F. Church and T. George, 169–81. Leiden: Brill, 1979.

———. "Luther and Hubmaier on the Freedom of the Will." In *Luther in Context*, 59–71. Bloomington, IN: Indiana University Press, 1986.

———. "Scholasticism and Radical Reform: Nominalist Motifs in the Theology of Balthasar Hubmaier." *Mennonite Quarterly Review* 45 (1971) 123–44.

Stephens, William Peter. *The Theology of Huldrych Zwingli*. Oxford: Clarendon, 1986.

Strübind, Andrea. *Eifriger als Zwingli: Die frühe Täuferbewegung in der Schweiz*. Berlin: Duncker & Humbolt, 2003.

———. "A New Paradigm in Anabaptist-Mennonite Historiography? A Response." *Mennonite Quarterly Review* 77 (2004) 308–17.
Sussdorf, Heinz-Gunther. "The Concept of Discipleship in the Theology of Balthasar Hubmaier." M.Th thesis, Baptist Theological Seminary, Ruschlikon-Zurich, 1988.
Swartley, Willard. "Biblical Interpretation (Hermeneutics)." In *The Mennonite Encyclopaedia*, Vol. 5, edited by Cornelius J. Dyck and Dennis D. Martin, 80–83. Scottdale, PA: Herald 1990.
———, editor. *Essays on Biblical Interpretation. Anabaptist and Mennonite Perspectives.* Text-Reader Series 1. Elkhart, IN: Institute of Mennonite Studies, 1984.
Teigen, Erling R. "The Clarity of Scripture and Hermeneutical Principles in the Lutheran Confession." *Concordia Theological Quarterly* 46 (1982) 147–66.
Torrance, Thomas F. "The Hermeneutics of Erasmus." In *Probing the Reformed Tradition: Historical Studies in Honor of Edward A. Dowey, Jr.*, edited by E. A. McKee and B. G. Armstrong, 48–76. Louisville, KY: Westminster/John Knox, 1989.
Troeltsch, Ernst. *The Social Teaching of the Christian Churches.* Translated by O. Wyon. London: Allen & Unwin, 1931.
Van Braght, Thieleman. *The Bloody Theatre or Martyrs Mirror of the Defenceless Christian.* Translated by Joseph F. Sohm. 16th English printing. Scottdale, PA: Herald, 1990.
Vedder, Henry C. *Balthasar Hubmaier: The Leader of the Anabaptists.* Heroes of the Reformation Series, 8. New York: Putnam, 1905.
Voth, Gay Lynn. "Anabaptist Liturgical Spirituality and the Supper of Christ." *Direction* 34.1 (2005) 3–14.
Walton, Robert C. *Zwingli's Theocracy.* Toronto: University of Toronto Press, 1967.
Weaver, J. Denny. "Discipleship Redefined: Four Sixteenth Century Anabaptists." *Mennonite Quarterly Review* 54 (1980) 255–79.
———. "Response to Snyder's 'The Birth and Evolution of Swiss Anabaptism.'" *Mennonite Quarterly Review* 80 (2006) 685–90.
Wenger, John C. "An Early Anabaptist Tract on Hermeneutics." *Mennonite Quarterly Review* 42 (1968) 26–44.
Williams, George Hunston. *The Radical Reformation.* Philadelphia: Westminster, 1962.
———. *The Radical Reformation.* Sixteenth Century Essays and Studies XV. 3rd ed. Kirksville, MO: Sixteenth Century Journal, 1992.
Williamson, Darren. "Erasmus of Rotterdam's Influence upon Anabaptism: The Case of Balthasar Hubmaier." PhD diss., Simon Fraser University, Canada, 2005.
Windhorst, Christof. "Anfänge und Aspekte der Theologie Hubmaiers." In *The Origins and Characteristics of Anabaptism/Les Debuts et les caracteristiques de l'Anabaptisme*, edited by M. Lienhard, 148–68. The Hague: Nijhoff, 1975.
———. "Balthasar Hubmaier: Professor, Preacher, Politician." In *Profiles of Radical Reformers: Biographical Sketches from Thomas Muntzer to Paracelsus*, edited by Hans-Jürgen Goertz and translated by Walter Klaassen, 144–57. Scottdale, PA: Herald, 1982.
———. *Täuferisches Taufverständnis: Balthasar Hubmaiers Lehre zwischen traditionaller und Reformatorischer Theologie.* Studies in Medieval and Reformation Thought 26. Leiden: Brill, 1976.
Wiswedel, Wilhelm. "The Inner and the Outer Word: A Study in the Anabaptist Doctrine of Scripture." *Mennonite Quarterly Review* 26 (1952) 171–91.

Bibliography

Wolf, Ernst. "Uber 'Klarheit der Heiligen Schrift' nach Luthers 'De servo arbitrio.'" *Theologische Literaturzeitung* 92.10 (1967) 721–30.

Yoder, John Howard. "Balthasar Hubmaier and the Beginnings of Swiss Anabaptism." *Mennonite Quarterly Review* 33 (1959) 5–17.

———. "The Hermeneutics of the Anabaptists." *Mennonite Quarterly Review* 41 (1967) 291–308.

———. *The Legacy of Michael Sattler*. Classics of the Radical Reformation. Scottdale, PA: Herald, 1973.

York, Tripp. "Martyrdom and Eating Jesus: Two Neglected Practices?" *The Conrad Grebel Review* 22.1 (2004) 71–86.

Zeman, Jarold Knox. *The Anabaptists and Czech Brethren in Moravia 1526–1628: A Study of Origins and Contacts*. Studies in European History 20. The Hague: Mouton, 1969.

Name Index

Aberli, Heinrich, 22, 93, 156
Adelphi, Johann, 14
Aldridge, John, 54, 385
Aquinas, Thomas, *See* Thomas Aquinas.
Arkleb, of Boskovic, 316
Aristotle, 71, 104, 282
Armour, Rollin, 36–37, 120, 174–76, 277, 385
Augustine, Saint, 45, 47, 118, 121, 142, 144, 146, 149, 170, 178, 196, 199, 200, 204, 219, 284, 306, 310, 349, 390–91

Basil (the Great), Saint, 175, 201
Bainton, Roland, 10, 28, 49, 50, 385
Beachy, Alvin, 385
Beckh, Marcus, 24, 335
Bender, Harold, 26–27, 38, 57, 276, 386
Bergsten, Torsten, 1, 9–20, 22, 24–25, 32–34, 43, 75, 78, 82, 92, 100, 106–7, 135–38, 156–58, 165, 169, 174, 177–78, 180, 193–98, 202, 204, 207–8, 214–15, 224, 236, 239, 245, 253–55, 260, 268–69, 276–77, 279–80, 288–89, 299, 315–16, 329, 334–37, 351, 366, 385–86
Bernard of Clairvaux, 40, 46, 59
Beza, Theodore, 10
Biel, Gabriel, 11, 278, 390
Biesecker-Mast, 59, 386
Binder, Georg, 156
Blabhans, Laien, 15

Blaurock, George, 137, 143, 210
Bluntschli, Anna, 22
Bluntschli, Fridli, 157
Boethius, 104
Bonaventura, Saint, 11
Bornkamm, Heinrich, 51, 386
Brandenburg, Friedrich van, 11
Brandenburg-Ansbach, George, 280
Brewer, Brian, 35, 45, 46, 60, 386
Bromiley, Geoffrey, 93, 129, 385, 386
Bullinger, Heinrich, 52, 171–72, 345, 361, 386, 387
Burger, Edward, 38, 386
Busser, Fritz, 53–54, 386

Calvin, John, 5, 10, 25, 50, 52–53, 386–87, 390–91
Caner, Emir, 35, 59–60, 386
Capito, Wolfgang, 136, 165, 169
Castleberger, Andreas, 114
Christ, Christine, 54, 386
Chrysostom, John, 147
Clasen, Claus-Peter, 386
Cooper, Brian, 45, 49, 386
Cyprian, Saint, 242
Cyril, Saint, 147

Davies, Rupert, 50, 386
Davis, Kenneth, 29, 40–41, 291, 386
DeMolen, Richard, 55, 387
Denck, Hans, xi, 2–3, 22, 28–29, 38–39, 43, 55–56, 194, 276–79, 283, 288–89, 293, 299–300, 308–9, 312–14, 328–29, 360, 363, 366, 371, 383, 390

395

Name Index

Deppermann, Klaus, 28, 386, 392
Dipple, Geoffrey, 31, 387
Dolan, John, 38, 387
Donatus, Aeilus, 199
Dubcansky, Jan, 194, 253–54
Duns Scotus, 11, 71
Dyck, Cornelius, 387, 393

Ebeling, Gerhard, 52, 387
Eck, Johann, ix, 10–12, 18–19, 25, 39, 56, 60, 78, 81, 88, 102–3, 108, 215, 217, 246, 277–78, 330, 336, 339, 384, 390
Endres, Ernst, 387
Erasmus, Desiderius, xi, xii, 2–3, 13–14, 35–39, 41, 47–48, 53–55, 57, 71, 92, 144, 147, 175, 230, 235–36, 258, 266, 275–79, 281–82, 284, 287–99, 301–6, 308–9, 311–14, 342, 360–61, 363–64, 366–67, 373–74, 379, 383–87, 391, 393
Estep, William, 9–10, 34, 335, 380, 386–87
Eusebius of Caesarea, 147, 348
Evans, Gillian, 387

Fabri, Johann, 13–14, 19–20, 24–25, 144, 146, 151, 187, 197–98, 315–16, 324, 335–38, 341, 383
Fast, Heinold, 172, 276, 387
Ferdinand, of Austria, 23, 134, 334–37, 354, 357–58, 361
Ferrario, Fulvio, 54, 387
Finger, Thomas, 31, 387
Forstmann, H. Jackson, 52, 387
Franzmann, Martin, 53, 387
Friedmann, Robert, 34, 235, 387
Friesen, Abraham, 38, 387
Fuchs, Tegen, 208
Furcha, Edward, 65, 385, 388

Gansfort, Wessel, 278
Garside, Charles, 205, 388
George, Timothy, 51, 108, 388
Gingerich, Ray, 32, 388
Glaidt, Oswald, 194–95, 214, 221, 288, 326

Glarean, Heinrich, 14
Goertz, Hans-Jürgen, 28–29, 40–43, 388–89, 392–93
Goldingay, John, 53, 388
Goncharenko, Simon, 35, 388
Gonzalez, Antonia, 25, 45, 47–48, 388
Göschl, Martin, 196, 224–25
Graffagnino, Jason, 45, 48–49, 388
Grant, Robert, 51, 388
Grebel, Conrad, 7, 16, 19, 26–28, 31–32, 36–38, 40–42, 45, 63, 93, 106, 113, 137, 141–43, 180, 187, 208, 210, 246, 257, 332, 383, 386, 392
Gross, Jakob, 208
Gynoraus, Peter, 158, 170, 194

Hall, Thor, 37, 39, 276, 388
Harder, Leland, 16, 21–22, 63, 65, 67, 76, 93, 97, 106, 115–17, 124–25, 127, 129, 137–39, 141, 143, 145, 147, 151, 153–54, 157, 180, 187, 210, 246, 257, 383
Harwood, Adam, 388
Hätzer, Ludwig, 194
Hayden-Roy, Priscilla, 53, 388
Hegendorf, Christoph, 175
Hershberger, Guy, 386, 388
Hoen, Cornelius, 278
Hofmann, Melchior, 28, 56
Hofmeister, Sebastian, 16, 18, 31, 136, 156, 169–73, 180
Holland, Robert, 55, 388
Hora, Erna, 316
Hottinger, Margaret, 137, 143
Hubmaier, Elsbeth, ix, 24, 26, 158, 254, 334–35, 337, 351
Hugline, Elsbeth, *See* Hubmaier, Elsbeth
Huss, Jan, 49
Hut, Hans, 2, 8, 22–23, 26, 28–29, 41, 43, 194, 315–16, 326, 328–29, 335–36, 344, 347, 356–57, 359–60, 363, 365–66, 371, 379–80, 389, 392
Hutterian Brethren, 26, 316, 329, 334, 359, 384

Janz, Denis, 225–26, 278, 388

Name Index

Jerome, Saint, 71, 144, 146–47, 175, 204, 302, 349
Jud, Leo, 19, 64, 93, 113, 156, 169–73, 180

Karlstadt, Andreas, 20, 36, 42, 93, 96, 111, 214, 216, 278, 390, 392
Klaassen, Walter, 30, 37, 55, 57–58, 229, 326–28, 375–77, 384, 388, 393
Klager, Andrew, 45, 47–48, 389
Klassen, Herbert, 315, 326, 389
Klassen, Ryan, 35, 389
Klassen, William, 29, 55, 229, 311, 384, 389
Koehler, Walther, 276
Kreider, Robert, 37, 389
Künzli, Edwin, 53–54, 389

Leo I, Pope, 199
Liechtenstein, Hans von, 195, 202, 207, 225, 230, 334, 365, 380
Liechtenstein, Leonhard von, 23, 195, 202, 207, 214, 221–22, 225, 334, 365, 380
Lienhard, Marc, 389, 393
Lingg, Martin, 137, 143
Littell, Franklin, 389
Lindberg, Carter, 389
Lombard, Peter, *See* Peter Lombard
Loserth, Johann, 9–11, 14, 25, 239, 268, 389
Luther, Martin, ix, xi, 2–4, 6–7, 10, 13–15, 25–26, 36, 38–41, 43–45, 50–54, 57, 59–60, 64, 66, 75–77, 92, 102, 108, 111–12, 129, 132–33, 147, 162, 176, 183, 195, 203, 218–19, 222, 226, 229, 235, 239, 247, 260, 266, 276–80, 282, 285, 287, 290–92, 294–99, 301–14, 317, 325, 328, 342, 349, 351, 360–61, 363–68, 370–75, 378–80, 383–84, 386–88, 390–92, 394

MacGregor, Kirk, 19, 35, 40, 45–46, 49, 59, 389
Macoskey, Robert, 32–34, 389
Mantz, Felix, 7, 26–28, 31, 45, 97, 106, 113, 137, 143, 210
Marpeck, Pilgram, 49, 55–56, 229, 311, 384, 386, 389, 391
Marti, Paul, 54, 389–91
Mau, Wilhelm, 9, 390
Maximilian I, Emperor, 11–12
McClendon, James, 34, 390
McDill, Michael, 35, 390
McGrath, Alister, 47, 50, 53, 390
McMullen, William, 390
Melanchthon, Philip, 14
Moore, Walter, 39, 277, 390
Müller, Hans, 20
Munro, Marita, 390
Müntzer, Thomas, 19, 28, 36, 41, 45, 141, 180, 257, 260, 392–93
Murray, Stuart, 57, 59, 390
Myconius, Oswald, 113, 156, 169–73, 180

Nam, Samuel Beyung-Doo, 35, 45–46, 390
Newman, Albert, 34, 390
Nicolas II, Pope, 117, 146–47

Oberman, Heiko, 47, 390
Occam, William *See* William of Occam
Oecolampad, Johannes, 19, 22, 93–94, 96–97, 102, 106, 135–36, 175–77, 179–82, 187–88, 190, 193, 198, 216, 219, 228, 354, 369, 377, 384
Origen, 3, 6, 147, 175–76, 184, 200, 278, 302–3, 349
Oyer, John, 60, 390

Packull, Werner, 28–29, 41, 194, 315–16, 328, 335–44, 347, 356, 390, 392
Parker, Thomas, 10, 390
Pater, Calvin, 390
Payne, Ernest, 34, 390
Payne, John, 54–55, 391
Pelagius, 199
Pelikan, Conrad, 14
Pernstein, Johann von, 239, 254
Peter Lombard, 11
Pike, E. C., 15–16, 22, 210, 391

Name Index

Pipkin, Wayne Walker, 1, 34–35, 60, 71, 75, 82, 85, 89, 99–100, 138, 156–57, 169, 174–76, 197–98, 204, 215, 239, 254, 260, 269, 274, 300, 312, 317, 335, 383–85, 388, 391–92
Poettcker, H., 55, 391
Potter, George, 10, 203, 391
Preus, James, 52–53, 391

Rabanus of Metz, 201
Raeder, Siegfried, 53, 391
Randall, Ian, 34, 391
Reinke, D. R., 53, 391
Rempel, John, 372, 376, 391
Reublin, Wilhelm, 19–20, 37, 40, 100, 106–7
Rhegius, Urbanus, 112, 177, 183, 194
Rhenanus, Beatus, 14
Ricker, J., 236, 391
Roth, John, 391, 392
Rothkegel, Martin, 32, 49, 391
Runia, K., 53, 391
Rupp, E. Gordon, 278, 383–84, 391
Rychard, Wolfgang, 13–15

Sachsse, Carl, 9, 14, 174, 177, 239, 391
Salzer, Ambrosius, 24, 335
Sapidus, Johannes, 14
Sattler, Michael, 2, 23, 28, 45, 52, 143, 320, 322, 385, 394
Schappeler, Christopher, 16
Schlaffer, Hans, 356
Schmid, Konrad, 113
Schwenckfeld, Caspar, 25–56, 288
Scott, Tomas, 18, 391
Scotus, Duns, *See* Duns Scotus
Seebass, Gottfried, 29, 392
Seewald, Gerd, 34, 276–77, 288, 392
Simons, Menno, 49, 55, 386, 391
Sider, Ronald, 392
Snyder, C. Arnold, 28–31, 40, 43–45, 48, 58, 114–15, 183, 261, 392
Sobek, Burian von Kornice, 195, 254, 260, 265
Spittelmaier, Hans, 194–95, 214, 221, 316

Stayer, James, 28–29, 31–32, 316, 391–92
Steinmetz, David, 39, 277–78, 313, 349, 392
Stephens, William Peter, 51–53, 112, 115, 258, 261, 373, 392
Strübind, Andrea, 30–31, 392
Strumpf, Simon, 16, 63, 65, 137
Sussdorf, Heinz-Gunther, 393
Swartley, Willard, 55–56, 393

Teck, Ulrich, 137, 143, 208
Teigen, Erling, 53, 111, 393
Theophylact, 175, 199
Torrance, Thomas, 55, 258, 393
Troeltsch, Ernst, 393

Vadian, 15–16
Van Braght, Thieleman, 26, 393
Veddder, Henry, 9–12, 16, 22–23, 34, 393
Voth, Gay, 35–36, 393

Walton, Robert, 137, 393
Watt, Joachim von *See* Vadian
Weaver, J. Denny, 31–32, 393
Wenger, John, 52, 393
Westin, Gunnar, 1, 34, 169, 385
Widerker, Anna, *See* Bluntschli
Wiedemann, Jacob, 380
William of Occam, 11, 71, 349
Williams, George Hunston, 10, 12–13, 28, 137, 344, 358, 392–93
Williamson, Darren, 35, 38–39, 393
Windhorst, Christof, 10–11, 13–15, 19–20, 39–40, 66, 115, 117, 174, 256, 393
Wiswedel, Wilhelm, 34, 55, 393
Wolf, Ernst, 53, 394

Yoder, John Howard, 1, 27–29, 52, 71, 75, 82, 85, 89, 99–100, 137–38, 156–57, 169, 171–72, 174–76, 197–98, 204, 215, 239, 254, 260, 269, 300, 312, 317, 322, 335–36, 345, 350, 383, 385, 387, 394
York, Tripp, 35, 394

Name Index

Zeman, Jarold, 23, 34, 48, 195, 225–26, 254–55, 335, 347, 394

Zwingli, Huldrych, ix, xi, 2–5, 7–8, 10, 15–22, 25–31, 34, 37–38, 41–42, 45–46, 50–54, 57, 63–71, 74, 76–82, 85, 88, 92–96, 101–4, 106, 111–54, 156–59, 161–62, 165–66, 169–73, 175–77, 182–87, 189–95, 197–98, 200, 203, 205–6, 209–10, 214–16, 218, 228–30, 235, 240, 243–45, 250, 256–58, 261, 265, 270, 276–78, 297, 303, 306, 314, 316–22, 324–25, 328–29, 341, 345–46, 348, 351, 360–61, 363–68, 370–75, 377–80, 384–93

Scripture Reference Index

A digitally searchable copy of all Hubmaier's Scripture references and usage can be purchased directly from the author.

Genesis

1–3	312
1	258, 353
2	242, 353
2:7	280, 283
3–4	327, 343
3	370
3:15	290
3:16	318
4:5ff	292
4:10	212
6:3	290, 340
7	201
8:1ff	150
14:14ff	320
17	242
17:23–27	124
20:17	348
22	340
22:18	290
26:4	290
28:12	222
28:14	290
32:29	302
41:2–3	184, 216
41:26–27	216

Exodus

2:8–11	353
2:12	320
8	184, 355
9:16	303
19:8	184
20	252, 292
20:4–6	62, 68, 232
20:8–11	203
20:23ff	184
24:6–8	184
28	83
28:15ff	83
28:30	83
32:31ff	348
34:20	266

Leviticus

11	279
11:3	323
11:4	279

Numbers

11:4f	348
25:7f	320

Deuteronomy

1:16	74
1:16–17	210
1:16–18	74
1:17	75, 77
1:39	184, 192

Scripture Reference Index

4:2	83, 151–52, 191
5	252
5:6–10	62, 68, 232
5:7ff	184
5:12–15	203
5:14	353
5:32	191, 197
6:8	266
7:25	62
10:12	340
11:26ff	293
12:30	151
12:32	63, 68, 72, 83, 152, 191
17:19–20	74, 77
18:15	82, 211
25	80
25:5ff	80
27:15	62, 68
27:26	243, 355
28:1	211
30:11ff	290
30:11	293
30:15	294
30:19	294
33	82–83
34:6	72

Joshua

10:12–13	353
24:27	340

1 Samuel

1:11ff	348
5:2ff	212
8:5	326

2 Samuel

5:2ff	207
6	352
6:6	231, 352
12:13	204, 212, 342
18:14	284

1 Kings

8:22f	348
17:1	348
19:18	237

2 Kings

22	80
22:13	355

2 Chronicles

34	80

Job

1:21	168
3:3	110, 173, 182, 184, 192, 291, 345
6:16	89, 110
41	88
41:19	88

Psalms

1:1	89
2:7	198
25:10	340
32:1	266
37:21	266
37:26–27	266
51	204, 212, 302
51:5	110, 192, 290–91, 311, 345
51:7	173, 182, 184
51:17	342
62:11	326
107:20	283, 286, 310, 349
116:10	266
118:22	150
119:7	286
119:11	286
119:25	283, 286
119:105	286
119:107	286

Proverbs

7:1–3	355
8:34	89
30:6	151–52

Ecclesiastes

2:1	358

2:16	358
15:14ff	281, 290
15:14	290, 292, 305, 358

Isaiah

1:10–23	210
1:17	322, 326
1:19	294
1:23	252
2:19f	352
7:14	211, 343
8:20	211
29	145
29:10–12	306
29:13	151, 191, 204, 211
30:1–2	191
30:10	184
40:3f	150
40:8	258, 286
40:13	150
43:24ff	126
44:9	63
45:7	306
54:1	352
54:13	85
55	130
55:1f	148
55:10	64, 69
55:11	258, 286
58:13	203
66:4	162
66:23	203

Jeremiah

6	258, 286
7	286
10:23	349
18	304
18:8	294, 342
18:10	294, 342
20:14	110, 173, 182, 184, 192, 291, 345
21:12	322, 326
22:3	322, 326
23:25–32	72
23:29	258, 286
31:34	293
36	89

Ezekiel

18	302
33–31f	205
38–39	352
44:23–24	75, 77, 210–11

Daniel

3	358
9	348
9:24	272–73
11:31	231, 237
11:38	206, 212
12:7	347

Hosea

10:8	352

Joel

2	83

Amos

5:23	205

Micah

6:8	326

Nahum

3:1ff	326

Habakkuk

2:4	181, 184

Zephaniah

3:1f	326

Zechariah

7:9f	326
14:8	148

Scripture Reference Index

Malachi
1:2f	303
1:6	340
2:8	205

Matthew
1:20f	211–12
1:20	202
2:16ff	182
2:16	185
3	265
3:3f	150
3:3	244
3:12	244
3:17	82
4:1–11	252, 322
4:4	166
5	327
5–7	252
5:13	145
5:17ff	191, 340
5:18	144, 150, 241, 244
5:19	185, 191
5:21	322–23
5:23f	349
5:25	79, 345
5:38ff	328
5:40	141, 208, 320
5:43f	323
6	348
6:5ff	203
6:9–13	166
6:25	110
6:34	306
7:4ff	250
7:7	348
7:12	96
7:15	83, 244
10:23	209
10:28	87, 90, 110
10:32–33	110
10:34	182, 185, 322
11:1	356
11:25–27	203
11:25	183
12:1–8	204
12:30	185
12:32	79, 345
12:36	250
13	89
13:24–30	39
13:25	89
13:29ff	87
13:36–43	39
15	85, 103
15:1ff	152
15:1–13	151
15:8–9	204
15:9	204, 211
15:11	203
15:13	63, 68, 71–72, 85, 151, 175, 178, 184–85, 191, 197–98, 306
15:14	89
15:28	302
16:13–20	79, 396
16:16	162, 269, 274
16:17f	344
16:18–19	269
16:18	181, 185, 191, 197
16:23	204, 249
17:5	185, 191
17:20	148, 150
18:13–20	39
18:15ff	83, 161, 244, 249, 250, 274, 318
18:15–18	355
18:16	263
18:18–20	76
18:34	79
19	351
19:12	351
19:13	176
19:14	95
19:17	72, 234, 289, 294
21:25–26	128
22	80
22:23ff	80
22:44	266
24	347–48
24:4	83
24:15	237
24:36	347
25:34ff	162–63, 263
25:34–36	159, 236
25:35ff	173
24:35	244

/ Scripture Reference Index

24:42	264
25:13	264
25:40	159
25:42	285
26:26–28	64
26:26	219
26:36ff	348
26:39	348
26:41	280
26:52–54	324
27:46ff	348
28:18ff	116, 122, 128–129, 240, 244, 333
28:18–19	175
28:18–20	185, 191–92
28:18	240
28:19–20	39
28:19ff	196–97, 269
28:19	94, 142, 150, 198, 259
28:20	179

Mark

1	128
1:1–5	128
1:2–4	140
1:11	82
1:15	107
1:27	185
10:13f	143, 145, 147–48, 150, 152, 154, 185
10:14	148, 185, 190, 218
10:29	218
10:38	340
12	80
12:18ff	80
13	347
13:32f	347
14:22–24	64
14:25	218
15:11	203
16:15f	240, 244, 259, 333
16:15–16	175, 191
16:15	197–98, 301
16:16	129, 150, 181, 185, 192, 196, 328

Luke

1:13	348
1:42	202
1:43	344
1:46	280
1:50	340
2:34	182
2:36ff	84
2:14	295
3	128, 265
3:4ff	150
6	208
6:27ff	328
6:29	75, 77
6:30ff	252
6:30	249
6:42	250
7:37	342
8:21	339
9:35	82
9:50	151, 198
9:54	90
8:4–15	216
9:23	294, 340
9:54–56	319
10	212
10:7	203
10:34ff	205
11	197, 348
11:1ff	203
11:23	197
11:45–52	197
12	85
12:5	340
12:13f	319–20
12:14	320
12:47	210, 240
12:48	212
12:52f	182
12:57–59	79
12:50	142
14:11	175
14:26	218
15:21	204
16:2	264
16:29	210–12
17:4	272
17:6	148, 150

405

Scripture Reference Index

18	348
18:1–7	203
18:13	204, 348
19:8	342
20	80
20:27ff	80
21	347
21:33	144, 152
22:19ff	64
22:19	97, 99
22:25f	320–21, 327
23:29–30	352
23:34	167, 290
23:46	168, 348
24:31ff	264

John

1	196, 333
1:1	181, 192, 197
1:9	301
1:11–12	295, 311
1:12–14	192
1:12	162, 292, 296, 301
1:13	281
1:14	162, 181, 197
1:23	150
1:26	128
1:29–31	122
1:29	122
1:31	122
1:32	270
2:5	356
2:12	191
3	333
3:3–7	192
3:5–6	121, 142
3:5	148
3:16	110, 301
3:22	141
4:1ff	83
4:2	141
4:13ff	147–48
4:46f	348
5:8	355
5:29	347
5:39f	62
5:39	75, 77, 102–3, 186, 191, 210–11
6:26ff	147
6:27	148
6:32–35	166
6:45	85
6:63	85
6:53ff	259
6:67	290, 296
7:14	202
7:37f	148
8:10ff	318
8:31f	283, 297
8:36	340
9:6f	201
9:6	202
10:9	356
10:10	90
12:47–48	75–77, 210–11
12:48	103, 209
13–17	266
13–14	265
13:15	117
14	196
14:6	103, 191, 197, 356
14:14	203
14:15	294
15	265
15:1	103
15:5	305
15:20	117
16–17	265
16	348
18:22–23	186
18:36	317
16:23–24	167
19:11	90
19:25	344
19:27	202
20:20–23	79
20:21	321
20:22ff	245, 270, 274
20:22	341

Acts

1:9	274
2	170
2:1ff	270
2:37–38	244
2:36	348

2:38–41	192
2:38	196, 200, 240, 245, 259
2:41	196
2:42	257, 259
3:1	348
5:29	75, 208, 210
7:48ff	220
7:55	207
7:59ff	348
8	185, 241
8:1–4	184, 192
8:9ff	245
8:12	196
8:13	149
8:20	249
8:35–38	192
8:38	196
9	211
9:1–19	192
9:18	184
10	241, 352
10:9–16	203
10:3	348
10:10	352
10:44ff	129
10:44–48	192
10:47–48	196
11:4–9	203
11:13–18	192
15	84
15:20	203
15:29	203
16	123, 196, 241
16:14–15	192
16:15	184, 196
16:32–33	192
16:33	196
17:18	185
18	241
18:8	196
19:1ff	118, 129, 206, 243–44
19:1–7	192
19:19	91
19:23ff	232
21:5	348
21:9	84
22	211, 241
22:1–16	192
22:16	184, 196
26	211
28:22	185

Romans

1	258
1:17	181, 184
2:7	267
4:5	267
4:8	266
4:15	151
4:25	227
5:1ff	162
5:12ff	162
5:12	267
5:19	162
6:3–4	123, 175, 191
7:18f	295
7:18	234, 238, 267
7:15ff	267
8	340
8:1	267
8:6	340
8:11	267
8:13	340
8:16–17	163
8:17	162–63, 206
8:32	267
8:34	356
9–11	303
9:3	267
9:13	303–4
9:17	302
9:18	301
9:19	302
9:20	302
9–21	304
10:5–8	267
10:9ff	164
10:9–10	122, 267
10:10–11	191
10:10	229, 338–39, 368
10:13	121, 131
10:15	152
10:17	181, 196
11:3	150
11:4	237
11:32	328

Scripture Reference Index

12	252
12:9–21	267
12:19f	323
13	322, 327
13:1ff	267, 324, 327, 357
13:1	263
13:4	75, 87, 90, 207, 209–10, 213, 327
13:13	203
14:1–6	204
14:3	267
14:14	203
14:20	353
14:23	63, 68, 181, 200, 341
15:4	191
16:17–18	83–84

1 Corinthians

1:13ff	129
1:19	198, 241
2	170
2:9	162
3	197
3:8	339
3:11–12	181
3:11	197
5	355
5:1f	267, 271
6:1–6	321
6:7f	320
7	351
7:2	240, 244–45
8:8	203
8:9	267
9:27	267
10	98–99, 265–66
10:1–5	140
10:1	123
10:2	170
10:4	97–98
10:13	167, 283
10:16	99, 261
10:17	99
10:21	207
11	99, 265
11:19	90
11:23–26	64
11:23ff	263
11:26	109, 111, 220
11:26a	99
11:26b	99
11:27	99
11:28	99, 196
12:6	306
12:12	267
13:6	180
14	267
14:20	148
14:26	205
14:29–37	76
14:26	79
14:34f	261
15:22	182, 192, 285

2 Corinthians

2	355
9:6	312
9:7	295, 342
10:4f	322

Galatians

1	202
1:8f	197
1:8	179, 204
2:11	113
2:14	249
3:5	152
3:15	151–52, 191
4:8	232
5	340
5:1	232
5:13f	339
5:24f	340

Ephesians

2:3	182, 192, 252, 290–91
4:14	148
5:19	205
6:1–2	263
6:14f	322

Philippians

1:6	255
2:8	110

2:13	233
3:19	72

Colossians
2:11f	141
2:12	123
2:16	203
3:16	205
3:20	263

1 Thessalonians
4:16ff	347
5:1ff	347
5:17	203
5:23	280

2 Thessalonians
3:6	355

1 Timothy
1:3	203
1:9	340
1:20	355
2:1f	357
2:4	302, 311, 328
2:5	203, 356
2:8	348
4:3	203
5:3ff	351
5:20	249

2 Timothy
1:15	274
2:6	301
2:15	167
2:20	305
3:12	206
3:15	191
4:10	274
4:14	274

Titus
3:1	257
3:10	91, 355

Philemon
	295

Hebrews
1:5	198
1:22	196
4:12	258, 280
6:4-6	309, 312
7	64
9	64
9:9-10	121
9:16f	219
10:22	191
10:26-31	309, 312
12:29	152, 191

James
1:5f	348
2:10	243-44, 340
5:9	348
5:13f	349
5:14ff	205
5:14	205

1 Peter
1:3-7	163
1:3	192
1:23	296
2:7	150
2:12	163
2:13f	263
2:13-17	357
2:16	340
2:23	164
3:20f	140, 341
3:20-21	130, 175, 191
3:20	123, 150, 201
3:21	196, 244, 252
4:3f	232
4:5ff	163

2 Peter
2	296
2:1	179, 191, 197-98
2:4	309

Scripture Reference Index

1 John

1:8–10	192
1:8	116
2:1	203, 356
2:2	301
2:4	355
3:18f	339
4:1	84, 204
5:8	96
5:21	232

2 John

10	269, 274, 355

Revelation

3:9	197
7:1ff	356
12	257
13:5	347
14:4	351
20	352
21:8	160, 162
22:18f	152
22:18	179, 191, 197

Wisdom

3	352
3:13	358

Ecclesiasticus (Sirach)

2:1	358
2:16	358
15:14ff	281, 290
15:14	292, 305, 358

Baruch

237

www.ingramcontent.com/pod-product-compliance
Lightning Source LLC
Chambersburg PA
CBHW071228290426
44108CB00013B/1324